CARING FATHERS IN THE GLOBAL CONTEXT

Edited by
Petteri Eerola, Katherine Twamley,
Henna Pirskanen and Pedro Romero-Balsas

With a foreword by
Margaret O'Brien

First published in Great Britain in 2025 by

Policy Press, an imprint of
Bristol University Press
University of Bristol
1-9 Old Park Hill
Bristol
BS2 8BB
UK
t: +44 (0)117 374 6645
e: bup-info@bristol.ac.uk

Details of international sales and distribution partners are available at policy.bristoluniversitypress.co.uk

Editorial selection and editorial matter © Petteri Eerola, Katherine Twamley, Henna Pirskanen and Pedro Romero-Balsas 2025

The digital PDF and ePub versions of this title are available open access and distributed under the terms of the Creative Commons Attribution-NonCommercial-NoDerivatives 4.0 International licence (https://creativecommons.org/licenses/by-nc-nd/4.0/) which permits reproduction and distribution for non-commercial use without further permission provided the original work is attributed.

British Library Cataloguing in Publication Data
A catalogue record for this book is available from the British Library

ISBN 978-1-4473-7242-4 paperback
ISBN 978-1-4473-7243-1 ePub
ISBN 978-1-4473-7244-8 ePdf

The right of Petteri Eerola, Katherine Twamley, Henna Pirskanen and Pedro Romero-Balsas to be identified as editors of this work has been asserted by them in accordance with the Copyright, Designs and Patents Act 1988.

All rights reserved: no part of this publication may be reproduced, stored in a retrieval system, or transmitted in any form or by any means, electronic, mechanical, photocopying, recording, or otherwise without the prior permission of Bristol University Press.

Every reasonable effort has been made to obtain permission to reproduce copyrighted material. If, however, anyone knows of an oversight, please contact the publisher.

The statements and opinions contained within this publication are solely those of the editors and contributors and not of the University of Bristol or Bristol University Press. The University of Bristol and Bristol University Press disclaim responsibility for any injury to persons or property resulting from any material published in this publication.

Bristol University Press and Policy Press work to counter discrimination on grounds of gender, race, disability, age and sexuality.

Cover design: Nicky Borowiec
Front cover image: Adobe Stock/Purrga

Contents

List of figures and tables	v
Notes on contributors	vi
Acknowledgements	viii
Foreword by Margaret O'Brien	ix

PART I Introduction to caring fatherhood

1. Why study fathers and care? ... 3
   Katherine Twamley, Petteri Eerola, Pedro Romero-Balsas and Henna Pirskanen

2. The who, what and how of care in caring fatherhood: an ecological care ethics approach ... 21
   Andrea Doucet

PART II Understandings and practices of good fatherhood and care

3. 'He is our handyman': young people's narratives on caring fatherhood and family life in the Faroe Islands ... 45
   Firouz Gaini

4. Changing fatherhood and gender roles in Somali families: experiences of being fathered in Somalia and in the diaspora ... 62
   Marja Tiilikainen

5. Moving beyond the narrative of marginalised fatherhood: Russian fathers' accounts of nonresident fathering after family separation ... 79
   Ekaterina Ivanova

6. Hegemonic, caring or hybrid fathers? The case of Polish fathers of adult children in 'the empty nest' ... 97
   Magdalena Żadkowska, Radosław Kossakowski and Bogna Dowgiałło

7. Berry-picking fathers and burdened mothers: parenting modes in dual-income households of urban China during the COVID-19 pandemic ... 114
   Guanli Zhang, Bingyi Zhang and Lichao Yang

PART III Exploring what facilitates or inhibits fathers' care

8. Fathers on the 'night shift'? Understanding caring fatherhood through parents' interpretative repertoires of night-time care ... 135
   Petteri Eerola, Armi Mustosmäki and Henna Pirskanen

9. What happens when fathers are at home? Learning from families' accounts of COVID-19 lockdown in the UK and South Africa ... 153
   Katherine Twamley and Sadiyya Haffejee

10	'Being there' as providers and caregivers: caring masculinities in parenting and partnering among young fathers in the UK *Anna Tarrant, Linzi Ladlow and Laura Way*	175
11	Gendered framings of responsibility for care and the availability of leave policies for fathers from a global perspective *Alison Koslowski*	195
12	Gender role attitudes, perceptions of parenthood and father's parental leave use in Finland *Miia Saarikallio-Torp, Johanna Lammi-Taskula, Anneli Miettinen, Johanna Närvi and Ella Sihvonen*	212

PART IV Minoritised fathers and care

13	Syrian refugee dads in the UK: gendered practices of 'involvement' *Tina Miller and Esther Dermott*	233
14	Reconstruction of fatherhood in a strange land: exploring fathering practices of Chinese migrants in Spain *Mengyao Wu and Alberto Del Rey Poveda*	249
15	Refugee fathers' parenting to protect, nurture and train under resettlement in Sweden *Disa Bergnehr*	266
16	Queer fathers and parents' caring path to parenthood in the Netherlands and Switzerland *Carole Ammann*	282
17	Fathers caring in families with children with disabilities *Jesús Rogero-García, Gerardo Meil and Pedro Romero-Balsas*	301
18	Accounting for lack of emotional engagement: adults reconceptualising fatherhood *Ann Phoenix*	321
19	Conclusions: Towards more nuanced understandings of fathers' care *Petteri Eerola, Henna Pirskanen, Pedro Romero-Balsas and Katherine Twamley*	338

Index   349

List of figures and tables

Figures

9.1	Smith Mum, diary entry, June 2020	161
9.2	Smith Dad, diary entry, May 2020, with caption: 'Smith Mum takes lunch up to me when I don't have time to go downstairs'	162
9.3	Bheki Dad, diary entry, July 2020	166
9.4	Bheki Mum, diary entry, July 2020	166
9.5	Bheki Mum, diary entry, July 2020	167

Tables

4.1	Focus group interviews	66
7.1	Basic information on participants and their families	117
8.1	Parents' interpretative repertoires of barriers and enablers related to the father's night-time care and shared care practices	141
11.1	Labour force participation rates for women and mothers	199
11.2	Total amount of statutory 'well-paid' leave available to parents in the first 18 months of a child's life: April 2023	206
12.1	The characteristics of fathers included in the analysis and the mean values and standard deviations for attitudinal dimensions by background variables	219
12.2	The results from the multinomial logistic regression (odds ratios and their statistical significance) (reference category = father has used only birth-related leave)	221
14.1	Demographic characteristics of respondents (N = 15)	254
15.1	Overview of interview data	271
16.1	Research participants' demographics	288
17.1	Daily minutes of childcare help provided by different agents depending on the presence of a child in special need with daily activities due to disability or chronic illness	307
17.2	Logistic regression models on daily time spent by the father and the mother, and the difference between the two	308
17.3	Weekly hours of paid work and degree of compatibility of working hours with family commitments, according to sex and presence of children in special need of help with daily activities	311
17.4	Different indicators of family satisfaction and conflict, according to sex and presence of children in special need of help with daily activities	313
17.5	Logistic regression models on daily time spent on childcare by noncouple agents	314

Notes on contributors

Editors

Petteri Eerola, Senior Lecturer at the University of Jyväskylä, Finland, and Honorary Associate Professor at the University College London, UK, is a social scientist with broad experience in research on fatherhood, parenting, and family life. Recently, he has studied the consequences of fathers' parental leave take-up, fathers' motivations and barriers to parental leave, and couples' negotiations on the parental division of labour. In his current work, he is studying gendered inequalities in night-time care in families with young children and parenting practices during the COVID-19 pandemic.

Katherine Twamley is Professor of Sociology at the Social Research Institute and Chair of the University College London (UCL) Sociology Network at UCL, UK. Her research focuses on gender, love and intimacy, and family, with a geographical focus on the UK and India. She recently led the 'Families and Community in the Time of COVID-19' project, which explored the experiences of families with children in ten different countries.

Henna Pirskanen works as Associate Professor of Social Work at the University of Lapland, Finland. Her research areas include childhood, youth and families, vulnerable life situations and sensitive topics. Her current research project investigates children's, young people's and professionals' perspectives on experiences of sorrow and grief in family and close relationships in Finland and Spain.

Pedro Romero-Balsas is Associate Professor of Sociology at the Autonomous University of Madrid, Spain. His research field covers fathering, work and family balance, parental leave use, masculinities and families. He is currently working on a research project about work and family balance among Spanish parents. He also serves as the leader of the Sustainable Parental Leave Terminology Working Group within the COST Action project CA21150 Sustainability@Leave.

Authors

Carole Ammann, ETH Zurich
Disa Bergnehr, Linnaeus University
Izram Chaudry, University of Lincoln

Notes on contributors

Alberto del Rey Poveda, University of Salamanca
Esther Dermott, University of Bristol
Andrea Doucet, Brock University
Bogna Dowgiałło, University of Gdansk
Petteri Eerola, University of Jyväskylä
Firouz Gaini, University of the Faroe Islands
Sadiyya Haffejee, University of Johannesburg
Ekaterina Ivanova, University of Melbourne
Alison Koslowski, University College London
Radosław Kossakowski, University of Gdansk
Linzi Ladlow, University of Lincoln
Johanna Lammi-Taskula, Finnish Institute for Health and Welfare
Gerardo Meil, Autonomous University of Madrid
Anneli Miettinen, The Social Insurance Institution of Finland
Tina Miller, Oxford Brookes University
Armi Mustosmäki, University of Eastern Finland
Johanna Närvi, Finnish Institute for Health and Welfare
Margaret O'Brien, University College London
Ann Phoenix, University College London
Henna Pirskanen, University of Lapland
Jesús Rogero-García, Autonomous University of Madrid
Pedro Romero-Balsas, Autonomous University of Madrid
Miia Saarikallio-Torp, Social Insurance Institution of Finland
Ella Sihvonen, Social Insurance Institution of Finland
Anna Tarrant, University of Lincoln
Marja Tiilikainen, Migration Institute of Finland
Katherine Twamley, University College London
Laura Way, University of Roehampton
Mengyao Wu, University of Salamanca
Lichao Yang, Beijing Normal University
Magdalena Żadkowska, University of Gdansk
Bingyi Zhang, Beijing Normal University
Guanli Zhang, Beijing Normal University

Acknowledgements

This volume is the product of a deeply collaborative effort, and we are grateful to the many individuals and institutions that made it possible.

First, we extend our heartfelt thanks to *UCL Global Engagement* for providing the funding that facilitated this collaboration. Their support enabled the editors to work together and with other colleagues, vital exchanges which shaped this book.

We also express our gratitude to *UCL* for funding the open-access fees, ensuring that this work remains freely available to readers worldwide.

In addition, we would like to extend our sincere thanks to the Kone Foundation for making it possible to finalise the manuscript in the calm, inspiring, and beautiful environment of the Saari Residence in Mynämäki, Finland.

Special thanks go to the attendees of the *ISA World Conference of Sociology 2023*, who participated in our two workshops on caring fatherhood and whose insightful feedback and active engagement in discussion provided valuable perspectives and enriched the development of this project.

Finally, we owe a deep debt of appreciation to all the *contributors* for their exceptional chapters. Your scholarship, dedication and creativity have made this book a compelling and rigorous collection of work.

Petteri Eerola, Katherine Twamley,
Henna Pirskanen and Pedro Romero-Balsas
Tampere, London, Jyväskylä and Madrid
20 December 2024

Foreword

Margaret O'Brien

In the Global North's first wave of fatherhood research during the 1970s and 1980s, there was optimism that greater involvement in the care of children by fathers would significantly contribute to the demise of patriarchy. At the time, researching fatherhood was a minority topic in the academy, with even feminist scholars asking, what could men tell us about family life? Aren't they unreliable narrators, irrelevant subjects, distant or absent, and when at home disciplinarian and oppressive towards women and children?

Studies from that first wave and this impressive new collection on caring fathers edited by Petteri Eerola, Katherine Twamley, Henna Pirskanen and Pedro Romero-Balsas contest that deficit narrative. *Caring Fathers in the Global Context* displays an abundance of insights into the diverse ways in which fathers care for children night-time and day, when young and old, navigating migration, and through a wide range of cultural and economic adversities.

The editors have curated a volume which describes and interprets fathers' situated caring practices in diverse contexts, moving beyond a vision where provisioning and direct child caring are conceptualised as incompatible and binary. In their conclusion they argue that 'a discourse of caring, intimate and emotionally engaged fatherhood has global reach, beyond the normative, middle-class, white Anglo-European contexts', but caution the ideal is not all-pervasive. Indeed, several chapters in the book show that caring masculinity norms can lie uneasily with men's sense of self and worth, particularly when not combined with opportunities to earn money for children's economic welfare.

This book succeeds in advancing earlier conceptualisation in fatherhood research by foregrounding the relationality between caring and earning. In a quest to discover whether fathers indeed had the capacity to care and to be emotionally attentive to children, classic concepts of 'father involvement' explicitly excluded economic provision, foregrounding direct caregiving. At the time, it was known that fathers could 'breadwin' – indeed, earning a family wage was an indispensable aspect of good fatherhood, especially prior to the rise of female employment in the 1970s. What was not so well known was whether men were able and 'competent' to be involved in the everyday care of children when they became fathers. A preoccupation concerned how fathers measured up on the dominant tripartite father involvement typology of engagement, accessibility and responsibility, which excluded financial provisioning. The field has moved on, as represented by this collection.

Another welcome contribution by this book is its institutional focus on how governments and states can facilitate fathers' care through macro-public policy measures, such as paternity and parental leave. An in-depth study of how fathers use parental leave in Finland and a comparative examination of parental leave in the diverse contexts of Australia, Chile, Japan, South Africa, Sweden and the US show the heterogeneity of global provision and highlight assumptions about 'deserving' fathers worthy of support and those 'undeserving' fathers excluded by explicit or implicit design features.

The work of Petteri Eerola, Katherine Twamley, Henna Pirskanen, Pedro Romero-Balsas and all the contributors to this tremendous collection represent the next generation of sociological scholars of fatherhood and fathering practice. They have shown that fatherhood is not a singular institution or experience, but a rich set of diverse and complex practices bounded by historical and cultural legacies, thus deepening our understanding of fathers' care in contemporary societies.

PART I
Introduction to caring fatherhood

1

Why study fathers and care?

*Katherine Twamley, Petteri Eerola,
Pedro Romero-Balsas and Henna Pirskanen*

The last 20 years have seen a burgeoning scholarly interest in fathers and fatherhood in fields such as sociology, social policy, gender studies and masculinity studies. This research has shown how cultural understandings, discourses, and ideals of 'good fatherhood', as well as men's practices in care, have changed over recent decades (Dermott, 2008; Johansson and Klinth, 2008; Eerola and Huttunen, 2011; Miller, 2011a; Brannen et al 2023). Increasingly fathers are expected to be more 'involved' in their children's lives, going beyond the traditional breadwinner role (Dermott, 2008; Eerola 2014; Ranson, 2014; Eerola and Mykkänen, 2015; Doucet, 2017; Brannen et al, 2023). Time use studies confirm that fathers are increasing their involvement in childcare and domestic work across countries (Sullivan, 2019). Nonetheless, men's involvement in such tasks does not match women's and in many studies it is clear that mothers continue to take on the bulk of parental responsibility (Miller 2011b; Rose et al, 2014; Eerola et al, 2021). A key concern then of this body of research has been to understand this 'stalled gender revolution' (Eydal et al, 2015; Friedmann, 2015; Petts, 2022; Edlund and Öun, 2023) and how to prompt more radical gendered transformations in family life.

In this book, we argue for a focus on care as a conceptual tool which can help us understand these processes better. We understand care as potentially transformative since it may foster what Elliott (2016) describes as caring masculinities. This concept entails the 'rejection of domination' and the 'integration of care values, including positive emotion, interdependence, and relationality' (Elliott, 2016: 241). In other words, the hope is that men's engagement in care will bring about transformative practices and perspectives on masculinities, extending beyond just the couple relationship. A focus on care has never been more vital. We are witnessing a time of multiple overlapping societal crises and turbulences (Tammelin et al, 2025), including the worldwide COVID-19 pandemic, eco-catastrophes and environmental crises, ongoing and new wars and conflicts, and increasing economic hardship and child poverty. Focusing on care and understanding it better creates possibilities for new socially sustainable realities that benefit individuals, communities and societies globally.

However, while many studies during the last few decades have explored men's understandings and practices of 'new', involved, and caring fatherhood, this research has often lacked a conceptual understanding of care. Fathers' involvement in care has more predominantly been studied through the distribution of time spent on caregiving tasks and fathers' personal understandings of their own role as parents (Dermott, 2008; Craig and Mullan, 2011; Miller 2011b; Eerola, 2014; Ylikännö et al, 2015). Even when the concept of care has been applied, it has been utilised inconsistently, and care has mainly been understood as something that is obvious and based on common sense. There has also been an implicit understanding that more involvement means more care, which might not always be so, as conceptually involvement differs from caring (Doucet, 2020; Doucet, Chapter 2, this volume).

This is where this book comes in. To achieve a more nuanced understanding of fathers' care, tools linking the broad body of sociological research on contemporary fatherhood with theoretical conceptualizations of care are needed. This more precise focus can enable an examination of when and how fathers' 'involvement' may be conceptualised as care, the implications of such care, and the circumstances in which care may be encouraged. We draw here in particular on the work of Andrea Doucet, who gives a comprehensive overview of feminist care literature and its relevance for fatherhood research in the following chapter as a starting point in this endeavour. Drawing on the work of Tronto (1993, 2013), she writes that care is inherently processual and relational, and thus should not be evaluated based on time or specific tasks completed. Instead, care should be seen as a 'habit of mind' in an individual who is concerned about others' needs (care about), ready to address those needs (care for), and actively meeting them through tangible actions (caregiving). Such a definition helps to move beyond the individual task-based approach to studying fatherhood and aligns with Elliott's (2016) theorisations of transformative care practices.

In this book we have called upon scholars of fatherhood to engage deeply with concepts of care. We have sought contributions from as wide a net as possible, thereby examining the intersection of care and fatherhood from diverse perspectives and in diverse circumstances. We drew on our own networks, but also hosted a conference panel and circulated a call for contributions. Mindful of publication bias towards scholarship of and from the Global North, and the dearth of fatherhood literature beyond that undertaken with white middle-class men, we were particularly keen to include chapters with diverse fathers and from multiple voices (therefore also including research with children about their experiences of fatherhood, for example). We have aimed as a minimum to include a chapter from each region of the world. Inevitably, we cannot cover all locations, potential forms of fatherhood and fathering, or methodological approaches and participants, but we are confident that together the volume addresses some key gaps which we have identified in the literature. In the conclusion we return to some of the remaining gaps and future directions for work in this field.

In the rest of this chapter, we outline the key issues and gaps in research on fathers and care, as we have identified them. First, a brief introduction to the previous research on the care of fathers is provided. After that, the transformative potential of fathers' care and the evidence around factors that facilitate fathers' involvement in care are discussed. The chapter concludes with summaries of the chapters included in this volume.

What do we know about how fathers care?

While there has been considerable research on fatherhood over the last 20 years, the bulk of this research has been undertaken in the Global North with white fathers in mixed-sex relationships. This literature shows that fathers spend more time on care activities than before, and how both the ideals and practices of fathers' care have become more nurturing and 'involved'. These studies have shown fathers have moved towards the 'emotional core' of the family (Dermott, 2008), challenging the prevailing stereotype of the distant and disengaged father. Research with fathers shows that they are keen to be more 'involved' in their children's lives than their fathers before them (Eerola and Huttunen, 2011; Miller, 2011a; Fletcher, 2020), and that younger generations of men are advocating for flexible work schedules in order to 'be there' for their children (Gattrell et al, 2015). There has also been an increase in dual-earner families and more families where the father takes the lead care role and works fewer paid hours than the mother (Hunter et al, 2017; O'Brien and Wall, 2017; Hodkinson and Brooks, 2018; Beglaubter, 2021; Pinho et al, 2021; Brannen et al, 2023).

However, even when fathers are primary or equal carers (according to their own definitions or relative paid work hours compared to mothers/ partners), the moral responsibility of parenthood tends to lie with mothers, meaning that women take on more of the 'mental load' in care (Rose et al, 2014; Eerola et al, 2021). This can mean that fathers are engaging in caregiving, but without other elements of care which involve monitoring and identifying care needs. In other words, evidence of direct care tasks and new ideals of intimate fatherhood does not necessarily evidence a caring mindset. Further to this, the bulk of studies show that men continue to hold the greater responsibility in breadwinning or provisioning for families. Fathers tend to organise care around their paid work, while mothers more often reduce their paid work hours to meet children's needs (Craig, 2006; Oláh and Gähler, 2014; Rose et al, 2014; Twamley, 2024). These studies signal the differing moral responsibilities that women and men continue to be held to in their parenting (Ralph, 2016).

The extent to which breadwinning may be considered a form of care work is contested. The gendered division of care has been a key motivation behind much research on mothers and fathers, in part to address women's historical exclusion from paid work and public life. This has resulted in paid work being treated as oppositional to care work. Commonly time use studies, for example, do not include earning as care provision, but rather as evidence of a lack of involvement in care. This does not always reflect how families themselves view paid work, which may be considered a key aspect of care that fathers (or, less commonly, mothers) provide (Eerola, 2014; Eerola and Mykkänen, 2015; Twamley, 2024). However, increasingly scholars are beginning to question this dichotomy (Schmidt 2018; Doucet, 2020). For example, drawing on the work of Tronto (1993), Schmidt (2018) argues that with a 'caring disposition' earning may be considered care work – that is, identifying the financial need and assuming responsibility to meet it to ensure economic wellbeing for the family. But Tronto (2013) herself argued that conceptualising men's care as 'providing' allows men to justify avoiding practical caregiving tasks traditionally associated with mothers. Such avoidance can reinforce the boundaries between men and caregiving, perpetuating inequalities rooted in the patriarchal gender order (Jordan, 2020). These discussions highlight that the relationship between caring and provisioning-oriented masculinities requires careful examination to understand how masculinities and care are negotiated in daily life and to explore the potential for dismantling gender inequality.

In addition to these gendered differences regarding moral responsibilities, studies also observe that when fathers are undertaking hands-on care tasks, these care practices do not always mirror those of women, either in activities taken or in the meanings attributed to them. Fathers typically engage in more physical play with children (Craig, 2006; Doucet, 2018), for example. Other scholars note that fathers tend to engage in the more enjoyable aspects of childcare and less in routine tasks or hygiene practices (Johansson and Klinth, 2008; Flaquer et al, 2019). This ability to opt in to particular forms of care and to fit care around leisure and unpaid work reflects men's superior bargaining power, as well as the limited transformations of gendered care responsibilities (Rose et al, 2014; Ralph, 2016; Eerola et al, 2021; Twamley, 2021).

However, there is a need to go beyond the norms and practices of fatherhood among the 'majority' population (Liversage, 2015) and complement this body of research by focusing on differently positioned men, as we aim to do in this volume. Fathers live and experience various societal divisions, backgrounds and statuses, such as social class, ethnicity, sexuality and racialization, which result in divergent capabilities and opportunities for fathers to be involved in care (Liversage, 2015). It is important to consider the intersectional power dynamics of how care is constituted and practised. In the intersections of social divisions, care may need to be negotiated, both within the family as well as in relation to cultural and institutional norms and expectations.

Minoritisation or marginalisation of fathers is interconnected with power and different intersectionalities in society. Studies which attend to diversely positioned fathers reveal different resources, aspirations, strategies and practices available to fathers (Mitchell and Lashewicz, 2016; Davies et al, 2024). For example, studies on fathers with disabilities suggest that being disabled can place constraints on the male breadwinner role. Additionally, time to care for their children is experienced as short if there are complex situations with health, impairment and stress (Kilkey and Clarke, 2010). Nonetheless, the onset of the fathers' ill health or impairment can mark a development of a positive relationship with the child, with some fathers perceiving themselves as having a new level of 'involvement' in the day-to-day care of their children, as long as sufficient support is in place for them.

Studies on how class intersects with family life have argued that working-class and middle-class families have different cultural logics of childrearing (Duncan et al, 2003). For example, working-class parents' care has been found to more often adhere to the cultural logic of natural growth, presuming that their children will spontaneously grow and thrive, and focusing on their children's enjoyment of childhood. In contrast, middle-class parents have been shown to more commonly adhere to the cultural logic of concerted cultivation, investing considerably in many aspects of their children's lives such as education and leisure-time activities to prepare for future careers and attainment (for example, Lareau, 2003, Wheeler, 2018). In other words, for working-class fathers, care can be preparing children to be working class, while middle-class fathers prepare their children for a middle-class life. Care can also manifest in minoritised fathers' need to create mechanisms to build resilience for them and their families, as suggested by Carroll (2018) in her study on gay fathers and in Cooper et al's (2020) research on African-American fathers. Care for these men included preparing their children for homophobic and racial discrimination before their children have direct experiences of it and empowering their children to handle these encounters. These studies demonstrate the importance of casting a wide net in research with fathers, since only focusing on white middle-class fathers in the Global North can result in a narrow understanding of fathers' care.

Different care practices that fathers engage in may be valorised in different ways and by different people. This has shaped the care activities in which men and women engage, as well as the ways in which care has been researched and supported by policy makers and practitioners (Gillies 2008). As is clear, fathers may practise care differently depending on their social positioning.

However, policy makers and practitioners who are meant to support families often draw on classed notions of care with little appreciation for the material circumstances in which families are living. In the UK and the US, scholars have argued that this has resulted in the demonisation of working-class fathers as 'feckless' for failing to live up to idealised notions of white middle-class parenting ideals which require economic investment and educational involvement from fathers (and mothers) (Gillies, 2008; Cammett, 2014; Tarrant, 2021; and Tarrant et al, Chapter 10 in this volume).

What do we know about what facilitates fathers' involvement in care?

Given the transformative potential of fathers' care, it is important to consider the circumstances which may support their involvement in care. Men's access to parental leave and flexible working have been two dominant foci of research and policy intervention, indicative of the perceived need to support men in combining paid and unpaid work (and indeed their partners' continued employment) as more families move to a dual-earner structure.

Gender-neutral parental leave schemes began in the 1970s in the Nordic countries, but the greatest shift in men's uptake of leave was observed after the introduction of a fathers' quota, which was first implemented in Norway in 1993 (Brandth and Kvande, 2009). Although the experience in the Nordic countries in promoting fathers in childcare through public policies has influenced the subsequent development of public policies in several European countries, national policies have also been shaped by the previous trajectory of parental and family policy design that had been implemented in the 20th century (Moss, Duvander and Koslowski, 2019). As such, the design of parental leave has been evolving across countries, as observed in the annual reports of the International Network on Leave Policies and Research (Blum et al, 2023). Different leave designs produce different effects on fathers' uptake. Where leave is gender neutral or lowly remunerated, men are less likely to take it (Meil et al, 2018; Eerola et al, 2019; Blum et al, 2023). Leave eligibility is also a key issue, which may be tied to citizenship, employment circumstances or the partner's employment status, thus in turn impacting which fathers are able to take parental leave (O'Brien and Wall, 2017; Blum et al, 2023). Such regulations concerning eligibility also signal which fathers' care is supported and valorised, as well as its relative importance to paid work (as discussed by Koslowski in Chapter 11 in this volume). For example, unemployed mothers in the UK are eligible for a maternity allowance for up to 39 weeks, while unemployed fathers are not eligible for any state support to facilitate care for their families.

Working conditions are also a key factor in fathers' take-up of parental leave (Bygren and Duvander, 2006; Geisler and Kreyenfeld, 2011; Romero-Balsas et al, 2012; Halrynjo and Mangset, 2022; Twamley, 2024). Leave information is also relevant, and the lack of communication or perceived complexity of the leave may decrease its utilisation (Tremblay and Genin, 2011; Birkett and Forbes, 2019; Twamley and Schober, 2019). Such policies are more effective in encouraging men's leave uptake in labour markets with more established rights and where most new fathers are already integrated into the labour market. Thus, most of this research comes from Global North contexts.

In examining the influence of fathers' leave on care, the literature has tended to focus on discrete care tasks, such as reading to or bathing children. These studies show that men's participation in parental leave is associated with greater levels of involvement in childcare tasks and to a lesser extent housework after the leave period ends (Haas and Hwang, 2008; Meil, 2013; Almqvist and Duvander, 2014; Rehel, 2014; Schober, 2014; Romero-Balsas, 2015; Eerola et al, 2022). There are also observed benefits for women's career outcomes. These include a reduced household gender wage gap (Andersen, 2018; Druedahl et al, 2019) and an increased likelihood that women are in paid work (Andysz et al, 2016; de la Corte Rodríguez, 2018). Men's leave alone is more likely to have an impact on his participation in care than leave taken at the same time as the mother, which may in fact reinforce gendered divisions of labour (O'Brien, 2009; Gangl and Ziefle, 2015; Romero-Balsas, Meil and Rogero-García, 2022; Twamley, 2024).

Beyond fathers' involvement in discrete tasks, research in this area has also demonstrated the transformative potential of fathers' leave alone. Brandth and Kvande found that when men took periods of leave alone they developed more of a caring disposition similar to that of the mothers, reporting that the men who took leave alone were more attentive and responsive to their children's needs (1998, 2001). Men (and women) have also reported that men feel more confident in their caring abilities, have a greater awareness of and respect for the demands of care work, and report a deeper relationship with their child due to the leave alone experience (Brandth and Kvande, 2003; O'Brien and Wall, 2017; Twamley, 2024). There is little attention in this research to other forms of care, such as care within the community or for the environment.

However, it isn't always the case that leave alone challenges hegemonic forms of masculinity (Connell, 1995) or transformations in family care relationships and responsibilities (O'Brien and Wall, 2017; Twamley, 2024). Leave alone is only one of many factors which may shape men's participation in care, and after the leave period is over, the work context can again pull men away from unpaid care. Flexible working policies are then one further avenue through which men's involvement in care may be facilitated. The flexibilisation and reduction of working hours are being adapted to and becoming part of male identities, as the type of labour flexibility is incorporated into the discourse of parental involvement, as noted by Ewald et al (2024) in the case of Australia. In an analysis of the literature on the effect of flexible working on fathers, Ewald et al (2020) conclude that these modifications to working hours have predominantly negative effects, including the stigma associated with flexibility, the invisibility of fathers' caregiving responsibilities, negative consequences for finances and career progression, and the failure of flexible working policies to include men in the discussion (see also Chung, 2022).

Summaries of the chapters

This book is divided into four parts: Part I includes this introduction and a chapter by Andrea Doucet that lays out the theoretical framework for the book. The chapters in Part II explore understandings and practices of good fatherhood and care; in Part III they examine factors which facilitate or impede fathers' participation in care; and in Part IV, the focus is on care in the lives of minoritised fathers. Although we have divided the chapters in this way, inevitably chapters within the sections also speak to themes in other sections.

In her chapter, 'The who, what and how of care in caring fatherhood: an ecological care ethics approach' (Chapter 2), Andrea Doucet lays out how caring fatherhood is understood and practised. In this conceptual piece, she raises questions as to who is a caring father, what is the care in caring fatherhood and how to measure the care in caring fatherhood. She introduces feminist, relational and ecological approaches to narratives, genealogies of concepts, and knowledge making. In addition, she maps historical and conceptual narratives about paid and unpaid work, gender divisions of labour, and caring fatherhood, and offers an alternative conceptual framing for research on fathering and care that is embedded in care ethics concepts. This chapter is central to theorisation of the book and from which later empirical chapters draw.

The first chapter in Part II, '"He is our handyman": young people's narratives on caring fatherhood and family life in the Faroe Islands' by Firouz Gaini (Chapter 3), is based on the analysis of 32 individual essays written by young people aged 14–15. The chapter delves into the multilayered question about men's ambivalent roles and identities in Faroese society today, and the ways in which young people experience and co-construct fathers' care.

Similarly, Chapter 4, 'Changing fatherhood and gender roles in Somali families: experiences of being fathered in Somalia and in the diaspora' by Marja Tiilikainen, explores Somalis' experiences of being fathered in diverse locations. Tiilikainen argues that children's expectations of care have deviated from their fathers, particularly in Somalia, but in Finland and Canada there is evidence of changing practices of care by fathers. She delves into how fatherhood is understood among Somalis and why these changes may be observed. These two chapters are unique in their attention to contemporary voices of children and young people as they narrate their views on being fathered.

In Chapter 5, 'Moving beyond the narrative of marginalised fatherhood: Russian fathers' accounts of nonresident fathering after family separation' by Ekaterina Ivanova, the experiences of separated fathers in Russia are explored. Through semi-structured interviews with non-resident Russian fathers, the chapter demonstrates how fathers are constrained by but also uphold policies which prioritise co-residence with the mother after parents' separation. The chapter beautifully illustrates how in-depth research can destabilise cultural narratives of 'detached' fathers.

In Chapter 6, 'Hegemonic, caring or hybrid fathers? The case of Polish fathers of adult children in the "empty nest"', Magdalena Żadkowska, Radosław Kossakowski and Bogna Dowgiałło explore transformations in fathering models when children are grown up and are no longer living under the same roof as their parents. Through a qualitative analysis of interviews with 40 Polish fathers, the authors identify changing practices of fatherhood when children are adults, sometimes opening spaces for new orientations to care.

In Chapter 7, 'Berry-picking fathers and burdened mothers: parenting modes in dual-income households of urban China during the COVID-19 pandemic', Guanli Zhang, Bingyi Zhang and Lichao Yang draw on qualitative data collected in China. The results show how pandemic lockdowns brought new challenges for families, changes in parenting modes and some new divisions of labour, but these were usually limited and temporal. The authors consider what this says about local understandings of fatherhood and motherhood.

Part III begins with the chapter 'Fathers on the "night shift"? Understanding caring fatherhood through parents' interpretative repertoires of night-time care' by Petteri Eerola, Armi Mustosmäki and Henna Pirskanen (Chapter 8), in which they conduct a qualitative analysis of the discourses Finnish fathers and mothers draw onregarding fathers' role in night-time care. They show how justifications for gender roles based on biological and situational factors uphold the gendered separation of care at night.

The next chapter, 'What happens when fathers are at home? Learning from families' accounts of COVID-19 lockdown in the UK and South Africa' by Katherine Twamley and Sadiyya Haffejee (Chapter 9), explores what can be learned about fathers' care through a detailed case study analysis of two families' experiences during pandemic lockdowns. The authors draw on qualitative interviews and multimodal diary data collected during the height of the COVID-19 pandemic in two different country contexts: the UK and South Africa. The chapter gives an insight into how the 'presence' of fathers is not enough either to be considered or to provoke transformations in care, and they explore some of the reasons why this may be.

In Chapter 10, '"Being there" as providers and caregivers: caring masculinities in parenting and partnering among young fathers in the UK', Anna Tarrant, Linzi Ladlow and Laura Way report on a longitudinal qualitative study of young fathers (aged 25 and under) in the UK. They provide an original perspective of analysing fathers' discourses at the moment of becoming parents and some years later. The chapter explores how young fathers navigate stereotypes of problematic and marginal fatherhood, and the tensions inherent between expectations associated with traditional and caring masculinities.

In Chapter 11, 'Gendered framings of responsibility for care and the availability of leave policies for fathers from a global perspective', Alison Koslowski compares the parenting leave system in Australia, Chile, Japan, South Africa, Sweden and the US. The results show how the design of different national parenting leave schemes implies different roles for fathers regarding childcare and paid work, and thus sets the scene for the diverse capabilities of fathers to care at this critical transitional moment.

In Chapter 12, 'Gender role attitudes, perceptions of parenthood and fathers' parental leave use in Finland', Miia Saarikallio-Torp, Johanna Lammi-Taskula, Anneli Miettinen, Johanna Närvi and Ella Sihvonen carry out a quantitative analysis where they assess the link between attitudes and use of parental leave by fathers in Finland. Their results show that reported gender role and caring attitudes have no effect in the use of the fathers' quota. Meanwhile, traditional attitudes are linked to a reduced use of shared parental leave. The implications here are the structural issues, such as policy design and earnings, are more important in promoting men's uptake of parental leave than attitudes, thus signalling the transformative potential of parental leave policies.

The first chapter in Part IV, 'Syrian refugee dads in the UK: gendered practices of "involvement"' by Tina Miller and Esther Dermott, analyses the experiences and practices of Syrian refugee fathers who have moved to the UK. The authors show that by focusing on minoritised fathers, further insights are gained into the complex relationships between fatherhood and masculinity, and cultural expectations around family and care.

In Chapter 14, 'Reconstruction of fatherhood in a strange land: exploring fathering practices of Chinese migrants in Spain', Mengyao Wu and Alberto Del Rey Poveda address the caregiving practices of Chinese self-employed migrant fathers in three different cities in Spain. Using a qualitative methodology, with a sample of 15 fathers, they document the experiences of reconciliation and caregiving of these fathers, which are affected and reconfigured by migratory experiences and labour reconfigurations in the destination country.

In Chapter 15, 'Refugee fathers' parenting to protect, nurture and train under resettlement in Sweden', Disa Bergnehr analyses interviews and diary notes collected in Sweden with Middle Eastern refugee fathers. The chapter aims to widen understandings of fathering and parenting under resettlement; how fathers protect, nurture and train their children. She describes how fathers who struggle with limited economic and cultural capital partly change their care practices and paternal or parental thinking.

In Chapter 16, 'Queer fathers and parents' caring path to parenthood in the Netherlands and Switzerland', Carole Ammann explores the deliberate and extended preparation of queer people for fatherhood and parenthood. Using a qualitative approach, she shows how the fathers undergo a lengthy period of preparation for parenthood, outlining how this preparation may be conceived of as a form of prefatherhood care work that is unique to queer fathers and parents.

In Chapter 17, 'Fathers caring in families with children with disabilities', Jesús Rogero-García, Gerardo Meil and Pedro Romero-Balsas analyse the impact of having a child with disabilities on the childcare provided by fathers, the distribution of care within the couple, and the level of participation of nonparental agents in childcare. In an online survey of parents with at least one child under seven years of age and living in Spain, a novel methodological approach of a 'childcare diary' was used to collect information on the time used in childcare activities. The authors conclude that in households with children with disabilities, there is less involvement of the father in their care. This is compensated by a greater dedication of the mother and the use of paid caregivers.

In Chapter 18, 'Accounting for lack of emotional engagement: adults reconceptualising fatherhood', Ann Phoenix draws on research with adults raised in 'non-normative' minoritised ethnic group households, who look back and interpret the fathering they experienced. She explores the disconnect between ideals of 'new fatherhood' and the actual practices of fathers, as well as how these practices are perceived by their children. The chapter emphasises the need to contextualise fatherhood in various ways, including through historical and intersectional lenses.

In the book's final chapter, 'Conclusions: Towards more nuanced understandings of fathers' care', the editors (Petteri Eerola, Henna Pirskanen, Pedro Romero-Balsas and Katherine Twamley) consider how together the volume has addressed the initial aims and questions proposed for the volume. We finish with a discussion about the limitations of the volume and some suggested future directions of research in this field. The discussion of this final chapter is built on the novel contributions provided by the authors of this book.

References

Almqvist, A.-L. and Duvander, A.-Z. (2014) 'Changes in gender equality? Swedish fathers' parental leave, division of childcare and housework', *Journal of Family Studies*, 20(1): 19–27. https://doi.org/10.5172/jfs.2014.20.1.19

Andersen, S.H. (2018) 'Paternity leave and the motherhood penalty: new causal evidence', *Journal of Marriage and Family*, 80(5): 1125–1143. https://doi.org/10.1111/jomf.12507

Andysz, A., Jacukowicz, A., Stańczak, A. and Drabek, M. (2016) 'Availability and the use of work–life balance benefits guaranteed by the Polish Labour Code among workers employed on the basis of employment contracts in small and medium enterprises', *International Journal of Occupational Medicine and Environmental Health*, 29(4): 709–717. https://doi.org/10.13075/ijomeh.1896.00745

Beglaubter, J. (2021) '"I feel like it's a little bit of a badge of honor": fathers' leave-taking and the development of caring masculinities', *Men & Masculinities*, 24(1): 3–22. https://doi.org/10.1177/1097184X19874869

Birkett, H. and Forbes, S. (2019) 'Where's dad? Exploring the low take-up of inclusive parenting policies in the UK', *Policy Studies*, 40(2): 205–224. https://doi.org/10.1080/01442872.2019.1581160

Blum, S., Dobrotić, I., Kaufman, G., Koslowski, A. and Moss, P. (2023) *19th International Review of Leave Policies and Related Research 2023*. https://www.leavenetwork.org/fileadmin/user_upload/k_leavenetwork/annual_reviews/2023/Blum_etal_LPRN_full_report_2023.pdf

Brandth, B. and Kvande, E. (1998) 'Masculinity and child care: the reconstruction of fathering', *Sociological Review*, 46(2): 293–313. https://doi.org/10.1111/1467-954X.00120

Brandth, B. and Kvande, E. (2001) 'Flexible work and flexible fathers', *Work, Employment and Society*, 15(2): 251–267. https://doi.org/10.1177/09500170122118940

Brandth, B. and Kvande, E. (2003) 'Father presence in child care', in A.M. Jensen and L. McKee (eds) *Children and the Changing Family: Between Transformation and Negotiation*. London: Routledge Falmer, pp 61–75.

Brandth, B., and Kvande, E. (2009) 'Norway: the making of the father's quota', in S. Kamerman and Peter Moss (eds) *The Politics of Parental Leave Policies*. Bristol: Policy Press, pp 191–206.

Brannen, J., Faircloth, C., Jones, K., O'Brien, M. and Twamley, K. (2023) 'Change and continuity in men's fathering and employment practices: a slow gender revolution', in C. Cameron, A. Koslowski, A. Lamont and P. Moss (eds) *Social Research for our Times: Thomas Coram Research Unit Past, Present and Future*. London: UCL Press.

Bygren, M. and Duvander, A.-Z. (2006) 'Parents' workplace situation and fathers' parental leave use', *Journal of Marriage and Family*, 68(2): 363–372.

Cammett, A. (2014) 'Deadbeat dads and welfare queens: how metaphor shapes poverty law', *Boston College Journal of Law & Social Justice*, 34(2): 233–265.

Carroll, M. (2018) 'Gay fathers on the margins: race, class, marital status and pathway to parenthood', *Family Relations*, 67(1): 104–117.

Chung, H. (2022). *The Flexibility Paradox: Why Flexible Working Leads to (Self-)Exploitation.* Bristol: Policy Press.

Connell, R.W. (1995) *Masculinities.* Cambridge: Polity Press.

Cooper, S., Burnett, M., Johnson, M., Brooks, J., Shaheed, J. and McBride, M. (2020) '"That is why we raise children": African American fathers' race-related concerns for their adolescents and parenting strategies', *Journal of Adolescence,* 82: 67–81.

Craig, L. (2006) 'Does father care mean fathers share? A comparison of how mothers and fathers in intact families spend time with children', *Gender and Society,* 20(2): 259–281. https://doi.org/10.1177/0891243205285212

Craig, L. and Mullan, K. (2011) 'How mothers and fathers share childcare: a cross-national time-use comparison', *American Sociological Review,* 76(6): 834–861. https://doi.org/10.1177/000312241142

Davies, A., Rix, J. and Robb, M. (2024) 'Fathers' Relationships with Their Disabled Children: A Literature Review', *Disability Studies Quarterly,* 43(3). https://dsq-sds.org/index.php/dsq/article/view/8744/8134

De la Corte Rodríguez, M. (2018) 'Child-related leave and women's labour market outcomes: towards a new paradigm in the European Union?', *Journal of Social Welfare and Family Law,* 40(3): 376–393. https://doi.org/10.1080/09649069.2018.1493657

Dermott, E. (2008) *Intimate Fatherhood,* Abingdon: Routledge.

Doucet, A. (2017) 'The ethics of care and the radical potential of fathers "home alone on leave": care as practice, relational ontology, and social justice', in M. O'Brien and K. Wall (eds) *Comparative Perspectives on Work-Life Balance and Gender Equality: Fathers on Leave Alone.* London: Springer Open, pp 11–28.

Doucet, A. (2018) *Do Men Mother? Fathering, Care, Parental Responsibilities,* 2nd edn. Toronto: University of Toronto Press.

Doucet, A. (2020) 'Father involvement, care, and breadwinning: genealogies of concepts and revisioned conceptual narratives', *Genealogy,* 4(1): 14. https://doi.org/10.3390/genealogy4010014

Druedahl, J., Ejrnas, M. and Jorgensen, T.H. (2019) 'Earmarked paternity leave and the relative income within couples', *Economics Letters,* 180: 85–88. https://doi.org/10.1016/j.econlet.2019.04.018

Duncan, S., Edwards, R., Reynolds, T. and Alldred, P. (2003). 'Motherhood, paid work and partnering: values and theories', *Work, Employment and Society,* 17(2): 309–330. https://doi.org/10.1177/09500170030170020

Edlund, J. and Öun, I. (2023) 'Equal sharing or not at all caring? Ideals about fathers' family involvement and the prevalence of the second half of the gender revolution in 27 societies', *Journal of Family Studies,* 29(6): 2576–2599. https://doi.org/10.1080/13229400.2023.2179531

Eerola, P. (2014) 'Nurturing, breadwinning and upbringing: paternal responsibilities by Finnish men in early fatherhood', *Community, Work & Family,* 17(3): 308–324. http://dx.doi.org/10.1080/13668803.2014.933774

Eerola, P. and Huttunen, J. (2011) 'Metanarrative of the "new father" and narratives of young Finnish first-time fathers', *Fathering*, 9(3): 211–231. https://jyx.jyu.fi/handle/123456789/40643

Eerola, P. and Mykkänen, J. (2015) 'Paternal masculinities in early fatherhood: dominant and counter narratives by Finnish first-time fathers', *Journal of Family Issues*, 36(12): 1674–1701. http://dx.doi.org/10.1177/0192513X13505566

Eerola, P., Närvi, J. and Lammi-Taskula, J. (2022) 'Can fathers' leave take-up dismantle gendered parental responsibilities? Evidence from Finland', *Journal of Family Research*, 34(3): 958–982. https://doi.org/10.20377/jfr-723

Eerola, P., Närvi, J., Terävä, J. and Repo, K. (2021) 'Negotiating parenting practices: the arguments and justifications of Finnish couples', *Families, Relationships and Societies*, 10(1): 119–135. https://doi.org/10.1332/204674320X15898834533942

Eerola, P., Lammi-Taskula, J., O'Brien, M., Hietamäki, J. and Räikkönen. E. (2019) 'Fathers' leave take-up in Finland: motivations and barriers in a complex Nordic leave scheme', *SAGE Open*, 9(4): 1–14. https://doi.org/10.1177/2158244019885389

Elliott, K. (2016) 'Caring masculinities: theorizing an emerging concept', *Men and Masculinities*, 19(3): 240–259. https://doi.org/10.1177/1097184X1557620

Ewald, A., Gilbert, E. and Huppatz, K. (2020) 'Fathering and flexible working arrangements: a systematic interdisciplinary review', *Journal of Family Theory & Review*, 12(1): 27–40.

Ewald, A., Gilbert, E. and Huppatz, K. (2024) 'Knowing your place: the role of occupational status in fathers' flexible working', *Community, Work & Family*, 27(4): 454–471.

Eydal, G.B., Gíslason. I.V., Rostgaard, T., Brandth, B., Duvander, A.-Z. and Lammi-Taskula, J. (2015) 'Trends in parental leave in the Nordic countries: has the forward march of gender equality halted?', *Community, Work & Family*, 18(2): 167 181. https://doi.org/10.1080/13668803.2014.1002754

Flaquer, L., Navarro-Varas, L., Antón-Alonso, F., Ruiz-Forès, N. and Cónsola, A. (2019) 'La implicación paterna en el cuidado de los hijos en España antes y durante la recesión económica', *Revista Española de Sociología*, 28(2). https://doi.org/10.22325/fes/ res.2018.61

Fletcher, T. (2020) *Negotiating Fatherhood: Sport and Family Practices*. London: Palgrave Macmillan.

Friedmann, S. (2015) 'Still a "stalled revolution"? Work/family experiences, hegemonic masculinity, and moving toward gender equality', *Social Compass*, 9(2): 140–155. https://doi.org/10.1111/soc4.12238

Gangl, M. and Ziefle, A. (2015) 'The making of a good woman: extended parental leave entitlements and mothers' work commitment in Germany', *American Journal of Sociology*, 121(2): 511–563. https://doi.org/10.1086/682419

Gatrell, C., Burnett, S., Cooper, C. and Sparrow, P. (2015) 'The price of love: the prioritisation of childcare and income earning among UK fathers', *Families, Relationships and Societies*, 4(2): 225–238.

Geisler, E., and Kreyenfeld, M. (2011) 'Against all odds: fathers' use of parental leave in Germany', *Journal of European Social Policy*, 21(1): 88–99.

Gillies, V. (2008) 'Childrearing, class and the new politics of parenting', *Sociology Compass*, 2(3): 1079–1095.

Haas, L. and Hwang, P. (2008) 'The impact of taking parental leave on fathers' participation in childcare and relationships with children: lessons from Sweden', *Community, Work and Family*, 11(1): 85–104. https://doi.org/10.1080/13668800701785346

Halrynjo, S. and Mangset, M. (2022) 'Parental leave vs. competition for clients: motherhood penalty in competitive work environments', *Journal of Family Research*, 34(3): 932–957. https://doi.org/10.20377/jfr-751

Hodkinson, P. and Brooks, R. (2018) 'Interchangeable parents? The roles and identities of primary and equal carer fathers of young children', *Current Sociology*, 68(6). https://doi.org/10.1177/0011392118807530

Hunter, S.C., Riggs, D.W. and Augoustinos, M. (2017) 'Hegemonic masculinity versus a caring masculinity: implications for understanding primary caregiving fathers', *Social & Personality Psychology Compass*, 11(4). https://doi.org/10.1111/spc3.12307

Johansson, T. and Klinth, R. (2008) 'Caring fathers: the ideology of gender equality and masculine positions', *Men and Masculinities*, 11(1): 42–62. https://doi.org/10.1177/1097184X06291899

Jordan, A. (2020) 'Masculinizing care? Gender, ethics of care, and fathers' rights group', *Men and Masculinities*, 23(1): 20–41. https://doi.org/10.1177/1097184X18776364

Kilkey, M. and Clarke, H. (2010) 'Disabled men and fathering: opportunities and constraints', *Community, Work & Family*, 13(2): 127–146. https://doi.org/10.1080/13668800902923738

Lareau, A. (2003) *Unequal Childhoods: Class, Race, and Family Life*. Berkeley: University of California Press.

Liversage, A. (2015) 'Minority ethnic men and fatherhood in a Danish context', in G. Eydal and T. Rostgaard (eds) *Fatherhood in the Nordic Welfare States: Comparing Care Policies and Practice*, Bristol: Policy Press, pp 209–230.

Meil, G. (2013) 'European men's use of parental leave and their involvement in child care and housework', *Journal of Comparative Family Studies*, 44(5): 557–570. https://doi.org/10.3138/jcfs.44.5.557

Meil, G., Romero-Balsas, P. and Rogero-García, J. (2018) 'Parental leave in Spain: use, motivations and implications', *Revista Española de Sociología*, 27(3): 27–43. http://dx.doi.org/10.22325/fes/res.2018.32

Miller, T. (2011a) *Making Sense of Fatherhood: Gender, Caring and Work*. Cambridge: Cambridge University Press.

Miller, T. (2011b) 'Falling back into gender? Men's narratives and practices around first-time fatherhood', *Sociology*, 45: 1094–1109.

Mitchell, J.L. and Lashewicz, B. (2016) 'Generative fathering: a framework for enriching understandings of fathers raising children who have disability diagnoses', *Journal of Family Studies*, 25(2): 184–198. https://doi.org/10.1080/13229400.2016.1212727

Moss, P., Duvander, A.-Z. and Koslowski, A. (eds) (2019) *Parental Leave and Beyond: Recent International Developments, Current Issues and Future Directions*. Bristol: Bristol University Press.

O'Brien, M. (2009) 'Fathers, parental leave policies, and infant quality of life: International perspectives and policy impact', *Annals of the American Academy of Political and Social Science*, 624(1): 190–213. https://doi.org/10.1177/0002716209334349

O'Brien, M. and Wall, K. (2017) *Comparative Perspectives on Work-Life Balance and Gender Equality: Fathers on Leave Alone*. SpringerOpen. https://library.oapen.org/bitstream/handle/20.500.12657/28116/1/1001878.pdf

Oláh, L. and Gähler, M. (2014) 'Gender equality perceptions, division of paid and unpaid work, and partnership dissolution in Sweden', *Social Forces*, 93(2): 571–594. https://doi.org/10.1093/sf/sou066

Petts, R. (2022) *Father Involvement and Gender Equality in the United States: Contemporary Norms and Barriers*. Abingdon: Routledge.

Pinho, M., Gaunt, R. and Gross, H. (2021) 'Caregiving dads, breadwinning mums: pathways to the division of family roles among role-reversed and traditional parents', *Marriage & Family Review*, 57(4): 346–374. https://doi.org/10.1080/01494929.2021.1875102

Ralph, D. (2016) '"Who should do the caring"? Involved fatherhood and ambivalent gendered moral rationalities among cohabiting/married Irish parents', *Community, Work & Family*, 19(1): 63–79. https://doi.org/10.1080/13668803.2014.1000266

Ranson, G. (2014) *Fathering, Masculinity and the Embodiment of Care*. Dordrecht: Springer.

Rehel, E.M. (2014) 'When Dad stays home too: paternity leave, gender, and parenting', *Gender and Society*, 28(1): 110–132. https://doi.org/10.1177/0891243213503900

Romero-Balsas, P. (2012) 'Fathers taking paternity leave in Spain: which characteristics foster and which hampers the use of paternity leave?', *Sociologia e politiche sociali*, 3: 106–131. https://doi.org/10.3280/SP2012-SU3006

Romero-Balsas, P. (2015) 'Consecuencias del permiso de paternidad en el reparto de tareas y cuidados en la pareja/Consequences Paternity Leave on Allocation of Childcare and Domestic Tasks', *Reis*: 87–109. http://dx.doi.org/10.5477/cis/reis.1

Romero-Balsas, P., Meil, G. and Rogero-García, J. (2022) 'Is Spanish parental leave "traditionalising" the gender distribution of childcare and housework?', *Journal of Family Research*, 34(3): 983–1001. https://doi.org/10.20377/jfr-745

Rose, J., Brady, M., Yerkes, M.A. and Coles, L. (2014) '"Sometimes they just want to cry for their mum": couples' negotiations and rationalisations of gendered divisions in infant care', *Journal of Family Studies*, 21(1): 38–56. https://doi.org/10.1080/13229400.2015.1010264

Schmidt, E.-M. (2018) 'Breadwinning as care? The meaning of paid work in mothers' and fathers' constructions of parenting', *Community, Work & Family*, 21(4): 445–462. https://doi.org/10.1080/13668803.2017.1318112

Schober, P.S. (2014) 'Parental leave and domestic work of mothers and fathers: a longitudinal study of two reforms in West Germany', *Journal of Social Policy*, 43(2): 351–72. https://doi.org/10.1017/S0047279413000809

Sullivan, O. (2019) 'Gender inequality in work–family balance', *Nature Human Behaviour*, 3(3): 201–203. http://dx.doi.org/10.1038/s41562-019-0536-3

Tammelin, M., Repo, K. and Eerola, P. (2025). 'Families with children in a turbulent era: setting the scene', in M. Tammelin, K. Repo and P. Eerola (eds) *Families with Children in a Turbulent Era*. Cheltenham: Edward Elgar, pp 1–8.

Tarrant, A. (2021). *Fathering and Poverty: Uncovering Men's Participation in Low-Income Family Life*. Bristol: Policy Press.

Tremblay, D.G. and Genin, É. (2011) 'Parental leave: an important employee right, but an organizational challenge', *Employee Responsibilities and Rights Journal*, 23: 249–268. https://doi.org/10.1007/s10672-011-9176-0

Tronto, J. (1993) *Moral Boundaries: A Political Argument for an Ethic of Care*. New York: Routledge.

Tronto, J. (2013) *Caring Democracy: Markets, Equality, and Justice*. New York: New York University Press.

Twamley, K. (2021) '"She has mellowed me into the idea of SPL": unpacking relational resources in UK couples' discussions of shared parental leave take-up', *Families Relationships and Societies*, 10(1): 67–82, https://doi.org/10.1332/204674320X15986394583380

Twamley, K. (2024) *Caring Is Sharing? Couples Navigating Parental Leave at the Transition to Parenthood*. London: UCL Press.

Twamley, K. and Schober, P. (2019) 'Shared parental leave: exploring variations in attitudes, eligibility, knowledge and take-up intentions of expectant mothers in London', *Journal of Social Policy*, 48(2): 387–407.

Wheeler, S. (2018) '"Essential assistance" versus "concerted cultivation": theorising class-based patterns of parenting in Britain', *Pedagogy, Culture & Society*, 26(3): 327–344. https://doi.org/10.1080/14681366.2017.1401551

Ylikännö, M., Pääkkönen, H. and Hakovirta, M. (2015) 'Time use of Finnish fathers – do institutions matter?', in G. Eydal and T. Rostgaard (eds) *Fatherhood in the Nordic Welfare States: Comparing Care Policies and Practice*, Bristol: Policy Press, pp 103–120.

2

The who, what and how of care in caring fatherhood: an ecological care ethics approach

Andrea Doucet

Introduction

I've been researching fathering, care and caring fatherhood for almost 30 years. My research journey began in southwest England in the early 1990s, with a qualitative doctoral research project on mother/father couples who self-identified as shared caregiving couples; this was followed by three overlapping qualitative longitudinal projects (2000–2016) focused mainly on Canadian fathers who self-identified as stay-at-home and/or primary or shared primary caregivers and fathers who took extended parental leave.[1] I spent the first two decades grappling with the meanings, processes, practices, challenges and generative effects of fathers' caregiving. In my third decade of researching fathers and care, I reached an impasse in my thinking.

This impasse had two main instigators. The first occurred when I revisited and re-interviewed fathers and mothers roughly ten years after our first interviews. I soon realised I was also revisiting how I was defining, interpreting and measuring unpaid care work. The second source of my intellectual block sprang from my work on a parallel research programme, which entailed mapping a feminist, relational and ecological approach to narratives, concepts and knowledge making *about care* and *with care*. With each passing year, my questions about *what* I was studying became more deeply connected to *how* I was studying. It became clear that to move beyond my impasse, I had to interweave these two research programmes – one on care and one on *how* to research care.

This chapter aims to interrogate how caring fatherhood is understood and practiced, especially in Global North contexts. Specifically, I focus on the 'care' in caring fatherhood by asking: (1) *who* is a caring father?; (2) *what* is the care in caring fatherhood?; and (3) *how* do we measure the care in caring fatherhood?

I have organised the chapter into four sections. First, I share my analysis of two stages of interviews across ten years with one case study couple, Don and Yvonne and how re-interviewing them contributed to my intellectual impasse. Then, I briefly detail the broad feminist, relational and ecological approach to narratives, concepts and knowledge making that underpin this chapter. Third, I provide a mapping of historical and conceptual narratives about paid and unpaid work, gender divisions of labour and caring fatherhood. Finally, I offer one alternative conceptual framing for research on fathering and care. It is embedded in concepts of care ethics and ecological care ethics and what I call the '3 Rs' of care: relationalities, responsiveness and responsibilities.

What is a caring father? (Don and Yvonne, 2004–2014)

Don and Yvonne: 'stars' of my study?

To begin with my story about Don and Yvonne, I take you back to the early 2000s, when a younger version of me, a mother of three young children, would often see Don in my neighbourhood. He was hard to miss, always with his four sons under the age of five in tow. I remember standing in line to sign my daughters up for summer camp at our local community centre and hearing his voice – a recognisably lone male voice amid a chorus of mothers' voices – discussing sleepless nights, spit, vomit and poo.

Don and his common-law partner, Yvonne, both white, middle-class engineers, participated in my study on fathers (single dads and/or stay-at-home dads) who self-defined as primary or shared primary caregivers (for example, Doucet, 2006). He was my study's 104th dad and the 69th stay-at-home dad; he and Yvonne were the 14th participating couple. I conducted an in-person interview with Don, one with Yvonne and then a couple interview with both, using a participatory visual method called the Household Portrait, which facilitates conversations about gender divisions of domestic labour and unpaid work (see Doucet, 2001; see also Christopher, 2020).[2]

In my analysis and writing, Don and Yvonne stood out as being similar to what Francine Deutsch (1999: 7) called 'equal sharers' or 'the stars' in her study of shared caregiving couples. Don was undoubtedly one of the 'star' fathers of my study. In my mind, he embodied and displayed what it meant to be a caring father at home, in the workplace and in the community.

At *home*, Don was not only a stay-at-home father for five years, but he also did most of the day-to-day caregiving for the couple's four young boys and was responsible for much of the family's care and community-based parenting work (that is, volunteering in and leading community parent-child groups, volunteering in school and participating in children's extracurricular activities).

In his community, Don was at the cutting edge of a new generation of fathers pushing for public recognition of their competence as caregivers of children – fathers who challenged 'masculine work norms' and community-based norms about mothering and fathering. In contrast to some fathers, who described parent-toddler groups as 'estrogen-filled worlds' (Doucet, 2006), Don not only participated in these groups but was also elected group coordinator.

At his paid *work*, Don pushed for his parental leave rights and faced the consequences of his self-advocacy. He increased his leave time from six weeks for their first son, to ten weeks for their second, to 25 weeks for their third. He told me that he 'hated the first two leaves because they were too short'. When preparing for his third leave, he received what he called 'veiled threats' from company management. After their fourth child was born, he took the couple's full entitlement of 35 weeks of parental leave and Yvonne took her 17 weeks of maternity leave. Shortly after, Don accepted a severance package; his company was downsizing and, as he said when I revisited him a decade later: 'I'll just return [to work] later … Enjoy those years and not let them slip by.'

Revisiting: and so, is Don still a caring father?

A great deal had changed in Don and Yvonne's household when I revisited them in late December 2014. That night, I conducted three interviews at their kitchen table: one with each of them and then an interview with them as a couple. In their individual interviews, we traced their home and employment lives with a method called the Lifeline (Davies, 1996, Doucet, 2018a), which took them back to their teenage selves after secondary school, through the years of working and raising their four boys, and to their future hopes and ideal worlds.

In their couple interview, we used the Household Portrait method again to map Don and Yvonne's work and care lives. I had brought their earlier Household Portrait with me – two long sheets of now partly crumpled paper, with coloured cards denoting what I soon realised was a very different allocation of household work and childcare. Constructed with me in 2004, it depicted a primary caregiving father and a primary breadwinning mother. Don was devoting most of his time to the day-to-day care work and responsibilities of family and household life, and Yvonne was prioritising breadwinning responsibilities while being highly involved in household and care work.

A decade later, it was stunningly clear in Don and Yvonne's new Household Portrait that responsibilities for care had moved from Don to Yvonne, and the primary breadwinning responsibilities were now Don's. He had shifted from being a stay-at-home dad to working overtime while Yvonne worked flexibly around the children's needs and schedules. Using the terminology of the field of gender divisions of labour, they had *reverted* from a version of 'equal sharing' or 'stars of the study' to a 'traditional' division of domestic labour.

As I sat with Don and Yvonne, an uneasy feeling came over me. It seemed like there were two distinct stories that I could tell about them in my research writing. On the one hand, there was the 'data on the page' – the decided shift in their Household Portraits. On the other hand, Don and Yvonne's reflections and rationale for how they organised their paid and unpaid work in 2014 reflected their consistent and shared commitment to caring.

Comparing their two Household Portraits, Don and Yvonne talked about what had changed and why, and how they each felt about it. It was clear in their individual interviews, their Lifeline maps and their couple interview that they accepted this shift in pattern as a temporary and necessary arrangement. Yvonne laid out how she had worked long hours in a private engineering firm when the boys were little, especially in the five years when Don was at home. This allowed her to gain the experience she needed to advance in her career and to eventually move from the private to the public sector, where she could take advantage of what they referred to as 'leave with income averaging' during the summer months.

Don rationalised his heavier paid workload and reduced family time in 2014, pointing out: 'It's not that hard and it benefits [us] a lot – the family, financially. And it gets us to retirement a lot quicker.' He further clarified, 'We still take time together and we take more vacations, I would say, more than most full-time employed families.' Don also noted that he was planning to reduce his work hours in the upcoming year, delegating responsibilities to other employees so that he could take on more responsibilities at home. He wanted to retire from full-time work within a couple of years. He told me: 'I want to be around the kids before they move out. And now that Andrew is in grade eleven, I think it's an important time to be around, not be too stressed and, you know, be there for them.' He also spoke about the four boys taking a gap year after high school, as he and Yvonne had done, so that they could perhaps travel, learn about different cultures and engage in environmental protection work.

When I left their home that cold winter evening, I remember sitting in my car for a long time. I asked myself: how do I characterise this household? If I refer to Don as a 'breadwinning father', would that override what I had previously written about him? Was he not still a 'caring father'? In the months and years that followed, I puzzled over a series of *who, what and how* questions. I asked: (1) *who* is a caring father?; (2) *what is* the care in caring fatherhood?; and (3) *how* do we assess and measure caring fatherhood?

Methodologies and epistemologies: mapping a knowledge-making approach *about care* and *with care*

To begin to answer the questions posed previously, I drew from and deepened my parallel research programme on narratives, concepts and knowledge-making practices, which bring together feminist, relational and ecological resources. Here, I draw mainly from the interwoven relational and ecological strands of this work. The relational thread is derived from relational sociology (for an overview, see Mauthner [2021]) and relational knowledge making approaches, with a strong focus on the work of American historical sociologist Margaret Somers, including her relational approach to narratives (for example, Somers, 1994) and concepts (Somers, 2008). My historical reading of fields as entangled historical and conceptual narratives is broadly rooted in epistemic reflexivity (Somers, 2008; see also Bourdieu and Wacquant, 1992), relational ontologies and historical epistemologies. Specifically, I am guided by the view that all historical narratives and concepts, including those about caring fatherhood, are 'cultural and historical objects' that 'lack natures or essences; instead, they have histories, networks and narratives' (Somers, 2008: 209). This means that I engage with 'relational patterns' (Somers, 2008: 204) of concepts with the aim of gaining a 'sense of *how we think and why we seem obliged to think in certain ways*' (Hacking, 1990: 362, cited in Somers, 2008: 254, emphasis added) while trying to figure out 'how to begin the process of unthinking' (Somers, 2008: 265).

The *ecological* part of my approach grows out of ecological theory and philosophy (for example, Ingold, 2011; Tsing, 2015; Haraway, 2016), especially Lorraine Code's ecological knowledge-making approach and my extension of her case study of ecological epistemologies in the work of the early 20th-century American ecological thinker Rachel Carson (for example, Doucet, 2021). In a nutshell (literally and metaphorically), an ecological approach embraces relational ontologies, multiple ontologies, and an urgent sense of the ethics and politics of knowledge making (see the overview given in Doucet [2018b]).

Relational ontologies refer to how what something *is* and *does* is shaped by and within a wide array of intra-affective contexts and habitats, as well as their methodological, conceptual and onto-epistemological measurement apparatuses. Intra-twined with relational ontologies, *multiple ontologies* move beyond an assumption of singularity in data, concepts and the scholarly narratives we craft (for example, Mol, 2002; Haraway, 2016). What this means for defining care and caring fatherhood is that different kinds of care and different understandings of caring fathers – all constituted by their complex habitats and measuring apparatuses – can exist simultaneously, and researchers sometimes need to comfortably (or uncomfortably) hold two positions at once.

Ecological theories, epistemologies and philosophies are partly informed by the escalating urgency of climate crises, which have made the 'ethical-political' (Code, 2006: 52) dimensions of knowledge making even more central. Ecological thinkers maintain that all knowledge-making practices are situated and that epistemic communities are not 'benign' (Code, 2006: v), but rather are 'opaque structures of vested interest' (Code 2020: 66). How does this affect the narrative I craft in this chapter? The historical narratives we tell are underpinned and made possible by specific conceptual narratives, and we need to acknowledge and take responsibility for these mappings and for the claims we make in specific socio-cultural and historical contexts and moments.

Historical and conceptual narratives of caring fatherhood

There are many ways to map historical and conceptual narratives, including those centred on ideals and practices of caring fatherhood. One good approach is drawn from Nancy Fraser's (2016, 2022) historical mapping of capitalism, care, and paid and unpaid work, which gives some attention to ecological and intersectional concerns. Fraser describes a critical shift in Global North countries from hegemonic norms and patterns of male breadwinner/female caregiver households (after the Second World War until approximately the 1980s) to ideals of 'two-earner households' as part of the late 20th and early 21st centuries' 'globalizing financialized capitalism' and related 'care crises' and 'care deficits' (Fraser, 2016: 100, 112). This shift encompasses several historical processes in gendered paid and unpaid work, including rising employment levels for mothers; recurring recessions with effects on male employment; inadequate state support for the care of children, the elderly and people with disabilities; accelerated levels of care work falling to mainly women, families, communities and transnational 'care chains'; and a 'dualized organization of social reproduction, commodified for those who can pay for it, privatized for those who cannot' (Fraser, 2016: 104).

This historical phase is also deeply tied to the rise of scholarship on fathers, to calls for men to be involved in childrearing, and to the seeds of concepts and categories of 'father involvement' and 'caring fathers'. Research on caring fatherhood has always been multifaceted. It has focused on many topics, including the influence of caring fathers on children's developmental outcomes (for example, Lamb et al, 1985; Barnett et al, 1992; Marsiglio, 1995; Lamb and Day, 2004), generative effects for fathers (for example, Hawkins et al, 1993; Hawkins and Dollahite, 1996), impacts on maternal employment and gender equality (for example, Fraser, 1994; Crompton, 1999) and on gender divisions of domestic labour (for an overview, see Doucet [2023a]).

I attend to two interconnected research fields that continue to develop in this ongoing historical context. The first is gender divisions of domestic labour; the second, closely tied to concepts of caring fatherhood, is research on father involvement. This overview is selective and for the sake of brevity, I mainly highlight research on two-parent (mother/father) households as these studies have dominated the field to date and have set the theoretical, conceptual, methodological and epistemological parameters of the wider fields of gender divisions of domestic labour and fathering research.

Gender divisions of domestic labour

Since its inception, the field of gender divisions of domestic labour has aimed at 'trying to understand what goes on inside the home and why the distribution of housework among heterosexual couples (has) remained so unequal' (Sullivan, 2018: 379). Its central questions have been 'Who does what?' (Berk, 1985: 15) and 'How much more are fathers doing at home?' (Hochschild with Machung, 1989: 4). Looking back to the 1980s and 1990s, there were many qualitative research studies on gender divisions, mainly about white mother/father families from varied social class locations in the UK and the US (for example, Pahl, 1984; Berk, 1985; Hochschild with Machung, 1989; Morris, 1990; Brannen and Moss, 1991; Deutsch, 1999). These studies investigated a wide array of care tasks. The work of Ray Pahl and others (see also Wallace and Pahl, 1985; Wallace, 2002; Crow and Ellis, 2017), for instance, highlighted broad conceptual and empirical definitions of unpaid work, the shifting meanings and boundaries within and between paid and unpaid work, the interplay between provisioning and meeting care needs, and the widening of unpaid and domestic work to embrace community-based work and volunteer work.

Qualitative studies on gender divisions of domestic labour have continued to flourish in the ensuing decades, but it is quantitative studies, national surveys, panel surveys and time-use studies (for example, time budgets, time-use diaries and time-use surveys) that have dominated the field. Their rapid growth through the 1980s and 1990s was partly a response to various socioeconomic, technological and political forces, such as the rise of big data, 'the availability of large sets of microeconomic data' (Hamermesh, 2016: 198) and the interest of national statistics agencies in how populations spend their time. The steep increase in time-use studies is also connected to the 1995 United Nations Fourth World Women's Conference, where the Beijing Platform for Action called for all national governments to conduct time-use studies to make visible women's unpaid domestic contributions to national economies.

Time-use studies are now widely regarded as the 'gold standard' for measuring unpaid work (Altintas and Sullivan, 2016: 456), while for feminist researchers, they have 'been invaluable in estimating the labor time contributed by household members and in measuring all forms of work' (Beneria, 2015: 369). At the same time, they have also set the conceptual, methodological, ontological and epistemological parameters of how *care work* – and, by association, caring fatherhood – is defined and measured.

Father involvement and caring fatherhood

In the 1980s, leading fathering scholars provided one of the most comprehensive definitions of involved or caring fathers (Lamb et al, 1985; see also Lamb, 2000). Lamb, with colleagues Pleck and Levine, envisioned fathering involvement as a set of three practices that aim to meet children's needs. These practices are:

(i) 'interaction' (later revised to 'engagement' [Lamb, 1987]), which refers to 'the father's direct contact with his child, through caretaking and shared activities' (Lamb et al, 1985: 884);
(ii) 'accessibility', or 'availability', which is defined as 'being present or accessible to the child' (Lamb et al, 1985: 884); and
(iii) 'responsibility', which refers to 'the role fathers take in making sure that the child is taken care of and arranging for resources to be available for the child' (Lamb et al, 1985: 884).

Although this approach has been tweaked slightly over the years and was widened considerably by Pleck (2010), it still influences many quantitative studies that measure caring fatherhood through surveys or time-use studies (for example, Petts and Knoester, 2018; Wray, 2020; Shafer, 2023). Perhaps less well known about Lamb and colleagues' work (1985) is that they clearly recognised the methodological and epistemological dimensions of involved fatherhood. Specifically, they knew that their definition of 'engagement' was conceptually connected to time-use methodologies that measured 'the amount of time spent in activities involving the child' and the 'father's direct contact with his child, through caretaking and shared activities' (Lamb et al, 1985: 884). They also acknowledged that accessibility and responsibility could not be measured by time. Pleck and other researchers consequently sought to widen what fathering engagement meant by developing new survey categories aimed at 'radically broadening engagement and the larger construct of involvement to include thoughts, affects, perceptions, and beliefs' (Pleck 2010: 63).

Despite some innovative developments, conceptual narratives about caring fatherhood in the fields of gender divisions of labour and fatherhood have remained fairly consistent.

Who is a caring father?

In the field of gender divisions of domestic labour, a caring father, implicitly or explicitly, is defined as a man who takes on an 'equal' share of housework and childcare tasks or time. Although qualitative research can explore fathers' and sometimes mothers' accounts of what this looks like in practice, there is nevertheless an assumption that equality means sameness, as measured by a limited set of (usually) domestic-bound tasks, and this frame determines who is called a 'caring father' (although see the critique by Twamley and Fairclough [2023]). Overall, time and care, as well as tasks and care, are conceptually and empirically conflated – that is, the time fathers report spending with their children (or being in the presence of their children) or doing tasks with and/or for their children (such as supervising them or assisting them with homework) is interpreted as synonymous with caring behaviours, indeed with *being* a carer or caring father. The assumption is that care can be reduced to a task or to time, with little or no consideration of how a task or unit of time is enacted or experienced by caregivers and/or care receivers.

What is the care in caring fatherhood?

In the fields of gender divisions of domestic labour and fatherhood studies, there are at least three key conceptual narratives about the 'care' in caring fatherhood. The first, concerning divisions between paid and unpaid work, bears an overwhelming assumption that care only includes fathers' direct care for their children. Thus, paid provisioning that supports unpaid care work in a family is excluded from the concept of caring fatherhood.

Second, there has been a decades-old debate in the field of gender divisions of labour about whether and how unpaid care work should include housework (for an overview, see Oakley [2019]; Sullivan [2018]). The dominant position has been that care work and housework should be divided so that care involves the direct care of children, while housework, even if it includes tasks like cooking for or tidying up after children, is usually not considered to include care tasks (but see Folbre [2006] on 'direct care' and 'indirect care').

The third dominant narrative of caring fatherhood is that other unpaid care tasks and responsibilities, such as caring for other family members, the elderly and community-based caring activities, are not included in measurements of care.

How is the care in caring fatherhood measured?

In the field of gender divisions of labour and especially in panel surveys (which have boomed since the COVID-19 pandemic), care and caring fatherhood are often measured through a narrow range of childcare tasks and responsibilities are often treated as measurable tasks. Yet, since the 1990s, many studies have highlighted that care responsibilities should not be measured by 'clock time', but rather conceptualised as 'process time' (for example, Davies, 1994; Coltrane, 1996). Although more recent studies (for example, Lareau and Weininger, 2008; Daminger, 2019; Doucet, 2023b) have argued that care responsibilities cannot be gleaned through tasks or time, there is still a growing body of quantitative research that attempts to use surveys and time-use studies to measure care responsibilities.

Care-centric conceptual narratives and caring fathers

To date, gender divisions of domestic labour research and fatherhood studies have barely connected with care ethics (although see Hanlon, 2008; Doucet, 2016, 2018a, 2023a; Elliott, 2016). In this final section of the chapter, I briefly review historical and conceptual narratives of care ethics. And I ask: what would it mean to approach caring fatherhood from a care ethics perspective?

Historical narratives of care

Care ethics – or feminist care ethics, as it is often called – is not a single field. Its trajectory is multiple, fluid and constantly changing in response to unfolding historical contexts, crises and research problematics. My summary here is likewise shaped by the narrative I am crafting in this chapter, which is selective and provisional and hinges on my specific questions. What I offer is one modest mapping.

Care ethics has unfolded in waves, beginning in the early 1980s with Carol Gilligan's (1982) first edition of *In a Different Voice*. Her book challenged leading theories and paradigms of human and moral development, as well as political and philosophical theories of justice, on conceptual, methodological, ontological and epistemological grounds. It also contested dominant liberal political and economic theories found in highly influential work on moral and human development (for example, Kohlberg, 1981) and critiqued abstract, generalised and individualised ideals of justice (for example, Rawls, 1971).

Each subsequent decade has widened and deepened the focus of care ethics. Briefly, throughout the late 1980s and 1990s, a second wave of care ethics attended to the political dimensions of care; connections between care and justice (for example, Gilligan, 1986; Held, 1995; Tronto, 1995); the sociopolitical dimensions and effects of how care is performed, delivered and managed (see Sevenhjuisen, 1992, 1998; Tronto, 1993); and some attention to racialised, classed and colonial dimensions of care (for example, Hill Collins, 1989; Narayan, 1995). These concerns continued into the 2000s, with greater attention to the overlaps between care and economies (Folbre, 2006), care and democracies (Tronto, 2013), and care and international relations (Mahon and Robinson, 2012; Robinson, 2019).

A third, 21st-century wave of care ethics is still emerging, slowly expanding concepts of care focused on human, more-than-human and ecological care (for example, Tsing, 2015; Puig de la Bellacasa, 2017; Krasny, 2023), Indigenous conceptions of care (Doucet et al, 2024; Jewell, 2024), queer care and crip care (for example, Karjevsky et al, 2020), racialised care (Prattes, 2022) and care ethics as methodologies (for example, Raghuram, 2019; Brannelly and Barnes, 2022) and epistemologies (for example, Robinson, 2020).

Several definitions, characterisations and insights have persisted in this selective mapping of research and writing on feminist care ethics, and they are encapsulated by what I refer to as the '3 Rs' of care ethics: *relationalities, responsiveness* and *responsibilities* (see Doucet, 2023a). These '3 Rs' are so tightly woven together that they are difficult to pull apart. For example, Gilligan (1982: 16–17) writes that the ethic of care involves 'sensitivity to the needs of others and the assumption of responsibility for taking care' as well as 'an overriding concern with relationships and responsibilities'. She also characterises responsiveness as 'response-abilities' or the ability to respond (see also Tronto, 2020).

Feminist care ethics – and these '3 Rs' – moves between the empirical, theoretical, epistemological, ontological and ethical. This is no small point; it is perhaps what distinguishes care ethics from the large and impactful bodies of theoretical and empirical research on care, unpaid work, or social reproduction. Care ethics is more than tasks and time, activities, practices or theories. I shine a spotlight on these '3 Rs' in relation to the *who, what* and *how* of care ethics, and suggest ways they can be centred or applied in work on care and caring fatherhood.

Who is a caring father?

A relational subject

From the outset, care ethics has posited a relational understanding of human nature and human subjectivities. As Tronto (2013: 30) has long argued, it has 'a different starting point' because 'individuals are conceived of as being in relationships'. Care ethics conceives of subjectivity as embedded in relationships, attentive and responsive to the needs of others, and responsible for both human and nonhuman care in ways that demands personal and collective responsiveness for care services, supports and policies. A subject is also embodied, vulnerable and interdependent, sometimes balancing relationalities and 'relational autonomy' (Friedman, 1993), 'independent in some ways while being (more) dependent in other ways' (Friedman, 2014: 59).

A subject who is responsive to multiple, context-specific responsibilities

Care ethics advocates responsiveness to contextuality and particularity. At this moment in history, when families and nations face a 'polycrisis' (Torkington,

2023) comprising crises of care, ecologies, the cost of living, housing and health, to mention just a few, we need to be responsive to how people will care and provide for their families. Rather than viewing humans as caregivers *or* earners, a care ethics approach views all humans as needing to provide and be provided for, to care and be cared for, at varied points across the life course. This perspective acknowledges the 'secondary dependence in those who care for dependents' (Kittay, 1995: 11) and the critical role of resources, services and policies (such as childcare and employment leave policies and social protections for parents) for sustaining the provisioning activities needed to support caregivers and the work of caring.

A care ethics approach to concepts and practices of caring fatherhood would focus on fathers' and families' responsibilities for to a wider array of activities, practices and identities. This could include, for example, paid work, provisioning activities, or investing time in caring for the planet or modelling such behaviour. Returning to the case study of Don and Yvonne, I could highlight Don's responsiveness to the changing needs of his growing children. His temporary focus on increasing his income was a response to a new phase of childrearing in which his four boys would soon be graduating. He wanted to fund their postsecondary education and support travel and alternative learning opportunities that could help them become good ecological and global citizens.

What is the care in caring fatherhood?

Relationalities between many types of care

To explain care from a care ethics perspective, I draw on Tronto and Fisher, who emphasise that 'caring includes everything that we do to maintain, continue, and repair our "world" so that we can live in it as well as possible' – a 'world [that] includes our bodies, our selves, and our environment, all of which we seek to interweave in a complex, life-sustaining web' (Fisher and Tronto, 1990: 40; see also Tronto, 2013: 19).

This ecological metaphor of a 'life-sustaining web' illustrates the multiple threads of care being interwoven in specific temporal and spatial processes. I have learned, for example, from my research with Black and Indigenous collaborators about the wide array of caring work in this web, including volunteer work that supports one's community, securing safe housing, teaching children to navigate racialised school and community settings (Goddard-Durant et al, 2023) or, in the case of Indigenous populations, cultural teaching about human-land connections (Jewell, 2024; Jewell et al, 2020). With some cautiousness (see Doucet 2020; see also Glenn, 2000), I suggest that provisioning and financial support are also part of this care web. In some contexts, they can be viewed as part of care responsibilities and part of 'indirect care'.

Responsiveness: care as labour and love, activities and 'habit of mind'

Care is more than tasks and time. It is more than activities and doings. Tronto (1993: 127) describes care ethics as combining two dimensions: 'a practice rather than a set of rules or principles ... [involving] particular acts of caring' and a 'general habit of mind'. This 'habit of mind' embraces attentiveness (to the needs of others), competence, responsiveness and responsibilities.

What are care responsibilities?

From the wide field of care ethics, I pull one well-cited passage that strongly demonstrates how care responsibilities are interconnected processes that embrace care as labour and highlight the emotional, cognitive, organisational, networking and responsive qualities and values involved in caring practices. In the early 1990s, Tronto and Bernice Fisher (1990) developed the idea that care involves four complex processes or interconnected phases that interweave *relationalities, responsiveness and responsibilities*. Tronto (2013) later identified a fifth phase, as well as what she calls 'moral qualities' and 'dispositions' (Tronto, 2013: 35, 19).

Taken together, these phases and their related moral elements are: (1) *caring about* someone's unmet needs (*attentiveness*); (2) *caring for* these needs (*responsibility*); (3) *caregiving* and making sure the work is done (*competence*); (4) *care receiving* and assessing the effectiveness of these care acts (*responsiveness*); and (5) *caring with*, which is about collective responsibilities for care that attends to the social and political, and for the creation of social policies that centre and support care (*plurality, communication, trust* and *respect*) (Tronto, 2013).

It is important to note that although Tronto uses the term 'responsibility' in just one part of her five phases of care, on my reading, these phases are all about more than care tasks – they are about the multilayered activities that constitute responsibilities for care. They involve building relationships with other caregivers and social institutions, making sure that care is 'good care', and assessing and modifying care as needed.

How do we research the care in caring fatherhood with care ethics?

The entanglement of care with methodologies and epistemologies is a small area of the care ethics field. Yet, it was already apparent in Gilligan's (1982: 19, emphasis added) earliest work, when she asserted that the ethics of care is partly a 'mode of thinking that is *contextual and narrative* rather than formal and abstract'. This implies that a care ethics approach prioritises qualitative research, but, more specifically, qualitative research that is centred on being *responsive* to particular research participants and their richly varied contexts, and being open to the complexities and varieties of care needs, practices and problems that occur in and for diverse populations. As care ethics is attentive to particularity, it does not advocate singularity or universality in principles or approaches.

Epistemologically, care ethics resists binaries and hierarchies (Robinson, 2020) of all kinds and calls for 'a move away from universalism and absolutism of modernist epistemology toward conceptions that emphasize particularity and concreteness' (Hekman, 1995: 2). This means, for example, interrogating the concepts and categories we use in research on families, fathering and care, and recognising that time and tasks are experienced and interpreted in multiple ways by both research participants and researchers (see Doucet, 2023a, 2023b; see also Sullivan, 2018).

An ecological care ethics approach also attends to relational ontologies, multiple ontologies, and the politics and ethics of knowledge making. Relational ontologies denote diversity, multiplicity and heterogeneity regarding what care tasks, care time and responsibilities *are*. This means that contexts and habitats matter in terms of whether and how we think about the relationship between care and earning or breadwinning. There are examples of this interplay in research on low-income fatherhood (for example, Edin and Nelson, 2013; Tarrant, 2021), Black fathering (for example, Reynolds, 2009), in discussions about 'providing as a form of involvement and care' (Christiansen and Palkovitz 2001: 99; see also Eerola, 2014; Schmidt, 2017), and in feminist work on how paid and unpaid work are 'interwoven' in mothers' everyday lives mothering (Hill Collins, 1994: 372; Garey, 1999: 191; see also Reynolds, 2001). In this chapter's case study of Don and Yvonne, thinking with relational ontologies denotes a recognition of their shifting relationalities between paid and unpaid work responsibilities across time. Paid work does not stand apart from and in opposition to unpaid work; rather, it supports unpaid work and can thus, in some instances, be considered a form of 'indirect care' (Pleck, 2010; Doucet, 2020).

Multiple ontologies imply multiplicity rather than singularity in narratives and worlds. There are many stories to tell about caring fathers, and whether and how we connect caregiving and breadwinning depends on the socioeconomic, cultural and intersectional contexts we work within, our research aims, our epistemic communities and audiences, and our full awareness of our ethical-political responsibilities as knowledge makers. Returning to Don and Yvonne, I am cognisant that there are many scholarly narratives that I can tell. This means moving beyond adding up who does what to consider the temporal, spatial and relational contexts and rationales of how both partners navigate and choreograph their lives of caring – for four sons, each other and themselves, their household and community lives and their shifting commitments and structured conditions of paid work.

Can a care ethics approach include quantitative research?

What implications does this have for quantitative research on caring fatherhood? Let me be clear. Care ethics *can* inform quantitative research on care and caring fatherhood, but I maintain that this process still needs to centre the '3 Rs'. Here are three modest and practical suggestions.

First, quantitative research on gender divisions of domestic labour, which typically measure one person's perceptions of who does what in units of tasks or time, can be useful for assessing the relationalities between women's unpaid work, employment levels and pay, autonomy and wellbeing; men's presence and activities in the home; and changes in women and men's paid and unpaid work practices and, possibly, their identities. However, it *does not and cannot* tell us much about care processes or caring fatherhood. Care is not a tally sheet (Doucet, 2023a).

Second, in-depth quantitative research that measures fathering actions, such as 'warmth' and 'responsiveness' (for an overview, see Pleck, 2010; see also Schoppe-Sullivan and Fagan, 2020; Shafer et al, 2021; Shafer, 2023), can tell us about men's perceptions of their practices and identities of caring fatherhood. However, the specificities of how (and why or why not) these apply to diverse populations, including low-income, new immigrant and refugee, racialised, Indigenous and LGBTQ populations, should always be an open question. Rather than imposing a measuring grid, ecological care ethics research calls for attention to complexity, multiplicity and particularities, seeking to ascertain 'the explanatory power of an attentive concentration on local particulars' and 'how those specificities work together', while seeking to 'generate responsible remappings across wider, heterogeneous epistemic terrains' (Code, 2006: 50).

Third, from an ecological care ethics approach, researchers must attend to their responsibilities as knowers. When conducting quantitative or qualitative research about particular groups or even nations, people with situated knowledges from those sites should, ideally, be invited to sit at the research design and implementation 'table'. Researcher responsibilities can also extend to being more precise about the wider implications of our research. In the context of Canada, for example, a Canadian father who takes parental leave is *not* necessarily a caring father. Rather, he is an employee in standard full-time employment with legal entitlements to take paid leave; he has the financial resources to do so, as the wage replacement rate in most jobs is 33–55 per cent; he often, but not always, has the support of his employers to take time off from paid work; and, to return to my case study of Don, he might be disrupting dominant norms about male breadwinning and female caregiving. In short, our responsibilities as knowers demand that we are clear about what we can say about care processes – and caring fatherhood.

Conclusions

This chapter tells the story of a fathering scholar's journey of getting stuck and unstuck in burgeoning and changing research fields. It is informed by and calls for space and time to reflect on the historical and conceptual narratives within which we do research on care. I shine a spotlight on the 'care' in caring fatherhood by asking: (1) *who* is a caring father?; (2) *what* is the care in caring fatherhood?; and (3) *how* do we measure the care in caring fatherhood? Rooted in a care ethics and an ecological care ethics approach, I focus on relationalities, responsiveness and responsibilities (the '3 Rs') and how these can remake contemporary conceptual narratives of caring fatherhood.

A care-centred approach is not only about *what* we study but also about *how* we study. Care needs to be analysed relationally to assess 'whether the care given was sufficient, successful, or complete'. It 'requires the moral quality of responsiveness', which 'will often involve noting that new needs emerge as the past ones are met. *Thus, the process continues*' (Tronto, 2013; 35, emphasis added).

Our work as researchers also demands a continuous process of reassessing. We need to be clear on what and how we are measuring and how we write and speak about care. In this time of global polycrisis, we need to rethink how we understand the *who*, *what* and *how* of care, caring and caring fatherhood.

Notes

[1] In these three Canadian projects, I personally interviewed 218 mothers and fathers. I revisited 15 couples after nine to ten years and six couples after five years (for an overview, see Doucet, 2018a; Doucet and McKay, 2020).

[2] The Household Portrait explores a wide array of childcare and household tasks: housework; caring work; community-based domestic work, including 'household service work' and 'kin work'; do-it-yourself work; financial management; household subsistence activities; and overall responsibility for housework and childcare. It works a little like a board game, with participating couples sorting color-coded cards correlated with the seven categories of tasks and responsibilities. For a conceptually reconfigured version of the Household Portrait, the Care/Work Portrait, see Doucet and Klostermann (2024).

References

Altintas, E. and Sullivan, O. 2016. Fifty years of change updated: cross-national gender convergence in housework. *Demographic Research*, 35, 455–470.

Barnett, R. C., Marshall, N. L. and Pleck, J. H. 1992. Men's multiple roles and their relationship to men's psychological distress. *Journal of Marriage and the Family*, 54, 358–367.

Beneria, L. 2015. Paid and unpaid work: meanings and debates. In L. Beneria, G. Berik and M. S. Floro (eds) *Gender, Development and Globalization: Economics as if People Mattered*. New York: Routledge, pp 179–226.

Berk, S. F. 1985. *The Gender Factory: The Apportionment of Work in American Households*. New York: Plenum.

Bourdieu, P. and Wacquant, L. J. D. 1992. *An Invitation to Reflexive Sociology*. Chicago, University of Chicago Press.

Brannelly, T. and Barnes, M. 2022. *Researching with Care: Applying Feminist Care Ethics to Research Practice*. Bristol: Policy Press.

Brannen, J. and Moss, P. 1991. *Managing Mothers: Dual Earner Households after Maternity Leave*. London: Unwin Hyman.

Christiansen, S. L. and Palkovitz, R. 2001. Why the 'good provider' role still matters: providing as a form of paternal involvement. *Journal of Family Issues*, 22, 84–106.

Christopher, E. 2020. Capturing conflicting accounts of domestic labour: the household portrait as a methodology. *Sociological Research Online*, 26, 451–468.

Code, L. 2006. *Ecological Thinking: The Politics of Epistemic Location*. New York: Oxford University Press.

Code, L. 2020. *Manufactured Uncertainty: New Challenges to Epistemic Responsibility*. New York: SUNY Press.

Coltrane, S. 1996. *Family Man: Fatherhood, Housework and Gender Equity*. Oxford: Oxford University Press.

Crompton, R. (ed.). 1999. *Restructuring Gender Relations and Employment: The Decline of the Male Breadwinner*. Oxford: Oxford University Press.

Crow, G. and Ellis, J. (eds). 2017. *Revisiting Divisions of Labour: The Impacts and Legacies of a Modern Sociological Classic*. Manchester: Manchester University Press.

Daminger, A. 2019. The cognitive dimension of household labor. *American Sociological Review*, 84, 609–633.

Davies, K. 1994. The tensions between process time and clock time in carework: the example of day nurseries. *Time & Society*, 3, 277–303.

Davies, K. 1996. Capturing women's lives: a discussion of time and methodological issues. *Women's Studies International Forum*, 19, 579–588.

Deutsch, F. M. 1999. *Halving It All: How Equally Shared Parenting Works*. Cambridge, MA: Harvard University Press.

Doucet, A. 2001. 'You see the need perhaps more clearly than I have': exploring gendered processes of domestic responsibility. *Journal of Family Issues*, 22, 328–357.

Doucet, A. 2006. *Do Men Mother? Fathering, Care and Domestic Responsibility*. Toronto: University of Toronto Press.

Doucet, A. 2016. The ethics of care and the radical potential of fathers 'home alone on leave': care as practice, relational ontology and social justice. In: M. O'Brien and K. Wall (eds) *Comparative Perspectives on Work-Life Balance and Gender Equality*. New York: Springer, pp 11–28.

Doucet, A. 2018a. *Do Men Mother? Fathering, Care, and Parental Responsibilities*, 2nd edn. Toronto: University of Toronto Press.

Doucet, A. 2018b. Feminist epistemologies and ethics: ecological thinking, situated knowledges, epistemic responsibilities. In: R. Iphofen and M. Tolich (eds) *The SAGE Handbook of Qualitative Research Ethics*. London: Sage, 73–88.

Doucet, A. 2020. Father involvement, care and breadwinning: genealogies of concepts and revisioned conceptual narratives. *Genealogy*, 4, 1–17.

Doucet, A. 2021. What does Rachel Carson have to do with family sociology and family policies? Ecological imaginaries, relational ontologies and crossing social imaginaries. *Families, Relationships and Societies*, 10, 11–31.

Doucet, A. 2023a. Care is not a tally sheet: rethinking the field of gender divisions of domestic labour with care-centric conceptual narratives. *Families, Relationships and Societies*, 12, 10–30.

Doucet, A. 2023b. 'Time is not time is not time': a feminist ecological approach to clock time, process time and care responsibilities. *Time & Society*, 32, 434–460.

Doucet, A., Jewell, E. M. and Watts, V. 2024. Indigenous and feminist ecological reflections on feminist care ethics: encounters of care, absence, punctures and offerings. In: S. Bourgault, M. Fitzgerald and F. Robinson (eds) *Decentering Epistemologies and Challenging Privilege: Critical Care Ethics Perspectives*. New Brunswick, NJ: Rutgers University Press, pp 109–127.

Doucet, A. and Klostermann, J. 2024. What and how are we measuring when we research gendered divisions of domestic labor? Remaking the household portrait method into a care/work portrait. *Sociological Research Online*, 29, 243–263.

Doucet, A. and Mckay, L. 2020. Fathering, parental leave, impacts and gender equality: what/how are we measuring? *International Journal of Sociology and Social Policy*, 40, 441–463.

Edin, K. and Nelson, T. J. 2013. *Doing the Best I Can: Fatherhood in the Inner City*. Berkeley: University of California Press.

Eerola, P. 2014. Nurturing, breadwinning and upbringing: paternal responsibilities by Finnish men in early fatherhood. *Community, Work & Family*, 17, 308–324.

Elliott, K. 2016. Caring masculinities: theorizing an emerging concept. *Men and Masculinities*, 19, 240–259.

Fisher, B. and Tronto, J. 1990. Towards a feminist theory of caring. In: E. K. Abel and M. K. Nelson (eds) *Circles of Care: Work and Identity in Women's Lives*. New York: State University of New York Press, pp 35–62.

Folbre, N. 2006. Measuring care: gender, empowerment and the care economy. *Journal of Human Development*, 7, 183–199.

Fraser, N. 1994. After the family wage: gender equity and the welfare state. *Political Theory*, 22, 591–618.

Fraser, N. 2016. Contradictions of capital and care. *New Left Review*, 100, 99–117.

Fraser, N. 2022. *Cannibal Capitalism: How Our System Is Devouring Democracy, Care and the Planet and What We Can Do about it*. New York: Verso.

Friedman, M. 1993. Beyond caring: the demoralization of gender. In: M. J. Larrabee (ed.) *An Ethic of Care: Feminist and Interdisciplinary Perspectives*. London: Routledge, pp 258–274.

Friedman, M. 2014. Relational autonomy and independence. In: A. Veltman and M. Piper (eds) *Autonomy, oppression and Gender*. Oxford: Oxford University Press, pp 42–60.

Garey, A. I. 1999. *Weaving Work and Motherhood*. Philadelphia: Temple University Press.

Gilligan, C. 1982. *In a Different Voice: Psychological Theory and Women's Development*. Cambridge, MA: Harvard University Press.

Gilligan, C. 1986. 'Reply by Carol Gilligan'. *Signs: Journal of Women in Culture and Society*, 11, 324–333.

Glenn, E. N. 2000. Creating a caring society. *Contemporary Sociology*, 29, 84–94.

Goddard-Durant, S. K., Doucet, A., Tizaa, H. and Sieunarine, J. A. 2023. 'I don't have the energy': Rrcial stress, young Black motherhood and Canadian social policies. *Canadian Review of Sociology*, 60, 542–566.

Hacking, I. 1990. Two kinds of 'new historicism' for philosophers. *New Literary History*, 21, 343–364.

Hamermesh, D. S. 2016. What's to know about time use? *Journal of Economic Surveys*, 30, 198–203.

Hanlon, N. 2008. *Masculinities and Affective Equality: Love Labour and Care Labour in Men's Lives*. Dublin: Equality Studies Centre, University College Dublin.

Haraway, D. 2016. *Staying with the Trouble: Making Kin in the Chthulucene*. Durham, NC: Duke University Press.

Hawkins, A. J. and Dollahite, D. C. 1996. *Generative Fathering: Beyond Deficit Perspectives*, Thousand Oaks: Sage.

Hawkins, A. J., Christiansen, S. L., Sargent, K. P. and Hill, E. J. 1993. Rethinking fathers' involvement in child care: a developmental perspective. *Journal of Family Issues*, 14, 531–549.

Hekman, S. 1995. *Moral Voices, Moral Selves: Carol Gilligan and Feminist Moral Theory*. Cambridge: Polity Press.

Held, V. 1995. The meshing of care and justice. *Hypatia*, 10, 128–132.

Hill Collins, P. 1989. The social construction of Black feminist thought. *Signs*, 14, 745–773.

Hill Collins, P. 1994. Shifting the center: race, class and feminist theorizing and motherhood. In: D. Bassin, M. Honey and M. M. Kaplan (eds) *Representations of Motherhood*. New Haven: Yale University Press, pp 56–74.

Hochschild, A. with Machung, A. 1989. *The Second Shift: Working Parents and the Revolution at Home*. New York: Avon.

Ingold, T. 2011. *Being Alive: Essays on Movement, Knowledge and Description*. Abingdon: Routledge.

Jewell, E. M., Doucet, A., Falk, J. and Fyke, S. 2020. Social knowing, mental health, and the importance of Indigenous resources: a case study of Indigenous employment engagement in Southwestern Ontario. *Canadian Review of Social Policy*, 80, 1–25.

Jewell, E. 2024. Towards an anti-colonial feminist care ethic. In: G. Starblanket (ed.) *Making Space for Indigenous Feminism*. Halifax: Fernwood Publishing, pp 168–192.

Karjevsky, G., Talevi, R. and Bailer, S. (eds). 2020. *Letters to Joan*. np: New Alphabet School, pp 33–49.

Kittay, E. F. 1995. Taking dependency seriously: The Family and Medical Leave Act considered in light of the social organization of dependency work and gender equality. *Hypatia*, 10, 8–29.

Kohlberg, L. 1981. *The Philosophy of Moral Development*. New York: Harper & Row.

Krasny, E. 2023. *Living with an Infected Planet: COVID-19, Feminism and the Global Frontline of Care,* Berlin: Transcript.

Lamb, M. E. (ed.). 1987. *The Father's Role: Cross-cultural Perspectives*. Hillsdale, NJ: Lawrence Erlbaum.

Lamb, M. E. 2000. The history of research on father involvement. *Marriage and Family Review*, 29, 23–42.

Lamb, M. E. and Day, R. D. (eds). 2004. *Reconceptualising and Measuring Father Involvement*. Hillsdale, NJ: Lawrence Erlbaum.

Lamb, M. E., Pleck, J. H., Charnov, E. L. and Levine, J. A. 1985. Paternal behavior in humans. *American Zoologist*, 25, 883–894.

Lareau, A. and Weininger, E. B. 2008. Time, work and family life: reconceptualizing gendered time patterns through the case of children's organized activities. *Sociological Forum*, 23, 419–454.

Mahon, R. and Robinson, F. 2012. *Feminist Ethics and Social Policy: Towards a New Global Political Economy of Care*. Vancouver: UBC Press.

Marsiglio, W. (ed.) 1995. *Fatherhood: Contemporary Theory, Research and Social Policy*. Thousand Oaks, CA: Sage.

Mauthner, N. S. 2021. Karen Barad's posthumanist relational ontology: an intra-active approach to theorising and studying family practices. *Families, Relationships and Societies*, 10.

Mol, A. 2002. *The Body Multiple: Ontology in Medical Practice*. Durham, NC: Duke University Press.

Morris, L. 1990. *The Workings of the Household: A US-UK Comparison*. Cambridge: Polity Press.

Neale, B. and Tarrant, A. 2024. *The Dynamics of Young Fatherhood: Understanding the Parenting Journeys and Support Needs of Young Fathers*. Bristol: Policy Press.

Narayan, U. 1995. Colonialism and its others: considerations on rights and care discourses. *Hypatia*, 10, 133–140.

Oakley, A. 2019. *The Sociology of Housework*. Bristol: Policy Press.

Pahl, R. E. 1984. *Divisions of Labour*. Oxford: Basil Blackwell.

Petts, R. J. and Knoester, C. 2018. Paternity leave-taking and father engagement. *Journal of Marriage and Family*, 80, 1144–1162.

Pleck, J. H. 2010. Paternal involvement: revised conceptualization and theoretical linkages with child outcomes. In: M. E. Lamb (ed.) *The Role of the Father in Child Development*, 5th edn. Hoboken, NJ: John Wiley & Sons.

Prattes, R. 2022. Caring masculinities and race: on racialized workers and 'new fathers'. *Men and Masculinities*, 25, 721–742.

Puig de la Bellacasa, M. 2017. *Matters of Care: Speculative Ethics in More Than Human Worlds*. Minnaeapolis: University of Minnesota Press.

Raghuram, P. 2019. Race and feminist care ethics: intersectionality as method. *Gender, Place & Culture*, 26, 613–637.

Rawls, J. 1971. *A Theory of Justice*. Cambridge, MA: Harvard University Press.

Reynolds, T. 2001. Black mothering, paid work and identity. *Ethnic and Racial Studies*, 24, 1046–1064.

Reynolds, T. 2009. Exploring the absent/present dilemma: Black fathers, family relationships and social capital in Britain. *Annals of the American Academy of Political and Social Science*, 624, 12–28.

Robinson, F. 2019. *Globalizing Care: Ethics, Feminist Theory and International Relations*. Abingdon: Routledge.

Robinson, F. 2020. Resisting hierarchies through relationality in the ethics of care. *International Journal of Care and Caring*, 4, 11–23.

Schmidt, E.-M. 2017. Breadwinning as care? The meaning of paid work in mothers' and fathers' constructions of parenting. *Community, Work & Family*, 21, 445–462.

Schoppe-Sullivan, S. J. and Fagan, J. 2020. The evolution of fathering research in the 21st century: persistent challenges, new directions. *Journal of Marriage and Family*, 82, 175–197.

Shafer, K. 2023. *So Close, Yet So Far: Fathering in Canada and the United States*. Toronto: University of Toronto Press.

Shafer, K., Petts, R. J. and Scheibling, C. 2021. Variation in masculinities and fathering behaviors: a cross-national comparison of the United States and Canada. *Sex Roles*, 84, 439–453.

Sevenhuijsen, S. 1992. Paradoxes of gender: ethical and epistemological perspectives in care in feminist political theory. *Acta Politica*, 2, 131–149.

Sevenhuijsen, S. 1998. *Citizenship and the Ethics of Care: Feminist Considerations on Justice, Morality and Politics*. Abingdon: Routledge.

Somers, M. R. 1994. The narrative constitution of identity: a relational and network approach. *Theory and Society*, 23, 605–649.

Somers, M. R. 2008. *Genealogies of Citizenship: Markets, Statelessness and the Right to Have Rights*. Cambridge: Cambridge University Press.

Sullivan, O. 2018. The gendered division of household labour. In: B. J. Risman, C. Froyum and W. Scarborough (eds) *Handbook of the Sociology of Gender and Social Research*. Dordrecht: Springer, pp 377–392.

Tarrant, A. 2021. *Fathering and Poverty: Uncovering Men's Participation in Low-Income Family Life*. Bristol: Policy Press.

Torkington, S. 2023. We're on the brink of a 'polycrisis' – how worried should we be? Retrieved from https://www.weforum.org/agenda/2023/01/polycrisis-global-risks-report-cost-of-living/

Tronto, J. 1993. *Moral Boundaries: A Political Argument for an Ethic of Care*. London: Routledge.

Tronto, J. C. 1995. Care as a basis for radical political judgments. *Hypatia*, 10, 141–149.

Tronto, J. C. 2013. *Caring Democracy: Markets, Equality and Justice*. New York: New York University Press.

Tronto, J. 2020. Afterword. Response-ability and responsibility: using feminist new materialisms and care ethics to cope with impatience in higher education. In: V. Bozalek, M. Zembylas and J. Tronto (eds) *Posthuman and Political Care Ethics for Reconfiguring Higher Education Pedagogies*. Abingdon: Routledge, pp 153–160.

Tsing, A. L. 2015. *The Mushroom at the End of the World: On the Possibility of Life in Capitalist Ruins*. Princeton: Princeton University Press.

Twamley, K. and Faircloth, C. 2023. Understanding 'gender equality': first-time parent couples' practices and perspectives on working and caring post-parenthood. *Sociological Research Online*. https://doi.org/10.1177/13607804231198619

Wallace, C. D. 2002. Household strategies: their conceptual relevance and analytical scope in social research. *Sociology*, 36, 275–292.

Wallace, C. D. and Pahl, R. E. 1985. Household work strategies in an economic recession. In: N. Redclift and E. Mingione (eds) *Beyond Employment*. Oxford: Basil Blackwell, pp 189–227.

Wray, D. 2020. Paternity leave and fathers' responsibility: evidence from a natural experiment in Canada. *Journal of Marriage and Family*, 82, 534–549.

PART II

Understandings and practices of good fatherhood and care

3

'He is our handyman': young people's narratives on caring fatherhood and family life in the Faroe Islands

Firouz Gaini

The many shades of the Faroese father

'If you try from day one to spend much time together with the child, you will soon be as closely attached to it as the mother breastfeeding it is', says GIGNI in instructions intended for Faroese fathers of small children on its website (gigni.fo). This state-funded institution, which provides preventive health services for children and young people, strives to catch the attention of hard-to-reach fathers in its diverse initiatives and services. As a father, GIGNI underlines, 'you can strongly benefit from *being there* during the [health visitor's] visit, so reflect on what you want to ask, talk to your beloved [partner], don't hold back. In this way, you are *participating* and can add the *father's role* into the meeting' (gigni.fo, emphasis added). GIGNI's alert calls for the father to be identified and embraced as a key caring person in the life of his young children. He needs to get out of the shadow of the mother-child dyad. For further information, GIGNI guides its website visitors to a Danish website tailored for fathers. The narratives disseminated through such websites – Faroese, Danish and others – are congruent with the dominant contemporary images of the responsible and caring (Nordic) father with a 'modern' and urban family life. This model encourages intensive and playful child-father social and emotional interaction in everyday life, which usually is, first and foremost in social science scholarship from the Global North, presumed to be the best of possible fathering practices (for example, Plantin, 2001; Farstad and Stefansen, 2015).

In this anthropological chapter, I interrogate this representation of hands-on caring fatherhood by examining its potential (in)congruence with cultural constructions of fatherhood and the child-father relationship. Drawing on extensive ethnographic research on Faroese fatherhood(s), I argue for an intergenerational and culture-centred analysis of the caring father: what characterises contemporary Faroese fathers' fathering styles compared to yesterday's practices seen from young people's narratives?

Even if the body of scholarly work on men and fatherhood is growing fast, very few critical (men and masculinity) studies from the Global North have considered the meaning of local cultural constructions of gender, parenthood and childcare in their representations of the new man/father. The premise of this chapter is that there are different types of culturally defined 'new fathers' with diversified fathering styles and values anchored in local communities in transition. Faroese fathers are reluctant when it comes to talking about their own parenting practices. Many men avoid spaces of public gender discussion. Therefore, I give the voice to the men's children (Gaini, 2022). The children serve, so to speak, as the father's spokesperson or representative, but their narratives represent another generation's perspectives. Based on an intergenerational approach giving the youth the opportunity to be part of the conversation on fatherhood and family life, a more nuanced understanding of care, culture and parenthood takes shape. Some fathers ponder the following question: who cares about the father's caring role? The youth does.

This chapter explores the cultural meaning of care in relation to fathering practices through the lens of adolescents' personal narrations. The family as a context of youth life represents a gap of knowledge in Nordic youth research (Gudmundsson, 2000). The absence of research exploring young people in families reflects the Global North's general definition of adolescence as a life stage characterised by expanding autonomy and independence from family ties (Hennum, 2002: 75). The study of parenthood (and fatherhood) is at the intersection of youth research, sociology of the family and gender studies. The image of youth is shaped by its context, and the perception of young people's 'transition' to adulthood is largely based on the sociological assumption that young people go through an individualised process (Hennum, 2002). The cultural and family-oriented aspects of young people's narratives on male parenthood and family life is at the core of this chapter's analysis.

From fishermen to nappy changers

The Faroe Islands, an island society located midway between Norway and Iceland in the Northeast Atlantic, is the context of this chapter. It is a self-governing country (a subnational island jurisdiction) under the external sovereignty of the Kingdom of Denmark. The Faroe Islands has a strongly fisheries-based export economy, roughly 55,000 inhabitants, and a total land area of 1,399 square kilometres. It is a society in the so-called 'father-friendly' Nordic region (Brandth and Kvande, 2003), but it has sometimes been presented as a Nordic 'exception' because of its conspicuous religious and conservative family values (Skorini et al., 2022). The small and sparsely populated society located far from the large urban hubs of the Nordic mainland has, together with many other Nordic rural communities, rarely has been the target of fatherhood research.

The Faroe Islands is a maritime society that is strongly connected to the sea, with the fisherman as a core national cultural icon (Gaini, 2020). From this perspective, the sea symbolises a masculine place (Hayfield, 2020). The fisherman has been (and continues to some extent to be) a symbol of the nation and a 'hero' in popular cultural narratives (Gaini, 2011, 2023). While the proportion of the male population working at sea has decreased since the 1980s, long-distance (offshore) work in maritime industries is still a reality shaping the everyday life of many Faroese families (Hovgaard, 2015). More than 3,000 Faroese men (approximately one in six working-age men) are long distance workers – on trawlers, freighters, oil rigs and so on. The special status of the fisherman is also affecting the stories in media, the political rhetoric in the Parliament, and the cultural conversation in school and arts institutions. The Faroe Islands is a member of the 'Nordic family' of states engaged in 'care and work-family policy initiatives to promote women's labour market participation, and fathers as carers' (Nielsen et al, 2020: 15). Nevertheless, the Faroe Islands has a higher level of 'familialism' in its societal fabric than the other Nordic countries: fewer women work full-time, more men have long-distance work, family networks are more central in the life of the citizens, the total fertility rate is higher, and paternity leave arrangements are less attractive (for example, Hayfield et al, 2016; Hayfield, 2018; Gaini, 2020). Faroese fathers spend fewer days on paternal leave on average than fathers in the other Nordic countries (Hayfield, 2020). A survey from 2020 reveals that many more people in the Faroe Islands – compared to the other Nordic countries – disagree with the proposal that parental leave should be *equally divided* between parents (Javnaðarflokkurin á Fólkatingið, 2020: 74).

The first time Faroese media shed light on Faroese fatherhood issues was in 1977, when a dispute on men's right to be present at births started (from the newspaper *14th September*, 1977). In the following years, many people participated in the public debate (pro and contra) on the presence of the father at birthing. It developed into an expansive conversation about the father–child relationship. 'To take care of and raise children is no longer a women only issue', the reader's post of a local newspaper stated (from the newspaper *14th September*, 1978). A few years later, in the early 1980s, the midwives at the Faroese hospitals started accepting fathers who wanted to participate in the birth of their children. Although the question about paternal leave slowly entered the public societal debate in 1978, it would take more than 20 years before the first Faroese parental leave law came into effect, some 30 years after the other Nordic countries had enacted national parental leave laws (Lammi-Taskula, 2008). Many Faroese men use the Facebook group 'Fathers in the Faroe Islands' with almost 1,000 members as a platform for ongoing discussions on paternal leave, custody, birth preparation and other important issues. At the beginning of 2023, Bjarni Kárason Petersen, the young Minister of Justice in the Faroese government, made history and headlines when he publicly announced that he was going on paternity leave. Bjarni, who was the first (male or female) minister ever to go on parental leave while being in the Faroese government (and who used this as an opportunity to draw attention to the sensitive political question on Faroese paternal leave legislation), says:

> The first time together with the child is special. We fathers also own this time, but we are maybe not very good at giving it high priority ... I hope that more fathers will see the value in taking paternal leave in the future, no matter if you are minister, artisan or teacher. (lms.fo, 2023)

Global fatherhood research

Fathering and parenting is a well-established research field in social and applied psychology, most prominently in the North American tradition of family psychology, and sociological and anthropological scholarship on male parenting in the Global North only emerged in publications towards the end of the 1990s (Eerola, 2014: 309). The early 1980s indicated an interesting shift in European and North American male parenting practices discussed in the work of scholars engaged in critical gender and family research. The scholars described a new and more 'sensitive and "hands-on" way of involvement [becoming] the dominant cultural conception of "good fatherhood"' (Eerola, 2014: 309). This trend hints at a turn in male parenting norms in Europe and North America at the turn of the century with so-called 'active caring fatherhood' becoming, broadly, 'culturally more accepted' (Eerola, 2015: 11; Twamley et al, Chapter 1 in this volume). Edley and Wetherell argue that this type of father, the 'new man' of the Global North, represents 'a softer, more sensitive and caring individual. He is the ideal partner for the modern, liberated woman' (Edley and Wetherell, 1999: 181).

The new father is discussed with vague reference to culturally accepted forms of parental practices among men, and the cultural context is rarely explicitly examined in interdisciplinary fatherhood studies. The introduction to the cultural context is missing, especially in studies from the Global North (compared to, for example, Lesejane, 2006; Lindegger, 2006; Tautolo, 2011; Philogene Heron, 2017; Powis, 2020) outlining caring fatherhood performance as the materialisation of dominant parenthood values and fathering ideals. In an anthology on global parenting, 21st-century Kenyan parenting is presented as a project 'maintaining traditional elements while simultaneously adapting to modern times' (Wadende et al, 2022: 9).

The use of a cultural lens in fathering studies is desired 'only when the definition of culture is expanded beyond ethnicity to include race, gender, sexual orientation, religion, and economic standing' (Miller and Maiter, 2008: 298). Local cultural norms, says Seward, 'proscribe how each man should go about enacting his family roles including fathering' (Seward, 1991: 228).

The difference between the Global North and the Global South is often exaggerated in (quantitative) fatherhood and masculinity studies (for example, Lamb, 1987). The new father exists in all parts of the world, but he is not necessarily the hegemonic type of father in his local community. Since the 1990s, almost all fatherhood research across cultures 'suggests some change in the direction of greater involvement by fathers' (Seward and Stanley-Stevens, 2014). Even in the Nordic countries, which are presented as the champions of caring fatherhood with fathers assumed 'to be loving, caring and capable of "mother-like" nurture, and to participate in early care' (Eerola, 2015: 20), 'cultural hindrances' blocking a full implementation of 'equal rights of both parents to earn and care' continue to exist (Eydal and Rostgaard, 2016: 398).

Very few studies have examined fathering in Nordic rural and small island communities. Fathering practices, says Brandth, are 'surprisingly absent from the international literature on men and masculinity in rural society' (Brandth, 2016: 435). It is also worth mentioning, as Eerola and others have emphasised in their work, that Nordic fathers, despite a 'father-friendly culture', continue to be at greater liberty to decide the terms of their engagement and participation (Eerola, 2015: 23; Brandth, 2016). While the severity of the problems related to parenting, care and gender equality might be very uneven across countries, there seems to be a growing global focus on responsible fatherhood.

By turning attention to young people's perspectives on caring fatherhood and family life, my intention is to destabilise and challenge monolithic images of the Faroese father, which have largely failed to apprehend the cultural construction of the father. Fathering style, or fathering practice, refers to the 'set of everyday practices performed by men in relation to their children', while fatherhood, in brief, refers to 'a society's collective understanding of what it means to be a man' (Edley, 2017: 99–100). Fathering is about the personal experiences of men 'as they engage in fathering practices' (Miller, 2011: 6).

Data and methods

The study

The anthropological project *Faroese Fatherhood in Transition: Exploring Everyday Life, Family Relations, and Masculinity across Two Generations of Men in Contemporary Faroe Islands* (2018–2022, funded by Research Council Faroe Islands) is the main source of data for this chapter focusing on the teenagers' narratives: individual essays written by eighth graders (aged 14–15) from a public (primary and lower secondary) school in a place we will call Blueville in this chapter in January and February 2020. The school project was conducted in collaboration with a teacher helping us to liaise with the pupils. Participation was voluntary and the pupils had the right to withdraw from the project at any time. We received informed consent from the participants who have been anonymised in all the material used in publications. The study complies with the ethical principles for good research practice (including All European Academies' European Code of Conduct for Research Integrity). The methods applied for data acquisition, research and evaluation conform to scientific criteria and are ethically sustainable. The project obtained approval from the Faroese Data Protection Agency. We received 32 essays from a balanced group of boys and girls. The introduction to the writing (essay) assignment was formulated (in Faroese) in this way:

> In this text you shall describe the Faroese father in 2020 through reflection on these themes of his life: children and family life, working life and career, masculinity and identity, equality and equal rights, and values and styles. You are welcome to combine and merge the topics as you like. Furthermore, you should say something about temporal change: what do you think has changed in the last three to four decades in the Faroes as regards the father's role and family life? You are welcome to discuss other additional questions illuminating the story about the Faroese father.

We received a varied collection of texts delving into questions – some general and some personal, some brief and some lengthy – about fatherhood and the father-child relationship. The essays contained from a couple of sentences and up to four pages of text. What all the participants seem to crave to do, despite their different lives and biographies, is to explain and defend the role of the father in the Faroese family. Essay writing is a solitary enterprise. Unlike other methods in qualitative research, for example, face-to-face individual interviews or participant observation, it does not request close communication between researcher and participant (Gaini, 2020: 21). Creative writing gives the author a sense of being more unrestrained and autonomous in relation to the themes and questions of the research project. It is, so to speak, easier to blur the line between personal real-life experience and imagined scenarios in the essay than in the (semi-)structured interview. The advantage of the essay method when it comes to young people's narratives on fatherhood and masculinity is that it accommodates multilayered and ambiguous perspectives at the same time as it, in the writing exercise itself, motivates young people to enhance their experimental writing (and critical thinking) skills (Trell and van Hoven, 2010).

The data analysis process started in the preparation of the essay assignment to pupils and continued until the writing of the results and conclusions of the project. In brief, the process contained these main steps: (a) reading and rereading the essays; (b) focused coding and arrangement of key words/concepts from the narratives across the essays; (c) abstracting themes contributing to the analysis of the research question; (d) mapping and modelling the relationship between the themes; (e) and critically examining these findings in relation to other information about Faroese fathers and families. Our prior knowledge on youth and parenthood in the Faroe Islands and the rest of the Nordic countries provided us with a framework for interpretation. The analysis was also informed by 'thick description' in anthropological research (Geertz, 1983).

The decision to use teenagers aged 14–15 in the project was based on the research objectives. People in this age group usually hold subjective feelings of autonomy and maturity in relation to important queries and decisions concerning their future, but at the same time, this age is a time of emotional confusion and frustration (Aagre, 2014). Teenagers under the age of 16 are between the child's spontaneity and creativity and the older adolescent's self-righteousness. The essay assignment method obtains its full potential when it is combined with other methods, which reflects the methodological strategy of *Faroese Fatherhood in Transition*. We triangulated the material from essays, interviews and surveys to critically assess the narratives in the essays. The essay is not interesting as style in our study, but as material introducing themes that the youth emphasise in conversation about fatherhood and family life (Hennum, 2002: 211).

Young people's narratives on fathers and care

Equal care

Now, we will take a closer look at equal care from young people's perspectives. When young people discuss fathering, the father–grandfather relationship is a part of the story about the father's caring fatherhood. Grandparents have an important position in families and in children's everyday lives in many cultures (Tautolo, 2011). The Faroese society, which has been defined as a 'family-oriented' and 'child-centric' society (for example, Gaini, 2013), is a good example of this. When the participants in our study talk about fathers, they tend to focus more on the child-father relationship than on the mother-father alliance.

Young people experience and reflect on contemporary men's new (altered) paternal identity endeavours, which is informed by yet different from the fathers' own experiences of being fathered (Miller, 2011: 82). The external view on the parents, from an insider (the teenage daughters and sons) of the family, reveals the predicaments of the present-day Faroese father with one leg in the local ('traditional father') and one leg in the global ('new father') model of fatherhood (Gaini, 2020). Jake writes in his essay about his parents who perform parenthood with an equal division of household chores:

> My mother and my father both have long [higher] education and work full time. I don't think there is a real difference on what is masculine and feminine today. In my family, it is for instance nothing strange that mother might wash the car and father wash the clothes, and I don't think this makes them feel more feminine or masculine. I think I was raised with the belief that men and women have opportunity to do the same things.

Jake portrays his family life as being organised around gender equal parenting and caring fathering. The fathers in our project underline their new roles in the family in contrast to common images of their fathers' and grandfathers' parenting styles, but they do also link their fathering practices to cultural values associated with Faroese manhood through generations (Gaini, 2020). This is also what their children, the pupils from the school in Blueville, explain in their written narratives.

Being supportive

Many young people present their fathers as supportive as well as caring in the Faroese study. Parenting is becoming increasingly stressful around the globe, says Selin, 'as parents try to balance their own lives and aspirations and those that they hold for their children, in an increasingly difficult world' (Selin, 2022: vi). Betty, the youngest of a group of five siblings from Blueville, writes about her 'modern' father:

> Daddy is such a good and modern father. He helps at home, taking care of chores together with mom, such as cleaning, hoovering, and washing the house. He also really likes keeping everything nice outside of our house. Together with mom, he frequently prepares nice and healthy dinners, on occasions to gather the whole family now counting eleven people. In fact, mom and dad go to great lengths to keep the family together. Furthermore, daddy is good at helping me with [school] homework and, for instance, when I need to rearrange my bedroom.

Betty is delighted to have a caring father that is active at home and eager to contribute to work promoting shared-caregiving fatherhood and even some kind of 'gender-free' parenting (Doucet, 2018: 23–25). The heteronormative father-and-mother-and-two-to-four-children family model with new focus on care and intimacy in emerging fathering practices does not, strictly speaking, request a peculiar child-father relationship, except for the generally caring and supportive role of the father. Frida writes about her father's personality and close relationship to his children:

> He is always there for me; and he is with me when I need it. Daddy makes everyone smile, even if they are not happy that day. I always had daddy as role model ... If someone asks daddy to do them a favour, he does it ... Daddy has taught me so many things that I am happy to know. For instance, I have learned to identify things in a car that are not working, or that need to be fixed. I usually help daddy repairing our car and our boat.

Frida talks about her young father who divorced her mother before she was of school age, and explains that she is happy that her father found himself a new woman to marry and have children with. The father is transmitting knowledge and cultural codes to the next generation, but first and foremost, he is a person who, according to the teenagers, is giving the children mental strength and the feeling of being protected.

Caring about the past

Amy reflects on changes in fathering practices and images of fatherhood in the Faroe Islands in her essay:

> We always hear stories about how tough and masculine men used to be. The stories always start with 'when I was young'. In the past, you got married, then you got children, and that was it, even if you did not love your partner ... You can imagine a father from the 1950s–1960s, wearing a coarse-knitted jersey, rubber boots, looking dirty and smelling of wind-dried meat ... My father is not like that. He is shopping, playing football, and other things like a modern father would do in his everyday life ... He is healthy, does a lot of training, and looks really happy.

Like many of her peers, Amy uses history and myths about the past to delimit and insulate representations of today's father. Her father is 'not like *that*', she stresses in emancipation from stereotypes of Faroese fatherhood. Oliver writes about the special role that the father has for his children in the family:

> It is the boys who profit from a father who is caring and present through life. You can only learn a small part from the mother, and the rest is learned from the father. If the father does a poor job in the upbringing of the son, then he has a bad influence on society. Life is a

rollercoaster with many swings, and you don't know what tomorrow will bring – and that is why it is good to have a person who can help you in the struggle that characterises the young manhood-years.

Oliver says that the father gives his child a different kind of care from the mother. Situated in a challenging life phase with many large decisions to be taken, he points out the special role of the father. Tom writes about the fisherman in his essay:

> In the Faroe Islands, many fathers have been fishermen, and therefore, they have only been at home for limited periods of time when the family was young … Nowadays, men are not at sea for more than three months at a time; I know that granddad was away for five-six months at a time, and then just came home for a very short visit before going back fishing, and my father, he is not away for more than four days at a time, but he is just sailing between two islands here in the Faroe Islands, so he is not far from home … Me and my father, we do a lot of things together.

As mentioned earlier, the seaman has for generations been a national hero in Faroese cultural narratives, but since the end of the 20th century, he has lost his high status among most groups of young people. 'Manly selfhood is not a thing or a constant; rather, it is an act that is ever in progress' (Inhorn and Wentzell, 2011: 803). Men continually negotiate their gender identities and male parental roles.

Softer dads

Betty believes that the father's paternal masculinity involves many qualities, including care and education that she in her essay presents as something 'good and modern' in relation to experiences from the father's and grandfathers' own adolescence. In her essay, Lena writes:

> Today's fathers are … not as masculine as their own fathers were, and they are much softer; they express more sentiments and are not afraid of revealing that they cry when something affects them. Today, some men can even cry while watching a movie, something which was unheard of in the past … Today, fathers also help much more at home, and they do all the chores together with the wife/partner. They are on paternal leave, they make food, they wash and help with homework.

In accordance with Betty, Lena endorses Faroese fathers' transition to a more emotional and caring fatherhood. She illustrates a contrast between today's father and yesterday's father, who is portrayed as a more 'masculine' type, mirroring the dominant societal representation of the Faroese fisherman's manhood (Gaini, 2020). The question of care is discussed in relation to an image of local (fisherman) fatherhood versus global (new and urban) fatherhood, but also in relation to divorce and family break-up. Linda writes about fathers and emerging masculinities in the Faroe Islands:

> It is more accepted today for fathers to show their soft side. All fathers are not masculine the way they were expected to be in the past. Today there are many ways of being masculine. It is OK – even encouraged – for fathers to take parental leave, to be at home with sick children, to be there emotionally, etc. At least this is the case in the younger generation. In the past, men were not supposed to show feelings, they should behave like 'men' ... In my point of view, it is a good thing that most men are not as 'masculine' as they used to be. Today a boy can talk to his father without just being told to 'man himself up', which can be very humiliating for the child.

Linda discusses the change in fathering styles in relation to a generational division. She considers the dominant masculinity of the past as an obstacle for caring and intimate fathering today.

Care, culture and fatherhood

Care in caring parenthood

In Faroese language, care is called *umsorgan*. To be caring is to be *umsorganarfullur*. It refers to a person who is careful, cautious and takes (good) care of others (people or animals). The word has many nuances and is used in many contexts, but rarely in discussions about male parenting.

Bekkengen talks about 'child-oriented masculinity' in her work on (caring) men wishing to spend more time at home (Bekkengen, 2002, 2003). The general image of fathers as carers is also influenced by structural conditions in society. Legal disenfranchisement, for instance, 'devaluates men's role as carers' (Dermott, 2008: 19). This is observed in the Faroe Islands as well as in many other countries.

The voice of the youth strengthens our understanding of the role and caring of the father in the family. It is important to try to understand care, which is a notion that has sometimes been associated with the antithesis of masculinity in its historic context (Brannen and Nilsen, 2006). In their sociological study on fatherhood in the UK, Brannen and Nilsen observed that some of the grandfathers did not distribute 'the practice of care' equally between themselves and their partners. Instead, they valued 'the relational aspect of care' (Brannen and Nilsen, 2006: 348–349). In other words, care attracts different connotations and meanings over time, which explains why men from different generations can relate to the concept in very different manners.

The father is the agent of a 'different' kind of protective care. Doucet says that fathers engage in the following types of nurturing, which are not only relevant for small children: 'fun and playfulness, a physical and outdoors approach, promoting children's considered risk taking, and encouraging children's independence' (Doucet, 2018: 110). This is in accordance with my material from the Faroe Islands, as many teenagers see the father as the prime parent as regards intergenerational transmission of cultural knowledge and nature-related activities.

Practical caring

The narratives of the youth reveal that one of the most central aspects of being a good father is to spend time with your children – and 'be there' for your children. The youth's images of the Faroese father have resulted in a kind of 'open-endedness' concerning the father's position between the 'new' and 'old' father model from fatherhood research in the Global North. Young people talk about what we usually call the 'modern' father at the same time as they value the fathers' bonds to the Faroese fathers of the past. Rather than talking directly about a 'new father', the youth traces new practices of caring fatherhood with strong local cultural anchorage. Today, young people in many countries, including the Faroe Islands, seem to look at their fathers (as well as mothers) as 'managers or coaches' helping them with their self-realisation projects (Hoikkala, 1998).

The 'plasticity of contemporary fathering', says Dermott, referring to practical caring, allows 'the development of a close relationship that is disassociated from equal co-parenting and shared childcare' (Dermott, 2008: 19–20). 'Nurturing fatherhood' is therefore an option without the precondition of radical change in local fathering practices. This is concurring with what we have observed in the essays written by Faroese teenagers. Young people say in the essays that the father-child relationship is based on a fathering style creating patterns of communication and emotional ties aiming for the elaboration of children's autonomy. While the public support for the 'rhetoric of paternal essentiality' is far from universal (Pleck, 2013), it is coming to the Faroe Islands.

Fathers comply with a range of practices and expectations associated with different masculinities, says Powis (2020: 22). The Faroese father embodies some of the practices and qualities branding the Nordic-style reflexive and intimate fatherhood (Johansson and Andreasson, 2017), but, as the participants from Blueville have demonstrated, he is also shaping his fathering style and father-child relationship on robust local knowledge linked to traditional cultural values. 'It often takes men a lifetime to realise fatherhood', says Philogene Heron talking about men from Dominica, West Indies. This is because it is not until he ages and becomes a grandfather, until he is freed from 'immediate masculine imperatives', that man normally realises fatherhood (Philogene Heron, 2017: 205). In the Faroe Islands, fatherhood is normally instantly apprehended and appreciated. There is rarely any noteworthy conflict between the paternal masculinity and any other local masculinity. In one of the interviewed fathers' words as he waited for his first child to be born, 'you just throw yourself into it' (Gaini, 2022).

The Faroese study informing my article reveals that the youth generation is engaged in conversation about changing fatherhood values and new fathering practices with a focus on four main themes influencing the father-child relationship and everyday life of the family in general. Equal care is at the core of their narratives, no matter how young people portray their fathers' working life and identity. The question of care is linked to the discussion about the supportive father who protects and inspires his children (Phoenix, Chapter 18 in this volume). According to the young people, the supportive father is often forgotten in the debate about parenthood and caring fatherhood in the Faroe Islands. The study also reveals the essential and active role of the past – the past generations of fathers – in narratives about contemporary Faroese caring fathers. The combination of the cultural values of equal care, being supportive and caring for the past, leads to the images of softer dads prioritising hands-on caring at the same time as they sustain cultural bonds to the styles of their own fathers and grandfathers.

The 'new father' (Dowd, 2000) is a notion largely based on Nordic welfare states' novel 'ideal of caring and present fathering practices' (Johansson, 2011) corresponding to the predominant 'new man' model promoting involved fatherhood and the repudiation of 'old' forms of masculinity (Farstad and Stefansen, 2015: 55). As pointed out by Phoenix (Chapter 18, this volume), it is important to conduct research investigating the gap between 'new father' models and fathers' everyday practices and how these are interpreted by children and adolescents.

Conclusion

The young essay writers discuss the 'new' father with various terms and formulations disconnecting him from the past generations' father model. However, they are not propagating a dichotomous fatherhood perception presenting 'old' fatherhood as the antithesis of what the qualities of the new father – hence, as authoritarian and unloving (Dermott, 2008: 23). Rather, young people's perspectives give us a more nuanced understanding of the multilayered child-father dyad, uncovering a deep creative and emotional relationship based on care in its widest meaning, that too often seems to be veiled and silent compared to the public attention pointing at the child-mother dyad. The Faroese father is sometimes exoticised as an icon of something 'authentic' in a globalising world, but he is also portrayed as the (handy) man struggling to find the perfect balance between being at home and being away. 'Daddy is our handyman', writes one of the Blueville teenagers in a positive representation of the father. Therefore, when GIGNI uses its website as a platform in the quest to convince young fathers to put effort into becoming 'as close to [the baby child] as the mother breastfeeding it', they rightly believe that they can make a difference in advancement of a paternal masculinity benefitting the family of the 21st century. In this chapter I have explained how this message can be interpreted in relation to culture, generations and care in the child-father relationship.

References

14th September (newspaper) (1977). *Frágreiðing frá føðiumstøðarbólkinum*, 12 May.

14th September (newspaper) (1978) *Luttakarir í føðireiking: Pápar eiga at fáa loyvi at vera hjástaddir undir føðingini*, 11 November.

Aagre, W. (2014). *Ungdomskunnskap – hverdagslivets kulturelle former*, 2nd edn. Bergen: Fagbokforlaget.

Bekkengen, L. (2002). *Man får välja – om föräldraskap och föräldraledighet i arbetsliv och samhälle*. Malmö: Liber.

Bekkengen, L. (2003). Föräldralediga män och barnorienterad maskulinitet. In T. Johansson and J.J. Kuosmanen (eds) *Manlighetens många ansikten – fäder, feminister, frisörer och andra män*. Malmö: Liber, pp 181–203.

Brandth, B. (2016). Rural masculinities and fathering practices. *Gender, Place and Culture*, 23(3), 435–450.

Brandth, B. and Kvande, E. (2003). *Fleksible fedre: maskulinitet, arbeid, velferdsstat*. Oslo: Universitetsforlaget.

Brannen, J. and Nilsen, A. (2006). From fatherhood to fathering: transmission and change among British fathers in four-generation families. *Sociology*, 40(2), 335–352.

Dermott, E. (2008). *Intimate Fatherhood: A Sociological Analysis*. Abingdon: Routledge.

Doucet, A. (2018). *Do Men Mother?*, 2nd edn. Toronto: University of Toronto Press.

Dowd, N.E. (2000). *Redefining Fatherhood*. New York: New York University Press.

Edley, N. (2017). *Men and Masculinity: The Basics*. Abingdon: Routledge.

Edley, N. and Wetherell, M. (1999). Imagined futures: young men's talk about fatherhood and domestic life. *British Journal of Social Psychology*, 38, 181–194.

Eerola, P. (2014). Nurturing, breadwinning, and upbringing: paternal responsibilities by Finnish men in early fatherhood. *Community, Work & Family, 17*(3), 308–324.

Eerola, P. (2015). Responsible fatherhood: a narrative approach. PhD dissertation. Jyväskylä: University of Jyväskylä.

Eydal, G.B. and Rostgaard, T. (2016). Introduction. In G.B. Eydal and T. Rostgaard (eds) *Fatherhood in the Nordic Welfare States: Comparing Care and Practice*. Bristol: Policy Press, pp 1–20.

Farstad, G.R. and Stefansen, K. (2015). Involved fatherhood in the Nordic context: dominant narratives, divergent approaches. *NORMA – International Journal for Masculinity Studies, 10*(1), 55–70.

Gaini, F. (2011). The adversity of the heroes of the past. In F. Gaini (ed.) *Among the Islanders of the North: An Anthropology of the Faroe Islands*. Torshavn: Faroe University Press, pp 163–198.

Gaini, F. (2013). *Lessons of Islands: Place and Identity in the Faroe Islands*. Torshavn: Faroe University Press.

Gaini, F. (2020). 'He understands me in a different way than others do': Faroese teenagers' narratives on fatherhood, masculinity, and family life. *Suomen Antropologi, 45*(2), 17–34.

Gaini, F. (2022). 'You just throw yourself into it': on fatherhood and family in the Faroe Islands. *Kritisk etnografi, 5*(1–2), 95–113.

Gaini, F. (2023). Man and manhood in the North Atlantic. In A. Gjestvang, *Atlantic Cowboy [Photo Book]*. London: GOST Books, pp 66–69.

Geertz, C. (1983). *Local Knowledge: Further Essays on Interpretive Anthropology*. New York: Basic Books.

GIGNI (2023). https://www.gigni.fo/smaboern/um-smaboern-0-2-ar/par lag-og-heimaliv and https://www.gigni.fo/smaboern/til-papar Accessed 4 November, 2023.

Hayfield, E.A. (2018). Family-centred work motility in a small island society: the case of the Faroe Islands. *Gender, Place & Culture, 25*(8), 1138–1153.

Hayfield, E.A. (2020). Parenting and islands: constructing gender and work in the Faroe Islands. In F. Gaini and H.P. Nielsen (eds) *Gender and Island Communities*. Abingdon: Routledge, pp 100–118.

Hayfield, E.A., Olavson, Ó. and Patursson, L. (2016). *Part-Time Work in the Nordic Region III*. Copenhagen: Nordic Council of Ministers.

Hennum, N. (2002). Kjærlighetens og autoritetens kulturelle koder: Om å være mor og far for norsk ungdom. PhD dissertation. Trondheim: NTNU. https://doi.org/10.7577/nova/rapporter/2002/19

Hoikkala, T. (1998). Aljosha and Tapio: two cases of compared fathering. *YOUNG, 6*(3), 19–32.

Hovgaard, G. (2015). 'Being away; being at home; being both': the case of Faroese maritime workers. In S.T. Faber and H.P. Nielsen (eds) *Remapping Gender, Place and Mobility*. Farnham: Ashgate, pp 175–189.

Inhorn, M.C. and Wentzel, E.A. (2011). Embodying emergent masculinities: men engaging with reproductive and sexual health technologies in the Middle East and Mexico. *American Ethnologist*, 38(4), 801–815.

Javnaðarflokkurin á Fólkatingi (2020). *Frágreiðing*. Copenhagen: Danish Parliament.

Johansson, T. (2011). The conundrum of fatherhood – theoretical explorations. *International Journal of Sociology of the Family*, 37(2), 227–242.

Johansson, T. and Andreasson, J. (2017). *Fatherhood in Transition: Masculinity, Identity and Everyday Life*. London: Palgrave Macmillan.

Lamb, M.E. (ed.) (1987). *The Father's Role: Cross-cultural Perspectives*. Hillsdale, NJ: Lawrence Erlbaum.

Lammi-Taskula, J. (2008). Doing fatherhood: understanding the gendered use of parental leave in Finland. *Fathering: A Journal of Theory, Research & Practice about Men as Fathers*, 6(2), 133–148.

Lesejane, D. (2006). Fatherhood from an African cultural perspective. In L. Richter and R. Morrell (eds) *BABA: Men and Fatherhood in South Africa*. Cape Town: HSRC Press, pp 173–182.

Lindegger, G. (2006). The father in the mind. In L. Richter and R. Morrell (eds) *BABA: Men and Fatherhood in South Africa*. Cape Town: HSRC Press, pp 121–131.

lms.fo (2023) https://www.lms.fo/fo/kunning/tidindi/landsstyrismadurin-i-logarmalum-fer-i-barsilsfarloyvi

Miller, T. (2011). *Making Sense of Fatherhood: Gender, Caring and Work*. Cambridge: Cambridge University Press.

Miller, M. and Maiter, S. (2008). Fatherhood and culture: moving beyond stereotypical understandings. *Journal of Ethnic and Cultural Diversity in Social Work*, 17(3), 279–300.

Nielsen, H.P., Hayfield, E.A. and Arnfjord, S. (2020). *Equality in isolated Labour Markets. Equal opportunities for men and women in geographically isolated labour markets in Læsø (DK), Suðuroy (FO), and Narsaq (GL)*. Copenhagen: Nordic Council of Ministers.

Philogene Heron, A. (2017). Fathermen – predicaments in fatherhood, masculinity and the kinship lifecourse. PhD dissertation. St Andrews: University of St Andrews.

Plantin, L. (2011). *Män, familjeliv och föräldraskap*. Umeå: Boréa.

Pleck, J.H. (2013). Foreword. In D.W. Shwalb, B.J. Shwalb and M.E. Lamb (eds) *Fathers in Cultural Context*. New York: Routledge Academic, pp xiv–xix.

Powis, R. (2020). Relations and reproduction: men, masculinities, and pregnancy in dakar, senegal. Arts and Sciences Electronic Dissertations 2232. St Louis: Washington University.

Prime Minister's Office 1 February, 2023: https://www.lms.fo/fo/kunning/tidindi/landsstyrismadurin-i-logarmalum-fer-i-barsilsfarloyvi

Selin, H. (2022). Introduction. In H. Selin (ed.) *Parenting across Cultures. Childrearing, Motherhood and Fatherhood in Non-Western Cultures*, 2nd edn. Cham: Springer, pp v–vi.

Seward, R.R. (1991). Determinants of family culture: effects upon fatherhood. In F.W. Bozett and S.M.H. Hanson (eds) *Fatherhood and Families in Cultural Context*. New York: Springer, pp 218–236.

Seward, R.R. and Stanley-Stevens, L. (2014). Fathers, fathering, and fatherhood across cultures. In H. Selin (ed.) *Parenting across Cultures. Childrearing, Motherhood and Fatherhood in Non-Western Cultures*, 2nd edn. Cham: Springer, pp 459–474.

Skorini, H.í., Sølvará, H.A. and Albinus, H. (2022). Færøerne mellem religiøs vækkelse og sekularisering: En Nordisk undtagelse bliver til. *Økonomi and Politik, 95*(1), 88–110.

Tamis-LeMonda, C.S., Uzgiris, I.C. and M.H. Bornstein (2002). Play in parent-child interactions. In M.H. Bornstein (ed.) *Handbook for Parenting. Volume 5*. Hillsdale, NJ: Laurence Erlbaum, pp 221–242.

Tautolo, A-S., 2011. Pacific fathers: cultivating the future. The health of Pacific fathers and their influence upon and involvement with their children. PhD dissertation. Auckland: Auckland University of Technology.

Trell, E-M. and van Hoven, B. (2010). Making sense of place: exploring creative and (inter)active research methods with young people. *Fennia: International Journal of Geography, 188*(1), 91–104.

Wadende, P.A., Lasser, J. and Fite, K. (2022). The Kenyan parent in changing times: an update. In H. Selin (ed.) *Parenting across Cultures. Childrearing, Motherhood and Fatherhood in Non-Western Cultures*, 2nd edn. Cham: Springer, pp 1–11.

4

Changing fatherhood and gender roles in Somali families: experiences of being fathered in Somalia and in the diaspora

Marja Tiilikainen

Introduction

'A father is like foreign ministry that takes care of decisions and duties regarding children outside [home], and a mother is like a ministry of the interior that takes care of everything and makes decisions at home', described a Somali Finnish mother. This understanding of gendered care responsibilities between a father and a mother reflects the Somali cultural understanding of harmonious family life, but also traditional Islamic norms and values (Velayati, 2016). In the patriarchal and patrilineal Somali society, the husband or father is considered the head of the household, protector and breadwinner of the family, whereas the wife's and mother's role is to manage domestic tasks and care of small children (Cabdi, 2005). However, these parenting ideals and practices are being renegotiated due to profound societal changes caused by long-term conflict, instability and poverty in Somalia, as well as extensive emigration and the formation of a global Somali diaspora.

In Somalia, the conventional roles of men and women were challenged after the collapse of the state in 1991 and the ensuing civil war, during which many men died, left the country or were traumatised and unable to work. Thus, women had to take over the financial responsibility in the household, which changed their role in the family and perhaps to some extent helped to improve their overall societal status (Warsame, 2001; Cabdi, 2005; El-Bushra and Gardner, 2016). However, Somali society remains male-dominated and many women in Somalia face violence from men both inside and outside the home (Bangura, 2021). In addition, their public and political participation remains contested (Horst, 2017). Forced displacement and international migration for its part (for example, to North America and Europe) and resettlement in new sociocultural and religious environments have transformed Somali parenting and traditional gender roles in families (Degni, Pöntinen and Mölsä, 2006; Osman et al, 2016; Haga, 2020; Tiilikainen, 2020a). It has been argued that Somali men in particular have been forced to reconsider their gender roles, respectable masculinity and fatherhood (Kleist, 2010; Tiilikainen, 2020b).

Migration significantly impacts family dynamics, roles and care relationships. For example, migrant parents may need to bring up children without the support of extended family networks; gender hierarchies change as women participate more than before in education and work life, which further impacts on intergenerational relationships; and children of migrants often experience social mobility and do better than their parents (Attias-Donfut and Cook, 2017: 120–125). Research in the past 20 years has produced important insights on transnational families, where family members live apart from each other, but do family and provide care to family members in transnational space (Mazzucato and Schans, 2011; Baldassar and Merla, 2014). The role of fathers in transnational families has remained rather invisible (Poeze, 2019). In addition, research on migrant fathers who are not geographically separated from their children but take part in care practices at home is scarce (although see Kvande and Brandth, 2016; Żadkowska et al, 2020; Bergnehr, 2022; Bungum and Kvande, 2022; Miller and Dermott, Chapter 13, this volume; Bergnehr, Chapter 15, this volume). This recent scholarship has enriched the picture on migrant men, who have primarily been seen through their role as breadwinners and whose relational attachments and involvement in the life of their children have been largely overlooked (Kilkey, Plomien and Perrons, 2013). For example, Bungum and Kvande (2022) have demonstrated how national parental leave rights for fathers in Norway support migrant fathers to care for and bond with their children. It has also been argued that as Western media has stereotyped Muslim men as patriarchal and violent, it has overshadowed the plurality of Muslim men as well as their everyday nurturing and caring practices (Inhorn and Naguib, 2018; Bergnehr, 2022).

This chapter will address a gap in the literature, namely children's views on parenthood and, in particular, fatherhood of migrant fathers (although see Omar, 2016; Ismail, 2020; Osman et al, 2021) by exploring the experiences and perceptions of a younger generation of Somalis regarding fatherhood both in Somalia and in the diaspora. How do Somali men and women describe care from and relationships with their fathers? How are fathers' care practices shaped by normative understandings of childhood and gender? Has migration transformed values guiding father-child dynamics as well as fathering practices?

Care by fathers is here understood widely, comprising different practices, such as fathers' role in children's education, financial and emotional support, and communication with children, interlinked with specific temporal and spatial processes. These practices are motivated by expectations that fathers have for their children's good future and based on cultural, religious and gendered family norms and values. However, cultural parenting orientations as well as parenting styles are changing in new contexts (Osman et al, 2016). In this volume (see Chapter 2), Andrea Doucet suggests that caring fatherhood is relational, responsive and responsible, which also helps to analyse changes in fathering practices and styles. According to Afua Twum-Danso (2009), cultural values of *respect*, *responsibility* and *reciprocity* guide African parent-child relationships. Children are being taught these values, which are seen as crucial for the social functioning of family and larger society. In this chapter I analyse how these values show in and guide care relationships between Somali fathers, their daughters and sons. I argue that these core values also impact Somali young people growing up in the diaspora, but at the same time fathering practices have developed towards intimate fatherhood (Dermott, 2003), including an ideal of a more emotionally close relationship with children and more open communication.

Data and methods

The chapter draws on multisited fieldwork and interview data that I collected in a research project 'Islam and security revisited: transnational Somali families in Finland, Canada and Somalia', funded by the Research Council of Finland (2012–2017). The main data were collected with 17 transnational families (originally 18, but one family withdrew from the research later on). To understand transnational family experiences on everyday security, I interviewed both the parental generation who had migrated from Somalia to either Canada or Finland, and some of their children, most of whom had been born either in Canada or in Finland, or were very small at the time of the migration. The socioeconomic background of the families varied. The data were collected in Toronto and Helsinki metropolitan areas. I also interviewed some of the family members in Somaliland and Puntland that are regions in northern Somalia (in this chapter I refer to these two regions as Somalia, even though Somaliland claims to be an independent state). Additionally, I conducted focus group interviews in all research sites. The participants were found with the help of research assistants, personal contacts and snowballing.

The parents had originally migrated to North America and Finland in the late 1980s or beginning of the 1990s to escape insecurity and civil war in Somalia. Hence, they had lived in their new countries for around 30 years or even longer. Among the studied 17 families, five couples had divorced, and the communication between children and fathers varied from non-existent to regular. Three fathers had died. Of the nine families where parents were together, two fathers were working in Somalia, but they also had Canadian/Finnish passports and active contact with their children. In this chapter I will discuss the 'diaspora experience' as a whole, and will therefore present the data details from both countries together.

For the purposes of this chapter, I draw on two datasets:

1. Interviews conducted with the children of migrant parents, so-called 'second generation', in the 17 study families. A total of 18 females and 15 males aged between 12 and 36 were interviewed. All were single, except for four of them, who were either married or divorced with children, and mostly lived with their parent(s). Over half of them were either students or applying to study. One participant was interviewed in Somalia. A total of 24 were interviewed individually, while nine participants were interviewed together with one or two siblings. The main themes covered during interviews were own life history, family, sense of security, role of religion, and transnational family connections. The language was either Finnish or English. The length of interviews was mostly between two and three hours, although the longest interview was three hours and 40 minutes.
2. The second set of data comprises eight focus group (FG) interviews: four in Somalia (two in Hargeisa, Somaliland and two in Garowe, Puntland); two in Helsinki; and two in Toronto (see Table 4.1). Focus groups were organised separately for women and men. The language of FG interviews in Somalia was a mix of English and Somali that was translated by a facilitator/research assistant. Other FG interviews were either in English or Finnish, but also the Somali language was used when needed with the help of facilitator/research assistant. The majority of participants were students, but the female FG in Helsinki as well as the male FG in Hargeisa were exceptions, as most of their participants were working. The main themes were participants' views on life and everyday security in the place where they were living; gender roles and family; transnational connections; aspirations for the future. The length of FG interviews was approximately one to three hours each. In Garowe, the FGs were organised with help of a group of students at the Puntland State University, and in Hargeisa with one female and one male research assistant.

All individual and FG interviews were digitally recorded and transcribed. For this chapter, I have analysed in particular the sections where young people speak about fathers. In quotations from transcripts I may have edited the language in order to make the meaning clear for a reader. I have also translated the Finnish quotations to English. To preserve anonymity of the participants, I do not provide detailed information such as age with quotations.

The datasets collected in Somalia on the one hand and in Canada and Finland on the other hand are not comparable, as the data from Somalia are more limited. However, these provide a backdrop against which to see changes, but also continuities, in parent-child relationships as well as fathering practices between Somali families that have migrated and those that have

Table 4.1: Focus group interviews

Focus group site	Participants	Number	Age
Garowe	Young women	8	18–21
Garowe	Young men	5	18–25
Hargeisa	Young women	4	20–30
Hargeisa	Young men	5	24–30
Helsinki	Young women	7	20–36
Helsinki	Young men	5	19–21
Toronto	Young women	5	20–21
Toronto	Young men	6	18–26

stayed in Somalia. These shifts are rooted not only in children growing up in the diaspora, but also their fathers' diaspora experience in the Global North.

Findings

Father's authority and gendered expectations in Somalia

Participants' reflections on the gendered expectations of their parents give some insights into gendered ideas about appropriate fatherhood (and motherhood). A deep gender divide was reported by both young women and men in Somaliland and Puntland, impacting opportunities and expectations towards them at home, in education as well as in the society at large. Girls were expected to take care of the household chores, even if they studied or worked, whereas their brothers learned early on that they were not supposed to do housework. Young men instead saw it as their main responsibility to prepare themselves for a breadwinner role:

> Normally in our culture boys are second to the father. They are expected to take the role of the father when he passes away or he retires or can't afford to breadwin. So, they are the breadwinners at the end of the day ... Boys have that kind of a role, they are leaders of the family. (FG, young men, Hargeisa)

In the absence of a pension system, boys' education in particular was seen as an investment for ageing parents' future. Children were expected to pay back the care and maintenance they had received during childhood, fulfil their expected responsibilities and contribute to the wellbeing of the family. This social contract (Twum-Danso, 2009: 427) also impacted choices regarding study fields. Parents typically recommended medicine or engineering as main subjects, likely leading to well-paid jobs that would even be useful for

Somali society. Arts was mentioned as an example of a subject that parents would not accept. 'If I want to learn arts, they will probably kick me out of the house. The thing is wasting time', said a young man in Garowe.

Fathers had the power to make decisions about children and their future, which was related to their perceived responsibility in ensuring present and future viability of the family, but also the authoritarian power held by them. A male student highlighted fathers having a final say in important decisions concerning the life of children:

> The most powerful decisions come from fathers. So if some young people graduated from the secondary school, and think like they can make their own decisions, when they consult their fathers about what they are going to study, the fathers could reject the idea … saying to them 'you are not going to study that and I am not going to pay your fee for that subject … so you are on your own [if you decide to do that]'. (FG, young men, Garowe)

He himself had initially wanted to study politics, but his father had rejected the idea because he considered politics to be a risky subject in Somalia, and the young man had finally chosen law instead.

Participants said that a father had the power to make decisions in an authoritative way. However, lack of communication and conversation was not present only in father-child relationships, but also parent-child relationships in general. Children reported that they had to obey their parents, who did not ask their opinions. Because parents did not spend much time with their children and thus did not know their wishes and needs, they easily responded 'no' to requests by their children. This was disappointing, but at the same time young participants explained noncommunication due to respect to their parents, which was also endorsed by Islam: they were supposed not to ask too many questions from their parents, keep quiet and accept their point of view: 'We believe whatever our parents say, we go through that and we should respect our parents. We believe that if you respect your parents and you believe whatever they say, you go to heaven. That we believe in' (FG, young men, Garowe).

According to Koshen (2007: 91), within Somali families, a formal and respectful way of communication with the head of the family is common, and another family member may act as a mediator when necessary. The focus group data also suggest that out of respect, children were not able to express themselves or discuss their concerns and problems freely with their parents (see also Twum-Danso, 2009: 421–422 about African children in general). Girls would not discuss their more personal and intimate things with their fathers, and hardly even with their mothers. On the one hand, young people reasoned the situation by culture and Islam, but on the other hand, they also found counterarguments from religion to contest parental behaviour and their lack of respect towards children:

> Religion tells you to show respect to your child and then he will respect you, that thing is not here at all in the culture ... All the time they [parents] are ordering them [their children]. But Islam says, give them du'a [pray for them]. Sometimes they [parents] curse their children when they fail, and Allah said don't curse your children ... Even Prophet Muhammed requested people to be friends with their children. In the future, I can discuss with my daughter or son any issue, what they want for the future, because of the knowledge that I gained from the Quran and studying religion. This allows me to discuss with them and sit at the table with them, ask about their future. I will also tell them my experiences from any side of life. The only thing that can change me is the studied knowledge of religion. (FG, young women, Hargeisa)

Thus, Islamic capital (Franceschelli and O'Brien, 2014) that young people had adapted, on the one hand, justified the status quo in intergenerational relationships, but, on the other hand, helped them to challenge and redefine the parental generation's ideals of responsible parenthood and fatherhood. The young woman quoted earlier re-interpreted religious sources based on the religious knowledge she had gained by actively studying Islam, and used religion as a tool for negotiating existing parenting practices and care. The young generation in Somalia thus had a different vision on desired parenting styles than the older generation. Young women in particular were vocal about the need to change patriarchal norms in the family and society, as they already witnessed women's increased participation in public places and financial contribution in families facing poverty. In addition, they were critical about fathers, many of whom used household money for buying khat (a plant that has a narcotic effect when its leaves are chewed) instead of responding to the needs of children.

Father involvement in the diaspora

Accounts from participants in Canada and Finland indicate that fathers' care is often focussed on supporting the educational development of their children. Some young people described how they always had books at home, and particularly the father gave them an example of a reading adult, which supported their own interest and learning. A young woman said:

> Everyone in our family reads, and we had bookshelves and books. My father bought old British classics [laughs]. I did not read them,

but he thought that as he was interested in them when he was a child, we might also be interested. We really read a lot of comic books and we borrowed a lot from the library. (Individual interview, Helsinki)

Highly educated parents, mostly the fathers, were to some extent able to support their children with homework, at least if they also mastered either Finnish or English language. But mostly this was not the case, due to language problems and different school systems. However, children appreciated that a father was interested, even if he was not able to help, asked how things were going and also engaged with teachers and school. Several young people also emphasised father's role in learning the Somali language: fathers demanded them to speak and respond in the Somali language at home, whereas mothers were more lenient about speaking Somali. One of the fathers was a member of the school board. Many participants said that parents expected them to continue their studies at high school and higher education, because they should use the opportunities that children growing up in Somalia did not have. Success in studies would make parents proud, whereas success in hobbies was not similarly appreciated. A young man said disappointedly: 'There are no parents that are showing up to kids' ball games or stuff like that. So, there isn't that sense of pride right there' (FG, young men, Toronto). Another young man related how his father did not initially like that he started playing football and spent so much time with it. 'Then he heard other people saying that "your son is really talented". I broke my leg and when I was again in shape, he supported me and said, just go back and play football [laughs]' (individual interview, Helsinki).

There is evidence that there are shifting gendered care practices among fathers in the diaspora (see also Miller and Dermott, Chapter 13, this volume; Bergnehr, Chapter 15, this volume). Young participants in Canada and Finland mostly noted that expectations regarding their duties at home as well as their future were pretty similar regardless of gender. Unlike in Somalia, boys and fathers were expected to participate in cleaning, cooking and taking care of small children. However, according to a few female participants, in practice they helped more with housework than their brothers. One young woman explained that she had reminded her brothers about the Prophet Muhammed, who always helped his wife, and even their father helped the mother, so cleaning was not meant for women only (individual interview, Helsinki).

Moreover, parents were seen to be more protective of daughters and there were more restrictions on girls – for example, boys were allowed to stay out later at night (also Osman et al, 2016). At the same time participants mentioned that fathers treated their daughters more 'softly' than their sons, even if they were angry with them. In general, young participants in the diaspora communicated significantly more with their parents than participants in Somalia did. According to interviewed girls, they were able to speak about 'everything' with their mothers, whereas in questions relating to their education, they discussed with their fathers. This may relate to Somali fathers being more educated than mothers, in addition to the impact of gender. According to Omar (2016), Somali young men also tend to seek advice from their fathers instead of mothers. This would take place when they went together to Friday prayer at a mosque, for example.

Even if there was a clear difference regarding how young people in the diaspora communicated with their parents in comparison to Somalia, respect and a certain distance were still present in their relationship with the older generation. In a focus group, three young men discussed how they spoke with parents when they had disagreements. They agreed that there was a big difference between a Finnish family and a Somali family in Finland. A Somali boy or a girl could never say 'fuck you' to a mother, but a Finnish young person could say so without consequences. The young men explained that how they spoke to their parents signified respect; the parents had raised them and supported them since they were small, and therefore they should respect them (FG, young men, Helsinki). Respecting parents and elderly people in general was also connected to Islam. Not all young participants in the 17 studied families practised religion, but for the majority, the primary identification was Muslim instead of, for example, Somali.

Among the participants in the diaspora, narratives about respect and authoritative fathers were balanced by narratives about emotional closeness. Open communication with a father and time spent with the child seemed to be the foundation for mutual trust and a supportive relationship. A young man explained how proud he was of his father, who had succeeded in guiding his children and concentrating on each of them: 'My father always speaks to me, supports me and asks. Our relationship is very good. We speak really often, perhaps more than anyone else in this home' (individual interview, Helsinki). The same young man also gave examples of how he and his father had been able to discuss difficult issues such as the death of the boy's mother when he was a small child or his smoking, which the father was not happy about. The father showed his emotions, the suffering that speaking about his deceased wife – the boy's mother – caused, and the disappointment caused by the boy's smoking. These moments brought the son and father close to each other. In addition, according to the boy, the father had given him freedom since he was a child, and he did not want to cheat, for example, by drinking alcohol. Also, another young man spoke about the importance of having a father who spent time with his children:

> As a boy you need a strong role model, a father needs to be also a pal. Not only a father, not only to give orders. If I become a father,

> I want to be like my father. I want to be a father who is present, like my own father was. I want to give opportunities. I will let you make mistakes, so that you can learn about them. Not like being right all the time. I remember when I was ten years old, he said, also adults make mistakes. If you notice that I am wrong, tell me … Stronger the father figure is, the easier it is to adapt to society. That you know what is right and wrong. That you do not need to find out everything yourself. Those who do not have a father who is present, they from a young age need to estimate themselves, what is right, what is wrong, because there is nobody guiding them. (Individual interview, Helsinki)

This man had lost his father to a serious illness. He told how the father in the presence of the boy's mother had tried to joke and speak about other things, 'but when we were alone, he spoke straight with me. I was really proud that he did that with me'. As an oldest child, he also had to take the responsibility over the family after the father's death:

> I was the last person with whom my father spoke. I was at the hospital. Before he died, he said, take care of the family. You are the head of the family, I know you can [do it]. After he had died, I had to call everyone, because my mom was not able to do that. I called her brother, cousins and relatives in the middle of the night. I had to take care of everything. My little sister asked, what happens to us now as father died. I said, nothing, we continue living. It was the toughest time in my life, but I was not able to show it. (Individual interview, Helsinki)

This example shows that while there is more intimacy between fathers and children, gendered ideas around the showing of emotions is limited to women by men. Oldest children, both sons and daughters, feel they have a responsibility to help with taking care of younger siblings. A young man described that when his father was away, his role was to keep discipline. 'If the younger ones do not obey mother, she cannot run after them around the house, and I always interfere. When father is away, I tell them to show more respect and listen to parents. Since I was child, father always taught us that you have to respect your parents' (individual interview, Helsinki).

Participants also contributed to household finances if their parents asked, for example, by paying bills or sending remittances to relatives in Somalia. Thus, in many families, children were also a financial resource (see also Twum-Danso, 2009: 425). The young people also saw it as their responsibility to take care of their ageing parents. One young man described it thus: 'Like just being able to cater to my parents' needs now especially at this older age opposed to them having to cater to my needs as I was growing up as a kid' (individual interview, Toronto). Hence, the young generation in the diaspora has at least to some extent internalised the cultural values of responsibility and reciprocity (Twum-Danso, 2009) that were also seen as the foundation for a viable family in Somalia. In addition to financial security, viability also meant social support and care. In Somalia, fathers had an authoritative parenting style to achieve these goals, whereas in the diaspora there was increased evidence of mutual communication, emotional closeness and intimacy with their children.

Geographical distance did not automatically mean absence or emotional distance: in the two families where the father was working in Somalia at the time of the interview, the children had close contact with him. In both cases, the transnational family had lived several years together in one place (Canada, Finland or Somalia) when children were small, which had created an intimate bond between the father and the children. Even though the father was now physically absent, he was available when he was needed: 'He's always just an email away and he always says we don't call enough', explained a daughter in Toronto (individual interview). However, among the families, there were also examples of emotionally distant fathers.

Some young participants described discontent with their fathers, and these accounts reveal important insights into young people's expectations of care from fathers. For example, one young man openly expressed unhappiness about his father's behaviour:

> My mother has helped me, my father no ... there ain't no fathers ... My father is more like tough, hardcore, that's like the male attitude to show dominance, you wanna teach a person how to be a man by showing how they wanna be a man right. I have issues with being with father and saying what's up, I may only see him maybe for an hour, two, and he's off to work for like 12-hour shifts. And then he would come back and then he'd be tired, he has to go to sleep, he has to maintain his medication, and you cannot find much time before he's heading off, or he's just coming back to bed with a 'hi'. That's all ... He may know vaguely what my mom would tell him, inform him of what's going on but yeah not that much like interaction. The work he's doing is challenging, it's hard, and at least trying to get paid to cover himself and the family and some things, at times he would go off for trips and we won't see him for a while, just out of the blue. At times it would be a bit hindrance not knowing what he's doing or where he is, or where he's going. You're like OK, he's off again, you don't care as much. (Individual interview, Toronto)

The young man described his mother as a 'super-mom', who was practically taking care of everything and dropping them to different places by car.

In another family, a mother had sent her son for a few months to her ex-husband, the son's father, who lived in an African country. The aim was to protect him from bad influences and company, and gun violence in Toronto. The young man was not pleased with the experience. When I asked him to name his family members, he did not include his father, and I asked why not. He responded:

> I don't consider him anything. For me it's [father is] a title. I've lived with him, I don't like him, I don't wanna have anything to do with him. His family's cool … We had problems when we lived together [during the visit in Africa]. I was mostly with his brother, my uncle. And this uncle was there for me more than he was. So, you know, and that whole trip, I even told him, if I came to live with you, I wouldn't even know it; I probably be thinking he's the guy that I came to visit because I'm with him every day, and me and him are the ones going out, not you and me, you know? So that whole trip opened up my eyes more. I'm happy; I'm genuinely happy I didn't live with him, because I know I wouldn't be the person I am today. I'd be a stuck-up snob if I was with him. I don't consider him family … Family means having each other's backs no matter what; unconditional love; hating each other, but knowing deep down you love each other. (Individual interview, Toronto)

The young man's father supported his ex-wife financially when she requested support, particularly for the needs of children. He also paid for the son's travel to him in Africa, but the breadwinner role was not enough for the son who expressed a need to spend time with his father.

Discussion

The analysis shows a strong intergenerational hierarchy between fathers and their children in Somalia. Young people in Somalia had an authoritarian view of fatherhood, expecting fathers to make decisions in the family with hardly any consultation with young people. For example, fathers might decide what children should study. Authoritative parenting as well as respect towards parents also led to lack of communication between children and their parents (see also Twum-Danso, 2009: 422).

In the diaspora, young people clearly experienced more intimate fatherhood (Dermott, 2003) from their fathers. In the data there were several examples of supportive fathers, who had a close relationship with both their daughters and sons. In particular, young men expressed the importance of having a caring father, a good role model who was accessible in their everyday life and interested in them. Time spent together as well as the ability to discuss personal things together brought children and fathers emotionally closer to each other.

There were probably several reasons for the change. First, unlike in Somalia, the welfare state structures in Canada and Finland provided parents with family and unemployment benefits that enabled Somali fathers to stay longer periods at home and take part in caring for small children. Helping mother at home was particularly important during the first years of resettlement, because most families did not have close relatives or other networks in a new country who could have supported them (Tiilikainen, 2020b). Also, Bergnehr (2022) found that long-term unemployed refugee men from the Middle East in Sweden contributed to caregiving more than before. It has also been suggested that the welfare state context may help migrant fathers to bond with their children (Bungum and Kvande, 2022). Second, fathers were exposed to different needs and ideas regarding fatherhood and raising children in a totally new sociocultural environment after migrating, and at least to some extent gradually changed their parenting practices. For example, Canadian-Somali parents realised that unlike in Somalia, children could not be let out alone as neighbourhoods were unsafe (Tiilikainen, 2020a), and Swedish-Somali parents expressed that they had learnt to listen to and respect their children's opinions (Haga, 2020: 120). Third, children growing up in Canada and Finland challenged the traditional authoritative, masculine father role, and wanted him 'to be also a pal, not only to give orders'. Breadwinning was seen as a kind of minimum expectation for a father, but children wished him to go beyond that. The need for better communication skills between parents and their children has also been expressed by young Somali men in Australia and the US (Omar, 2016) as well as Somali-born parents in Sweden (Osman et al, 2016). These examples of children's agency provoking change in fathering practices underline fatherhood being relational (Doucet, Chapter 2, this volume). However, the experiences of fatherhood and father's care practices in the diaspora were divided. Socioeconomic status and language skills impacted parental practices and opportunities.

Young people's accounts also reveal significant differences in how fathers in Somalia and in the diaspora perceive their own role as well as that of their children from a gender perspective. In Canada and Finland, fathers have stepped into the domestic sphere that in Somalia is usually managed by women. Consequently, their expectations for their daughters' future have expanded from care work in the family to higher education and paid work. Based on the interviews, fathers in the diaspora actively and equally supported the education of their sons and daughters. In families with two parents, fathers were usually more engaged with school than mothers; they discussed children's future plans with them and also taught them the Somali language. This change was impacted by long-term resettlement in Canada and Finland where ideals of gender equality are highly esteemed.

In addition, due to welfare society, fathers did not face similar financial constraints as in Somalia that would have reduced their capacity to care and educate their children.

In the absence of welfare state structures, families in Somalia were dependent on social security provided by their (extended) families. Children were expected to contribute to the wellbeing of family and fulfil the social contract with parents (Twum-Danso, 2009: 427) by, for example, taking care of their ageing parents. Interestingly, the values of reciprocity, respect and responsibility were also reflected in parent-child relationships in Canada and Finland. Fathers and mothers taught their children the importance of relationality between extended family members and kin, instead of individualism that they encountered in the Global North. These cultural values were seen as the foundation for a viable family unit not only in Somalia, but also in new diasporic contexts of Canada and Finland. Children respected their parents not only for their role as parent, but also for a number of other things – for example, because they knew what the parents had gone through during the civil war and when they brought the family out of Somalia. Or a father was respected for his qualities such as generosity in sending remittances and supporting relatives in Somalia, or being a hardworking man who took care of his family. Furthermore, young people took it for granted that they had a responsibility to reciprocally help their parents and older generation in general, siblings and other close family members in any way possible when this was needed.

The values of reciprocity, respect and responsibility were also enforced by Islam that parents passed on to their children. Islamic capital (Franceschelli and O'Brien, 2014) was used by young people both in Somalia and in the diaspora, on the one hand, to explain certain behaviour, such as respect to older people, but also, on the other hand, to challenge and change existing gender roles or relationships between parents and children.

Overall, this chapter enriches the literature on migrant Muslim fathers by providing examples of how fathers in the diaspora have cultivated their fathering practices towards more intimate fatherhood (Dermott, 2003) and have increased emotional involvement with their children (also Wu and Del Rey Poveda, Chapter 14, this volume). This perspective challenges stereotypical views of Muslim men (Grüner, 2021). Over the years living in the diaspora, patriarchal norms in Somali families seem to have decreased and gender divisions relaxed, which has also been observed in other migrant families (Attias-Donfut and Cook, 2017: 121).

Through contacts with transnational families, new ideas have also sparked discussion in Somalia regarding gender roles and intergenerational relationships. For example, in the focus groups in Somalia, participants expressed that females who had migrated abroad were better at sending remittances than males, and they also paid attention to youth from the diaspora, who were able to challenge the views of their parents. More research would be needed to study current parent–child relationships and how they may be changing in Somalia.

Acknowledgements
I thank all the participating families and individuals in Finland, Canada and Somalia who made this research possible. I am grateful to the Puntland State University, which hosted me during the fieldwork in Garowe, and in particular to Shucayb Mohamud Adan, Warsame Abdirizak Warsame, Farhia Osman Farah, Burhan Jama Muhammad, Maryama Nuradin Afrah and Sabirin Mohamud Mohamed, who helped me to organise the focus group interviews there. Finally, I thank the editors of the book for their insightful comments that helped me greatly to improve the text.

References
Attias-Donfut, Claudine and Joanne Cook (2017) 'Intergenerational relationships in migrant families: theoretical and methodological issues', in C. Bolzman et al (eds) *Situating Children of Migrants across Borders and Origins*. Dordrecht: Springer, pp 115–133.

Baldassar, Loretta and Laura Merla (eds) (2014) *Transnational Families, Migration and the Circulation of Care Understanding Mobility and Absence in Family Life*. New York: Routledge.

Bangura, Ibrahim (2021) 'Trapped in violence and uncertainty: patriarchy, women, and the conflict in Somalia', *African Conflict and Peacebuilding Review*, 11(1): 80–103.

Bergnehr, Disa (2022) 'Adapted fathering for new times: refugee men's narratives on caring for home and children', *Journal of Family Studies*, 28(3): 934–949. https://doi.org/10.1080/13229400.2020.1769708

Bungum, Brita and Elin Kvande (2022) 'Polish migrant fathers using parental leave in Norway', *Journal of Family Research*, 34(3): 912–931. https://doi.org/10.20377/jfr-753

Cabdi, Sucaad Ibraahim (2005) 'The impact of the war on the family', in *Rebuilding Somaliland. Issues and Possibilities*. Lawrenceville, NJ/Asmara, Eritrea: Red Sea Press, pp 269–293.

Degni, Filio, Seppo Pöntinen and Mulki Mölsä (2006) 'Somali parents' experiences of bringing up children in Finland: exploring social-cultural change within migrant households', *Forum Qualitative Sozialforschung/Forum: Qualitative Social Research*, 7(3), Article 8. http://nbn-resolving.de/urn:nbn:de:0114-fqs060388

Dermott, Esther (2003) 'The "intimate father": defining paternal involvement', *Sociological Research Online*, 8(4). http://www.socresonline.org.uk/8/4/dermott.html

El-Bushra, Judy and Judith Gardner (2016) 'The impact of war on Somali men: feminist analysis of masculinities and gender relations in a fragile context', *Gender & Development*, 24(3): 443–458.

Franceschelli, Michela and Margaret O'Brien (2014) '"Islamic capital" and family life: the role of Islam in parenting', *Sociology*, 48(6), 1190–1206.

Grüner, Jeppe Schmidt (2021) 'Emergent fatherhood: new articulations of fatherhood among Muslim men in Denmark', *Contemporary Islam*, 15: 233–247. https://doi.org/10.1007/s11562-020-00455-x

Haga, Rannveig (2020) 'Somali parents in Sweden: navigating parenting and child wellbeing', in Marja Tiilikainen, Mulki Al-Sharmani and Sanna Mustasaari (eds) *Wellbeing of Transnational Muslim Families. Marriage, Law and Gender*. New York: Routledge, pp 112–128.

Horst, Cindy (2017) 'Implementing the Women, Peace and Security agenda? Somali debates on women's public roles and political participation', *Journal of Eastern African Studies*, 11(3): 389–407. https://doi.org/10.1080/17531055.2017.1348000

Inhorn, Marcia C. and Nefissa Naguib (eds) (2018) *Reconceiving Muslim Men: Love and Marriage, Family and Care in Precarious Times*. New York: Berghahn Books.

Ismail, Abdirashid A. (2020) 'Transnational Finnish–Somali families and children's wellbeing', in Marja Tiilikainen, Mulki Al-Sharmani and Sanna Mustasaari (eds) *Wellbeing of Transnational Muslim Families: Marriage, Law and Gender*. Abingdon: Routledge, pp 129–146.

Kilkey, Majella, Ania Plomien and Diane Perrons (2013) 'Migrant men's fathering narratives, practices and projects in national and transnational spaces: recent Polish male migrants to London', *International Migration*, 52(1): 178–191. DOI: 10.1111/imig.12046

Kleist, Nauja (2010) 'Negotiating respectable masculinity: gender and recognition in the Somali diaspora', *African Diaspora*, 3: 185–206.

Koshen, Hawa Ibrahim A. (2007) 'Strengths in Somali families', *Marriage & Family Review*, 41(1–2): 71–99. DOI: 10.1300/J002v41n01_05

Kvande, Elin and Berit Brandth (2016). 'Individualized, non-transferable parental leave for European fathers: migrant perspectives', *Community, Work & Family*, 20(1): 19–34. DOI: 10.1080/13668803.2016.1270258

Mazzucato, Valentina and Djamila Schans (2011) 'Transnational families and the well-being of children: conceptual and methodological challenges', *Journal of Marriage and Family*, 73(4): 704–712.

Omar, Yusuf Sheikh (2016) 'Intergenerational conflict in the Somali diaspora: the perspectives of young Somali men in Australia and USA', *Somali Studies*, 1: 77–104.

Osman, Fatumo, Marie Klingberg-Allvin, Renée Flacking and Ulla-Karin Schön (2016) 'Parenthood in transition: Somali-born parents' experiences of and needs for parenting support programmes', *BMC International Health and Human Rights*, 16(7). DOI: 10.1186/s12914-016-0082-2

Osman, Fatumo, Eva Randell, Abdikerim Mohamed and Emma Sorbring (2021) 'Dialectical processes in parent-child relationships among Somali families in Sweden', *Journal of Child and Family Studies*, 30: 1752–1762. DOI: 10.1007/s10826-021-01956-w

Poeze, Miranda (2019) 'Beyond breadwinning: Ghanaian transnational fathering in the Netherlands', *Journal of Ethnic and Migration Studies*, 45(16): 3065–3084. DOI: 10.1080/1369183X.2018.15470

Tiilikainen, Marja (2020a) 'Raising children of Somali descent in Toronto', in Marja Tiilikainen, Mulki Al-Sharmani and Sanna Mustasaari (eds) *Wellbeing of Transnational Muslim Families: Marriage, Law and Gender*. Abingdon: Routledge, pp 147–163.

Tiilikainen, Marja (2020b) 'Finnish Somali fathers, respectability, and transnational family life', in Johanna Hiitola, Kati Turtiainen, Sabine Gruber and Marja Tiilikainen (eds) *Family Life in Transition: Borders, Transnational Mobility, and Welfare Society in Nordic Countries*. Abingdon: Routledge, pp 131–141.

Twum-Danso, Afua (2009) 'Reciprocity, respect and responsibility: the 3Rs underlying parent-child relationships in Ghana and the implications for children's rights', *Journal of Children's Rights*, 17: 415–432.

Velayati, Masoumeh (2016) 'Gender and Muslim families', in Constance L. Shehan (ed.) *The Wiley Blackwell Encyclopedia of Family Studies*. Chichester: John Wiley & Sons.

Warsame, Faiza A. (2001) 'The role of women in rebuilding Puntland', in *Rebuilding Somalia: Issues and possibilities for Puntland*. London: HAAN Associates, pp 259–302.

Żadkowska, Magdalena, Natasza Kosakowska-Berezecka, Tomasz Szlendak and Tomasz Besta (2020) 'When migrant men become more involved in household and childcare duties – the case of Polish migrants in Norway', *Journal of Family Studies*, 28(2): 401–421. DOI: 10.1080/13229400.2020.1712222

5

Moving beyond the narrative of marginalised fatherhood: Russian fathers' accounts of nonresident fathering after family separation

Ekaterina Ivanova

Introduction

Russian fathers have gained a certain representation in academic research as marginalised in the domestic sphere, by being practically uninvolved in parenting and superfluous for meaningful family routines; a position exacerbated after family separation (Ashwin and Lytkina, 2004; Chernova, 2012; Utrata et al, 2013; Utrata, 2015). This image of fatherhood stands in stark contrast to Western discourses, academic and public, which have increasingly centred around fathers' nonfinancial involvement and their role as carers (for more on this trend, see Twamley et al, Chapter 1, and Doucet, Chapter 2, this volume). The recognition of fathers as caring parents has been at the centre of contemporary political debates and legislation reforms regulating separated parenthood in the West, as well as in personal narratives of separated fathers (Collier and Sheldon, 2006; Fehlberg et al, 2011; Andreasson and Johansson, 2019; Jordan, 2020). Although it remains widespread for children to spend more time with their mothers after separation in Western countries (Smyth, 2017; Flaquer, 2021), 'being there' through co-parenting, organised as shared custody arrangements, has increasingly been seen as a prerequisite for good separated fathering (Philip, 2014; Andreasson and Johansson, 2019; Natalier and Dunk-West, 2019; Randles, 2020; Weber, 2020; Campo et al, 2021). In contrast, in Russia the themes of shared custody and co-parenting seem to be absent in public debates or institutional reflection (Kay, 2007a, 2007b). According to available data, more than 90 per cent of children reside with their mothers after family separation (Rzhanitsyna and Kalabikhina, 2012).

Using interviews with Russian fathers collected in 2015 and 2022, the chapter aims to provide a picture of Russian fatherhood that departs, sometimes significantly, from the image of a marginalised and detached father present in the current research on Russian fatherhood. In doing so, it follows the approach outlined by Doucet in Chapter 2 of this volume, which encourages us to understand caring fathering as a relational and moral practice deriving its meaning from its embeddedness in familial relationships and wider social contexts (see also Smart and Neale, 1999; Morgan, 2011; Philip, 2013, 2014). Family dissolution challenges the established parenting practices and relationships, and creates complex moral dilemmas for parents (Smart and Neale, 1999). Research demonstrates that when negotiating child support and custody, parents are guided by their understandings of the 'right', 'good' and 'fair', which are gendered and culturally specific (Duncan and Edwards, 1999; Philip, 2013; Keil and Elizabeth, 2017). Following this, the chapter investigates separated fathering against the backdrop of gendered, legal and cultural norms regulating parenthood and family separation in Russia.

In this chapter, particular attention is paid to Russian fathers' practices of child support as a gendered form of care. Doucet (2020) has pointed out that in fatherhood research conducted in Western contexts, breadwinning and care are often conceptually juxtaposed, with the former being portrayed as taking away from caregiving. However, there are contexts in which financial provision remains the main (if not the only) legitimate and socially acceptable form of masculine care. For instance, Hanlon (2012) demonstrated that for fathers in Ireland, caregiving was still considered unnatural and inconvenient, while their commitment to breadwinning was understood as the fatherly way of care, the masculine form of 'love labour' (2012: 116). I argue that Hanlon's observations are relevant for Russia, where breadwinning is central not only to Russian men's selfhood but also their ideas of good fatherhood (Kay, 2006; Utrata, 2015; Lipasova, 2017; Ukhova, 2022; Walker, 2022), as well as to the gendered construction of parenthood in Russia (Kay, 2007c; Shpakovskaya, 2015).

Unpacking the marginalisation narrative: research on Russian fatherhood

The marginalisation of Russian fatherhood has been a prominent narrative in academic research, the position commonly attributed to individual men's disinterest in parenting and their 'choices', such as excessive drinking, that pushed them to the margins of everyday family lives (Ashwin and Lytkina, 2004; Utrata et al, 2013; Utrata, 2015). In one of the first ethnographic research on Russian separated fatherhood after the collapse of the Soviet Union, Utrata demonstrated that Russian fathers, despite finding nonresident fatherhood inherently deficient, powerless and unsatisfactory (Utrata, 2008: 1305), did nothing to challenge this position, instead agreeing that 'they are at best not much more than "appendages" to single-mother families' (2015: 108). Utrata argued that men benefited from accepting such a deficient image of separated fatherhood, as they could stay unencumbered by parental responsibilities after separation, but still evaluate themselves as decent fathers (Utrata, 2008).

Other researchers, while supporting the marginalisation thesis, also emphasised the role of Russian and, before that, the Soviet state in pushing men to the margins of family lives (Kay, 2006, 2007a, 2007b; Chernova, 2012). According to them, the origins of paternal marginalisation can be traced back to the gender politics of the early Soviet state, which was argued to purposefully undermine fatherhood as a patriarchal institution through the demolishment of its legal and economic basis, such as religious marriage and private property (Kukhterin, 2000). Soviet fathers received little incentive from the state to be involved in domestic lives, and fatherhood was reduced to economic support, which the state enforced on men in the case of family separation (Chernova, 2012). After the collapse of the Soviet Union in 1991, the marginalised position of fathers and their invisibility as carers in state discourses and policies was 'inherited' by postsocialist Russia (Kay, 2007a; Bezrukova and Samoylova, 2020). At present, Russian law does not provide regulation and enforcement for joint physical custody, and legally only one parent can be granted physical custody of children (that is, the resident parent, typically the mother), while the other is obligated to contribute financially and is entitled to contact with their children (the nonresident parent, typically the father).

Recent research provides support for the marginalisation narrative to some extent, but also draws a picture of change. Some studies confirm that men do little when it comes to children (Kravchenko, 2012; Lipasova, 2017), while other depict fathers who share childcare responsibilities and identify themselves as involved fathers (Avdeeva, 2012; Bezrukova and Samoylova, 2019; Ukhova, 2022). In previous research of mine, fathers differed significantly in terms of their commitment after separation: while some practised shared parenting, others were satisfied with their role of 'Sunday dads' (Ivanova, 2017). Fathers' willingness to pay child support varied as well, and some provided financial support regularly and generously (Ivanova, 2018). A recent study by Bezrukova and Samoylova (2020) gave voice to fathers' dissatisfaction with their legal and social position after separation. This chapter thus further explores the divergence between the established narrative on Russian fatherhood as inherently marginalised and the evidence provided by recent studies that challenges the image of Russian men as detached and disinterested fathers.

Data and analysis

This chapter is based on two sets of semi-structured interviews with Russian fathers who experienced family separation and/or divorce with children under 18 years old. The first set of 18 interviews was collected in 2015 for my master's thesis research; 25 interviews were collected in 2022 for my PhD research. Demographically, the two samples were very similar, with the average age of participants being 35 in 2015 and 37 years old in 2022. In both samples, participants had separated or divorced, on average, five years before the interview. Children's ages varied from case to case in both samples, with the youngest being 2.5 years old in 2015 and one year old in 2022, and the oldest being 16 years old in both samples.

In 2015, all participants were recruited using snowball sampling. All participants lived in cities with a population over a million. Most had university education. Data on participants' income were not collected. In 2022, the majority of participants were also recruited via personal connections and snowballing. Additionally, I used the services of a professional recruiter to collect a more diverse sample. Sixteen fathers participating in my study in 2022 lived in cities with a population of over a million. Five participants lived in cities with a population of around 500,000–600,000; the remaining four were from smaller cities with a population between 100,000 and 300,000. The 2022 sample included participants from different income groups, which were calculated based on the state-provided stratification of income brackets. The median income in the sample fell between 75,000 and 90,000 rubles. Fourteen participants had an income higher than the national average. Nine participants had a secondary professional level of education (that is, vocational education), and the rest had university education.

Importantly, participants in both samples shared similar experiences of fathering. Fathers' contact with their children varied, but in most cases, children spent most of their time with their mothers after separation. It was common for fathers to see their children regularly, but only during the daytime. However, several participants had their children stay overnight, usually over the weekend, or for a longer period of time during children's school holidays. Notably, in 2015, as well as in 2022, there were fathers who shared time with their children equally with their ex-partners, and fathers who were resident parents for some time after separation. All participants negotiated parenting arrangements informally, with the exception of one father interviewed in 2022, who unsuccessfully attempted to gain full custody over his children through court litigation. The majority of fathers also had an informal agreement on child support.

Collected data were analysed using thematic narrative analysis (Riessman, 2008; Braun and Clarke, 2022). I identified and articulated the patterns of shared meaning (that is, themes), while also paying analytical attention to participants' narrative practice (that is, the ways in which fathers meaningfully organised and presented their experiences as culturally relevant and intelligible for the researcher). In the following sections, analysis is illustrated by interview excerpts that are provided with a brief information on each case. It includes a participant's pseudonym, residence/contact arrangements at the moment of the interview, the number and the age of children at the moment of separation, when initial arrangements were made, and the year in which the interview was collected.

Becoming a nonresident father: the moral script of family separation

According to the interviewed fathers, it was common for children to stay with their mothers after separation. Legally, all participants who were officially divorced were assigned the status of the nonresident parent during the divorce proceedings. Becoming a nonresident parent was taken for granted by most participants, both divorced and separated; in interviews, this arrangement was described as 'standard', 'normal' and 'natural'. In fact, it was common for fathers to admit they did not discuss children's resident arrangements whatsoever. Anatolii's response was very illustrative of this attitude. He explained: 'I believe, we both considered, we were certain of the standard course of events. No one discussed the fact that the child would stay with her mom' (Interview #5, Anatolii, occasional stayovers on the weekends and school holidays, two children from two marriages, five and three years old, 2015).

Nonresident parenting was understood not only as a standard postseparation scenario for fathers, but also as the right choice made in their children's best interests. Taking the story of Pavel, a nonresident father whose partner moved to a different city soon after separation and took their son with her. Pavel was stricken by his son's relocation, describing in the interview that learning about his ex-partner's decision felt like 'his balls were [cut off] with a reaping hook'. Nevertheless, he, a family lawyer himself, assured me of having no intention to obstruct this decision. Relocation likely contributed to the deterioration of Pavel's relationship with his son. Despite his attempts to visit the son at least once a month, Pavel eventually found himself on the margins of his son's life. When I asked Pavel why he did not try to challenge his ex-partner's decision, he explained that staying with the mother was in his son's best interests:

> Well … This is a complicated question. In my opinion, a child, of course, should be brought up by his mom. Not by the father but by his mother. And if divorce happens, it is preferable for a child to stay with his mom. Of course, there are different situations, and there were different situations in my legal practice. But she [the ex-partner] is a good mother. (Interview #2, Petr, weekly daytime visits, one child, six years old, 2015)

In Pavel's narrative, his interpretation of the child's best interests stemmed from the gendered division of labour in the family. Elsewhere in his interview, he referred to a stronger emotional connection mothers foster with their children when doing care work. Fathers, according to him, usually have a limited involvement in caring due to their greater commitment to paid employment. This was a common reasoning Russian fathers provided to me, and in many families, including Pavel's, fathers indeed spent more time doing paid work than mothers, especially when their children were little. However, underlying this reasoning was also a belief in fundamental and naturalised gendered differences in parenting, which was shared even by those fathers who reported being more engaged in childcare before and after separation. For example, Dmitrii, while legally being a nonresident parent, de facto practised shared parenting, having his daughter two nights a week after his separation. He nevertheless referred to his ex-partner's place as his daughter's home. When I asked him whether he ever considered having the daughter for more nights or even establishing her residence with him, he responded:

> Of course, I had. Maybe, like ... But no, it would be nonsense, of course. It was just my inner talk ... It was a sick fantasy that I could have taken over the responsibilities of a mother. I think this is not normal. A father who would raise a girl. (Interview #16, Dmitrii, two nights a week, one child, eight years old, 2022)

While for Dmitrii, having a daughter was a particularly strong rationale in favour of maternal residence, in the narratives of other Russian fathers, their children's wellbeing, irrespective of gender, was commonly linked to them staying with their mothers after separation. Subsequently, nonresident fathering was a moral script, following which fathers complied with the gendered expectations for good parenthood after separation. This script had a normative force and, as Dmitrii's excerpt suggests, even imagining alternative arrangements could create a sense of a 'gender vertigo' (Connell, 2005: 137).

The diversity of nonresident fathering

Embracing the position of the nonresident parent did not necessarily lead to fathers' lack of engagement in their children's lives after separation. Russian fathers' narratives of nonresident fathering were diverse, with several participants emphasising their dedication and commitment to stay as involved as their negotiations with their ex-partners and their personal circumstances would allow. For example, Yurii failed to negotiate co-resident arrangements for his two children with his ex-partner, and never had them to stay overnight. Yet, his whole narrative was centred on his neverending efforts to stay involved in his children's daily lives, even after he got married for the second time:

Life was organised this way. I remember when I met my future father-in-law for the first time, he asked me: Do you have any hobbies? And I was saying: You know, what? My only hobbies now are my children. I am raising my children. If I have free time, I spend it on my children, picking them up, giving them a lift, having a phone call, meeting with them. (Interview #3, Yurii, two children, 9 and 11 years old, 2015)

While not all men expressed such a strong commitment, nonresident fathers generally reported seeing children regularly, and having them to stay over, usually on the weekend, and/or spending winter or summer school holidays at their place or together in the countryside. This is how Anatolii described his involvement after divorce:

We tried to follow some kind of schedule. For example, I took the kid for a walk every Tuesday and Thursday evening. I also had her every second weekend because her mom also wanted to spend time with her daughter on the weekend. When the daughter started school, I obviously stopped taking her for evening walks as she did it by herself¹. There was a moment – still now, from time to time – when she spent significantly more time on the weekends with me than with her mother. During summer, she could stay with me for several weeks. So, there was a moment when she was here so often on the weekends that her mom was annoyed at her for that. (Interview #5, Anatolii, occasional stayovers on the weekends and school holidays, two children from two marriages, five and three years old, 2015)

As his daughter was getting older, they adjusted the schedule. Anatolii explained:

Life is changing. She has school on Saturdays now, as well. She is older now. To come by for a half an hour at night on the working week … The child should prepare her homework, have some rest, and prepare for bed. If she needs a lift, then of course, not a question. But come around just to sit with her or have a walk, to spend three hours driving just to spend an hour with her, this is a little odd. (Interview #5, Anatolii, occasional stayovers on the weekends and school holidays, two children from two marriages, five and three years old, 2015)

This excerpt demonstrates that this adjustment was made in consideration of his daughter's increased school load. It was also based on his daughter's changing preferences for spending her free time, as he explained elsewhere in the interview. While the exact number of hours Anatolii spent with his daughter weekly reduced, he did not feel he was missing out on their relationship, as he managed to make up for this time during longer summer breaks.

Flexibility was commonly reported by Russian fathers, with arrangements often reflecting children's age, work and other relationship commitments and relocation. The interview with Timur provided an example of complex and flexible arrangements, negotiated to accommodate his son's young age at the time of separation, as well as Timur's employment, requiring him to spend months travelling for work, and his ex-partner's decision to move to a different city:

> When we separated, I tried to come by and get the kid for a walk every day, almost every day. Then, I began to take him overnight for a couple of days. But he was young back then; it was a little hard for him. A year after separation, I took him at the beginning of June and gave him back at the beginning of July because I had a relatively work-free month. Then they moved to [name of city] in September. I was working till November and came to [name of city] to pick him up at the end of the month and took him to [name of city], where he was with me till the middle of December. Then I brought him back to [the name of city]. Then, again, I came to pick him up on 4 January and brought him back only now, at the end of January. (Interview #12, Timur, irregular periods of stayovers, one child, three years old, 2022)

With no institutional guidelines or a cultural scenario for shared parenting to follow, the arrangements for time and care reported by participants were diverse and negotiated on an ad hoc basis. Timur's description also illustrates that fathers' degree of involvement can be substantial and, not infrequently, fathers who described themselves as nonresident parents were in fact practising shared parenting. Moreover, several participants experienced being resident parents for some period after separation. At the time of the interview, three fathers had their children staying with them approximately half the time, and four fathers had their children living with them most or all the time. These participants were aware that their situation differed from the normative script for separated fathering and provided me with reasons for such arrangements to take place. Importantly, in the absence of the shared custody regime, these arrangements had to be negotiated in the shadow of the law, which continued to define fathers as nonresident parents.

Doing fatherly care through child support and property division

As nonresident parents, fathers were legally obliged to pay child support. In most cases, it was arranged informally, as private unregulated transactions between parents, an option that was legally available to separated parents.

Participants emphasised that financial support of their children after separation was their moral obligation rather than just a legal obligation, and tended to present themselves in the interviews as compliant payers and generous providers. For example, this is how Igor talked about child support:

> We decided not to formalise the payments, but from the point of view that this is my duty, I always feel that I have to give my child a fair amount ... For me, this is a kind of pleasure, I don't know, my social role in this life. (Interview #1, Igor, one night a week, one child, 8 years old, 2022)

In the interview, Igor emphasised his role as the primary breadwinner in the family before separation. After separation, he regularly had his son to stay overnight on the weekend, but believed his main contribution to his son's upbringing was through child support. Similarly, Mark, who separated when his son was about one year old, and who since then only occasionally had him overnight, admitted he was not interested in a greater involvement, but was willing to pay child support:

> A: [When we separated] I said I would help with money; at that point, I earned very little and could only help with very little sums. But I said I would, no one tried to make it formal, to get official alimony, we never did that ... At that point, it was something very minimal, like, 1000 rubles a month; then, with my income increasing I began to increase the payment as well. There were moments when the ex-wife asked me: 'oh, we also need money for this, transfer a little more, please'.
> Q: What percentage were you used to transfer, and what do you transfer now?
> A: It was ... 10 to 30 per cent of my salary. Now, I earn a little less, so I send her a larger percentage, actually.
> Q: So, there is a fixed sum of money that you send, rather than a fixed percentage?
> A: Mostly yes, the amount I found adequate.
> (Interview # 15, Mark, occasional stayovers, one child, one year old, 2022)

Mark's narrative demonstrates that when practising child support, he made adjustments to the payments based on the changing circumstances and the needs of his son. He also indicated that he followed not only legal guidelines but also his personal perception of fairness, and at some point, he paid more than 25 per cent of hid income, which was the legal norm. Alexey too 'personalised' child support payments by going beyond the amount required by law:

A: I've decided for myself: there is salary, there are formalities that clearly state who owes what to whom. Thus, I will pay what I must, plus a little bit on top [extras]. When it's a little with 'a crust', you flatter yourself: oh, how good I am. So, I am doing what I am supposed to do, plus a bonus on my behalf. This is how I perceive this money: 25 per cent is simply not my money. It does not belong to me. This is what I owe, in any case, and it's not mine. And what is extra – this is from me, from me personally.
Q: Like, from dad with love
A: Yeah, something like that.
(Interview #1, Alexey, irregular daytime visits, one child, ten years old, 2015)

These examples indicate that Russian fathers saw financial provision as a morally acceptable and socially legitimate way to express care and affection, a way to 'be there' for their children when they could not – or did not want to – share caregiving responsibilities with their ex-partners. However, this attitude was not exclusive to fathers who spent little time with their children. For example, Karim was the resident parent for his two sons for a few years after separation and was living with his older son at the time of the interview. Despite this, he still believed his primary way of showing care should have been through financial provision, something that he struggled with due to his chronic illness, which affected his employment:

A: The situation here in Russia is very simple: you plainly need to make money. If you earn something, you can show your love, and everything else. And ... With my illness, with all this hardship, I struggle with this currently. I really want to show my love, but I'm not always able to.
Q: So, you think for fathers specifically it is important to demonstrate financially ... to contribute?
A: Well, of course, of course.
Q: Is this important for any parent, mothers included? Or this is the father's thing.
A: What I'm saying is ... Love is love, and everyone loves them, they see it, that we love them very much but ... For self-validation even, that I am a good father, I would like to do many things. But not everything works out.
(Interview #22, Karim, one son lives with him, while he sees the other occasionally, 15 and 9 years old, 2022)

The moral way of doing fathering after separation also included certain expectations regarding property division. Russian law establishes the joint property regime in marriage, which is divided equally between the spouses in case of divorce, except as is otherwise provided in the notarised agreement. However, there was an understanding, frequently expressed in the interviews, that whenever possible, children should continue to live in the residence they did before separation. Subsequently, it was very common for participants to report that they left the property to their ex-partners, who stayed with the children. The following exchange with Arsenii provides an example of such a rationale:

Q: How did you solve the issues with the house?
A: They [the ex-partner with the son] stayed in the apartment, which was purchased during the marriage.
Q: Did you discuss this decision, to not divide the property?
A: Well, it wasn't like that, just – where else would they stay? They should live somewhere. This was perhaps not a very pleasant decision for me, but they should live somewhere, shouldn't they?
Q: Why not pleasant?
A: Well, I live in a rented property. Let's say, those opportunities … OK, I understand that opportunities are always the same but that level of financial success that I had in the 1990s and early 2000s is different from what I have now. And now it is a little, well, it is more difficult now.

(Interview #17, Arsenii, no contact, one child, six years old, 2015)

At times, it was legally and financially easier to leave the property to one parent rather than try to divide it, and in some cases, fathers seemed to benefit from this decision no less than their ex-partners and children . However, the allocation of property to the resident parent was also a moral decision, made with the children's best interests in mind. Nonresident fathers more often found themselves in a situation where they needed to find and organise a new place of living after separation. Residential uncertainty and (at least temporal) unsettledness was commonly expressed by fathers and affected their practices of parenting, particularly their ability to have children overnight.

Still keeping the bar low? Caring as voluntary commitment

Previous sections of this chapter have aimed to demonstrate that nonresident fathering was commonly understood by Russian participants as a moral way of doing good fathering after separation. However, participants' practices and interpretations of their experiences must be understood as embedded in the social and institutional context in which men experience little pressure to be accountable for involvement, even of a financial nature, after separation. Participants felt able to explicitly acknowledge that they had little desire or motivation to see their children more often and commit to shared parenting. Anatolii, whose parenting arrangements were described earlier in the chapter, corrected me when I referred to him as an involved and good father during our interview:

> I don't consider myself a good dad. At best, a typical one. There are people I know who spend more time with their children and engage in more educational activities. I mostly go with the flow. If there is an opportunity, I am involved. But I won't move mountains if there is no such opportunity. (Interview #5, Anatolii, occasional stayovers on the weekends and school holidays, two children from two marriages, five and three years old, 2015)

Alexey, who saw his son sporadically and never had him overnight, had a similar opinion about his fatherly 'performance'. Yet, narratively juxtaposing himself with the image of an absent father allowed him to justify his limited presence in his son's life:

> I presume that it's better to have a father like me than no father at all. I understand that … Well, I'm far from being an ideal dad. I'm quite far from this ideal. But it's better than if I just forget, leave behind, turn away, disappear. This would be the worst scenario. (Interview #1, Alexey, irregular daytime visits, one child, ten years old, 2015)

Such accounts resonated with Urata's earlier observations on Russian men opting out of a narrow fatherhood ideal (Utrata 2008). In this research, participants similarly expressed a strong sense of freedom to define their level of commitment to fathering after separation and did not feel moral repercussions if they were not particularly engaged in children's lives. However, a lack of involvement was often excused by a continuing financial provision, to which Russian fathers felt more accountability. Igor was very clear about this, explaining:

> Look, formally, right, if we take what the law requires, she has to spend all the time with him [Igor's son], and I can only pay child support and not even show up. This is the law, this is how it works here. Obviously, this is not the option for both of us, none of us would be pleased with this, and least so the son. I want to spend time with my son, I give him as much time as I can. I call her, I arrange the time, and we never argue about this. She accepts the situation as it is. She is happy I find time for him; I find quite a lot of time for him anyway. She had this

day off when she could do whatever she wants. I wouldn't say I always have a day when I can do whatever I want to do. (Interview #1, Igor, one night a week, one child, eight years old, 2022)

Importantly, the widespread use of informal employment and off-the-book salaries in Russia (Barsukova and Radaev, 2012) resulted in the official child support system failing to represent men's actual liability for financial provision (Ivanova, 2024). This left compliance with primarily informal arrangements at the discretion of fathers. Quite frequently, participants admitted they paid a sum that constituted a smaller percentage of their income than they would have been required to pay had they organised child support through the court. The minimisation of official child support through the understatement of income left mothers with little choice between accepting any support offered by fathers or enforcing official but usually meagre payments. While fathers typically reported discussing the sum of support with the mothers of their children, it was not infrequent for fathers to discretionarily decrease payments when the circumstances – of their work or personal lives – changed. The legal and social norms, and the structural conditions of the Russian economy thus allowed men to maintain discretion on deciding how much care – whether through direct involvement in caregiving or through financial provision – they were willing to provide.

Discussion and conclusion

This chapter has explored nonresident fathering in Russia, going beyond the image of detached, marginalised fatherhood prevalent in the contemporary academic literature (Ashwin and Lytkina, 2004; Chernova, 2012; Utrata et al, 2013; Utrata, 2015). It has demonstrated that, contrary to this image, most fathers whose experiences were discussed in this chapter remained very much connected with their children after separation, through regular contact and the practices of child support. While all participants who went through divorce procedure were granted a formal status of the nonresident parent, informal residence arrangements negotiated in the shadow of the law were more diverse. For many, nonresident parenting was an active practice; fathers put effort into maintaining their contact with children over the years, and negotiated and adjusted parenting arrangements when life circumstances – theirs or those of their children – changed. In several cases, Russian fathers shared time with children equally with their ex-partners or were de facto primary carers for their children.

This chapter has contributed to an understanding of caring fathering as contextual and relational practice and disposition, an approach advocated by Doucet in Chapter 2 of this volume and Philip elsewhere (Philip, 2014, 2013). Through this perspective, I have demonstrated that Russian fathers often perceived nonresident fathering as caring fathering. Participants believed it was most beneficial for their children's emotional and physiological wellbeing to stay with their mothers after separation. Moreover, fathers also believed this arrangement was fair to their ex-partners, who, in most cases, carried a larger responsibility and did more care work before separation. In navigating separation, participants presented themselves as relational subjects (Doucet, Chapter 2 in this volume), whose practices and interpretations of good fathering were formed at least partly in relation to their ex-partners' and their children's desires and requests.

My analysis argues for interpreting caring fathering beyond the practices of direct caregiving, and incorporating material dimension of care, an argument discussed by Doucet (Doucet, 2020; and Chapter 2, this volume) and by other authors in this volume (see Miller and Dermott, Chapter 13, and Bergnehr, Chapter 15 in this volume). My research demonstrated that for Russian fathers, material provision, organised through regular child support payments and property division, was a meaningful way of 'being there' for their children and a culturally exalted form of doing caring fathering. In their narratives, fathers presented themselves as compliant payers, and genuine and generous providers. This, as well as fathers' accounts on child support as a practice of active and ongoing involvement in children's lives, challenges the existing academic narratives, which commonly juxtapose involvement and financial support, and associate good fathering only with the former (Doucet, 2020).

I suggest that such observations are relevant to other contexts beyond Russia. As was mentioned in the introduction of this chapter, despite the normative emphasis on co-parenting (Krieken, 2005; Parkinson, 2011; Natalier and Dunk-West, 2019), and paternal involvement through shared custody, the majority of separated fathers in Western countries remain nonresident parents after separation (Smyth, 2017; Flaquer, 2021). Some (albeit limited) research also demonstrates that child support is considered a meaningful contribution and is interpreted as a form of caring not only by paying fathers, but also by resident mothers (Natalier and Hewitt, 2010; Cook et al, 2015; Keil and Elizabeth, 2017). More research is needed to understand the lived experiences of fathers who do not conform with the new ideal of postseparation parenting that prescribes shared custody and equal involvement in caregiving.

Understanding fathering as a contextually embedded practice suggests paying attention to the possibilities and constraints that this context imposes on fathers. It is important to note that structurally, fathers remain marginalised as carers in Russia, a point made earlier in the works of Kay (2007a, 2007b). In the absence of a shared custody regime, their participation in caregiving, when going beyond simple contact and visitation, is legally unintelligible and therefore inevitably informal. This limits a separated father's ability to negotiate and bargain over parenting arrangements, and essentially institutionalises a narrow ideal of separated fatherhood, centred on financial provision. However, interviews with Russian fathers also demonstrated that men frequently considered themselves as benefiting from such a position, since the 'low bar' for separated fatherhood allowed fathers to stay free from caregiving work without moral repercussions for their paternal identities. In this, my findings support the observations made earlier by Utrata (2008). While fathers felt more accountability in relation to their financial provision, they also retained significant discretion on how money will be managed after separation. Ultimately, fathers' compliance with child support was regulated by moral rather than legal norms, as the state struggled to implement effective enforcement in the circumstances of the widespread informal employment (Barsukova and Radaev, 2012; Ivanova, 2024). Overall, bringing social and legal context into the picture highlighted the complex intersections of care and gender power relations, and how they were produced and sustained by different institutions. Future research in this direction can provide more insights into how gendered inequalities are sustained by and, in their turn, sustain the ideals and practices of good fathering, unfolded in different national and cultural contexts.

Note

[1] Children in Russia start school at the age of seven. It is not uncommon to let children spend time outside on their own in the area adjacent to the apartment block in which they live.

References

Andreasson, J. and Johansson, T., 2019. Becoming a half-time parent: fatherhood after divorce. *Journal of Family Studies* 25, 2–17. https://doi.org/10.1080/13229400.2016.1195277

Ashwin, S. and Lytkina, T., 2004. Men in crisis in Russia: the role of domestic marginalization. *Gender & Society* 18, 189–206. https://doi.org/10.1177/0891243203261263

Avdeeva, A., 2012. Vovlechyonnoe otsovstvo v sovremennoi Rossii: strategii uchastiya v ukhode za det'mi '[Involved fatherhood' in present-day Russia: childcare strategies]. *Sotsiologicheskiye issledovaniya* 95–104.

Barsukova, S. and Radaev, V., 2012. Informal economy in Russia: a brief overview. *Journal of Economic Sociology* 13, 99–111. https://doi.org/10.17323/1726-3247-2012-2-99-111

Bezrukova, O.N. and Samoylova, V.A., 2019. Papi 'po lyubvi' i 'papi ponevole' ili pochemy rossiiskiye otsi ne idut v otpusk po ukhodu za rebeyonkom ['Eager dads' and 'dads against their will', or why Russian dads are reluctant to go on parental leave]. *Sotsiologicheskie issledovaniya*, 7: 90–101. https://doi.org/10.31857/S013216250005796-8

Bezrukova, O.N. and Samoylova, V.A., 2020. Materinskii geitkiping v Rosii: molodiye otsi o materiyah i barierah dostupnosti detei posle razvoda [Maternal gatekeeping in Russia: young fathers about mothers and accesability barierrs to children after divorce]. *Monitoring obshchestvennogo mneniya: ekonomicheskiye i sotsial'nyye peremeny* 3: 463–498. https://doi.org/10.14515/monitoring.2020.3.1680

Braun, V. and Clarke, V., 2022. *Thematic Analysis: A Practical Guide*. London: Sage.

Campo, M., Fehlberg, B., Natalier, K. and Smyth, B.M., 2021. Exploring separated fathers' understandings and experiences of 'home' and homemaking. *Journal of Social Welfare and Family Law* 43, 291–306. https://doi.org/10.1080/09649069.2021.1953857

Chernova, Z., 2012. The model of 'Soviet' fatherhood. *Russian Studies in History* 51, 35–62. https://doi.org/10.2753/RSH1061-1983510202

Collier, R. and Sheldon, S. (eds), 2006. *Fathers' Rights Activism and Law Reform in Comparative Perspective*. Oxford: Hart Publishing.

Connell, R. (2005). *Masculinities*. Cambridge: Polity.

Cook, K., McKenzie, H., Natalier, K., 2015. Mothers' experiences of child support: qualitative research and opportunities for policy insight. *Journal of Family Studies* 21, 57–71. https://doi.org/10.1080/13229400.2015.1011769

Doucet, A., 2020. Father involvement, care, and breadwinning: genealogies of concepts and revisioned conceptual narratives. *Genealogy* 4, 14. https://doi.org/10.3390/genealogy4010014

Duncan, S. and Edwards, R., 1999. Understanding lone motherhood: competing discourses and positions, in S. Duncan and R. Edwards (eds) *Lone Mothers, Paid Work and Gendered Moral Rationalities*. London: Palgrave Macmillan, pp 23–64.

Fehlberg, B., Smyth, B., Maclean, M. and Roberts, C., 2011. Legislating for shared time parenting after separation: a research review. *International Journal of Law, Policy & the Family* 25, 318–337. https://doi.org/10.1093/lawfam/ebr015

Flaquer, L., 2021. Shared parenting after separation and divorce in europe in the context of the second demographic transition. In A.-M. Castrén et al (eds) *The Palgrave Handbook of Family Sociology in Europe*. Cham: Springer International Publishing, pp 377–398.

Hanlon, N., 2012. *Masculinities, Care and Equality*. Basingstoke: Palgrave Macmillan.

Ivanova, E., 2017. 'Ya ne otnoshu sebya k khoroshim papam, v lutshem sluchae, k normal'nim': kak rossiiskiye muzhchini konstruiruyut obraz 'horoshego otsa posle razvoda ['I don't consider myself a good father, at best, an average one': how Russian men construct the image of the 'good father' after separation]. *Zhurnal sotsiologii i sotsialnoy antropologii [Journal of Sociology and Social Anthropology]* 20, 132–150.

Ivanova, E., 2018. Alimenty kaka mnozhestvenniye den'gi: contributsiya, obyazatel'stvo ili zabota? Issledovaniye praktik soderzhaniya rebenka otsami posle razvoda [Child support as multiple monies: contribution, duty, or care? Research on fathers' practices of child maintenance after divorce]. *Economicheskaya sotsiologiya* [*Ecomonic Sociology*] 19, 101–133.

Ivanova, E., 2024. Uklonenie ot alimentov. In Ledeneva A., Teague E., Matijevic P., Moisé G.M., Majda P. and Toqmadi M. (eds) *The Global Encyclopaedia of Informality*, volume 3. London: UCL Press.

Jordan, A., 2020. Masculinizing care? Gender, ethics of care, and fathers' rights groups. *Men and Masculinities* 23, 20–41. https://doi.org/10.1177/1097184X18776364

Kay, R., 2006. *Men in Contemporary Russia: The Fallen Heroes of Post-Soviet Change?* Farnham: Ashgate.

Kay, R., 2007a. Caring for men in contemporary Russia: gendered constructions of need and hybrid forms of social security. *Focaal* 2007, 51–65. https://doi.org/10.3167/foc.2007.500105

Kay, R., 2007b. 'In our society it's as if the man is just some kind of stud': men's experiences of fatherhood and fathers' rights in contemporary Russia. In R. Kay (ed.) *Gender, Equality and Difference during and after State Socialism*. Basingstoke: Palgrave Macmillan, pp 125–145.

Kay, R. (ed.), 2007c. *Gender, Equality and Difference during and after State Socialism*. Basingstoke: Palgrave Macmillan.

Keil, M., Elizabeth, V., 2017. Gendered and cultural moral rationalities: Pacific mothers' pursuit of child support money. *Women's Studies Journal* 31, 34–47.

Kravchenko, Z., 2012. Muzhchiny v zabote o detyah sravnitelnyy analiz rossii frantsii i norvegii (Men caring for their children: a comparative analysis of Russia, France and Norway). *Journal of Sociology and Social Antropology* 15, 65–85.

Krieken, R.V., 2005. The 'best interests of the child' and parental separation: on the 'civilizing of parents'. *Modern Law Review* 68, 25–48. https://doi.org/10.1111/j.1468-2230.2005.00527.x

Kukhterin, S., 2000. Fathers and patriarchs in communist and post-communist Russia. In: S. Ashwin (ed.) *Gender, State and Society in Soviet and Post-Soviet Russia*. London: Routledge, pp 71–89.

Lipasova, A., 2017. Fatherhood in the Russian provinces: a theoretical and empirical analysis. *Journal of Social Policy Studies* 15, 629–642. https://doi.org/10.17323/727-0634-2017-15-4-629-642

Morgan, D., 2011. *Rethinking Family Practices*. Basingstoke: Palgrave Macmillan.

Natalier, K. and Hewitt, B., 2010. 'It's not just about the money': non-resident fathers' perspectives on paying child support. *Sociology* 44, 489–505. https://doi.org/10.1177/0038038510362470

Natalier, K. and Dunk-West, P., 2019. What is a good post0separation relationship? The perspectives of Australian parents. *Journal of Social Welfare and Family Law* 41, 171–187. https://doi.org/10.1080/09649069.2019.1590901

Parkinson, P., 2011. *Family Law and the Indissolubility of Parenthood*. Cambridge: Cambridge University Press.

Philip, G., 2013. Relationality and moral reasoning in accounts of fathering after separation or divorce: care, gender and working at 'fairness'. *Families, Relationships and Societies* 2, 409–424. https://doi.org/10.1332/204674313X667407

Philip, G., 2014. Fathering after separation or divorce: navigating domestic, public and moral spaces. *Families, Relationships and Societies* 3, 219–233. https://doi.org/10.1332/204674314X14017856302453

Randles, J., 2020. The means to and meaning of 'being there' in responsible fatherhood programming with low-income fathers. *Family Relations* 69, 7–20. https://doi.org/10.1111/fare.12376

Riessman, C.K., 2008. *Narrative Methods for the Human Sciences*. London: Sage.

Rzhanitsyna, L. and Kalabikhina, I., 2012. *Alimenti v Rossii: analiz problem i strategiya v interesah rebenka* [*Alimony in Russia: Problem Analysis and the Strategy in the Interest of the Children*]. Moscow: IE RAN.

Shpakovskaya, L., 2015. How to be a good mother: the case of middle class mothering in Russia. *Europe-Asia Studies* 67, 1571–1586. https://doi.org/10.1080/09668136.2015.1101210

Smart, C. and Bren, N., 1999. *Family Fragments?* Cambridge: Polity Press

Smyth, B.M., 2017. Special issue on shared-time parenting after separation. *Family Court Review* 55, 494–499. https://doi.org/10.1111/fcre.12299

Ukhova, D., 2022. Doing Gender with class: gender division of unpaid work in Russian middle-class dual earner heterosexual households. *Journal of Family Issues* 43, 3244–3270. https://doi.org/10.1177/0192513X211042846

Utrata, J., 2008. Keeping the bar low: Why Russia's nonresident fathers accept narrow fatherhood ideals. *Journal of Marriage and Family* 70, 1297–1310.

Utrata, J., 2015. *Women without Men: Single Mothers and Family Change in the New Russia*. Ithaca, NY: Cornell University Press.

Utrata, J., Ispa, Dean.M. and Ispa-Landa, S., 2013. Men on the margins of family life. In D.W. Shwalb, B.J. Shwalb and M.E. Lamb (eds) *Fathers in Cultural Context: Cross-cultural Perspectives*. New York: Routledge, pp 279–302.

Walker, C., 2022. Remaking a 'failed' masculinity: working-class young men, breadwinning, and morality in contemporary Russia. *Social Politics: International Studies in Gender, State & Society* 29, 1474–1496. https://doi.org/10.1093/sp/jxac002

Weber, J.B., 2020. Being there (or not): teen dads, gendered age, and negotiating the absent-father discourse. *Men and Masculinities* 23, 42–64. https://doi.org/10.1177/1097184X17747082

6

Hegemonic, caring or hybrid fathers? The case of Polish fathers of adult children in 'the empty nest'

Magdalena Żadkowska, Radosław Kossakowski and Bogna Dowgiałło

Introduction

The chapter aims to present the various ways in which Polish fathers navigate their relationships with their adult children, particularly during the 'empty nest' phase. The analysis, based on qualitative interviews with Polish fathers, is guided by two key concepts of fatherhood: caring and protective. We also delve into the role of negotiation and reconstruction throughout the life course (Pfau-Effinger, 2004), which significantly influence these relationships. By dedicating a chapter to this specific phase, we aim to fill a gap in the academic literature, which has rarely focused on the situation of fathers (and their relationships with their children) during this crucial period of life. Studying the relationship of older fathers with their adult children can fit into the discussion on types of fatherhood in terms of historical changes in fatherhood (Hauser, 2015; Doucet, 2016). Indeed, the situation of fathers experiencing the empty nest phase can serve to reflect on existing, historically constituted types of fatherhood and its functions (Lamb, 2000), because without children at home the roles of the father – for example, that of the breadwinner – can be replaced or reformulated.

For many years, studies relating to fatherhood ignored the subcultural variations in the definition and conceptualisation of fatherhood (Lamb, 2000). Many studies devoted both to masculinity and fatherhood underline dichotomies: hegemonic versus marginalised masculinities (Connell, 1987), traditional/orthodox fathers versus 'new' fathers (Eerola and Huttunen, 2011) or protective versus caring (Wojnicka, 2021). Although both types of fatherhood – 'involved father' and 'good provider' –used to be qualified as examples of 'good fathering' (Marks and Palkowitz, 2004), nowadays the traditional, common ways of fathering are being questioned, leading to an increased uncertainty about being a 'good' father (Miller, 2011). Additionally, mothers' criticism of fathers' parenting is culturally more legitimate (Eorla et al, 2021).

In Poland, the generation of men born in the 1960s and 1970s grew up under the influence of patterns of protective masculinity (Wojnicka and Nowicka, 2021), which was understood as providing financial support and/or physical protection to dependent women and children (Wojnicka, 2021). Research on contemporary fatherhood practices shows a highly stereotyped world of mothers and fathers (Dotti, 2014) with still-existing gender-segregated *cultural repertoires* (Swidler, 1986). The development of the 'new' construction of fatherhood is still complicit with many standards of traditional masculinity. This is particularly apparent in fathers' firm disassociation from the 'feminine style' of parenting. Such strategies enable fathers to maintain a masculine identity in the context that was usually associated with traditional masculinity (Doucet, 2006; Hauser, 2015). Nevertheless, contemporary fathers are no longer disconnected from traditional feminine practices, particularly those concentrated on caring (Wojnicka, 2021), and their presence in the mainstream (public debate and social campaigns) influences the new practices of being a father.

To investigate more deeply the changes of fatherhood in Poland we decided to analyse the everyday life practices of Polish fathers in the empty nest phase. We focus on an in-depth analysis of the paternal practices of 40 Polish men aged 45–68 whose adult children have left the family nest, which aims to explore the concepts of 'caring' and 'protective' within the context of fathering adult children. In this chapter, we aim to answer the following research question: how does the departure of children from the home serve as a turning point in fathers' life trajectories, potentially initiating or altering their caring practices (Elliot, 2016)?

As to the theoretical approach, we apply the frame of life course studies (Elder, 2003; Cooney, 2022), a concept based on two assumptions: (1) the shape of later phases is influenced by previous events; and (2) the biographies of the family members are 'linked' (linked lives) and mutually influence each other (Trommsdorff, 2006). We also consider the 'emerging adulthood' concept (Arnett, 2000), giving fathers more space and time with adult children at home, an important factor in the reconstruction of parental roles (Żadkowska et al, 2024).

From our previous studies, we know that the 'male breadwinner' script weakens after children become independent (Żadkowska et al, 2024). Fathers feel less need to invest in the family's daily life and their children's future (Giraud et al, 2024). The freeing up of time and money and the resulting reconfiguration of the paternal role should therefore trigger a shift in parenting practices, especially since, as in the case of mothers (Żadkowska et al, 2024), there is a lack of models for being a father in an empty nest.

State of the current situation
Fatherhood

The understanding of fatherhood and fathers' involvement has evolved over time. The male breadwinner dominated family studies in the second half of the 20th century. In Western societies in the late 20th century, the long-term hegemony of that model related to the Parsonian vision of family, which started to go into decline (Esping-Andersen, 2009). Fathers started to spend more time with their children and they doubled the amount of time spent on housework and childcare (Smith, 2010; Marsiglio and Roy, 2012). With the emancipation of mothers, fathers are less often the sole or even the main providers of financial resources in their families (Raley et al, 2012). Changes in family policies (for example, paid paternity leave) are affecting the number of fathers at home (Suwada, 2021). Fathers feel greater sociocultural pressure than was the case in the past to become more involved in childcare (de Singly, 1996; Henwood and Procter, 2003). Practices of the 'new father' can be noticed in Poland (Sikorska, 2009; Suwada, 2021) and worldwide (Doucet, 2006; Banchefsky and Park, 2016; Eorla et al, 2021; Romero-Balsas et al, 2021).

Although sociologists note that the male breadwinner model has been replaced by the caring and involved father, gender biases still strongly influence fatherhood. Biological differences between mothers and fathers are still used by parents to explain the difference between maternal and paternal responsibilities (Suwada, 2017, 2021). Women remain the primary caregivers, while men 'help' or are seen as 'secondary caregivers' or 'supporters' (Kaufmann, 1992; Żadkowska, 2016). And the father's primary duty is to meet the family's economic needs.

New challenges and traditional scripts are not simply for fathers to 'choose' from, but rather for their coexistence; fathers are juggling parenting roles and defining their ways of acting and being men (Gottzén and Kremer-Sadlik, 2012) and the duality of orthodox and inclusive masculinities seems to be at the heart of contemporary middle-class fatherhood (Gottzén and Kremer-Sadlik, 2012).

These changes in contemporary fatherhood do not necessarily indicate an unequivocal transformation from traditional roles. Therefore, in our analysis, we employ two concepts that, at first glance, appear to be at opposite ends of the spectrum: the concepts of 'protective' and 'caring' masculinity. Both relate to masculinity and, in our assessment, provide a suitable interpretative framework for analysing fathers experiencing the empty nest. According to Wojnicka, 'protective masculinity is linked to external hegemony ... and physical power, and it defines the male role mostly in terms of providing financially' (2021: 3). Adopting this understanding would imply that the roles of the fathers in our study are limited to traditionally conceived power and dominance. However, such an interpretation of masculinity and its relationships with other actors (for example, wives or children) is restrictive and potentially biased – at least in relation to the empirical data we have obtained. Consequently, we have also incorporated the concept of 'caring' masculinity to interpret our data more comprehensively.

The concept of 'caring masculinities' emphasises embracing care and rejecting domination. A father's role adopts traits traditionally associated with femininity, such as emotional expression, sensitivity, symmetrical relationships, domesticity, interdependence, expressiveness and involvement (Elliot, 2016). Father involvement can be seen as a set of three practices that meet children's needs: 'interaction', meaning a father's direct contact with his child through caretaking and shared activities; 'accessibility', which is defined as being present or accessible to the child; and 'responsibility', which refers to the role fathers take in ensuring that the child is taken care of and arranging for necessary resources (Lamb, 2000).

This dual-concept approach allows for a more nuanced understanding of the complex dynamics of fatherhood in the context of the empty nest phase. The integration of 'protective' and 'caring' masculinity concepts in our analytical framework enables a more holistic examination of contemporary fatherhood's multifaceted nature. It acknowledges the potential coexistence of traditional provider roles with more nurturing and emotionally engaged paternal behaviours.

Empty nest

Existing research on the empty nest phase rarely focuses on the fathers' point of view (Żadkowska et al, 2024). Research in the early 1970s showed that the departure of children makes fathers more dependent on their professional role (Bart, 1972). Those who based their father's role on the breadwinner model and failed to establish a relationship with their children in the empty nest phase can feel guilty and find the 'empty nest stage' difficult to cope with (Barber, 1989). The perception of gender roles makes it difficult for fathers to express emotional distress (Lowenthal and Chiriboga, 1972), they become less authoritarian and directive, and their relationships with their adult children become more voluntary (Bozett, 1985).

Although recent research highlights the contemporary transformation of the father role (Coles et al, 2018; Bosoni and Mazzucchelli, 2019), little is known about how men respond to this change in the empty-nest phase. According to existing studies, men may find the experience of their children leaving home difficult (Sheriff and Weatherall, 2009). Other researchers have reported that fathers, unlike mothers, saw the children's departure as a stage that encouraged the children's maturity and, therefore, was positively associated with low levels of stress (Bouchard, 2018). Analysing the evolution of fatherhood suggests that an event such as adult children leaving home should have an impact on fathers, especially those who had acted as 'scaffolding' to help them to reach their goals and 'safety nets' to catch them before they fell too far in order to achieve a successful transition to adulthood (Swartz et al, 2011).

The Polish context

The 'vocation' associated with being a father is ever-present in Polish tradition. Even nowadays, the common saying that a man must plant a tree (interesting in times of sustainability), build a house and have a son is repeated. A father is supposed to pass on a tradition, a name, a legacy, an inheritance and a pattern along the male line.

Looking at the role of Polish fathers during the communist era (1945–1989), their role was limited to providing financially (Suwada, 2021) whereas women were more oriented towards the domestic sphere (Suwada, 2017, 2021). Polish family culture, which is based on explicit familialism (Szelewa, 2017) and is explicitly gendered (Suwada, 2017), era reinforced such a family model during the communist.

After 1990, parental patterns have not changed quickly, as Polish fathers have often remained absent and continued to lack involvement in everyday family life (Marody and Giza-Poleszczuk, 2000; Saxonberg, 2014; Stanisz, 2014). They were exposed to different ideals of fatherhood prompting attention to fatherhood as one of the elements co-creating their subjective identity (Stanisz, 2014: 206). The mother, who had direct emotional contact with the child under her control and was also the main person in the household to make decisions about the family (Stanisz, 2014). The new reality in Poland perpetuates the breadwinner pattern, but the 'new father' and 'engaged father' patterns are present even among fathers with adult and adolescent children.

The respondents who took part in the project were fathers who left home, married and had children at a young age. In Poland in the 1970s–1990s, moving in together was tantamount to getting married, and the average age of marriage was only 22. Thus, when their adult children leave the family nest, they are often relatively young and can take advantage of the situation to renew their direct relationship with their children and forge new forms of relationships and care practices with them.

In our project, Polish fathers generally did not express extreme emotional attitudes when their children left home. Instead, they tried to continue to assume roles and functions associated with traditional models of masculinity (Giraud et al, 2024). Nevertheless, their narration was not at all only 'traditional'/'orthodox'/'protective', which is why we have decided to have a deeper look at their stories.

Methodology

The project 'Till death do us part... Everyday life practices of 50–64-year-old couples with at least, 20 years of common life experience' (Sonata Bis 8, UMO-2018/30/E/HS6/00159), funded by the National Science Centre in Poland, was led by the University of Gdańsk. Empirical data were collected in Poland in two regions (pomorskie and wielkopolskie, both in urban settings of Gdansk and Poznan and in countryside) between 2019 and 2022.

In this chapter, we analyse the interviews with 40 Polish fathers of adult children in a long-term relationship, whose children have left home in recent months or years, or who are about to leave. The scenario of joint in-depth interview consisted of the following topics: the history of the couple and family's residence, the process of the children moving out, a comparison of practice and relationships before and after the children moved out, and plans for the future. The individual interview scenario conducted a year later online (in connection with the COVID-19 pandemic) with 25 of same male participants consisted of the following topics: changes in relationships with children and household practices after a year, discussion of personal time and space, discussion of time and space allocated to the marital relationship, and emotions related to the new phase of life. Participants were married and lived as heterosexual couples who had been in a relationship together for more than 20 years. As the population of Poland became nearly entirely ethnically homogeneous after the Second World War, the sample lacked ethnic diversity. The interviewees were a little more educated than the average for Poland, but still varied in terms of education: 12 per cent had been to primary or vocational school, 34 per cent had been to secondary school and 54 per cent had tertiary education. For the men, the youngest interviewee was 44, the oldest was 69 and the average age was 55. Their children were, on average, 26 (25 for daughters and 27 for sons). The average time since the children's departure was three years.

The interviews were recorded, transcribed, anonymised and then analysed mainly with the use of Maxqda software. Standard ethical rules (Mizielińska et al, 2018) used in sociology were introduced as the project was accepted by the Ethical Commission of the University of Gdańsk. Participants either signed a consent form or gave verbal consent to participate in the study, allowing the researchers to use anonymised quotes in publications. Data analysis was carried out using a three-step procedure. First, we have used thematic analysis (Braun and Clarke, 2021) to find themes related to the diverse types of father-child relations. In the second step, we have chosen two categories – 'protective model' and 'caring model' – to code the material again and find out in the deductive process if these models are visible in our samples. Both categories stem from the adoption of an interpretive framework relating to the concepts of 'protecting' and 'caring' masculinity. The analysis of empirical data enabled us to identify two distinct themes that bridge the aforementioned theoretical concepts with inductively treated research data: 'Protective father, but with blurring authority' and 'Caring father, but often in disguise'. The use of both inductive and conceptually oriented approaches influenced our analytical strategy to be 'abductive' (Thompson, 2022): existing theoretical concepts determined analytical themes, but did not close off the possibility of inductively discovering patterns in the existing empirical data.

Results

Protective father, but with blurring authority

This study is underpinned by two concepts of masculinity, while simultaneously maintaining an openness afforded by an inductive strategy. Our analysis indicates that the concept of 'protective' masculinity can only partly be used to describe the behaviours and attitudes of our respondents. The concept of 'protective masculinity' is based on power and control, and the specific interdependence between women and children and the men. The relevance of the use of this concept becomes meaningful in the conditioning of very strong gender relations existing in the family. In the case of men who are experiencing an empty nest, the realisation of this type of masculinity is limited – their control over the children can only be indirect. Adult children are more independent than younger children, and the level of power and control over children is possibly decreased as the children move out.

Nevertheless, it is possible to come across statements from the respondents that may indicate the characteristics of 'protective' masculinity. One of the fathers revealed his involvement as a 'protector' in organising the place and the idea of his son's first business. The following statement indicates that, despite referring to adult children, the interviewee continues to express a desire for dominance and personal decision-making authority in the context of his children's lives:

> I got to know the owner of the property – there was a huge parking space for truck drivers … And there's everything there! Restaurants, bars, shops. So, I came to an agreement, I said, well, I will build a little car workshop there for him. And he went on his own, so to speak. He rented a flat there and started working there. (Father 33)

Some fathers indicate performing gendered division of practices. Some of them are ready to help when it comes to 'masculine' topics: issues relating to building, renovating, repairing things or cars, or financial support.

In the case of 'female' and emotional support, they leave it to their wives as they used to:

> On the other hand, when it comes to some such more substantive, 'masculine' matters, my wife shows no willingness to get in the way and leaves that lot to me. On the other hand, matters of emotion, feelings, I see that the contact is quicker with mum than with dad … the relationship of the son with the mother will always be stronger and deeper than with the father. (Father 2)

Fathers still find themselves in traditionally defined duties and skills that belong to the masculine sphere (for example, repairing broken things or renovations), but interestingly, this dimension becomes a space for renegotiating masculinity and power relations. As the following excerpt shows, the younger man (son-in-law) asks for help, but he does it less and less often. He tries to repair things at home by himself and when he fails, he calls the father-in-law to make an intervention. This is a unique situation where the father can return to his 'protective' attitude:

> I mean, with my daughter it's a bit different, because there's a son-in-law who does the work, but he also calls and asks. Sometimes I do make a hydraulic repair, because he couldn't do it himself. I show him how to lay the tiles, right? But he's got a knack for it, right? More or less like me, he likes these things, yes? And when I showed him, well, first of all, instead of having a bathroom at home, I trained him on the terrace to lay tiles, so that he could learn at my place, right? … Now, he can do a lot of things himself, yes? (Father 14)

This excerpt shows that although the respondent was able to fulfil his supportive role, allowing the father to maintain control of his mentoring and expert status, he appreciates and points out that another male – in this case, the son-in-law – is also able to take on a controlling role in his family life (although he makes mistakes and asks for help).

In the next example, the protective attitude changes from one-way to two-way after the son moves out. It is the son who calls his father for advice, on a specific issue, deciding where he needs support and control:

> Well, and when he calls, he will call and say, 'does that sofa from Ikea have to be tightened up properly, or can it be a bit loose?', well I say, 'it has to be tightened up properly', then he says 'oh fuck, then we'll have to fix it again'. He always calls me when there's a problem. If he can't do something, something even mechanical, or if there's a bigger

problem. He calls about specific issues, right? He doesn't call to chat; he calls to deal with a specific issue. (Father 3)

The narrative of 'control' and its loss in the context of the relationship with the children resounds in the following words: 'The time of controlling or demanding, in my opinion, that is completely gone' (Father 12, answering the question about relational changes between him and his adult children). This statement is symptomatic in terms of the transformation from the 'standard' protective masculinity to its 'fading' dimension.

Although the supportive role is still strong in the respondents' narratives, it is clear that the previous character of 'protective' masculinity cannot be maintained. Therefore, it seems that the empirical case relating to men experiencing an empty nest is not only interesting in terms of transformations in the trajectory of men's lives, but also forces reformulations to the theoretical assumptions of the concept of 'protective' masculinity.

A caring father, but often in disguise

Not only is being a protective father more challenging when children leave home, but being a caring father also changes significantly compared to the full-nest stage. Previously, care was manifested through direct contact, shared activities, presence and responsibility (Doucet, 2016). In an empty nest, these expressions of care may no longer be necessary or culturally expected. Fathers must grapple with both a loss of control and the need to refrain from taking action, instead engaging in emotional work (Hochschild, 1983) to support their child's independence. Consequently, a father's involvement may need to be expressed in new ways. This process may involve adopting new strategies that we have named: invisible caring, caring in disguise, or fully embracing a caring role (a fully fledged caring).

The very act of stepping back from a protective role can be viewed as a form of care that requires emotional work. This 'invisible' care involves managing emotions such as fear, anxiety and impatience which are associated with a loss of control and do not align with traditional masculine ideals that portray men as active agents or doers (Hauser, 2015).

Father 12 discovered that his child was facing problems by chance, despite repeatedly asking if everything was alright and receiving reassurances that it was. This situation underscores the father's anxiety about being unable to help if he is unaware of the issues his children are dealing with and portrays a new context for being a father of an adult child:

A parent always wants to help their children, that's the case and that remains. But if they are in a really difficult situation, won't the lack of

> direct physical contact cause that we won't find out about it? Won't we be able to help them? Just a few days ago, by accident, we discovered that they were having problems. I kept on asking 'is everything OK?'. And he replied that it was. Officially we don't know but it concerns the state of health of our daughter-in-law. (Father 12)

This situation seems to be emotionally difficult. There is anxiety about the child and discomfort heightened by the fact that care for the children cannot take the form of concrete actions, but can only manifest itself in passivity at the level of activity (invisible caring). Officially, parents may pretend not to be aware of their children's problems. They are concerned and somewhat aware of these issues. They choose to act as if they do not know about them to respect their children's efforts to achieve independence. Although Father 12 does not take direct action to help, invisible caring represents in-depth emotional work (Hochschild, 1983). It involves managing his own concern and anxiety while not interfering in his children's lives. The father provides care without direct intervention, thereby maintaining a more symmetrical power relationship with the child. This can be challenging for fathers who were used to the active, hands-on approach of the protective father role, which involved taking concrete actions to help and guide their children.

The second strategy, 'caring in disguise', on a behavioural level resembles behaviours characteristic of hegemonic masculinity and, on an intentional level, implies bond building based on a symmetrical father-adult child relationship. Such an example that appears in fathers' statements could be the avoidance of frequent telephone contact, but a readiness to respond when children initiate communication:

> What I'm saying is that sometimes maybe she exaggerates. She is too interested ... In a way, as a mother, I understand that she's more concerned about how they live, how they cope. Maybe I don't show emotion as much – I am also sometimes worried about things, about failures that happen to kids. I think this is normal and natural. But I just try not to interfere so much – my wife sometimes accuses me of not calling often, but I think that if a child sometimes has such a need, I think that they, for their part, should call their mother or father if they want to. At least that's how I see it, it's like an unnecessary imposition, that's how they may perceive it. It can also be annoying for them at some point. I would perceive it that way, that someone is controlling me here, what I am doing, where I am going - a person also needs this privacy, I think ... Maybe I'm wrong here, but that's how I perceive it. (Father 5)

In this quote, the father, explaining why he does not call his children as often as their mother would expect him to, starts the explanation from the position of the hegemonic father – he refers to a calling order resulting from the hierarchical relationship between parents and children, according to which it is the adult children who should call their parents, but the statement goes on to indicate that refraining from calling the children is a form of working to maintain the relationship, a fear that the parent may be seen as 'nagging' and controlling. On the other hand, it is an acknowledgement of a certain maturity – after all, the child is now old enough and mature enough to decide on their own to make contact if necessary. Thus, the father deliberately refrains from contact, empathises with the child, recognises the child's right to privacy and, above all, 'tries' not to interfere too much in the child's life, which requires effort on his part and is paradoxically a form of care.

The stage of children distancing themselves from their parents may also present challenges for those fathers who took on the role of the caring father during the full-nest stage. Those who portrayed themselves as supportive, engaged, present and emotionally connected formerly refrained from some of the practices in the caring repertoire, treating this as a sign of caring towards adult children:

> Sometimes I think about it [the times he was small and wanted to be hugged], I'm trying to restrain myself from expression of emotions. I try not to let them come out ... I don't know, it's hard for me to say, because sometimes I do not know why, what happened. Of course, if I hug him, it's not a problem, but for him to come out with it. (Father 21)

The participant complains about the weakening of physical closeness with his adult son, specifically the inability to hug him as often as he would like to. He is doing emotion work (Hochschild, 1983) by constraining his own display of the emotions he feels in order to respect his son's expectations.

It is important to emphasise that caring practices are not always seen as difficult and based on holding back. For example, those fathers who manifested elements of a caring approach at the full-nest stage, even if they limited this role to play situations (see Kazura, 2000) by participating in physical games, acting as peers to their children and allowing the child to take the lead, make it clear that caring understood in this way can be a source of satisfaction:

> I had three sons. Because I have three siblings, I have a whole bunch of nieces and nephews. And I always enjoyed playing with them, I was such an elderly uncle. I also know that with my sons we also built such constructions with blocks, and we also invented some funny games. And ... I'm already sharpening my teeth here, that when there are grandchildren, I feel I'll again have lots of ideas on what to think of,

how to spend time and how to get young people involved in something, in thinking, in combining. Well, also those are the plans. (Father 1)

There are also examples of fathers who say that in the empty nest stage, caring can accompany a satisfying father–child relationship ('fully fledged caring').

> The role of the parent basically comes down to 'being around', whatever that means. The parent should be open to every attempt at contact between the child and the parent and show that this child is loved, supported by the parents, that with every form of contact they can count on support, on some kind of word, on being listened to. And that's how we try to make it work – we absolutely do not close ourselves to contact … No one can force anyone to do anything, so it's just a decision for both parties. It's an adult-to-adult relationship now, so it has to be respected. (Father 7)

This statement shows a reflective approach to caring fatherhood. While it requires work on emotions and competencies, it is also a source of satisfaction.

Transitioning to or continuing to function within the caring father model involves recognising and acknowledging appropriate strategies (caring in disguise, invisible caring, fully fledged caring) within microstructural (wife, children and family) and macrostructural (cultural and social norms) arrangements. Caring fathers may not involve themselves in care work, but they acknowledge the needs of adult children and modify their (paternal) actions accordingly. It is not accurate to say that men are incapable of showing care, but rather that they need to acquire the necessary skills. Caring requires letting go of the traditional masculinity concept and attitude, which can be challenging. Engaging in care transforms men, and it should be viewed as a process in which they employ various strategies, including concealed, invisible, or explicit (fully fledged) care.

Conclusions

This chapter deals with transformations in the role of the father by using the example of Polish men experiencing the 'empty nest' stage. Our conclusions are based on the narratives of respondents who are at a specific point in their lives, so we don't know what kind of fathers they were at the very beginning, or when they were living in a 'full nest' situation, although such threads of a biographical nature appeared in the interviews. However, our goal was not to compare the different stages of fatherhood in the lives of the respondents, but to describe how they now cope with their role as father. An additional limitation in making more general conclusions was the fact that most of the respondents in our pool were men who were relatively successful in life, both professionally and privately. These were men who generally found their way in the 'new' Poland after 1989, when communism ended and the process of developing a capitalist economy and liberal democracy began. Our respondents, although they came from both large urban and rural centres, belong primarily to the middle class.

The results of our study indicate that the concepts of caring and protective can be also seen as blurred and should be sensitised. It is very difficult to find ideal types of described concepts and our study shows that new subtypes of both concepts should be developed. Variables such as the man's age (older) and specific stage in life (children moving out) force a reconceptualization of the proposed models and suggest they would evolve. Our research can provide an impetus to sensitise conceptual efforts within critical masculinities studies, which tend to work on dichotomies (traditionally hegemonic versus progressively caring). Meanwhile, social reality generates a multitude of surprising variables that force constant reflection and reformulation of theoretical approaches. Therefore, we assume that the development of the themes we propose – inspired by theory, while grounded in the data – will provoke further discussion.

As such, we propose developing the existing concepts as follows: the concept of 'protective masculinity' as an initial one is transformed into 'blurring protective', because in the case of men in the empty nest experience, the 'protective' masculinity concept no longer plays such an important role, sometimes losing focus and sometimes no longer having virtually any meaning. 'Blurring' means that what may have constituted a man's hegemonic and protective attitude towards others (here primarily children) earlier now loses its importance and becomes blurred. The empirical data cited not only indicate objective reasons for the weakening of the 'protective' role but also point to the role of fathers' self-reflection in the process of realising that the time of 'control' and power is inevitably over. Some of the participants still show tendencies to be protective, but in most cases being 'protective' is already heavily 'softened' by the maturity and independence of the children. In many cases, even if fathers try to continue the former role, they must consider the subjectivity and independence of adult children. Many respondents consciously emphasise this in their interviews.

At the same time, the change in being 'protective' does not mean that the respondents go into a full 'caring masculinity' mode. We show in our study that the 'caring' mode is not unambiguous in the case of the respondents, that it is sometimes 'invisible', sometimes 'in disguise' and only sometimes can be called 'fully fledged'. Some respondents brought the praxis of 'caring' that still characterised them in earlier stages of family life, while some, coming out of the 'protective' role, transformed their attitude into a more or less visible 'caring'.

In both cases, the concepts of protective and caring became certain initial 'ideal types', verified in the process of empirical research. Changes in attitudes towards others, relations of power and control over others in the case of the studied fathers indicate that it would be reasonable to create a certain axis of both concepts – an axis resulting from the biographical transformations of a man's life. This would make it possible to apply both concepts and to place them on the fathers' life courses according to the biographical point in which the men find themselves.

We regard the proposals for conceptual resolution that result from our study as opening up a discussion not only on the situation of men entering a specific age and family life phase but also on how to sensitise concepts of masculinity.

While our research has not pinpointed the departure of children as a context where fathers routinely discuss emotions (as they typically name it a natural occurrence), they may still face a challenging transition into a new mode of fathering. On the one hand, they are accustomed to adhering to societal norms of masculinity, involving emotional avoidance, constant control and displays of strength. On the other hand, they observe a shift in expectations, taking on a new role in the family amid broader societal changes regarding 'new fatherhood'. Consequently, many men find themselves coping with the task of reconciling these conflicting expectations to establish a personally fitting fathering masculinity.

Funding

The research leading to these results has received funding from the Polish National Science Centre in the framework of Project Contract No Pol-UMO-2018/30/E/HS6/00159. PI dr Magdalena Żadkowska, 'Till death do us part ... Everyday life practices of 50–64 years old couples with at least, 20 years of common life experience'.

References

Arnett, J. J. (2000) 'Emerging adulthood: a theory of development from the late teens through the twenties', *American Psychologist*, 55, 469–480.

Banchefsky, S. and Park, B. (2016) 'The "new father": dynamic stereotypes of fathers', *Psychology of Men and Masculinity*, 17(1), 103–107.

Barber, C. E. (1989) 'Transition to the empty nest' in S. T. Bahr and E. T. Peterson (eds) *Aging and the Family*. Lanham, MD: Lexington Books, pp 15–32.

Bart, P. B. (1972) 'Depression in middle-aged women' in V. Gornick and B. K. Moran (eds) *Women in Sexist Society*. New York: The New American Library Inc, pp 163–168.

Bosoni, M.-L. and Mazzucchelli, S. (2019) 'Generations comparison: father role representations in the 1980s and the new millennium' *Genealogy*, 3(2).

Bouchard, G. (2018) 'A dyadic examination of marital quality at the empty-nest phase', *International Journal of Aging and Human Development*, 86(1), 34–50.

Bozett, F. (1985) 'Male development and fathering throughout the life cycle', *American Behavioral Scientist*, 29, 41–54.

Braun, V. and Clarke, V. (2021) 'One size fits all? What counts as quality practice in (reflexive) thematic analysis?', *Qualitative Research in Psychology*, 18(3), 328–352.

Coles, L., Hewitt, B. and Martin, B. (2018) 'Contemporary fatherhood: social, demographic and attitudinal factors associated with involved fathering and long work hours', *Journal of Sociology*, 54(4), 591–608.

Connell, R. W. (1987) *Gender and Power: Society, the Person and Sexual Politics*. Stanford: Stanford University Press.

Cooney, T. M. (2022) 'Introduction to special issue on "divorce and the life course"', *Social Sciences*, 11(202), 1–4.

De Singly, F. (1996) *Le soi, le couple et la famille*. Paris: Nathan.

Doucet, A. (2006) *Do Men Mother? Fathering, Care, and Domestic Responsibilities*. Toronto: University of Toronto Press.

Doucet, A. (2016) 'Is the stay-at-home dad (SAHD) a feminist concept? A genealogical, relational, and feminist critique'. *Sex Roles: A Journal of Research*, 75(1-2), 4–14.

Dotti Sani, G. M. (2014) 'Men's employment hours and time on domestic chores in European countries', *Journal of Family Issues*, 35(8), 1023–1047.

Eerola, P. and Huttunen, J. (2011) 'Metanarrative of the "new father" and narratives of young Finnish first-time fathers', *Fathering*, 9(3), 211–231.

Eerola, P., Närvi, J., Terävä, J. and Repo, K. (2021) 'Negotiating parenting practices: the arguments and justifications of Finnish couples', *Families, Relationships and Societies*, 10(1), 119–135.

Elder, G. H., Johnson, M. K. and Crosnoe, R. (2003) 'The emergence and development of life course theory', in J. T. Mortimer and M. J. Shanahan (eds) *Handbook of the Life Course: Handbooks of Sociology and Social Research*. Dordrecht: Springer, pp 3–22.

Elliott, K. (2016) 'Caring masculinities: theorizing an emerging concept', *Men and Masculinities*, 19(3), 240–259.

Esping-Andersen, G. (2009) *The Incomplete Revolution: Adapting Welfare States to Women's New Roles*. Cambridge: Polity Press

Giraud, C., Kossakowski, R., Żadkowska, M. and Dowgiałło, B. (2024) 'The empty nest as a phase of fatherhood', in M. Żadkowska, M. Skowrońska, C. Giraud and F. Schmidt (eds) *Reconfiguring Relations in the Empty Nest: Those Who Leave and Those Who Stay*. Dordrecht: Springer, pp 65–89.

Gottzén, L. and Kremer-Sadlik, T. (2012) 'Fatherhood and youth sports: a balancing act between care and expectations', *Gender & Society*, 26(4), 639–664.

Hauser, O. (2015) 'Maintaining boundaries: masculinizing fatherhood in the feminine province of parenting', *Qualitative Sociology Review*, 11, 84-104. DOI: 10.18778/1733-8077.11.3.06

Henwood, K. and Procter, J. (2003) 'The "good father": reading men's accounts of paternal involvement during the transition to first-time fatherhood', *British Journal of Social Psychology*, 42(3), 337–355.

Hochschild, A. (1983). *The Managed Heart: Commercialization of Human Feeling*. Berkeley: University of California Press.

Kazura, K. (2000) 'Fathers' qualitative and quantitative involvement: an investigation of attachment, play, and social interactions', *Journal of Men's Studies*, 9, 41–57.

Kaufmann, J. C. (1992) *La trame conjugale. Analyse du couple par son linge*. Paris: Nathan

Lamb, M. (2000) 'The history of research on father involvement', *Marriage and Family Review*, 29, 23–42. DOI: 10.1300/J002v29n02_03.

Lowenthal, M. F. and Chiriboga, D. A. (1972) 'Transition to the empty nest: crisis, challenge, or relief?', *Archives of General Psychiatry*, 26(1), 8–14.

Marks, L. D. and Palkovitz, R. (2004) 'American fatherhood types: the good, the bad, and theuninterested', *Fathering*, 2, 113–129.

Marody, M. and Giza-Poleszczuk, A. (2000) 'Changing images of identity in Poland: from the self-sacrificing to the self-investing woman', in S. Gal and G. Kligman (eds) *Reproducing Gender: Politics, Publics, and Everyday Life after Socialism*. Princeton: Princeton University Press, pp 151–175.

Marsiglio, W. and Roy, K. (2012) *Nurturing Dads: Social Initiatives for Contemporary Fatherhood*. London: Russell Sage Foundation.

Miller, T., 2011. *Making Sense of Fatherhood: Gender, Caring and Work*. Cambridge: Cambridge University Press.

Mizielińska, J., Stasińska, A., Żadkowska, M. and Halawa, M. (2018) 'Ethical dilemmas in research on intimate couples: experiences from the fieldwork', *Studia Socjologiczne*, 3(230), 41–69.

Pfau-Effinger, B., 2004. 'Socio-historical paths of the male breadwinner model: an explanation of cross-national differences', *British Journal of Sociology*, 55(3), 377–399.

Raley, S. B., Bianchi, S. M. and Wang, W. (2012) 'When do fathers care? Mothers' economic contribution and fathers' involvement in child care', *American Journal of Sociology*, 117, 1422–1459.

Romero-Balsas, P., Meil, G. and Rogero-García, J. (2021) 'Policemen on leave alone in Spain: a rift in hegemonic masculinity?', *Men and Masculinities*, 24(3), 483–500.

Saxonberg, S. (2014) *Gendering Post-communist Family Policies: A Historical-Institutional Analysis*. Neuviden: Palgrave.

Sheriff, M. and Weatherall, A. (2009) 'A feminist discourse analysis of popular-press accounts of post-maternity', *Feminist and Psychology*, 19, 89–108.

Sikorska, M. (2009) *Nowa matka, nowy ojciec, nowe dziecko*. Kraków: Wydawnictwa Akademickie i Profesjonalne.

Smith, R. (2010) 'Total Parenting', *Educational Theory*, 60(3), 357–369.

Stanisz, A. (2014) *Rodzina made in Poland. Antropologia pokrewieństwa i życia rodzinnego*. Poznań: Poznańskie Studia Etnologiczne.

Suwada, K. (2017) *Men, Fathering and the Gender Trap: Sweden and Poland Compared*. Dordrecht: Springer.

Suwada K. (2021) *Parenting and Work in Poland: A Gender Studies Perspective*. Dordrecht: Springer.

Swartz, T. T., Kim, M., Uno, M., Mortimer, J. and O'Brien, K. B. (2011) 'Safety nets and scaffolds: parental support in the transition to adulthood', *Journal of Marriage and the Family*, 73(2), 414–429.

Swidler, A. (1986) 'Culture in action: symbols and strategies', *American Sociological Review*, 51(2), 273–286.

Szelewa, D. (2017) 'From Implicit to explicit familialism: post-1989 family policy reforms in Poland', in D. Auth, J. Hergenhan and B. Holland-Cunz (eds) *Gender and Family in European Economic Policy: Developments in the New Millennium*. London: Palgrave Macmillan, pp 129–156.

Thompson, J. (2022) 'A guide to abductive thematic analysis', *The Qualitative Report*, 27(5), 1410–1421.

Trommsdorff, G. (2006) 'Parent-child relations over the lifespan: a cross-cultural perspective', in K. H. Rubin and O. B. Chung (eds) *Parenting Beliefs, Behaviors, and Parent-Child Relations: A Cross-cultural Perspective*. London: Psychology Press, pp 143–183.

Wojnicka, K. (2021) 'Men and masculinities in times of crisis: between care and protection', *NORMA*, 16(1), 1–5.

Wojnicka, K. and Nowicka, M. (2021) 'Understanding migrants' masculinity through an intersectional lens', *Men and Masculinities*, 25(2), 1–20.

Żadkowska, M. (2016) *Para w praniu. Codzienność, partnerstwo, obowiązki domowe*. Gdańsk: Wydawnictwo Uniwersytetu Gdańskiego.

Żadkowska, M., Skowrońska, M., Giraud, C. and Schmidt, F. (2024) *Reconfiguring Relations in the Empty Nest: Those Who Leave and Those Who Stay*. London: Palgrave Macmillan.

7

Berry-picking fathers and burdened mothers: parenting modes in dual-income households of urban China during the COVID-19 pandemic

Guanli Zhang, Bingyi Zhang and Lichao Yang

Introduction

This chapter introduces our research examining the impact of the COVID-19 pandemic on parenting modes in dual-income urban households in China. We conceptualise the parenting mode as the dynamic interplay of childcare responsibilities, practices and ideologies within a family, encompassing not only the division of childcare tasks but also the broader relational, responsive and responsible aspects of parenting as outlined by Doucet's '3 Rs' framework (Doucet, 2023). Rather than narrowly equating parenting mode with time allocation for household chores and childcare duties, we view it as a reflection of how families navigate their internal relationships, respond to members' needs and fulfil diverse caregiving responsibilities in relation to wider societal contexts. The shifts in parenting modes during the COVID-19 pandemic serve as an illuminating lens to examine the evolving roles and strategies of fathers in caregiving as well. Doucet's comprehensive and reflective framework for defining parenting enabled us to scrutinise fathers' caregiving practices, emotional engagement and perceptions of their parental responsibilities in response to the unprecedented pandemic. This perspective aligns with the central theme of this volume and contributes empirical evidence from the Chinese context.

How has the COVID-19 pandemic reshaped these parenting modes, reconfigured the existing fathers and mothers' roles, and exacerbated the existing gender inequalities in childcare? To address these questions, we conducted in-depth semi-structured interviews with 19 married couples across seven Chinese cities during the peak of COVID-19 infections between December 2022 and January 2023. This qualitative approach allows for a nuanced exploration of the lived experiences of parents during the pandemic, capturing changes in parenting practices, role expectations and the underlying gender dynamics. By focusing on dual-income urban households, we seek to understand how the unique circumstances created by the pandemic have interacted with pre-existing patterns of parental involvement and gender ideologies in contemporary urban China. This research contributes to the growing body of literature on the gendered impacts of COVID-19 on family life (for example, Twamley et al, 2023; Graham et al, 2021; Mooi-Reci and Risman, 2021), while also offering insights into the evolving nature of parenting modes in the context of rapid social change in China.

Chinese fathers' parental roles and parenting involvement

Recent research indicates that Chinese fathers' involvement in parenting has been increasing, though still insufficient. Urban Chinese fathers today demonstrate greater engagement in childcare compared to previous generations, spending more time with their children and showing higher enthusiasm for parenting (Li, 2020). Contemporary urban Chinese fathers have internalised the role norms of 'new fatherhood', acknowledging men's innate desire for parenting and developing a parenting mode characterised by relationality, freedom and independence (Li, 2016).

Regarding the content of parenting, Chinese fathers play a significant role in child-related decision making, especially concerning children's skill development (Cao and Lin, 2019). They are increasingly enthusiastic about leisure activities and communication with their children (Wu et al, 2024). Research by Lin, Li and Yang (2020) identified two orientations among Chinese fathers: 'pragmatic fathers' who prioritise preschool learning and language skills; and 'hedonistic fathers' who encourage sports to enhance children's physical abilities.

Chinese fathers primarily assume four responsibilities: providing economic support, caring for children, offering shelter and support for family members, and facilitating communication (Xu, 2017). Most urban fathers have abandoned the traditional 'men outside, women inside' division of labour, increasingly participating in childcare (Du and Dong, 2013). They engage in physical care, daily education, emotional comfort and companionship (Li, 2021), with a particular focus on children's educational issues (Xu, 2017).

In contemporary Chinese society, fathers' masculinity manifests in a hybrid form, encompassing both caring and dominating elements. The caring aspect is reflected in fathers' willingness to participate in everyday childcare, fostering close emotional relationships (Xu and O'Brien, 2014). The dominating element emphasises fathers' roles as disciplinarians, educators and role models, with many Chinese fathers preferring to express love nonverbally (Li, 2021).

Despite increased involvement, Chinese fathers' participation in childcare remains unequal. The distribution of childrearing responsibilities in terms of time and quality is not equal between fathers and mothers (Liu et al,

2022). Concepts of 'masculinised care' and 'selective parenting' (for example, Johansson and Klinth, 2008; Offer and Schneider, 2011) describe well Chinese fathers' parenting modes, since fathers' caregiving behaviours are often linked to their professional role, with breadwinning remaining central to their male identity. Consequently, fathers are more involved in decision making than in daily care. Their caregiving activities are commonly biased and selective, primarily taking the forms of play, communication and supervision (Craig and Mullan, 2011).

Factors influencing Chinese fathers' involvement in parenting operate at individual, family, cultural and policy levels. Well-educated fathers tend to be more involved in childcare-related tasks (Liu, Haslam, Dittman et al, 2022). Family factors include social class, internal division of labour and mothers' attitudes towards fathers' involvement (Li, 2020). Cultural traditions valuing 'scholarly temperament' encourage fathers to participate in children's education (Li, Hu, Huang et al, 2021). Recent evidence suggests that many urban Chinese fathers cite Western parenting concepts, such as the equal father–child relationship and fathers' warm and nurturant engagement, as reasons for active participation (Li and Lamb, 2012). Government advocacy for gender equality and family policies may also promote increased paternal involvement (Hong et al, 2022; Yu, 2024).

The COVID-19 pandemic has significantly impacted Chinese fathers' parenting involvement. It has disrupted previously stable work-family relationships, bringing fathers who used to work long hours back home and temporarily increasing their parenting time (Ni et al, 2024). Chinese fathers reported improved parent-child relationships during the pandemic (Zhang and Zhou, 2021), while mothers experienced increased parenting stress (Li and Wu, 2021). As the pandemic's influence on family life is complex, further research is needed to examine Chinese fathers' parenting involvement during this period.

Research methods and data

How has the COVID-19 pandemic affected father and mother's childcare roles and their parenting modes in dual-income urban families in China? To investigate this, our study examined 19 dual-income urban families across seven Chinese cities, each with one or more minor children aged 0–15. A respondent-driven sampling method was employed in this research due to the limited mobility during the lockdown and the prevailing stigmatisation of the infected for the time. Table 7.1 illustrates the educational and professional backgrounds of the participants, as well as their family compositions and financial statuses. Both the husbands and wives were invited for semi-structured in-depth interviews and were interviewed separately after informed consent. Each interviewee was interviewed between one and

Table 7.1: Basic information on participants and their families

Family No.	Husband/Father Male				Wife/Mother Female				Number, gender and age of child(ren)	Annual income*	Income ratio**
	Code	Age	Education	Occupation	Code	Age	Education	Occupation			
1	01M	36	Bachelor	Engineer	01F	33	Master	HR	1 daughter (1 yo.)	800	3:7
2	02M	33	College	Trainer	02F	43	Master	Banker	2 sons (5 yo.)	750	1:9
3	03M	36	Bachelor	Manager	03F	34	Bachelor	Storekeeper	2 sons (9 yo., 5 yo.)	200	3:1
4	04M	45	Master	College staff	04F	44	Master	Public servant	1 daughter (13 yo.)	500	1:3
5	05M	43	Master	Lawyer	05F	43	Master	Housewife	1 daughter (1 yo.)	550	1:0
6	06M	46	Master	Programmer	06F	44	Master	Manager	1 daughter (7 yo.)	750	3:7
7	07M	37	Bachelor	Legal counsel	07F	38	Bachelor	Piano teacher	1 daughter (1 yo.)	600	1:1
8	08M	46	Bachelor	Engineer	08F	44	Master	School teacher	1 daughter (15 yo.)	300	1:1
9	09M	35	College	Technician	09F	35	College	Train attendant	1 daughter (8 yo.)	200	1:1
10	10M	49	Doctor	Researcher	10F	44	Bachelor	Entrepreneur	1 son (12 yo.)	5000	1:16
11	11M	43	Bachelor	Accountant	11F	43	Master	Lawyer	1 son (10 yo.), 1 daughter (5 yo.)	1500	1:9
12	12M	45	College	Engineer	12F	43	Bachelor	TV producer	2 sons (12 yo., 5 yo.)	350	3:2
13	13M	45	Bachelor	Accountant	13F	45	Bachelor	Accountant	1 son (12 yo.)	1000	3:2
14	14M	42	Master	HR	14F	46	Bachelor	NGO officer	1 son (11 yo.)	500	2:1
15	15M	44	Master	Professor	15F	45	Master	Professor	1 son (8 yo.), 1 daughter (8 yo.)	300	1:1
16	16M	46	Bachelor	Public servant	16F	43	Bachelor	Public servant	1 son (15 yo.), 1 daughter (5 yo.)	750	4:3
17	17M	48	Doctor	Professor	17F	45	Doctor	Professor	1 daughter (11 yo.)	250	1:1
18	18M	42	Bachelor	Manager	18F	42	Bachelor	Public servant	1 son (14 yo.)	500	2:1
19	19M	48	Doctor	Manager	19F	45	Doctor	Professor	1 daughter (13 yo.)	1200	9:1

* All monetary values are reported in thousands of Chinese Renminbi (RMB). At the time of data collection, the exchange rate was approximately 1,000 RMB to £105 or US$140.
** The income ratio is defined as the proportion of the husband's reported annual income to that of the wives.

three times on the phone, lasting 40–150 minutes per session, in which they were encouraged to discuss their perceptions of gender/family relationships, sources of parenting knowledge, parenting concepts, goals, content, division of labour, and changes in these aspects before and after the pandemic.

Our study adopted an inductive, phenomenological epistemological standpoint. For data analysis, we employed Colaizzi's descriptive phenomenological method (Morrow, Rodriguez and King, 2015). This process involved text selection, meaning extraction and two rounds of thematic categorisation. Through this systematic coding approach, we developed a fundamental structure encompassing the representations, themes, changes and interviewees' attitudes towards parenting modes during the COVID-19 pandemic.

Emerging agenda and shifting challenges for parenting during COVID-19

The COVID-19 pandemic introduced novel dimensions and complexities to parenting practices and domestic labour division in dual-income urban Chinese households. This unprecedented period precipitated a reconfiguration of maternal and paternal modes, as well as overall family dynamics, across several critical domains. The pandemic engendered temporary familial separations, restructured temporal allocations and exacerbated parental anxiety levels. These transformations manifested in multifarious forms, ranging from modified living arrangements to recalibrated work-childcare paradigms. Families exhibited adaptive responses to rapidly evolving circumstances, revealing both resilience and strain in their parenting methodologies. The situation underscored the dynamic nature of familial systems in response to exogenous shocks, highlighting the interplay between societal disruptions and intrafamilial adaptations.

Temporary separations and the lack of support

The resurgence of the COVID-19 pandemic across China in late 2022 precipitated stringent restrictions on human mobility to enforce spatial segregation and mitigate viral transmission. Working parents altered their daily routine between work and home and consequentially their roles and responsibility of caring. While a mother in a participating family underwent a 40-day quarantine at her place of employment, her husband was left as the sole caregiver for their two children at home. Pandemic-induced restrictions precluded children from engaging in outdoor activities, compelling the father to adapt to prolonged periods of interaction with the children in confined indoor spaces. This abrupt shift in caregiving dynamics resulted in a marked increase in paternal fatigue. According to her husband:

The first few days were the hardest. My wife video called the children every day. Later, the whole family got adapted to the arrangement. She was at work, and I was at home with the two children. The children couldn't go out to play. They were so frustrated for being locked down at home not seeing their mothers for weeks, so they made troubles at home instead. I inevitably felt overwhelmed dealing with them every day, expecting my wife to come back and take over the job. (03M, 36 years old, two sons aged nine and five)

The suspension of intergenerational support, domestic services and institutional childcare due to pandemic-induced separation measures disproportionately affected families that were reliant on these systems. Parents reported heightened anxiety and an intensified sense of busyness as they shouldered previously distributed childcare responsibilities alongside professional obligations. This abrupt shift underscores the vulnerability of urban Chinese families to disruptions in established care networks and highlights the critical role of extended support systems in maintaining familial equilibrium during crises. As a father of two sons complained:

When the pandemic began, our younger son was only over three years old and about to start his kindergarten. We stopped hiring a nanny, but soon we realised that there were too many chores to do at home. We had to manage everything by ourselves – taking care of both the younger and the older one, picking them up, cleaning, cooking – it was totally overwhelming and beyond our capacity of management. However, when we decided to ask the nanny back, it became impossible as a consequence of the pandemic control policy. (12M, 45 years old, two sons aged 12 and five)

However, the pandemic-induced lockdown precipitated a significant shift in paternal involvement within urban Chinese households. Fathers, previously working for extended hours, were compelled to return home and modify their professional schedules. This resulted in reduced working hours or transitions to remote work, consequently increasing father-child interaction time. The absence of grandparental support further solidified nuclear family cohesion and augmented fathers' direct engagement in childrearing activities. Many fathers among the respondents reported a marked enhancement in parent-child relationship quality during this period, with the pandemic serving as a catalyst for increased familial communication. This phenomenon underscores the potential for external disruptions to recalibrate family dynamics, particularly in terms of paternal involvement and the strengthening of intergenerational bonds within the nuclear family unit. Just as a father explained in the interview:

If I had worked as if in the normal days, my time with the children would have been very short. Before COVID-19, it was common that the children were already asleep when I came back home from work at night. During the lockdown period, I had more contact with the children, spent more time with them, and our relationship became closer and tighter. (15M, 45 years old, twins aged eight)

Segmented time

The COVID-19 pandemic precipitated a widespread shift towards remote work and online education among urban Chinese households. This period saw a significant increase in the prevalence of telecommuting for parents and distance learning for children, transforming domestic spaces into multifunctional environments for professional and educational activities. The widespread adoption of remote work and online education led to a significant reduction in parental commute times and child transportation logistics. This shift resulted in an increase in discretionary time and enhanced schedule flexibility within households. Consequently, domestic routines became more fluid, characterised by delayed sleep and meal times. Notably, family dining patterns were recalibrated to accommodate children's virtual class schedules. As a father depicted the changes at his family:

During the pandemic, staying at home made us more relaxed. All the family members slept later at night and woke up later in the morning. Sometimes we combined breakfast and lunch. We ate when the children finished their classes. On weekends when the children didn't have classes, we were even more casual with time. (04M, 45 years old, one daughter aged 13)

Prior to the COVID-19 pandemic, dual-income Chinese parents typically experienced significant time constraints regarding childrearing due to professional obligations. The shift to remote work during the pandemic presented these parents with a more adaptable approach to reconciling occupational and familial responsibilities. Qualitative data from interviewed families consistently indicated that the transition to remote work resulted in increased discretionary time and enhanced scheduling flexibility for dual-income parents. This change facilitated greater parental engagement in child-centred activities and interactions, subsequently fostering more harmonious familial relationships and a more cohesive domestic environment. Notably, this phenomenon was characterised by increased paternal presence in the household, deeper involvement of fathers in childrearing practices and more frequent father-child interactions. A father of two saw the favourable impact of the pandemic on his parenting involvement as he explained to us:

> The pandemic was somehow a good thing for me. A lot of my business trips were cancelled and I got more chance to return home early to take care of the children. There was more interaction between me and the children. I took them to play in the communal areas every day, cooked what they wanted to eat, played games with them and even successfully taught the older one how to ride a bicycle. (12M, 45 years old, two sons aged 12 and five)

However, the transition to remote work significantly eroded the demarcation between professional and domestic spheres, exacerbating work-family balance challenges, particularly for working mothers. This phenomenon manifested prominently in the fragmentation of previously consolidated work periods by multifarious domestic responsibilities, including household management and childcare. The inefficacy of online learning modalities necessitated increased maternal involvement in educational support and supervision, further intensifying time and energy demands on working mothers. Domestic duties and childrearing became the predominant focus for these women during the home-based work period, relegating professional responsibilities to interstitial timeframes. While this arrangement afforded some temporal flexibility, it usually resulted in diminished productivity and the erosion of personal time and autonomy for working mothers. In contrast, paternal experiences diverged significantly. Fathers often maintained uninterrupted, focused work periods, largely insulated from the confluence of professional and caregiving demands. For instance, a father of two and professor at a university reported that the pandemic afforded him enhanced opportunities to engage in preferred work tasks, with the ability to work unencumbered in his designated workspace for extended periods. This gendered disparity in remote work experiences aligns with findings from international studies. Hjálmsdóttir and Bjarnadóttir (2021) documented similar patterns in their cross-cultural analysis, underscoring the global nature of this phenomenon.

Increasing level of anxiety

During the COVID-19 pandemic, countless families experienced fear and apprehension stemming from pervasive uncertainty. A father's recount of his infant daughter's COVID-19 infection vividly illustrates the excessive anxiety and psychological stress experienced by parents during the pandemic. His narrative, detailing the weeks leading up to the interview, exemplifies the heightened concerns and emotional toll on caregivers facing such health crises:

> What I worried the most is actually our baby. She hasn't been sick since birth. For her first infection in life, it was COVID. Nothing could be more awful. I was anxious all day long at that time and didn't know what to do.

The baby couldn't speak. She behaved very differently from usual after getting a temperature. Usually, she would play and explore the room a lot, but after the fever, she became listless and didn't want to move, which was heart-wrenching to see.' (05M, 43 years old, one daughter aged one)

Postpandemic, interviewed parents demonstrated an increased emphasis on children's health and wellbeing, with heightened attention to both physical and mental aspects. Among the interviewed families, fathers usually exhibited a more open approach to parenting, advocating for children's happiness and autonomy, predicated on economic stability and fostering an inclusive worldview. The pandemic-induced uncertainty prompted introspection among dual-income parents, resulting in prioritised family time and enhanced intrafamilial communication. Just as an interviewed mother moaned: 'After experiencing this pandemic, seeing many elderly and young people passing away quickly, I feel it's more important to spend more time with family, to accompany the elderly and children when there's time' (06F, 44 years old, one daughter aged seven).

The economic repercussions of the COVID-19 pandemic, manifested in reduced wages and heightened life pressures, negatively impacted the emotional wellbeing of several interviewees. Prolonged home confinement severed social connections beyond immediate family, accentuating the insularity of urban living spaces and exacerbating ennui among dual-income parents. A participating father, who was a fitness industry professional and was primarily responsible for weekday childcare, experienced severe income reduction and impending unemployment due to the pandemic. As will be seen from the following quotes, this situation precipitated prolonged mental exhaustion and depressive symptoms for him, culminating in diminished patience in childrearing interactions:

We couldn't go anywhere and didn't know when the pandemic would end. We could only stay at home with a bunch of trivial matters, dealing with the children every day. Sometimes I would feel quite depressed and have no patience with the children. Sometimes after saying something twice, I wanted to beat them up if I had to say it again. Before the pandemic, I was always more patient to them. The children were younger back then and didn't understand much, so I would explain things to them time and again. Now if I say something twice and they don't listen, I become very impatient.' (02M, 33 years old, twins aged five)

The coexistence of confusion, anticipation and anxiety emerged as a prevalent psychological state among individuals confronting heightened global uncertainty. Urban dual-income parents in China, who were previously confident in their career and family management, experienced a sudden erosion of efficacy in their life experiences when faced with unprecedented external uncertainties. This paradigm shift compromised their ability to offer meaningful life guidance to their offspring, consequently elevating parental anxiety levels.

Persistence of fundamental parenting paradigms

Despite the significant disruptions caused by the COVID-19 pandemic, it is noteworthy that the division of parental labour among the 19 families interviewed did not undergo substantial alterations. The pre-pandemic patterns of parental role distribution largely persisted, even as families navigated the challenges of lockdowns, remote work and online schooling. Mothers continued to maintain their position as primary coordinators of parenting responsibilities, adapting their holistic planning and management of childrearing activities to the new pandemic context within urban familial units.

The pandemic-induced restrictions on mobility and access to external support systems highlighted existing patterns of childcare distribution. In households that previously relied on domestic workers and grandparental support, the temporary absence or reduced availability of these auxiliary caregivers during lockdowns often resulted in a re-allocation of daily childcare duties among parents. However, this re-allocation typically followed pre-existing patterns, with mothers often shouldering a higher proportion of quotidian caregiving responsibilities, especially in families that already lacked such support systems before the pandemic.

Chinese middle-class families have consistently placed a high value on their children's education (Chen-Bouck, Duan and Patterson, 2017; Beck and Nyíri, 2022). Parents often provide supplementary educational guidance for their offspring, a phenomenon referred to in the literature as 'shadow education' (Zhang, 2020). Accordingly, all interviewed families emphasised the indispensability of parental involvement in educational oversight, behavioural guidance and interactive companionship – aspects that became even more crucial during periods of home confinement and online learning. Parents demonstrated active engagement in educational supervision, adapting to the challenges of remote education. This maternal approach, characterised by refinement, stringency and calculated strategies, persisted and often intensified in response to the demands of home-based learning.

Notably, several fathers who assumed primary responsibility for educational supervision pre-pandemic maintained this role, exhibiting a strict demeanour that occasionally elicited trepidation in their children. While these fathers provided specific guidance on academic content, adapting to online learning formats, they generally continued to exhibit less involvement in habit formation and behavioural guidance, even as the importance of these aspects increased during prolonged periods at home.

The pandemic did create opportunities for increased parental presence, particularly for fathers who transitioned to remote work. However, this did not necessarily translate into fundamental changes in parenting roles, as the following quote from an interviewed mother exemplifies:

> He [my husband] hardly communicates with the child about anything other than tutoring schoolwork. Although he has taken on a lot of specific knowledge guidance, especially during online classes, I still provide more support to our daughter in terms of how to develop good habits, what kind of person to be, and how to view and handle things in life, which became even more important during lockdowns. (19F, 45 years old, one daughter aged 13)

The interviewed parents exhibited a relatively equitable distribution of engagement in companionship interactions with their children, a pattern that continued and often intensified during periods of home confinement. The dual function of companionship – emotional and instrumental – became more pronounced during the pandemic, with high-quality, responsive interactions recognised as crucial for maintaining children's cognitive development and sense of security in an uncertain time.

A typical participating family's 'strategic' division of parental labour, while challenged by pandemic restrictions, adapted within its existing framework. When rural-based grandparents were unable to provide daily care due to travel restrictions, parents absorbed these responsibilities according to their pre-established roles. The mother, possessing the highest educational attainment, continued to oversee educational supervision and habit formation, now within the context of home-based learning. Both parents engaged in companionship interactions during their discretionary time, which often increased due to remote work arrangements.

In essence, while the COVID-19 pandemic introduced new challenges and temporarily altered some aspects of family life, it did not fundamentally change the underlying patterns of parental labour division in these urban Chinese families. Instead, existing parenting strategies were adapted and often intensified to meet the demands of the new reality, underscoring the resilience and stability of established familial roles and responsibilities.

Inherent inequalities amid pandemic parenting

In many participants' eyes, the COVID-19 pandemic, an exogenous and contingent factor, induced temporary and superficial changes. An interviewed mother articulated profound philosophical insights based on her lived experience during the pandemic: 'The pandemic was merely an interlude; much remained unchanged and pre-existing issues persisted. The pandemic also served as a magnifying glass, bringing these problems into sharper focus' (08F, 44 years old, one daughter aged 15).

While discussing the pandemic's impact on parenting practices, it is crucial to note what remains unchanged – that is, the longstanding structural gender inequalities in urban Chinese dual-income families' childrearing practices remained largely unshaken. These inequalities manifested in two primary aspects: physical participation and mental engagement.

Physical participation inequality: ever-present mothers versus intermittently involved fathers

Childcare typically lacks clear demarcations of beginning and end, resembling a perpetual state of readiness that demands attention, patience and responsiveness. The physical presence of caregivers is indispensable. When interviewed mothers described their daily routines during home confinement, children's schedules permeated their narratives, while paternal involvement was seldom mentioned. This begs the following question: where were the fathers? As an interviewed mother noted, pre-pandemic, fathers primarily assumed childcare responsibilities only when working mothers were physically unavailable due to professional obligations: 'My husband's demanding work schedule naturally results in less attention to family matters compared to me. However, when my work occasionally requires overtime or travel, he can take on the responsibility of caring for the family and children' (13F, 45 years old, one son aged 12).

During the pandemic-induced work-from-home period, mothers who were already more involved in childcare pre-pandemic found themselves spending even more time with their children. Paternal absence seemed to become a tacit norm, with fathers' roles only becoming apparent when mothers were physically separated due to quarantine measures. On the contrary, we noticed that a participating family in this study presented an alternative scenario of intermittent paternal involvement: while the mother was constantly physically present, children became adept at navigating her various parenting strategies. In such instances, when the father, who was usually disengaged, suddenly intervened in disciplinary matters, his involvement proved remarkably effective. Although this family did not intentionally establish paternal authority in daily life, the father's infrequent yet impactful participation in childcare was closely related to the power dynamics silently formed between the couple, both adhering to traditional gender ideologies.

Mental load inequality: overburdened mothers versus much-anticipated fathers

Both before and during the pandemic, a significant gender disparity existed in the mental load associated with childcare among urban Chinese dual-income parents. While an interviewed mother greatly appreciated her husband's hands-on care and companionship with their daughter during the home confinement period, reflecting on pre-pandemic daily life, she angrily recounted:

> Both parents are in the school's WeChat group, but fathers seem oblivious to any information shared by teachers. My husband often says, 'you just arrange it', which is essentially shirking responsibility. This is common among my friends' families too. A father is considered highly competent if he can simply execute the mother's arrangements. Moreover, mothers must provide extremely detailed instructions for fathers to complete tasks; merely outlining general directions is insufficient. (17F, 45 years old, one daughter aged 11)

Another mother participating in our study also strongly criticised her husband's disregard for their child's class WeChat group, believing he had never genuinely invested in parenting. Conversely, the father explained to us that following his wife's arrangements, whether for household chores or childcare, was the optimal choice for maintaining family harmony under the principle of seeking common ground while reserving differences: 'I follow her [my wife's] arrangements. I do as much as she tells me to. I'm not good with details and she might not be satisfied with how I do things anyway, so it's better if I just act on her instructions' (12M, 45 years old, two sons aged 12 and five).

In all interviewed families, mothers invested substantial mental energy in comprehensive childcare planning, remaining the de facto 'worrier' even when they were physically absent. Regardless of gender power relations, income disparities or household labour division, mothers were responsible for overall childcare coordination. Some fathers held biologically deterministic views on motherhood, believing maternal love and initiative were innate, thus relegating themselves to auxiliary roles in parenting.

In families where fathers were the primary breadwinners, they tended to neglect childrearing due to work commitments. Conversely, when mothers were primary earners, grandparents and domestic workers primarily undertook daily care. However, mothers, irrespective of their work commitments, remained highly invested in children's education, habit formation and interactive companionship. The maternal identity, unrestricted by time and space, imposed a high-intensity mental load on women, persisting even as children became more independent.

Mothers engaged deeply in children's education, extracurricular activities and moral development. Even when fathers' participation in daily care or education exceeded that of mothers, their consideration of children's futures was comparatively limited. Mothers consistently expected fathers to bear parenting responsibilities and prioritise childcare, despite often excusing them from household chores. Previous research indicates that working mothers, despite recognising gender inequality in childcare division, often willingly expend more energy on personal childcare due to mistrust in fathers' parenting quality (Bianchi and Milkie, 2010). Consequently, working mothers continue to bear an excessive mental load in childcare amid work–family conflicts, balancing expectations and disappointment in fathers' heartfelt parenting participation.

The structural inequality and its root in Chinese family and society

The persistent and deeply entrenched gender structural inequalities in urban Chinese dual-income families' parenting practices during the COVID-19 pandemic reflect the intertwining of modern gender equality concepts, individualistic tendencies, traditional Confucian patriarchal ideologies, gender norms and Marxist gender equality ideals in contemporary Chinese society (Ji, 2015a). On the one hand, urban dual-income couples, generally highly educated ones, have been influenced by concepts of modernity and neoliberalism amid market economic transitions and globalisation. They have formed modern gender equality views and individual rights consciousness, strongly supporting trends towards gender equality. There is a consensus that both spouses should participate in economic labour and cooperate in family responsibilities. In particular, highly educated women possess stronger notions of gender equality and personal development (Ji, 2015b), simultaneously pursuing equal rights in the labour market and within the family. The view that 'women must have careers' frequently emerged in interviews with both fathers and mothers. Work allows mothers to temporarily step out of the family domain, achieve a degree of financial independence and experience feelings of confidence, independence, value and accomplishment. As a mother of two and professor at a university noted:

> The monthly salary for our domestic helper is 4,000 yuan, which my salary alone cannot cover. However, I firmly believe that it's necessary to free me from the household chores and allow me time for my own careers. Work gives me a sense of achievement, housework does not. (12F, 43 years old, two sons aged 12 and five)

The principle of 'whoever is capable does it' guides some interviewed families in negotiating the division of housework and childcare based on the couple's work commitments and contributions to family income. As both spouses recognise the importance of external work and family care, arrangements where women are breadwinners and men are primary caregivers are also accepted as a negotiated model of childcare division in contemporary China. Some working mothers view the economic rewards and social resources linked to their work as fundamental to family childcare. Adhering to this belief, working mothers not only acknowledge the importance of work for their independence but also associate their careers with their children's interests and welfare, viewing work as an indispensable option and rejecting the traditional image of the virtuous wife and good mother.

On the other hand, traditional Confucian patriarchal ideologies and gender norms in China have not automatically faded with rapid socioeconomic changes. They continue to exist in urban Chinese dual-income families, with men's family values being more deeply influenced by traditional patriarchal culture (Ji, 2015b) and resistant to change. The traditional gender notion of 'men work outside, women manage the home' still guides their parenting practices. This phenomenon is particularly evident in the division of parenting responsibilities among some interviewed families raising sons. One interviewed father persistently held gender stereotypes such as 'men enjoy and excel at sports more than women' and 'men are more playful than women', believing that his 'high-quality' companionship with his son could foster independence and a sense of responsibility. As he stated:

> Although my wife handles most of the daily childcare, I make sure to spend quality time with our son, especially on weekends. I often take him to the park to play football or go cycling. It's not just about having fun – I think it's important for boys to learn physical skills and develop a sense of independence. Plus, I'm naturally more energetic and playful than my wife, so these outdoor activities come easily to me. I feel it's my role to teach my son how to be a man and prepare him for the responsibilities he'll face in the future. (14M, 42 years old, one son aged 11)

Moreover, the promotion and influence of Marxist gender equality ideas, such as 'women can hold up half the sky', have played a positive role in women's acceptance of gender equality concepts (Cheung and Halpern, 2010; Li, 2023). Current public discourse continuously shapes the ideal image of the perfect mother – a career woman who can balance work and life, 'grasping with both hands, excelling in both areas'. Working mothers set perfectionist standards for themselves in all aspects: striving to outperform men in their careers while aspiring to be virtuous wives and good mothers at home, surpassing even full-time mothers. The intertwining of these ideologies makes it challenging for urban Chinese dual-income couples to alter the gender structural inequalities in their parenting practices.

Conclusion

This chapter has examined the COVID-19 pandemic's impact on parenting modes in dual-income urban Chinese families, focusing on fathers' roles compared to those of mothers. Two primary findings emerged. First, the pandemic introduced new challenges to parenting practices, including temporary separations, time fragmentation and increased anxiety. While parents experienced multidimensional reflections on emotional responses and family dynamics, the overall parenting modes and division of labour did not undergo substantial changes, maintaining characteristics of diversified subjects, refined content and strategic participation. Second, analysis of parental roles, commitments and involvement during the pandemic elucidated inherent gender inequalities in parenting modes among the researched families. It resonates with Twamley and Haffejee's observation on the gendered divisions of labour of care during the pandemic in the UK and South Africa (Chapter 9, this volume), which has by and large become entrenched. While pandemic-related parenting practices were observable, the longstanding structural gender inequalities, characterised by the coexistence of physical participation and mental load, would be a key factor to consider in the promotion of gender equity in parenting in contemporary China.

Our qualitative study yields valuable insights into childcare division in urban dual-income Chinese families during the pandemic, offering an opportunity to reflect on the aforementioned changed and unchanged elements of parenting modes. The analysis of interviews with fathers and mothers reveals significant gender differences in their parenting modes. Mothers typically focus on caregiving details and express more anxiety, while fathers emphasise parenting purposes and methods, often downplaying the crisis. Both parents are influenced by societal gender stereotypes, though some mothers tend to challenge these notions. In addition, fathers' narratives suggest they enjoy more advantages in time allocation and work-life balance. Applying Doucet's '3 Rs' framework, we found divergent understandings and practices of relationalities, responsiveness and responsibilities between fathers and mothers. Bridging these gendered disparities is crucial for promoting equitable parenting practices. These findings contribute to our understanding of parenting dynamics during crises and illuminate persistent gender inequalities in caregiving, informing future research and policy initiatives.

This chapter proposes two key considerations for dual-income urban Chinese families in the postpandemic era. First, as families remain the primary locus of childrearing, efforts should focus on dismantling traditional gender role expectations, encouraging couples to collaboratively support each other in parenting based on their specific circumstances. Second, the decline of work unit systems and public childcare has shifted childcare responsibilities back to families, primarily mothers. The government's inadequate support for family parenting warrants critical reflection. Given China's low fertility rates nowadays, childcare possesses crucial public value. The government and society should collectively support families by establishing comprehensive parenting and family support systems. This includes effective public policies, extensive public childcare services, dual-parent parental leave policies, flexible work arrangements and childcare allowances. Additionally, communities and social organisations should provide flexible, multifaceted parenting assistance to dual-income families.

References

Beck, F. and Nyíri, P. (2022). 'It's all for the child': the discontents of middle-class Chinese parenting and migration to Europe. *China Quarterly*, *251*, 913–934.

Bianchi, S. M. and Milkie, M. A. (2010). Work and family research in the first decade of the 21st century. *Journal of Marriage and Family*, *72*(3), 705–725.

Cao, S. and Lin, X. (2019). Masculinizing fatherhood: negotiation of Yang and Jiao among young fathers in China. *Journal of Gender Studies*, *28*(8), 937–947.

Chen-Bouck, L., Duan, C. and Patterson, M. M. (2017). A qualitative study of urban, Chinese middle-class mothers' parenting for adolescents. *Journal of Adolescent Research*, *32*(4), 479–508.

Cheung, F. M. and Halpern, D. F. (2010). Women at the top: powerful leaders define success as work+ family in a culture of gender. *American Psychologist*, *65*(3), 182–193.

Craig, L. and Mullan, K. (2011). How mothers and fathers share childcare: a cross-national time-use comparison. *American Sociological Review*, *76*(6), 834–861.

Doucet, A. (2023). Care is not a tally sheet: rethinking the field of gender divisions of domestic labour with care-centric conceptual narratives. *Families, Relationships and Societies*, *12*(1): 10–30.

Du, F. and Dong, X. Y. (2013). Women's employment and child care choices in urban China during the economic transition. *Economic Development and Cultural Change*, *62*(1), 131–155.

Graham, M., Weale, V., Lambert, K. A., Kinsman, N., Stuckey, R. and Oakman, J. (2021). Working at home: the impacts of COVID 19 on health, family-work-life conflict, gender and parental responsibilities. *Journal of Occupational and Environmental Medicine*, *63*(11), 938–943.

Hjálmsdóttir, A. and Bjarnadóttir, V. S. (2021). 'I have turned into a foreman here at home': families and work–life balance in times of COVID-19 in a gender equality paradise. *Gender, Work & Organization*, *28*(1), 268–283.

Hong, X., Wang, J. and Zhu, W. (2022). The relationship between childcare services participation and parental subjective well-being under China's three-child policy – based on the mediation effect of parenting stress. *Sustainability*, *14*(24), 16425.

Ji, Y. (2015a). Asian families at the crossroads: a meeting of East, West, tradition, modernity and gender. *Journal of Marriage and Family*, 77(5), 1031–1038.

Ji, Y. (2015b). Between tradition and modernity: 'leftover' women in Shanghai. *Journal of Marriage and Family*, 77(5), 1057–1073.

Johansson, T. and Klinth, R. (2008). Caring fathers: the ideology of gender equality and masculine positions. *Men and Masculinities*, 11(1), 42–62.

Li, X. (2016). The 'nursing dad'? Constructs of fatherhood in Chinese popular media. *Intersections: Gender and Sexuality in Asia and the Pacific*, 39, 1–15.

Li, X. (2020). Fathers' involvement in Chinese societies: increasing presence, uneven progress. *Child Development Perspectives*, 14(3), 150–156.

Li, X. (2021). How do Chinese fathers express love? Viewing paternal warmth through the eyes of Chinese fathers, mothers and their children. *Psychology of Men & Masculinities*, 22(3), 500–511.

Li, X. and Lamb, M. E. (2012). Fathers in Chinese culture: from stern disciplinarians to involved parents. In *Fathers in Cultural Context*. Abingdon: Routledge, pp 15–41.

Li, X. and Wu, X. (2021). Same city, different depression: gender, class and mental health disparities during the COVID-19 pandemic [同城异郁：新冠疫情下的性别、阶层与心理健康差异]. *China Population and Development Studies*, 27(6), 95–105.

Li, X., Hu, Y., Huang, C. Y. S. and Chuang, S. S. (2021). Beyond WEIRD (Western, educated, industrial, rich, democratic)-centric theories and perspectives: masculinity and fathering in Chinese societies. *Journal of Family Theory & Review*, 13(3), 317–333.

Li, Y. (2023). Modernisation, Confucianism and gender justice in rural and urban China: the lived experience of women with children. Doctoral dissertation, University of Bristol.

Lin, X., Li, H. and Yang, W. (2020). You reap what you sow: profiles of Chinese fathers' play beliefs and their relation to young children's developmental outcomes. *Early Education and Development*, 31(3), 426–441.

Liu, Y., Haslam, D. M., Dittman, C. K., Guo, M. and Morawska, A. (2022). *Predicting Chinese father involvement: parental role beliefs, fathering self-efficacy and maternal gatekeeping: developmental*. *Frontiers in Psychology*, 13 (2022), 1066876.

Mooi-Reci, I. and Risman, B. J. (2021). The gendered impacts of COVID-19: lessons and reflections. *Gender & Society*, 35(2), 161–167.

Morrow, R., Rodriguez, A. and King, N. (2015). Colaizzi's descriptive phenomenological method. *The Psychologist*, 28(8), 643–644.

Ni, P., Hong, P., Pan, L., Han, X., Zhai, S. and He, J. (2024). Work arrangements and father involvement during COVID-19 lockdown: a mixed methods study. *Family Relations*, 73(1), 54–73.

Offer, S. and Schneider, B. (2011). Revisiting the gender gap in time-use patterns: multitasking and well-being among mothers and fathers in dual-earner families. *American Sociological Review*, *76*(6), 809–833.

Twamley, K., Iqbal, H. and Faircloth, C. (2023). *Family Life in the Time of COVID: International Perspectives*. London: UCL Press.

Wu, A., Tian, Y., Chen, S. and Cui, L. (2024). Do playful parents raise playful children? A mixed methods study to explore the impact of parental playfulness on children's playfulness. *Early Education and Development*, *35*(2), 283–306.

Xu, Q. (2017). *Fatherhood, Adolescence and Gender in Chinese Families*. Dordrecht: Springer.

Xu, Q. and O'Brien, M. (2014). Fathers and teenage daughters in Shanghai: intimacy, gender and care. *Journal of Family Studies*, *20*(3), 311–322.

Yu, J. (2024). The impact of the two-child policy on urban family dynamics in Beijing: parental roles, child development and family economic strategies. *Studies in Social Science & Humanities*, *3*(6), 23–33.

Zhang, C. and Zhou, J. (2021). Gender differences in work and family relationships and their impact on negative emotions during the COVID-19 pandemic [国内新冠肺炎疫情下的工作、家庭关系及其对负面情绪影响的性别差异]. *Collection of Women's Studies*, *164*(2): 40–52.

Zhang, W. (2020). Shadow education in the service of tiger parenting: strategies used by middle-class families in China. *European Journal of Education*, *55*(3), 388–404.

PART III

Exploring what facilitates or inhibits fathers' care

8

Fathers on the 'night shift'? Understanding caring fatherhood through parents' interpretative repertoires of night-time care

Petteri Eerola, Armi Mustosmäki and Henna Pirskanen

Introduction

In this chapter, we provide a new perspective on caring fathers by analysing Finnish fathers' and mothers' accounts of fathers' night-time care. We focus on the 'parental night shift', which includes late-evening and early-morning routines, night awakenings, child feeding, anticipating infant night-time needs, 'sleep training' and other parental responsibilities undertaken outside waking hours. It is often borne by mothers, and fathers may not even be aware of it (Maume et al, 2010; Burgard, 2011). The 'night shift' is not limited to infancy and can continue for years, manifesting, for example, as night-time care for a sick child or sleepless nights of emotional labour worrying about one's child(ren) and family matters (for example, Ruppanner et al, 2021; Coles et al, 2022). We understand night-time hours – often neglected by mainstream sociology as well as family and parenting research – as a prism through which inequalities in parenting, family wellbeing and daily family life of parents and children can be reflected on and examined from a novel point of view. The study takes place in Finland, a country characterised as a dual-earner welfare state with a long history of supporting shared and equal parenthood (Lammi-Taskula, 2017).

In this chapter, we study parents' – both fathers' and mothers' – interpretative repertoires produced to enable or constrain fathers' care during the intimate, 'hidden hours' between late evenings and early mornings. In addition, we explore the interpretative repertoires parents used to account for sharing night-time care. We analyse qualitative interviews with Finnish fathers (n = 8) and mothers (n = 23) of children under six years old collected in 2022. The study is part of the multidisciplinary research project 'The parental night shift: gendered inequalities in night-time care' (2022–2027) funded by the Kone Foundation.

Background
Evenings, nights and mornings: a new perspective on gendered care

Research on gendered parenting and care suggests two key trends in Western societies in recent decades. First, research highlights changes in fatherhood and men's care. In other words, contemporary fathers provide more care for their children than the fathers of earlier generations and they have moved closer to the intimate and emotional core of families (for example, Dermott, 2008; Eerola, 2015; Miller, 2017). Cultural images of fatherhood and societal expectations put on fathers have also transformed, with contemporary fathers expected to be actively involved in hands-on care of their children from the start of parenthood (Ralp, 2016; Miller, 2017). However, traditional breadwinning mentalities still coexist with the more caring ideals of fatherhood (Eerola, 2015; Kelland et al, 2022; see also Twamley and Haffejee, Chapter 9 and Rogero-García et al, Chapter 17 in this book).

Second, studies have also highlighted that strong gendered divisions still exist in care, even when fathers are actively involved (Rose et al, 2014; Eerola et al, 2021). Mothers engage in more practical and mundane routine care tasks than fathers, who spend relatively more time on different kinds of leisure, educational and recreational activities (for example, Craig, 2006; Rose et al, 2014; Ralph, 2016). According to Rose et al (2014), these gendered divisions are often discretionary and largely taken for granted, and fathers can opt out of tasks they find too challenging or feel uncomfortable with (see Rogero-García et al, Chapter 17 in this volume). Several studies have also shown how mothers 'orchestrate' parenting by taking care of the mental labour and managerial side of family life and childcare (Walzer, 1996; Ralph, 2016; Miller, 2017; Daminger, 2019). These examples of existing gendered divisions in care labour reflect a culture of intensive mothering, where the expectations placed on mothers in particular have become significantly more burdensome (Faircloth, 2014).

Extant social science research on parental care and its gendered manifestations has concentrated almost exclusively on responsibilities, tasks and activities taking place during the daytime hours. To date, only four empirical studies on night-time parenting have been published (in the English language), including two qualitative articles from the UK and the US (Venn et al, 2008; Maume et al, 2010) and two articles based on the American Time Use Survey (Burgard, 2011; Ruppanner et al, 2021). The topic has also been addressed to a limited extent in a few other publications with a more general focus on either sleep or parenting (for example, Hislop and Arber, 2003; Meadows et al, 2008; Rauch, 2024). Although the overall picture based on these few papers remains limited, evidence of gendered inequalities embedded in night-time care was observed in all studies (Venn et al, 2008; Maume et al, 2010; Burgard, 2011; Ruppanner et al, 2021). A qualitative study based on interviews of UK couples (n = 25) with children of various ages found that both parents expected mothers to take care of their children's needs during the night (Venn et al, 2008). An interview study of US couples (n = 25) with children of various ages reported the 'night shift' as a burden that fathers may not even be aware of (Maume et al, 2010). Both qualitative studies also found that parents did not explicitly negotiate night-time care practices (Venn et al, 2008; Maume et al, 2010). Studies based on the nationally representative American Time Use Survey revealed that US mothers, including working mothers, buffer fathers' sleep from disruption (Burgard, 2011; Ruppanner et al, 2021) and are considerably more likely to get up at night and provide care that interrupts their own rather than the fathers' sleep (Burgard, 2011). In particular, mothers with children under two years of age suffered from fragmented sleep (Burgard, 2011). However, the gender disparity persists thereafter, with mothers of older children (aged 3–17) providing significantly more night care than fathers (Burgard, 2011). A qualitative UK study on the gendered nature of sleep disruption among midlife women reported that many mothers experienced long-term cumulative sleep deprivation and tiredness caused by night-time care that affected their working lives (Hislop and Arber, 2003).

The connections among sleep, care, wellbeing and gender have been studied more extensively in the fields of biomedical research, neurophysiology, epidemiology and psychology than in the social sciences. The results have shown that continuous night sleep is critical for maintaining and promoting wellbeing and mental health (Dement, 2000; Luyester et al, 2012; Coles et al, 2022). Although the need for sleep varies among individuals and across the lifecycle, becoming a parent is for most people the most salient event affecting sleep (Richter et al, 2019; Coles et al, 2022). Total sleep time, the duration of continuous sleep and sleep satisfaction all decrease after the transition to parenthood, which increases the risk of greater stress and declining physical and mental health (Medina et al, 2009; Richter et al, 2019; Coles et al, 2022). However, the effects of childbirth on parents' sleep patterns vary for men and women. Poor sleep quality and insufficient sleep have been found to be common among parents, especially mothers with young children, and sleep disturbances are linked to weakened postpartum mental health and other maternal health risks (Dement, 2000; Richter et al, 2019). A German study based on population-representative panel data found that both mothers' and fathers' sleep satisfaction and sleep time did not fully recover for up to six years after the birth of their first child (Richter et al, 2019). The findings of a recent meta-analysis of 29 studies showed that fathers with children who slept poorly had worse general health and wellbeing than fathers with children who slept well; however, associations of children's poor sleep with depression were fewer and less frequent for fathers than those reported for mothers (Coles et al, 2022).

Fathers' care and gendered parenting in Finland

This study took place in Finland, a Nordic dual-earner welfare state. It has a long history of supporting shared and equal parenthood, including promoting women's participation in the labour force and encouraging fathers to take greater responsibility for childcare (Eydal et al, 2015; Lammi-Taskula, 2017; Eerola et al, 2019). Finland, along with Norway, was the first country in the world to introduce postbirth paternity leave to be taken simultaneously with the mother in the late 1970s, and it was the second country after Sweden to introduce sharable parental leave in the mid-1980s. The current Finnish leave scheme introduced in 2022 provides fathers with income-related fathers' parental leave of six months, of which a maximum of ten weeks is transferable to the child's other parent. Additionally, fathers are eligible for childcare leave up to the child's third birthday with a flat-rate benefit (for more about the Finnish leave scheme, see the chapter by Saarikallio-Torp et al, Chapter 12 in this volume).

Research on Finnish fathers highlights how during recent decades, fathers' own accounts of fatherhood have become more care- and nurture-oriented, focusing on sensitive and emotionally involved ways of fathering (Eerola, 2015). Cultural expectations of fathers' roles in care have also shifted, as fathers are expected to be involved with their children's lives from the very beginning of parenthood. During the pregnancy and baby year, most Finnish fathers attend maternity and child welfare clinics at least occasionally with their child's mother. Through the first two decades of the 2000s, increasing interest in fatherhood has also been seen in public discourse (Eerola, 2015). In addition, the amount of time spent by Finnish fathers in caring for their children almost doubled between the late 1980s to early 2010s; in families with two working parents, men performed over 40 per cent of all childcare in 2010 (Ylikännö et al, 2015; more recent statistics were unavailable at the time of writing). According to time-use research, there were no gendered differences across various forms of care, as men took an equal share in both hands-on and indirect care.

Although during recent decades Finland has seen a change in cultural expectations towards fatherhood and an increase in time fathers spend in providing care, the division of caregiving responsibility between parents remains far from equal. Take-up of parental leave is highly gendered, as fathers take only 10 per cent of all parental leave available to parents, meaning young children are cared for at home mostly by their mothers (Eerola et al, 2019). Overall responsibility for routine care often falls on mothers, who also bear the main responsibility for the mental labour related to the family and household chores. It has been argued that existing gendered divisions of care in Finnish families are reinforced by cultural ideals, which, despite the increasing dominance of the understanding of caring fatherhood in Finnish parenting culture, still emphasise the mother's role as primary carer (Eerola et al, 2021). However, according to an earlier study based on interviews with Finnish couples, tensions and disagreements seem to emerge especially when couples are negotiating household duties rather than childcare (Eerola et al, 2021).

Data and analysis

We analysed qualitative interviews of Finnish parents with children under the age of six conducted in the autumn of 2022. As the focus of the chapter is on the father's care role, interviews of fathers (n = 8) and mothers (n = 23) living in different-sex relationships with the other parent of their child(ren) were examined, whereas interviews with mothers living in same-sex relationships and single mothers collected for the project were excluded from the analysis. Our sample included parents who were either on parental or childcare leave with their child (mothers = 6), working full-time (mothers = 12; fathers = 5), working part-time (mothers = 1; fathers = 1), studying (mothers = 1) or combining parental/childcare leave with work or studies (mothers = 4; fathers = 2). The ages of the interviewees varied from 27 to 47 years old. In total, 22 of the interviewed parents had a BA or higher (MA, PhD) education. Most of the interviewees were living in urban areas in and around major Finnish cities. All the interviewed parents had at least one child under six; however, most of the interviewees were parents of infants under two years of age. Of the interviewees, 20 had more than one child, either from their current or a previous relationship.

Calls for parents to participate in an interview were circulated primarily through newsletters and social media accounts of Finnish nongovernmental organisations (NGOs) and networks such as Mothers in Business, Diverse Families and Rainbow Families Finland. Interviews were conducted in person (n = 10) or online (n = 21) according to the interviewees' wishes and lasted for an hour on average. In-person interviews took place at locations chosen by the interviewees, mainly in family homes. Interviews were semi-structured with narrative features. The interview guide focused on the interviewees' personal experiences and narratives of care and parenting in the late evenings, night-time hours and early mornings. In the interviews, parents broadly discussed their current situations but also their earlier experiences regarding night-time care; retrospective talk was common, especially among those with older children. Interviews were conducted by two female and a male researcher in Finnish, except for one interview with a non-Finnish-speaking informant conducted in English. The interviews were recorded with the consent of the interviewees and transcribed before the analysis. Finnish National Board on Research Integrity ethical research guidelines were followed.

This study is anchored in the broad tradition of discursive research methods. We consider interviewees to adopt language to 'make sense' of their everyday life experiences and practices related to night-time care and that these accounts are produced through social interaction. When familiarising ourselves with the data and reading the transcripts, we started to see varying reasons and accounts related to the father's role in night-time care. We approached these accounts and reasons as 'interpretative repertoires', a concept originally coined by Potter and Wetherell (1987) to explore the use of language to construct and express meaning in social interactions. They defined interpretative repertoires as 'a lexicon or register of terms and metaphors drawn upon to characterise and evaluate actions and events' (Potter and Wetherell, 1987, p 138). This means that interpretative repertoires are culturally available units or frames through which people develop explanations, descriptions and versions of different phenomena. It is also notable that the same people may use several repertoires and move between them in complementary or contradictory ways.

We started the analysis with each author reading about a third of the interviews. After reading through and discussing the preliminary findings, the researchers agreed on the four main interpretative repertoires used to account for how night-time care is (not) divided in the families according to the aspects affecting the division of care: *biological, individual/situational, work-related* and *institutional*. These repertoires were employed to account for why the mother was taking the lead in care (barriers to the father's care), when and why the father was taking the night shift (enablers of the father's care) and what kind of practices of sharing of night-time care the parents had arranged. In the second round of analysis, which was more detailed, the second author compiled a table into which each co-author then inserted excerpts from the interviews wherein parents described who was caring at night and why. After examining all the data together and adjusting the repertoires, the second author wrote up the first draft of the analysis, which the first and third authors complemented to finalise the work.

Results

In terms of the results, we will first discuss the interpretative repertoires parents used when accounting for barriers to fathers' care. Following this, we will describe how the same repertoires were used to account for enablers of fathers' care. Finally, we will examine the parents' practices for sharing night time care. The interpretative repertoires and their different uses are presented in Table 8.1.

Table 8.1: Parents' interpretative repertoires of barriers and enablers related to the father's night-time care and shared care practices

Interpretative repertoires	Barriers to fathers' care	Enablers of fathers' care	Shared care practices
Biological	*Father* cannot breastfeed *Father's* lack of hormones	*Mother's* health issues *Child's* age and weaning	Chronobiological rhythms
Individual/situational	*Mother's* role as primary carer *Child* prefers the mother *Father's* sleep habits	*Mother* a 'heavy sleeper' *Father* a 'light sleeper'	Taking turns in tasks (for example, father reads bedtime story every other evening) Dividing care tasks (for example, mother sleeps with the baby, father cares for older child/children at night)
Work-related	*Father's* role as wage earner *Father* absent evenings/nights due to shiftwork	*Mother's* return to work *Mother's* work (shifts, travel)	*Work from home* enables more flexibility for fathers to engage in care *Office hours* (9–5 jobs allow more participation for fathers)
Institutional	*Mother's* leave as payment for caring for the child day and night	*Father's* leave Sleep training as institutional praxis highlights *father's* role	–

Why do fathers not engage in care at night?

The majority of the interviewed parents, both mothers and fathers, described relatively inegalitarian and gendered parenting practices, with mothers taking care of their young children at night. The reasons given for why it was mothers who cared, or alternatively why fathers did not, varied from biological and child-related to work-life and institutional factors that had shaped how children's needs were addressed at night.

Biology was a common interpretative, culturally available repertoire that both mothers and fathers drew from when justifying why it was practical and 'natural' for mothers to take care of the child at night. These included women's biological capabilities and conditions related to breastfeeding, waking up and staying awake at night. These reasons were often naturalised and essentialised, and thus unproblematised descriptions. A mother might simply comment: 'I'm the one who breastfeeds', whereas fathers could justify why they were not caring for the child at night simply by saying 'I cannot breastfeed'. This was particularly the case when the parents had young children under a year old. The descriptions of the mothers' primary role were at times more elaborate, making reference to hormones that mothers were developing from the birth and breastfeeding that made it easier for them to wake up at night. The lack of these hormones was thought to make it more difficult for fathers to hear the baby crying or wake up at night. According to a one of the interviewed mothers: 'My husband had difficulties in falling asleep again if he woke up at night, and I know, well yeah, that the hormones while breastfeeding are such that for me, it is relatively easy. I do fall asleep again quite quickly' (Mother 29 years old, child one year old, four older children 4–18 years old, on childcare leave, studying and working part time).

One of the mothers described herself as 'being so high on hormones that I went all crazy' (Mother, 35 years old, child one year old, working full time) after the birth that her husband thought she was like a mother lion, acting as if she were the only one (in her own mind) who knew how the baby should be cared for, including deciding whether the baby was breastfed or given formula. This mother described how she thought 'formula was poison', leading to her very determined attitude towards breastfeeding; for her, there was no other option than to breastfeed, day and night, no matter how exhausted she was. She described how in hindsight, she felt that she was dominating at home when the baby was young, not giving equal opportunities for the father to step in to share in the night-time care.

The child's preference for the mother was generally described as one of the other main reasons for mothers taking the night shift. Parents often connected this attachment to biological factors related to breastfeeding. Since the mothers were generally the primary caregivers during the day, this bond was described as not being easy to break at night. Some mothers said they had happily chosen the night-caregiver role as breastfeeding was perceived as the easiest and most convenient way to soothe the baby, so that everyone in the family, including the mothers themselves, could get more sleep. Mothers described arrangements, such as sharing the bed with the baby, to maximise the amount and quality of their own sleep. These mothers described how they could easily feed the baby sleeping next to them and continue sleeping without too many interruptions, such as leaving the bed. However, at times, the infants' preference for breast over bottle could strain mothers if they would have liked to share the caregiver responsibilities with the father:

> It came as a little bit of a surprise that when we wanted to share caring responsibilities more equally, we found that the baby prefers me [the mother] and soothes a lot more easily with me. Lately, when I have tried to leave the house in the evenings to spend some leisure time on my own and left my husband to put the baby to sleep, the baby has decided not to take the bottle anymore. (Mother 31 years old, child four months old, on parental leave)

Children's preference for the mother was also described as straining and frustrating for those fathers who would have wanted to care for the baby at night and provide opportunities for the mother to rest and get more sleep:

> When the baby stopped accepting the bottle (formula), I felt somewhat powerless, as no matter how much I wanted and tried, it would not, the baby would not soothe before having breast milk. That was a time when I felt I could not do as much as I would have wanted. (Father 47 years old, child one year, eight months old, working full time)

At times, mothers pointed to individual qualities, such as their own or their spouses' chronobiological rhythms, that made it easier for mothers to stay awake at night or wake up early in the morning compared to fathers. Some mothers explained that they had decided to take the night shift as they felt they could handle tiredness a lot better than the fathers. Restless nights caused problems for the father, such as stress, being tense and cranky, or more severe health issues such as insomnia. Often the fathers themselves, as well as the mothers, described the fathers failing to hear their children crying or making noise since they sleep so heavily that they 'just don't wake up' (father 37 years old, child one year, four months old, working full time). In these descriptions, the fathers' deep sleep was considered natural and not questioned.

Work-life related interpretative repertoires were often employed to highlight the father's role as worker and earner and as a barrier to caring for the child. Both mothers and fathers referred to paid work as one key reason why the mother, who was often at home with the young child (or children), was the one taking the responsibility for the night shift. As fathers were mostly working during the day, they were described as needing to rest at night so that they would be able to work. One father described this situation as follows: 'I'm the one who is going to work in the morning, doing cognitive labour, and that is why it is my wife who wakes up to care for the child at night. We have discussed that it is not helpful for both of us to get burned out' (Father 37 years old, child one year, four months old, working full time).

In addition to daytime work, shiftwork was described as preventing fathers from caring for their children at night. One mother (30 years old, children four months and 2.5 years old, on parental leave) said: 'He is working shifts, so when he has an evening shift, he cannot be here to put the kids to bed. If he has night shifts, he cannot be here to wake up at night.' Some mothers also described how they had to arrange for fathers doing shift work to sleep in the mornings and during the day, which affected their ability to rest during the day. Some mothers appeared to be understanding and willing to take care of the child, but some expressed their frustration concerning the division of childcare, especially if they had tried to negotiate some sharing of night-time or morning care. For example:

> Yes, we have negotiated, but these negotiations have not led anywhere, or there has been no change in our situation. Last time, I tried to ask him to get up with the baby, when the baby wakes up at six, even sometimes when he has a day off, could he get up. But he just mumbles something, and then I get all frustrated, ok, it is a 'no' then. … The father is also quite tired on the weekends, and he knows he should take care of the baby, but it appears that he does not have the energy. (Mother 41 years old, children one and three years old, working full time)

Interpretative repertoires highlighting the role of institutional factors, mainly the mother's parental and childcare leave, were also used to explain why it was the mother's responsibility to take the 'night shift'. One mother (35 years old, child one year old, working full time), for example, described her situation as follows: 'the father was paid to do the waged work, whereas, in a certain way, I was paid for being at home and doing the care work'. Also, some fathers justified their withdrawal from night-time care by referring to the mothers' parental or childcare leave and their own role as wage earners. Thus, the work-related and institutional repertoires are used in connection with each other and forming barriers to the father's engaging in childcare.

When do fathers engage in care at night? Enablers of fathers' night-time care

Despite the various reasons why mothers mainly care for their children at night, in some families there were fathers who took on an important, or even primary, role in the night shift. The interpretative frames for the fathers' childcare role were similarly related to biological, individual/situational, work-life and institutional factors, as was the case when justifying the mothers' childcare, but they were constructed and used somewhat differently as enablers of fathers' childcare. Often, the father's role was described as increasing with the child's age as it became less dependent on breastfeeding and the mother was returning to work from leave. The father's take-up of parental leave was also seen as an enabler of the father's night-time care by some parents.

Biology as an interpretative repertoire was drawn on when different kinds of physical, embodied and health-related factors had affected families' situations and decisions, and led to the father taking the night shift. These biological repertoires often intersected and were entangled with individual/situational repertoires.

In some cases, it was recovery from a difficult labour or the mother's poor health that prevented her from caring for the baby and made the father the primary carer. These situations could be short term and the mother's role in night-time care increased after the first days or weeks when her health improved. At times, the mother's poor health, such as sleeping problems or mental health issues, was described as lasting for a long time and the father continued with the night shift on a more permanent basis. The father's role in the beginning could also lead to a more permanent pattern of the father's primacy during the night, as one father described:

> Yeah, most of the time, it's me that takes care of him [the second child] and it's OK, yeah. Because I think I'm a light sleeper, … Sometimes when our second child came, there were some complications, so I started off that way … Because the first child came by Caesarean section, so the mother was bedridden most of the time. So, I started taking that responsibility from the beginning of our parenthood. So, it has always been like that. (Father 35 years old, children one year, eight months and 4.5 years old, working full time)

In this description, the mother's health issues and the father's personal qualities – being a light sleeper – were described as creating the division of care where the father was taking most of the responsibility during the night. As the father had learned how to care for an infant and was accustomed to taking the night shift, the father's care continued to be important when the second child was born.

Mothers could also describe themselves as heavy sleepers who do not wake up easily or are just too exhausted, leading to the father being the night-time caregiver. Thus, it was not just fathers who were heavy sleepers – it could be the reverse, as revealed by one mother's details of her family's childcare arrangement:

> I suppose more equal division of care would be better, but I have to deal with my exhaustion first of all. Although if I wake up and get out of bed before my husband does, then surely, I do it, take care of the child, but I simply do not wake up [laughs]. (Mother 39 years old, children three and 11 years old, working full time)

The mother's health as the reason for the father's primacy in night-time care was also described in the following example, wherein the father (33 years old, child one year, six months old, four older children 5–18 years old, on childcare leave and studying) narrated himself as more capable of responding to the child's needs at night due to the mother's impaired eyesight: 'it is a lot easier for me to care for the small baby at night, as there is need to bend down and see in the dark what one is doing and all this … we have ended up with this arrangement after trial and error'. Also, in this extract, it is clear how families might try different roles and divisions of care tasks, and the father's care role is a result of a longer process of repetition and learning.

However, in many cases, the father's role in night-time care was described as increasing in importance when the child became a bit older and was less dependent on breastfeeding and thus the mother's body. Often weaning and calming down the child at night required effort and the conscious decision to shift the responsibility for nights to the father. When the baby no longer has a 'biological need' for breastmilk at night, families could start weaning at night. This could be done through 'sleep training', the aim of which is for the baby to learn to sleep through the night without waking up to be fed. In this process, the father's role in many families was described as essential as the baby is thought to respond to the mother's body and the smell of milk and wanting to breastfeed in order to continue sleeping. Thus, the role of the father was to take up the night-time care with the aim of soothing the child back to sleep without milk. One of the mothers described this situation: 'We ended breastfeeding during the night with the help of sleep training, and that was quite textbook-like, as the father was taking care of the nights and I was able to sleep at night on the living room couch' (Mother 33 years old, children two and five years old, working full time).

In this quote, the mother's description of the 'textbook-like' implementation of sleep training refers to sleep training guides with instructions drafted by healthcare professionals to support new sleeping routines and habits. Thus, along with biological and individual repertoires, parents also drew on institutional repertoires when accounting for the father's growing role during the night shift. Many of these highlight the father's role in weaning and teaching the baby or infant to sleep throughout the night. Sleep training, especially if successful, was described by several mothers as a relief, giving them a culturally and socially acceptable and institutionally supported possibility of sleeping in a separate room or at a hotel without interruptions.

Work-related interpretative repertoires, such as the mother's return to work from leave, were also used to account for the father's increasing role during the night. It could be coupled with sleep training and weaning or it could happen later when the child was a little older. When the mother was returning to work, she was described as needing more rest and sleep than when she was on leave taking care of the child (or children). If both parents were working, it was perceived to equalise the situation at home and lead to new negotiations and practices about how to share childcare at night. Sometimes, it was described as happening effortlessly after the child was weaning: 'It has become more equal as I returned to work. Also, because I ended breastfeeding when the child was a year and a month old. It has calmed down the nights, and the father is taking more responsibility for the nights now' (Mother 35 years old, child one year old, working full time).

Working outside the home might also mean that the mother works nights or travels for work and goes on overnight work trips, which shifts the responsibility to the father. The father's role in night-time care could also be supported institutionally via the father's parental leave. The father's take-up of parental leave could coincide with the mother's return to work, and thus it has the potential to reverse the night-time care role, which was discussed by an interviewed mother:

> I returned to work, well, and we split the parental leave so the father was at home with the child when the child was 6 months old and they bonded so that I, as a mother, wasn't good for anything, I wasn't the child's favourite anymore [laughs]. (Mother 39 years old, children three and 11 years old, working full time)

Spending time with the child with the support of parental leave could create new patterns of night-time care in the family, making room for more caring fatherhood.

Taking night shifts: practices for sharing night-time care

Many families also created their own patterns of sharing night-time care from the early days of parenthood, thereby enabling both parents to take on the childcare responsibilities. When accounting for their sharing practices, the parents used similar interpretative repertoires referring to biology, individual/situational and work-related reasons. However, we could not find institutional factors employed to account for why the parents were sharing tasks.

Chronobiological rhythms were described as influencing many parents' practices related to sharing childcare at night. In these cases, biological repertoires were interwoven with repertoires also referring to individual and personal qualities. In other words, parents would adjust the care according to their own chronotypes and sleep cycles that were perceived as natural. For instance, if the father liked to stay up late, he would care for the baby's needs late in the evening and the mother could sleep without interruptions and then wake up early with the baby. According to one mother:

> As my husband is a night owl, he could stay up with the baby in the late evening and take care of part of the night shift while I was sleeping heavily between 10 pm and 3 am ... Early mornings were clearly my shifts then since for my husband, the mornings were so difficult. (Mother 36 years old, child three years old, working part time)

Chronotypes could also be reversed in the couples, with the mother being the night owl and the father an early riser. In these cases, the care was then divided accordingly. Taking turns waking up early in the morning could also be a practice that enabled each parent to sleep later on the weekend: 'Nowadays, what we do is that one gets to sleep later on Saturdays and the other on Sundays; that also has become a kind of unwritten rule' (Mother 31 years old, child five years old, working full time).

These descriptions of taking turns were also common for evening routines, with fathers taking responsibility for putting the child (or children) to bed. The children became accustomed to these practices so that they were described as knowing 'it's mom's or dad's turn to read the bedtime story' (mother 43 years old, children four and eight years old, working full time). These sharing practices were sometimes narrated to include taking turns with other household tasks – for example, one parent was cleaning the kitchen while the other was taking care of the children's evening routine.

Parents also described taking turns in caring for the baby if they noticed the other parent appeared too tired. This was described as a way of supporting each other, especially in the challenging and strenuous situations and phases involving babies and toddlers. Also, parents whose baby had suffered colic detailed taking turns holding and rocking the crying and restless baby throughout the night. One father described evenings when the infant had trouble falling and staying asleep. In such a case, the parents could take turns soothing the child:

> Before, it was a very big issue between us, who does it, puts the baby to sleep each night, and if it was difficult, we switched every half hour between us, who was the parent who was rocking the child, getting through this strenuous situation. And even in the middle of night, we could switch, so that each of us could get a couple of hours of proper sleep a night. (Father 47 years old, child one year, eight months old, working full time)

Additionally, older children were described as having phases when they slept poorly, were ill, were afraid of the dark or had restless nights. Parents talked about figuring out varying solutions to these situations; some, for instance, took turns sleeping by the child's bed, providing the other parent – both mothers and fathers – with the chance to sleep in another room.

According to the participants, another common arrangement in families was dividing the responsibility of night-time care for each child. The mother could be taking care of the baby (for example, because of the breastfeeding) while the father took care of the older children's needs during the evenings and nights. In blended families, it was often the biological parent who took more responsibility for the care of their biological child (or children).

The father's role of waking up early with the child and providing the mother with the chance to sleep a little longer in the morning was described in many interviews. His role was connected to work-related interpretative repertoires in which working fathers were described as spending time with their child (or children) before going to work in the morning. Working from home gave fathers even better possibilities for this morning childcare shift (and mothers to sleep). Some parents also talked about how fathers working shifts had days off during the week and could then take care of the child on those days, providing the mother with an opportunity for rest.

Some couples divided household and care tasks so that the mother would be mainly providing childcare at night and the father was in charge of other household tasks, such as grocery shopping, evening and morning routines, taking children to daycare and school or all cognitive labour in the family. These shared practices were perceived to be relatively fair as each type of responsibility was strenuous in its own way.

Conclusions

In this chapter, we examined the interpretative repertoires Finnish fathers and mothers use to account for the father's role in night-time care. As a result, barriers, enablers and shared childcare practices constructed on biological, individual/situational, work-related and institutional repertoires were identified. As no prior study to date has examined the topic, this study contributes novel information on Finnish fathers' care outside normal waking hours. In addition, the study has yielded valuable insights into not only fathers' but also mothers' experiences and perceptions of fathers' care.

The study was conducted in Finland, a Nordic dual-earner welfare state with a long history of supporting shared parenting, in which fathers are encouraged to take responsibility for childcare from the onset of parenthood and cultural expectations emphasise involved fatherhood (for example, Eerola et al, 2015; Lammi-Taskula, 2017). Finnish fathers identify themselves as oriented towards being caring and nurturing (see Eerola, 2015), which was also evident in the accounts of the fathers interviewed for this study. However, the division of caregiving between Finnish parents is not equal (see, for example, Ylikännö et al, 2015; Eerola et al, 2021), and this gendered division of care recurs in parents' accounts of who is responsible for childcare during the late evening, night and early morning.

The reasons produced by the parents, whether related to barriers, enablers or negotiated practices, are inevitably intertwined with cultural ideals of parenthood and care. In the interviews, these cultural ideals are echoed, reiterated and constantly present. In other words, while enablers of the father's care and negotiated practices reflect how cultural ideals of fatherhood have become care- and nurture-oriented (Eerola, 2015), parents' accounts of barriers to the father's care mirror more gendered aspects of childcare, highlighting the notions of the mother's primacy and intensive mothering. (Eerola et al, 2021). Thus, the results demonstrate how in Finnish society, different gendered practices of night-time childcare between fathers and mothers coexist and are experienced as relatively culturally acceptable.

Although our analyses reveal that fathers provide night-time care in many different ways, the results suggest that in many families, mothers are still the primary carers for their child (or children), be it day or night, as implied in earlier studies (Craig, 2006; Maume et al, 2010; Rose et al, 2014; Ralph, 2016; Plage et al, 2016; Miller, 2017; Rupanner et al, 2021). We cannot conclude whether night-time care was, for example, more equally shared in families in which the mother did not breastfeed, but it appears that in many parents' accounts, the role of fathers in night-time care increases as the child grows. On the basis of previous research (for example, Plage at el, 2016; Rupanner et al, 2021), there are grounds to ask whether the night-time shift has a division of household labour similar to that at other times of the day or whether it is a zone wherein the responsibilities are shared and negotiated (and justified) differently. Our analysis also provides indications that among families, temporal changes in night-time care may occur, but to explore this systematically, a different methodological approach would have been needed. A direct answer cannot be obtained from the data of this study, but it does suggest that in the Finnish context, there is also good reason to suppose that ideals and expectations related to the father's daytime care and nurture-oriented fatherhood and shared parenting practices are stronger than for their night-time childcare.

This chapter provides new insights into the role of fathers in night-time care and how parents understand and justify barriers and enablers related to fathers' care. It also makes a novel contribution to a body of research on gendered parental care by shedding more light on the negotiations on and practices of sharing night-time care in families with young children. The results of the study are policy-relevant and can be utilised by, among others, policy makers and practitioners working with parents, for example, at maternity and child welfare clinics. We did not investigate the consequences of the night shift on the parents' perceptions of the quality of family life or spousal relationships, but our results signal the need for more such studies delving into parental wellbeing.

Nevertheless, the night shift can be argued to have effects on the wellbeing of parents, especially because care at night is not only required in infancy but can also extend over a long time period, and patterns of care may become permanent during those years. Hence, the results extend our understanding of the father's role and responsibilities during the night, which covers approximately one third of a 24-hour day, including increasing our knowledge of caring and sharing fatherhood and how it is enabled.

Acknowledgements

The authors wish to thank PhD candidates Erika Grigorjew and Inka-Liisa Kuusiaho for conducting the analysed interviews alongside the first author of this chapter.

Funding

This research is part of the multidisciplinary research project 'The parental night shift: gendered inequalities in night-time care' (2022–2027), funded by the Kone Foundation.

References

Burgard, S. (2011). The Needs of Others: Gender and Sleep Interruptions for Caregivers. *Social Forces* 89(4), 1189–1216.

Coles, L., Thorpe, K., Smith, S., Hewitt, B., Ruppanner, L., Bayliss, O., O'Flaherty, M. and Staton, S. (2022). Children's Sleep and Fathers' Health and Wellbeing: A Systematic Review. *Sleep Medicine Reviews* 61, 101570.

Craig, L. (2006). Does Father Care Mean Fathers Share? A Comparison of How Mothers and Fathers in Intact Families Spend Time with Children. *Gender and Society* 20(2), 259–281.

Daminger, A. (2019). The cognitive dimension of household labor. *American Sociological Review* 84(4), 609–633.

Dement, W. (2000). *The Promise of Sleep: The Scientific Connection between Health, Happiness, and a Good Night's Sleep*. New York: Palgrave.

Dermott, E. (2008). *Intimate Fatherhood*. Abingdon: Routledge.

Eerola, P. (2015). *Responsible Fatherhood: A Narrative Approach*. Jyväskylä: Jyväskylä Studies in Education, Psychology and Social Research.

Eerola, P., Närvi, J., Terävä, J. and Repo, K. (2021). Negotiating Parenting Practices: The Arguments and Justifications of Finnish Couples. *Families, Relationships and Societies* 10(1), 119–135.

Eerola, P., Lammi-Taskula, J., O'Brien, M., Hietamäki, J. and Räikkönen. E. (2019). Fathers' Leave Take-up in Finland: Motivations and Barriers in a Complex Nordic Leave Scheme. *SAGE Open* 9(4), 1–14.

Eydal, G. B., Gislasson, I. V., Rostgaard, T., Brandth, B., Duvander, A.-Z. and Lammi-Taskula, J. (2015). Trends in Parental Leave in the Nordic Countries: Has the Forward March of Gender Equality Halted? *Community, Work & Family* 18(2), 167–181.

Faircloth, C. (2014). Intensive Parenting and the Expansion of Parenting. In E. Lee, J. Bristow, C. Faircloth and J. Macvarish (eds), *Parenting Culture Studies*. London: Palgrave Macmillan, pp 25–50.

Hislop, J. and Arber, S. (2003). Sleepers Wake! The Gendered Nature of Sleep Disruption among Mid-life Women. *Sociology* 37(4), 695–711.

Kelland, J., Lewis, D. and Fisher, V. (2022). Viewed with Suspicion, Considered Idle and Mocked: Working Caregiving Fathers and Fatherhood Forfeits. *Gender, Work & Organization* 29(59), 1578–1593.

Lammi-Taskula, J. (2017). Fathers on Leave Alone in Finland: Negotiations and Lived Experiences. In M. O'Brien and K. Wall (eds) *Comparative Perspectives on Work–Life Balance and Gender Equality: Fathers on Leave Alone*. London: Springer, pp 89–106.

Luyster F. S., Strollo P. J., Zee P. C. and Walsh J. K. (2012). Sleep: A Health Imperative. *Sleep* 35(6), 727–734.

Maume, D., Sebastian, R. and Bardo, A. (2010). Gender, Work–Family Responsibilities, and Sleep. *Gender & Society* 24(6), 746–768.

Medina, A. M., Lederhos, C. L. and Lillis, T. A. (2009). Sleep disruption and decline in marital satisfaction across the transition to parenthood. *Families, Systems, & Health* 27(2), 153–160.

Miller, T. (2017). *Making Sense of Parenthood: Caring, Gender and Family Lives*. Cambridge: Cambridge University Press.

Plage, S., Perales, F. and Baxter, J. (2016). Doing Gender Overnight? Parenthood, Gender and Sleep Quantity and Quality in Australia. *Family Matters* 97, 73–81.

Potter, J. and Wetherell, M. (1987). *Discourse and Social Psychology: Beyond Attitudes and Behaviour*. Thousand Oaks: Sage.

Ralph, D. (2016). 'Who Should Do the Caring'? Involved Fatherhood and Ambivalent Gendered Moral Rationalities among Cohabiting/Married Irish Parents. *Community, Work & Family* 19(1), 63–79.

Rauch, C. (2024). The social structures of sleep: effects of work-related and family constraints on sleep duration and regularity among French workers. *Sociological Research Online* 29(3), 729–749.

Richter, D., Kramer, M., Tang, N., Montgomery-Downs, H. and Lemola, S. (2019). Long-Term Effects of Pregnancy and Childbirth on Sleep Satisfaction and Duration of First-Time and Experienced Mothers and Fathers. *Sleep* 42(4), 1–10.

Rose, J., Brady, M., Yerkes, M. A. and Coles, L. (2014). 'Sometimes They Just Want to Cry for their Mum': Couples' Negotiations and Rationalisations of Gendered Divisions in Infant Care. *Journal of Family Studies* 21(1), 38–56.

Ruppanner, L., Maltby, B., Hewitt, B. and Maume, D. (2021). Parents' Sleep across Weekdays and Weekends: The Influence of Work, Housework, and Childcare Time. *Journal of Family Issues*. https://doi.org/10.1177/0192513X21101793

Venn, S., Arber, S., Meadows, R. and Hislop, J. (2008). The Fourth Shift: Exploring the Gendered Nature of Sleep Disruption among Couples with Children. *British Journal of Sociology* 59(1), 79–97.

Walzer, S. (1996). Thinking about the Baby: Gender and Divisions of Infant Care. *Social Problems* 43(2), 219–234.

Ylikännö, M., Pääkkönen, H. and Hakovirta, M. (2015). Time Use of Finnish Fathers: Do Institutions Matter? In G. B. Eydal and T. Rostgaard (eds) *Fatherhood in the Nordic Welfare States: Comparing Care Policies and Practice*. Bristol: Policy Press, pp 103–120.

9

What happens when fathers are at home? Learning from families' accounts of COVID-19 lockdown in the UK and South Africa

Katherine Twamley and Sadiyya Haffejee

Introduction

In March 2020 the United Nations (UN) declared a worldwide pandemic caused by the COVID-19 virus. Without any available cure or vaccine, the public health response initially focused on social distancing measures to control the spread of the virus. In many countries this resulted in prohibitions against travel and limitations on leaving one's home, as well as the closure of hospitality businesses, schools and other childcare institutions. As various scholars and commentators have noted, the closure of educational and childcare facilities led to children's care being 'reprivatised' to the family (Daly, 2021). This created extra labour for parents, but also the potential for a radical shift in how family life was organised. In particular, some scholars and activists saw the increased presence of men in the home as a potential stimulus towards less gendered divisions of care and a surging of caring masculinity (Barker et al, 2021; Wojnicka, 2022). However, time-use and survey studies suggested otherwise, showing that women continued to spend more time on childcare tasks and domestic work than men during and after lockdown periods (Sevilla and Smith, 2020; Obioma et al, 2023).

This chapter draws on data from the international consortium project 'Families and Community in the Time of COVID (FACT-COVID)'. FACT was a longitudinal qualitative study exploring the experiences of families with children during the peak of the COVID-19 pandemic across ten different countries (Twamley, Iqbal, and Faircloth, 2023). We focus here on South Africa and the UK as countries in the Global South and North with different sociocultural profiles that nonetheless experienced similar gendered impacts over the course of the pandemic. In this chapter we discuss the evolving interplay of fatherhood, family dynamics and policy frameworks, within a time of significant worldwide turmoil and policy transformation. We contextualise the 'pandemic moment' of lockdown within the embedded gendered dynamics of family life and consider how local policies exacerbated or challenged these dynamics. We argue that the pandemic functioned as a 'breaching experiment' (Scambler, 2020: 140) that can provide social scientists with a rare opportunity to examine day-to-day practices under new conditions of living. We show that despite fathers' extended time at home with children during lockdown periods, gendered divisions of labour were largely upheld, and consider the reasons for this continuity in two different social and cultural contexts.

Fathering, care and COVID-19

In both the UK and South Africa, there has been evidence of shifting discourses around what it means to be a father, with higher expectations around men's involvement in childcare emerging in the last twenty years (van den Berg and Makusha, 2018; Brannen et al, 2023). At the same time, 'breadwinning' or financial provisioning remains a central part of fatherhood for many men in both contexts (Le Roux and Lesch, 2023; Twamley, 2024), even when more and more mothers are in paid employment (Connolly et al, 2016; Sullivan, 2019). This is particularly acute in South Africa where female-headed households are the norm rather than an exception. In both countries this results in a high labour load for women, a 'second shift' of unpaid work after a working day, as well as contributing to gendered differences in employment progression (Costa Dias et al, 2020; Maharaj and Dunn, 2022).

The COVID-19 pandemic provoked two major changes to everyday family life in the UK and South Africa. First, with childcare institutions shut and the risks of being infected high, children and adults were mostly confined to their homes for long periods of time. Second, while some parents were able to work from home, many (particularly in South Africa) lost their jobs or were no longer able to receive a salary when their employers shut down (Spaull et al, 2021). Arguably the response to the second issue was addressed more forcefully than the first in both countries. In the UK a Coronavirus Job Retention Scheme – 'Furlough' – provided employers with a means to cover 80 per cent of employees' salaries while they were unable to work. Studies later showed that furlough intensified already-gendered differences in employment, with more women than men offered and taking furlough (Andrew et al, 2022). Those who were not eligible for employment or business-related support had recourse to 'Universal Credit' (UC), except those with limited residency rights. In South Africa, the Presidential Stimulus Package, valued at approximately R500 billion (£21.6 billion), was launched with the aim of alleviating poverty, increasing economic activities and strengthening the country's ability to manage the pandemic (Bhorat et al, 2021). In addition to augmenting health and essential services, a substantial portion of this budget was allocated to providing economic support via the unemployment insurance fund (UIF) and the temporary employer/employee relief scheme (TERS), providing financial relief to those not able to work and who were placed on temporary furlough or had their working hours reduced. As with the UK, women in South Africa suffered more job losses than men, constituting two thirds of the total, and their recovery was slower compared to men when the economy started to reopen (Parry and Gordon, 2021). As many more women are employed in the informal economy, they also did not benefit from the unemployment insurance fund or the COVID-19 Social Relief Distress (SRD) Grant at the same rate as men did (Spaull et al, 2021).

The shutting of childcare institutions resulted in high levels of care labour gaps; in their place, parents were expected to be able to take up the care for their children, often while juggling new modes of working from home. A time-use study found that in the first UK national lockdown, parents were doing childcare during nine hours of the day, and housework during three, often in addition to paid work hours (Andrew et al, 2022). Parents and children had to negotiate issues which were unproblematic or non-existent before the pandemic, while isolation and confinement to the home disrupted previously taken-for-granted family routines and rituals (Prime et al, 2020). These issues were magnified for families from disadvantaged backgrounds. For example, in some parts of rural South Africa, schoolchildren had no access to electricity or the internet to continue with their education after schools closed, leaving parents to step in as best they could (Dube, 2020). There was also increased 'COVID labour' associated with managing risk, which was shown to exacerbate already-existing inequalities, including those related to gender (Twamley, Faircloth and Iqbal, 2023a).

The radical shift in everyday parents' work and home lives during pandemic lockdowns provoked debates about the potential impact on gender inequalities. Some scholars and commentators suggested that the crisis presented a chance to accelerate progress towards gender equality through promoting and expanding men's roles in caregiving and household responsibilities (Barker et al, 2021; Wojnicka, 2022). Men's exposure to care – for example, through parental leave or unemployment – has been shown to shift their attitude to care and sometimes their later participation in care work (Chesley, 2011; Meil et al, 2023; Norman et al, 2023; Twamley, 2024). Since 'traditional' gender role attitudes are a key barrier to the take-up of extended leave by men, even in countries that rank high in gender equality overall (see, for example, the case of Finland in Saarikallio-Torp et al, Chapter 12 in this volume), bypassing the opt-in for fathers to be at home has the potential for widespread transformation.

However, previous evidence is mixed regarding the impact of fathers' increased presence in the home with their children (Meil et al, 2023;

Twamley, 2024). In terms of job loss, there is also evidence that when men become unemployed, women may take on *more* housework and emotion work to support men as they deal with their change in situation (Legerski and Cornwall, 2010). And when women lose their jobs, they may take on more household labour to 'make up' for their job loss (Damaske, 2021), while also experiencing pressure to 'enjoy' their newfound time to spend with their children (Rao, 2020). In terms of parental leave, the type of leave (whether at the same time as the mother or not) is also of key importance in provoking transformation in gendered care roles (Twamley, 2024).

Ultimately a whole host of empirical studies evidenced the endurance of gendered inequalities during the pandemic (Sevilla and Smith, 2020; Obioma et al, 2023; Wojnicka and Kubisa, 2024). Such findings were certainly borne out in findings from across the FACT-COVID study (Twamley, Iqbal and Faircloth, 2023). In this chapter, we examine the data from the UK and South Africa, illustrated through the experiences of one family in each country, and consider how factors in the two contexts and wider policy responses during the pandemic contributed to these outcomes.

The FACT-COVID study

The FACT-COVID study was conducted across ten different countries between 2020 and 2021. Each country had a principal investigator who led the data collection and analysis for their respective context, but the same research questions and design were implemented in each location. The overall findings of the project have been published elsewhere (Twamley, Iqbal and Faircloth, 2023). In this section, we outline the theoretical and methodological approach of the study, before detailing the particularities in sampling and methods applied in the UK and South Africa.

Across all ten country case studies, we aimed to uncover the challenges that families with children faced and their strategies for addressing them during the first year of the COVID-19 pandemic. The concept and design of the study were developed incorporating insights from two principal theoretical frameworks: the dynamics of families, relationality and personal life (Twamley et al, 2021), and the sociology of everyday life with a focus on family practices (Morgan, 2011). Relationality is also considered key in understanding gender (Connell, 2005), with motherhood and fatherhood understood as contingent upon and interrelated with ideas of femininity and masculinity (Mac an Ghaill and Haywood, 2007). With a focus on relationality, we draw on data from various family members in examining meanings, experiences and practices associated with fatherhood and care. To understand how these shifted over time in relation to changes in policy and public health outcomes and the circulation of the virus, we conducted a longitudinal study.

The two main forms of data collection were multimodal diaries and in-depth interviews. In all countries we sought to recruit families as locally understood. In practice, this often meant household members who were related to one another and lived together, but in some instances grandparents who lived apart also took part and/or household members not related (such as lodgers). The diaries consisted of regular prompts from researchers to participants about everyday life and the shifting situation. We asked participants about their daily lives, sources of and responses to information about the pandemic, and, pertinent to this chapter, care activities within and beyond the household. Some diary prompts were planned according to our research questions, while others were issued in response to specific events (such as a shift in national policy). These 'mobile methods' facilitated the collection of data in situ and increase the temporal closeness of self-reporting, as participants receive a 'text' each time a new diary prompt or question is uploaded (Boase and Humphreys, 2018). All data collection was conducted virtually/online. The different types of data (images, interviews, and diary entries) were transcribed and analysed using thematic analysis techniques (Braun and Clarke, 2006). Coding was both inductive and deductive, in that we applied theoretical codes from our literature review, while also generating new codes directly from the data. In examining gender and care, we developed codes from research around responsibilities in different forms of care, such as caring about, caring for, caregiving, care receiving and caring with (from Tronto [2013], as discussed in Doucet, Chapter 2 in this volume).

Data collection and recruitment in the UK

In the UK, data collection started in May 2020 and ended in June 2021. We recruited 38 families with children living in various parts of the UK through a short recruitment survey distributed via social media and outreach organisations. Not all families lived permanently within the same household, and we had some children and grandparents living across or in separate households. All family member participants are given the same pseudonym to make their connection clear. A total of 11 families reported a household income of over £90,000 per annum, 14 between £30,000 and £90,000, and 13 less than £30,000. These incomes are based on parents' estimations (therefore, grandparents who live separately are not included in this 'household' income). There were eight single mother households (no single fathers) in the UK sample. Most parents identified as heterosexual. There were an average of 1.7 children in each household at the beginning of the study (three babies were born over the course of the project). Only children aged 12 and over were invited to individually participate. Overall, we had 73 individuals participating: 13 young people, eight grandparents and 52 parents. A total of 18 of the 59 adults came from a visible minority ethnic background. Participants completed individual multimodal diaries and a final family level online interview in May/June 2021. For the diaries we used a data collection application (https://indeemo.com/) that facilitates entries via text, video and photos. Photos and videos are shared with permission from participants and images were blurred to protect anonymity, in line with guidance from our university ethics committees. More details on methods and ethical dilemmas of research during a pandemic can be read elsewhere (Faircloth et al, 2022).

Data collection and recruitment in South Africa

In South Africa, data collection began in June 2020 and concluded in March 2021. Participants were recruited via social media platforms, community WhatsApp groups, existing community networks and referrals from community-based partners. We collected digital diaries from 20 families and supplemented these with one-time telephonic interviews with an additional 21 individuals. In total, the study included 64 participants, comprising 16 children (11 girls and five boys) and 48 adults. The mean age of children was 14.1 years. The majority of participants (80 per cent) were Black South African. All participants resided in Gauteng Province. Most families had access to basic amenities, including water and electricity. Three families lived in informal housing, with only outside access to water and a toilet. Nearly a third of the adult participants were unemployed. Of those employed, approximately 50 per cent received a monthly wage, while the rest were self-employed or worked part-time or 'piece' jobs. We did not ask participants to disclose their household income. Education levels among participating adults ranged from high school-entry level to university level. All households identified as heterosexual.

For the diary entries, we used the WhatsApp messaging application. WhatsApp is more accessible and cost-effective in the South African context. Mobile data vouchers were provided to participants to facilitate their engagement in the study. Two additional check-in telephone calls were conducted at two-time points (December 2020 and March 2021). One-off in-depth interviews were conducted telephonically. The interview questionnaire used in the one-off interviews was aligned with the prompts used for the multimodal diaries. More details on the methods are published elsewhere (Haffejee et al, 2023).

Findings

For this chapter, we have selected the accounts of one family from each country case study. The families selected are illustrative of broader findings across the two project sites and were chosen due to the rich data from various family members. We focus on just one family in each site to better demonstrate the contextual and relational nature of their accounts, and the interplay between broader policies and everyday practice. Issues of validity and reliability feature in criticisms of case study research (Priya, 2021). We address this by avoiding generalising to the broader population (Yin, 2009), instead using this approach to illustrate findings from across the two studies and to look in more depth at the factors which shaped care practices during the pandemic.

The Smith family (UK)

The Smith family are composed of Smith Mum, Dad, Daughter (12 years old) and two other children aged ten and eight who did not individually participate in the study. They live in a small coastal city in England. At the onset of the COVID-19 pandemic, both parents were in paid work: Mum worked three days a week in a charity (paid work) and the other two days she was studying for a masters. Despite both ostensibly working full time, Smith Mum took primary responsibility for the house and children, as they described in their initial diary entries:

> I am a partner in a law firm at [city in England] and pre-lockdown I used to spend around 45–60 hours a week at the office. So, I don't have lot of time for much else, just coming home to see the family. A couple of days a week I would try to pick up the girls from an activity, they do Guides and that kind of thing, but I was really busy in the last year with work, so sometimes that was difficult, which is sad. (Smith Dad, diary entry May 2020)

> Before lockdown Smith Dad would take the kids to school once a week (sometimes more), he's almost always around in the mornings so we did have breakfast together. I did all the after school stuff, he often has to work late … I basically do almost everything in the week and we share it in the weekends. (Smith Mum, diary entry May 2020)

Smith Dad's long work hours frame their description of everyday life pre-pandemic, giving rise to a normative gendered split in care and domestic work.

With the onset of the pandemic, Smith Dad switched to working from home, which in other research has been posed as a potential mechanism through which men may become more involved in care work, particularly during the pandemic (Mallett et al, 2020). However, the Smith family gendered dynamic stayed much as it was, with more reported negative repercussions than positive:

I'm struggling with fewer boundaries meaning you're 'always on' as there isn't that natural break you get from physically leaving the office. Even though I will often work at home it feels worse at the moment! (Smith Dad, diary entry May 2020)

Now he [Smith Dad] is at home all the time it's almost worse because he doesn't need to be somewhere at a set time anymore … The kids are finding it weird that dad is at home but not available (he tries to have lunch/dinner with us but often misses lunch and sometimes dinner). Son was asking me all these questions about who would look after them if something happened to me – he'd worked out how he could help Daughter (8) with school work if I wasn't there – he didn't seem to register that Smith Dad would be there for him – it was a sad conversation to have. (Smith Mum, diary entry May 2020)

Smith Mum reflected that her husband is both present and not present, creating some confusions and tensions. She noted that her children do not view their father as someone who 'looks after' them. Indeed, Smith Daughter (12) expressed similar feelings in her final project interview:

Smith Daughter:	He just slept up in the loft and didn't come downstairs to stop, he just kept working.
Smith Mum:	He's always been like this. It's always been an ongoing battle between us.
Smith Daughter:	But working in the office he had to come home at some point, whereas he doesn't now.

Here we can say that Smith Dad does not apparently actively participate in much 'caregiving' (Tronto, 2013). The situation was further compounded by Smith Mum's furlough, meaning that she was not undertaking her job for the first six months of the pandemic, though still undertaking her (part-time) masters degree:

My job enabled me to be doing something for me and I paid for some childcare to enable this which I can't do now, but now all I do is look after the kids, do laundry and cook, clean – I'm getting more used to it and less resentful as time goes by. Smith Dad does hate the situation too but that doesn't mean anything ever changes. My job has always been less well paid and I've changed careers several times/had three children/work part time, etc so it has to be my role that is affected – not his. Which of course means I remain the less paid/lower-on career ladder person! Tricky how to change this – our lives have become how they are and ways of being become embedded.

Being furloughed has meant there really isn't any choice but if I hadn't been furloughed I would have reduced my hours right down anyway and Smith Dad would not have changed his. (Smith Mum, diary entry May 2020)

Smith Mum poses furlough as part of the accounting of how she is taking on the majority of the care and domestic work, but also recognises that their divisions were 'embedded' and that she would have taken furlough even if she had not been offered it. This is the important context which is often missing from other studies about gendered divisions of labour during the pandemic. Although lockdown was viewed by some as a moment with transformational potential, it needs to be contextualised within the established everyday practices of families. Women such as Smith Mum expect from a young age to experience future challenges in combining paid work and care (Patterson and Forbes, 2012) and may even choose career paths long before pregnancy that will enable the combination of care and paid work (Twamley, 2024). This further consolidates the gender pay gap (Chambraud et al, 2018) that encourages the lower-earning mother to take furlough. Although provisioning may be considered an aspect of 'care', it is a gendered responsibility more often associated with men, then further consolidated when the father earns more than the mother. Thus, the circumstances before and during the lockdown period are not conducive to change, as Smith Mum says that even when Smith Dad would like to see change, it 'doesn't mean anything ever changes'.

The accounts and pictures of everyday life from Smith family demonstrate how this pans out in a day-to-day basis. Smith Mum and Smith Daughter uploaded photos of various activities they are doing with one another and the other children, such as this one posted by Smith Mum (Figure 9.1).

Figure 9.1: Smith Mum, diary entry, June 2020

In her caption beside this photo, she noted the few men they see with other children out and about:

> Caption: Go on about a 4 km walk (me walking and the 3 kids on roller skates) delivering party bags round to 5 of Daughter (8) friends. We stop and have a quick chat from the roadside with each family. We see mainly mums, although one family we see a dad! (Smith Mum, June 2020)

Meanwhile, Smith Dad posted very few pictures, all of which reflected his absence in the family, such as the following (Figure 9.2).

Smith Mum reported struggles with this division of labour during lockdown:

> I am not someone [who] enjoys being at home and making a nice house, so I think I take that out from the kids sometimes; having no focus (since I have been furloughed) means I have lost my temper with them, lose my temper with them too much. (Smith Mum, Diary entry September 2020)

Indeed, other research noted the heightened stress and anxiety experienced by mothers during the pandemic as compared to men (Pierce et al, 2020). Later, Smith Mum returned to work, but reported this as an even more difficult time, as she struggled to accomplish her paid work while also taking all the responsibility for the house and children, when the schools were again closed.

Examining the ways in which care is narrated by Smith Mum and Dad, it's clear that Smith Mum is the primary carer in both literal and ideological

Figure 9.2: Smith Dad, diary entry, May 2020, with caption: 'Smith Mum takes lunch up to me when I don't have time to go downstairs'

ways. In the terms of Tronto (2013), she cares for and about the family and household, taking the responsibility for the needs of the children, and undertaking most of the caregiving, while also working to reduce her 'resentment' as time goes by. She often discussed in her diaries her worries and thoughts about her children, about how they were coping during the pandemic and how she was trying to address their needs:

> Daughter 3 (8 years old) has found everything hardest I think – I have moments where homeschooling is really hard. She finds learning harder than her siblings – and she gets very frustrated when she gets things wrong/makes mistakes … I've had the most rows with Daughter 3 and I feel awful about it because she's only little. (Smith Mum, diary entry June 2020)

Smith Dad participated less overall in the study, but when he did, his entries were dominated by references to his paid work. Articulations about 'care' more often arose in relation to a responsibility to his colleagues and employees. For example, in discussing his long work hours, he wrote: 'There is also the added pressure that knowing as a business – I am one of approximately 90 partners and we employ 700 people – we need to pull together to make the best of the economic situation' (Smith Dad, diary entry June 2020).

Although Smith Dad had always worked long hours, during the months of lockdown and its associated uncertainty, the sense of responsibility and need to work long hours was further bolstered. As such, it became 'logical' that Smith Mum would take on ever-increasing responsibilities for care and home, which in her final interview she reported had 'intensified' over the period of the study.

The Bheki family (South Africa)

The Bheki Family are composed of Mum, Dad and three children. Mum and Dad (both 34 years old) and their two older children (15 and 10 years old) participated in the study. The youngest child attends preschool, and the family resides in a small, low-income town on the outskirts of Johannesburg. Housing in the town comprises both government-subsidised housing and informal dwellings, with the Bheki family residing in one of these subsidised houses. The town has amenities like running water and sanitation, electricity, partially tarred roads, a primary and high school, a clinic, an early childhood development centre and churches.

Prior to the pandemic, Bheki Dad was employed full time as a construction worker, and Mum worked part time as an assistant in an early childhood development centre (ECD) while also training to become a nail technician. With the closure of all ECDs, Mum lost her job and Dad's company closed temporarily, forcing the family to rely on unemployment benefits. When he was able to work, conditions were challenging, with projects starting and stopping abruptly:

> Currently, regarding the COVID, it affected me so bad that we were stopped at work and before that my life was normal … So things turned when we were stopped due to lockdown … And in my company we started to have less projects and even now as I'm speaking they are busy with retrenchments. So it really affected me so bad. (Bheki Dad, diary entry July 2020)

The pandemic and the resultant lockdown had a devastating impact on employment and household food security in South Africa. Approximately 40 per cent of households reported losing their main source of income in the initial lockdown and 47 per cent reported that their household ran out of money to buy food by the second month of the pandemic (Wills et al, 2023). For the Bheki Family, the lack of income was a constant worry which framed their experiences of the pandemic:

> I have been not working, it has been very difficult to ensure everything needed in the house is available, especially when u have young kids who don't understand but anyway, the little I have been getting at work and the TERS/UIF has kept us surviving, our grocery has to change, yes when you are used to certain routine and food as a need so [it] is difficult to adjust to it, now because of the financial stress, I can't buy things I like. (Bheki Dad, diary entry August 2020)

Bheki Dad's anguish around their change in financial circumstances is palpable. He spoke of trying to ensure the family's basic needs were met, and characterised their family as 'surviving'. Other research showed an increase in depressive symptoms in those who lost employment during the pandemic (Oyenubi and Kollamparambil, 2020).

In other entries, he discusses how his children are adapting:

> I'm so glad and feel blessed to have an amazing family that is so understanding; even my last born surprised me. I promised to buy him a puppy and it was before lockdown started but he never put pressure on me, even though he would ask me 'dad, month end you are bringing the dog home?' and finally I got him one. They are a strong team and my strength. (Bheki Dad, diary entry October 2020)

His entries suggested that financial provisioning was his responsibility in the family and he was even surprised that his son was understanding about the challenges he faced in fulfilling it. He demonstrates that he cares for his children and family, but does not take responsibility for direct caregiving.

When discussing the division of tasks in the household since the lockdown, Bheki Dad noted that he doesn't get involved in housework:

> I don't have much with that [housework] because really like I was always indoors if I am home, make sure that I don't touch many things at home. Just sit at home, watch my TV and my series and that's it. So it was really bad because remember we as man we like to be handy, fixing things but then it was difficult at this current period for me because I wasn't doing anything. (Bheki Dad, diary entry July 2020)

At the onset of the pandemic, Bheki Dad stayed mainly indoors, as he wasn't working. While he was used to being hands-on around the house, he found himself restricted, only engaging in passive activities like watching TV. He preferred to involve himself with chores like household maintenance, but as many of the stores were closed and he did not have excess cash, he was not able to do any of this. He said:

> Getting bored, really, I am getting bored. I don't want to lie because I cannot stay at home 24 hours, 7 days a week doing nothing. I am one person who likes to do home chores, work and do all those things. So, I have to stay at home because working as well, it needs me to go buy stuff to come and fix the house or fix the car and all those things. So, I really get bored watching TV the whole day. So that's really bothering [me] a lot. (Bheki Dad, diary entry July 2020)

Bheki Dad clearly sticks to 'masculine' domestic tasks (Christopher, 2024), in which, as he explains, he can no longer partake. Images shared by the family reflect Bheki Dad's solitary activities: him driving to work, at a mall and watching television. Figure 9.3 was shared by Bheki Dad as an illustration of how he spent his time.

Although she was also earning prior to the pandemic, Bheki Mum did not express the same level of responsibility around provisioning in the household. The accounts show that she took responsibility for housework and childcare. Bheki Mum primarily engaged with the study via images. These demonstrate how on an everyday level, she was primarily engaged in housework, entertaining the children and visiting her sick mother. Bheki Mum's experience was different from that of the single mums in the study, who were primarily concerned with securing finances for the family.

In Figure 9.4 we see her sitting with her children around a gas stove (as there is no electricity) keeping warm and having supper, while in Figure 9.5,

Figure 9.3: Bheki Dad, diary entry, July 2020

Figure 9.4: Bheki Mum, diary entry, July 2020

Note: Bheki Mum added the text in the triangle '14/07/2020 Having supper around the heat no electricity with family'

she is seen entertaining one of the children. In both these instances, no mention is made of Bheki Dad.

In spite of the economic challenges faced by the family, the pandemic is not reported as having strained relationships in the family. Bheki Dad wrote that his relationship with his wife was good:

> We never had a time where we fought with my partner. Only, yes, stress was there because we couldn't do or we couldn't accumulate some of the things that we do on a monthly basis. So, that may have stressed

Figure 9.5: Bheki Mum, diary entry, July 2020

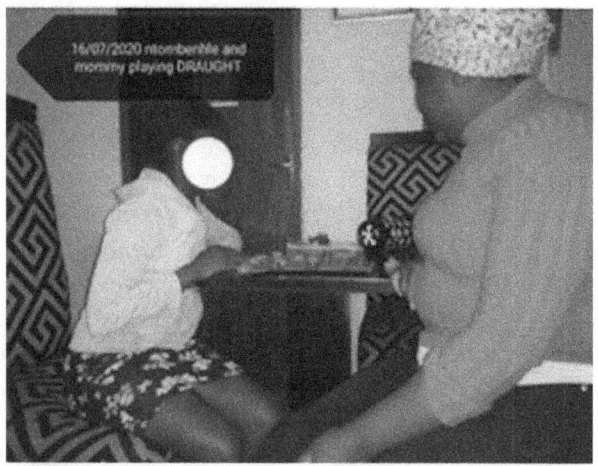

Note: Bheki Mum added the text in the black arrow '16/07/2020 Daughter and mommy playing draught'

us a bit, but everything was fine, also the kids were fine. (Bheki Dad, diary entry September 2020)

It is difficult to assess without an account from Bheki Mum, but data from other families suggest that women accepted gendered divisions of labour as the norm and did not attempt to shift practices during this time. Bheki Dad also spoke of the opportunities for connecting as a family that the lockdown afforded:

It gave us time to spend with our families because we are at home most of the time, we are at home 24/7. So, it gave us time to interact with our families, to know them better and spend time with them. So, in that case it's an advantage. (Bheki Dad, diary entry July 2020)

Nonetheless, the increased exposure and reported closer relationships were not enough to shift the gendered division of the labour in this family. Bheki Mum seems to have shouldered the burden of domestic labour, while Bheki Dad lamented his inability to financially provide for the house and to continue in previously male-typed tasks, such as fixing things around the house. This is consistent with other studies in South Africa, which show that even when co-resident, men may not necessarily take on the primary caregiving duties traditionally associated with mothers, although they may contribute to childcare in a supportive or secondary role (Hatch, 2024). In this family and others in South Africa, the pandemic appeared to be experienced as a moment out of time, one of survival and 'boredom', which must be endured before things can shift back to the way they were before.

Discussion and conclusion

This chapter gives a snapshot of two families' experiences at the height of the COVID-19 pandemic in the UK and South Africa respectively. We selected the families as illustrative of broader findings across the case studies. We focused on families with co-resident fathers, since nonresident fathers did not participate in the study. However, it was clear from single mothers' accounts that pandemic policies around social distancing exacerbated nonresident fathers' disengagement from their children (as discussed in Haffejee et al, 2023; Twamley et al, 2023b). In examining co-resident parent families, in this chapter we have explored how wider policies in response to the COVID-19 pandemic impacted gendered care and domestic work practices within the participant families. As with wider studies, we found limited shifts in gendered care practices and in fact more evidence that such divisions were further entrenched. In this section, we bring together the findings to unpack why this might be the case.

In both countries, women's employment were more negatively affected than men's during the pandemic (Andrew et al, 2022; Casale and Shepherd, 2022). These disparities meant that men were more often still engaged in work and/or receiving unemployment benefit than women. These circumstances reflect the gendered nature of the employment market, women's previous engagement in paid employment, and pandemic policy responses. However, in both the UK and South Africa, it was also clear that the meanings attributed to men's and women's earning were not the same. In both case studies, for example, the fathers felt and enacted financial provisioning as their responsibility. They spoke about earning as a form of care for their families (see also Tarrant, Chapter 10 in this volume) and, as in the case of Smith Dad, also for colleagues and employees. This was established before the pandemic and exacerbated during it by their partners' lack or lower income and the uncertainties surrounding their own work. In contrast, women's caring was discussed in relation to hands-on care work and housework.

On the other hand, the lockdown precipitated men's presence in the home in ways that had not been experienced previously. Fathers reported closer relationships with their families due to increased proximity, particularly in the case of Bheki father who worked fewer paid hours. However, this increased proximity did not provoke a shift in the division of care and domestic work undertaken by men and women. This was true across the samples in both countries and observed in other studies (Cameron et al, 2023; Wojnicka and Kubisa, 2024). That other responsibilities did not arise was particularly striking in the case of Bheki Dad, given his few paid work hours over the course of the study. His account highlights his attachment to gendered ideas of appropriate responsibilities and domestic work – he recounted being bored when he was unable to do 'DIY' work, but did not apparently assist his wife in other more 'feminine' domestic tasks (Christopher, 2024), such as cooking and cleaning. These findings reflect those uncovered in parental leave research, which shows that in order for truly transformative change to occur in gendered family practices, fathers need to spend time *alone* at home with their children (for example, Twamley, 2024). When mothers and fathers are on leave together, gendered responsibilities are more likely to be reinforced than challenged (Twamley, 2024). Moreover, parental leave typically occurs around the time of birth, a point in time when practices are more likely to be newly established with lasting consequences (Norman et al, 2023), suggesting less relevance for the participant families, none of whom was recruited at the transition to parenthood. It is also worth noting that studies on the impact of parents' unemployment show a more complex picture than those around parental leave. Indeed, a study comparing the impact of fathers' unemployment with parental leave take-up in Spain found that only parental leave resulted in men's long-term increased participation in care work (Meil et al, 2023). And, as noted in the introduction, women may in fact increase their care labour when their partners experience unemployment (Legerski and Cornwall, 2010). These studies point to the importance of the gendered context in which shifts in fathers' presence at home may occur. Together with our findings, we posit that the definition and social understanding of policies are relevant for their transformative potential. Parental leave is designed to encourage increased fathers' participation in care, whereas the various COVID-19 policies were primarily concerned with reducing the risk of infection while ensuring the continuation of the economy through employer support mechanisms. Indeed, the UK response was criticised for its failure to consider the gendered consequences of its various policies and public health messaging (Buchan, 2021).

In addition to these factors, we can see that in both families, various anxieties around the pandemic, both financial and relational, were expressed by parents. As reported in many studies, this was a time of heightened mental ill-health, stress and uncertainty (for example, Posel et al, 2021). During such times, it is unlikely that entrenched habits will be challenged; rather, individuals are more likely to continue with established practices in an effort to maintain a sense of personal and familial security (Smeets et al, 2019). While women expressed a sense of resignation around gendered divisions of labour in both studies (both within and beyond the cases discussed), they also expressed a sense that a pandemic was not a time to work on shifting such established family practises, but rather a time to 'get through'. Calarco et al (2021) gathered similar accounts from couples in the US. They argued that only where parents were committed to shifting gendered parenting norms did the pandemic offer an opportunity for change. We add that commitment from *both* partners is necessary, as well as other structural support mechanisms, in particular support for women's employment during times of crisis and a political response which centres care needs (as also argued by Zhang et al, Chapter 7 in this volume). We therefore see that policies, previous gender attitudes and practices around familial responsibilities and the experience of the pandemic all coincided to consolidate rather than challenge gendered divisions of care and domestic work in the UK and South Africa. This research, while conducted during the height of the COVID-19 pandemic, has relevance beyond that period. We have demonstrated that men's presence at home is not enough to shift gendered relations and that any policies which aim to improve gendered divisions of labour need to consider how those policies may interact with established gendered norms and attitudes relating to care.

References

Andrew, A., Cattan, S., Costa Dias, M., Farquharson, C., Kraftman, L., Krutikova, S., Phimister, A., and Sevilla, A. (2022). The gendered division of paid and domestic work under lockdown. *Fiscal Studies*, 43(4), 325–340.

Barker, G., Burrell, S., and Ruxton, S. (2021). COVID-19 and masculinities in global perspective: reflections from Promundo's research and activism. *Men and Masculinities*, 24(1), 168–174.

Bhorat, H., Oosthuizen, M. and Stanwix, B. (2021). Social assistance amidst the COVID-19 epidemic in South Africa: a policy assessment. *South African Journal of Economics*, 89(1), 63–81.

Boase, J. and Humphreys, L. (2018). *Mobile Methods: Explorations, Innovations, and Reflections*, vol. 6. London: Sage, pp 153–162.

Brannen, J., Faircloth, C., Jones, C., O'Brien, M. and Twamley, K. (2023). Change and continuity in men's fathering and employment practices: a slow gender revolution. In C. Cameron, A. Koslowski, A. Lamont and P. Moss (eds) *Social Research for Our Times: Thomas Coram Research Unit Past, Present and Future*. London: UCL.

Braun, V. and Clarke, V. (2006). Using thematic analysis in psychology. *Qualitative Research in Psychology*, 3(2), 77–101.

Buchan, L. (2021). Government 'stay at home' advert showing women doing chores pulled amid backlash. *The Mirror*, 20 January. https://www.mirror.co.uk/news/politics/breaking-government-stay-home-advert-23401319

Calarco, J. M., Meanwell, E., Anderson, E. M. and Knopf, A. S. (2021). By default: how mothers in different-sex dual-earner couples account for inequalities in pandemic parenting. *Socius*, 7, 23780231211038783. https://doi.org/10.1177/23780231211038783

Cameron, C., Hauari, H., Hollingworth, K., O'Brien, M. and Whitaker, L. (2023). Young children's lives in East London through the pandemic: relationships, activities and social worlds. *Children & Society*, 37(4), 1102–1118.

Casale, D. and Shepherd, D. (2022). The gendered effects of the COVID-19 crisis in South Africa: evidence from NIDS-CRAM waves 1–5. *Development Southern Africa*, *39*(5), 644–663.

Chambraud, C., Nagamootoo, N., Radcliffe, L., Schaefer, A., Nowak, V., Walne, S., Hardy, C. and Mokhtar, D. (2018). Equal lives: parenthood and caring in the workplace. *Business in the Community*. https://www.bitc.org.uk/report/equal-lives-parenthood-and-caring-in-the-workplace/

Chesley, N. (2011). Stay-at-home fathers and breadwinning mothers: gender, couple dynamics, and social change. *Gender & Society*, *25*(5), 642–664.

Christopher, E. (2024). 'It's a man's job': doing gender and male gatekeeping in the division of household labor. *Journal of Family Issues*, *45*(11), 2851–2874.

Connell, R. W. (2005). *Masculinities*. 2nd edn. Berkeley, CA: University of California Press.

Connolly, S., Aldrich, M., O'Brien, M., Speight, S. and Poole, E. (2016). Britain's slow movement to a gender egalitarian equilibrium: parents and employment in the UK 2001–13. *Work, Employment and Society*, *30*(5), 838–857.

Costa Dias, M., Joyce, R. and Parodi, F. (2020). The gender pay gap in the UK: children and experience in work. *Oxford Review of Economic Policy*, *36*(4), 855–881.

Daly, M. (2021). The concept of care: insights, challenges and research avenues in COVID-19 times. *Journal of European Social Policy*, *31*(1), 108–118.

Damaske, S. (2021). *The Tolls of Uncertainty: How Privilege and the Guilt Gap Shape Unemployment in America*. Princeton: Princeton University Press.

Dube, B. (2020). Rural online learning in the context of COVID-19 in South Africa: evoking an inclusive education approach. *Multidisciplinary Journal of Educational Research*, 10(2), 135–157.

Faircloth, C., Twamley, K. and Iqbal, H. (2022). 'Er, not the best time': methodological and ethical challenges of researching family life during a pandemic. *Families, Relationships and Societies*, *11*(1), 39–43.

Haffejee, S., Mwanda, A. and Simelane, T. (2023). South Africa: COVID-19 and family well-being. In K. Twamley, H. Iqbal and C. Faircloth (eds) *Family Life in the Time of COVID: International Perspectives*. London: UCL Press, pp 147–172.

Hatch, M. (2024). An unbalancing act: gender and parental division in childcare in South Africa. *Families, Relationships and Societies*, *13*(1), 86–104.

Le Roux, M. and Lesch, E. (2023). Exploring the caring of fathers in low-income, rural communities in South Africa. *Journal of Family Studies*, *29*(3), 1198–1221.

Legerski, E. M. and Cornwall, M. (2010). Working-class job loss, gender, and the negotiation of household labor. *Gender & Society*, *24*(4), 447–474.

Mac an Ghaill, M. and C. Haywood. (2007). *Gender, Culture and Society: Contemporary Femininities and Masculinities.* London: Palgrave Macmillan.

Maharaj, P. and Dunn, S. (2022). 'It's not easy being a mom especially when you are unemployed': navigating childcare, a necessary social service in South Africa. *Journal of Social Service Research*, 48(4), 472–484.

Mallett, O., Marks, A. and Skountridaki, L. (2020). Where does work belong anymore? The implications of intensive homebased working. *Gender in Management: An International Journal*, 35(7/8), 657–665.

Meil, G., Rogero-García, J., Romero-Balsas, P. and Díaz-Gandasegui, V. (2023). The impact of paternity leave compared to unemployment on child care and housework distribution in Spain. *Journal of Family Issues*, 44(3), 633–653.

Morgan, D. (2011). *Rethinking Family Practices.* Dordrecht: Springer.

Norman, H., Elliot, M. and Vanchugova, D. (2023). How important is early paternal engagement? Deriving longitudinal measures of fathers' childcare engagement and exploring structural relationships with prior engagement and employment hours. *Journal of Family Issues*, 0192513X231214642.

Obioma, I. F., Jaga, A., Raina, M., Asekun, W. A. and Hernandez Bark, A. S. (2023). Gendered share of housework and the COVID-19 pandemic: examining self-ratings and speculation of others in Germany, India, Nigeria, and South Africa. *Journal of Social Issues*, 79(3), 907–934.

Oyenubi, A. and Kollamparambil, U. (2020). COVID-19 and depressive symptoms in South Africa. In National Income Dynamics Study (NIDS) – Coronavirus Rapid Mobile Survey (CRAM), Wave 2. Cape Town: Southern Africa Labour and Development Research Unit (SALDRU), University of Cape Town.

Parry, B. R. and Gordon, E. (2021). The shadow pandemic: inequitable gendered impacts of COVID-19 in South Africa. *Gender, Work and Organization*, 28(2), 795–806. https://doi.org/10.1111/gwao.12565

Patterson, L. and Forbes, K. (2012). 'Doing gender' in the imagined futures of young New Zealanders. *Young*, 20(2), 119–136.

Pierce, M., Hope, H., Ford, T., Hatch, S., Hotopf, M., John, A., Kontopantelis, E., Webb, R., Wessely, S. and McManus, S. (2020). Mental health before and during the COVID-19 pandemic: a longitudinal probability sample survey of the UK population. *The Lancet Psychiatry*, 7(10), 883–892.

Posel, D., Oyenubi, A. and Kollamparambil, U. (2021). Job loss and mental health during the COVID-19 lockdown: evidence from South Africa. *PloS one*, 16(3), e0249352.

Prime, H., Wade, M., and Browne, D. T. (2020). Risk and resilience in family well-being during the COVID-19 pandemic. *American Psychologist*, 75(5), 631–643.

Priya, A. (2021). Case study methodology of qualitative research: key attributes and navigating the conundrums in its application. *Sociological Bulletin*, *70*(1), 94–110.

Rao, A. H. (2020). *Crunch Time: How Married Couples Confront Unemployment*. Berkeley: University of California Press.

Scambler, G. (2020) Covid-19 as a 'breaching experiment': exposing the fractured society. *Health Sociology Review*, *29*(2), 140–148.

Sevilla, A. and Smith, S. (2020). Baby steps: the gender division of childcare during the COVID-19 pandemic. *Oxford Review of Economic Policy*, *36*(Supplement 1), S169–S186.

Smeets, T., van Ruitenbeek, P., Hartogsveld, B. and Quaedflieg, C. W. (2019). Stress-induced reliance on habitual behavior is moderated by cortisol reactivity. *Brain and Cognition*, *133*, 60–71.

Spaull, N., Daniels, R. C., Ardington, C., Bassier, I., Benhura, M., Bridgman, G. and Zizzamia, R. (2021). Synthesis Report: NIDS-CRAM Wave 3. https://cramsurvey.org/wp-content/uploads/2021/02/1.-Spaull-N.-Daniels-R.-C-et-al.-2021-NIDS-CRAM-Wave-3-Synthesis-Report.pdf

Sullivan, O. (2019). Gender inequality in work-family balance. *Nature Human Behaviour*, *3*(3), 201–203.

Tronto, J. C. (2013) *Caring Democracy: Markets, Equality, and Justice*. New York: New York University Press.

Twamley, K. (2024). *Caring Is Sharing? Couples Navigating Parental Leave at the Transition to Parenthood*. London: UCL Press.

Twamley, K., Doucet, A. and Schmidt, E.-M. (2021). Introduction to special issue: relationality in family and intimate practices. *Families, Relationships and Societies*, *10*(1), 3–10.

Twamley, K., Faircloth, C. and Iqbal, H. (2023a). COVID-19 labour: Making a 'livable' life under lockdown. *Sociological Review*, *71*(1), 85–104.

Twamley, K., Faircloth, C. and Iqbal, H. (2023b). United Kingdom: inclusions and exclusions in personal life during the COVID-19 pandemic. In K. Twamley, H. Iqbal, and C. Faircloth (eds) *Family Life in the Time of COVID: International Perspectives*. London: UCL Press, 223–248.

Twamley, K., Iqbal, H. and Faircloth, C. (2023). *Family Life in the Time of COVID: International Perspectives*. London: UCL Press.

van den Berg, W. and Makusha, T. (2018). *State of South Africa's Fathers 2018*. Cape Town: Sonke Gender Justice & Human Sciences Research Council.

Wills, G., van der Berg, S., and Mpeta, B. (2023). Household resource flows and food poverty during South Africa's lockdown: short-term policy implications for three channels of social protection. https://papers.ssrn.com/sol3/papers.cfm?abstract_id=4331504

Wojnicka, K. (2022). What's masculinity got to do with it? The COVID-19 pandemic, men and care. *European Journal of Women's Studies*, *29*(1), 27S–42S.

Wojnicka, K. and Kubisa, J. (2024). The COVID-19 pandemic and caring masculinity: new prospects or a wasted opportunity? *Gender, Work and Organisation*, *31*, 1723–1737.

Yin, R. K. (2009). *Case Study Research: Design and Methods*, vol. 5. London: Sage.

10

'Being there' as providers and caregivers: caring masculinities in parenting and partnering among young fathers in the UK

Anna Tarrant, Linzi Ladlow and Laura Way

Introduction

This chapter presents analyses from a qualitative longitudinal study called 'Following Young Fathers Further' (FYFF, grant ref: MR/S031723/1) to explore how young fathers in the UK narrate their experiences and understanding of fathering, fatherhood and co-parenting in the context of recent cultural and generational shifts towards engaged fatherhood. Aged 25 and under when they conceive a first pregnancy or become a parent for the first time, these young men's experiences of fatherhood are often assumed to be problematic and therefore subject to stigma. The prevailing and problematic view that they are absent, feckless, irresponsible and, indeed, uncaring (Tarrant, 2021) sustains assumptions that young fathers lack commitment to their children, their partners and/or co-parents, and are more likely to uphold traditional gendered commitments and values that stall progress towards gender equality among parents, as well as parenting equity (see Neale, 2016; Neale and Tarrant, 2024).

Seeking to interrogate and counter the persistence of such pervasive views through an analysis of evidence generated from a qualitative longitudinal study of young fathers, we argue that commitments towards 'caring masculinities' (Eliott, 2016) are in evidence among this diverse cohort of otherwise marginalised young fathers. These are expressed through narratives of their sustained participation in their children's lives and development and their understanding of the necessity of establishing patterns of effective co-parenting over time. However, despite foregrounding self-representations as caring fathers (see also Doucet, Chapter 2, this volume), young fathers also express tensions between 'being there' for their children as engaged fathers and financial providers, which are often heightened for those in more challenging socioeconomic, co-parenting and caregiving circumstances. These tensions reflect the uneven dynamics of change and continuity in gendered relations in the context of the rapid socioeconomic and welfare changes characterising the past decade, which require a more nuanced explanation of the gradual and uneven realisation of engaged fatherhood and transformations in male identities among diverse cohorts of men as-fathers.

Elaborating a framework of *socially engaged fatherhood* that aims to account for, and explain, the challenges of young fatherhood as well as its emancipatory potential, we present analyses of a core feature of these young men's narratives of parenting and partnering – namely, how they seek to reconcile and realise both their own and societal expectations of 'good' fatherhood (see also Ivanova, Chapter 5, and Żadkowska et al, Chapter 6, this volume). Conceptualising their parenting and partnering practices over time as caring masculinities, we consider the extent to which this cohort of fathers' caring practices and ideologies align or diverge and explore the conditions that support and/or constrain them in their intentions to 'be there' for their children as 'caring fathers'. We find that the potentials of caring masculinities, while in evidence, are achieved over time as part of a dynamic, transitory process, shaped by the intersections of societal perceptions of parenting at a young age (and associated expectations around fertility decisions and timings), interpersonal resources and co-parenting relationships, and socioeconomic barriers and welfare conditions.

Towards a socially engaged model of young fatherhood

We begin with a brief overview of the existing research about young fathers to account for the theoretical frameworks that have shaped the existing evidence base and produced alternative understandings of their lives and experiences. In doing so, we argue for the emergence of a socially engaged young fatherhood (Neale and Tarrant, 2024) that incorporates the caring and nurturing aspects of involved fatherhood, albeit contextualised by the wider systemic processes that either support or undermine young men's enactment of caring masculinities in their relationships with their children and co-parents.

Since young fathers first began to receive empirical attention, predominantly in the UK and the US, different frameworks have developed that reflect and reproduce particular constructions, and therefore views, of young fatherhood (Neale and Tarrant, 2024). These are the orthodox, yet problematic 'social problems' framework, that developed from the 1980s onwards in association with wider social and political concerns about teenage pregnancy, and the more recent 'social engagement' framework that has been informed by more sophisticated and even optimistic theories, including involved fatherhood and caring masculinities (Neale and Tarrant, 2024).

Early young fatherhood scholarship was situated within wider academic, practice and policy concern about teenage parents. An accompanying 'social problems' perspective emerged that prioritised attention to the antecedent risk factors that may result in teenage or early parenthood. Predominantly based on the studies of young vulnerable fathers, a risk profile was identified that explained the prevalence of teenage parenting among this cohort, as well as the continued impacts of these upon their parenting efforts. These include: biographies of socioeconomic disadvantage; complex childhood histories featuring incidence of parental separation and divorce, neglect or abuse and/or upbringing in small, fragmented family networks; regular house moves and insecure housing trajectories; care or criminal justice experiences; and/or street and neighbourhood violence (for a fuller review, see Glikman, 2004; Lemay et al, 2010; Berger and Langton, 2011; Lewin et al, 2015; Pirog et al, 2018; SmithBattle et al, 2019; Neale and Tarrant, 2024; Kiselica, forthcoming). Having entered parenthood, young fathers often report disrupted education and employment trajectories, acute financial pressures, issues securing housing and continued dependency on (grand) parents or other family members. Where such challenges reflect the wider exosystem (Deslauriers and Kiselica, 2022) or 'shaky ground' (SmithBattle et al, 2019) through which young fathers seek to establish their identities as parents, they may also inadvertently support deficit perspectives of these young men, and discourses that portray them as 'absent, criminal, violent and socially excluded' (Johannson and Hammarén, 2014: 367).

A more nuanced set of findings, largely based on qualitative evidence generated with young fathers themselves, has been defined elsewhere as the 'social engagement' framework (Neale and Tarrant, 2024). This framing, to which our own analyses here most strongly align, simultaneously captures the antecedent challenges and risks associated with young fatherhood, alongside the capacity of young fathers to care for and sustain engagements with their children and co-parents, often in spite of other difficulties (Neale, 2016; Neale and Davies, 2016). While young fathers navigate a unique and complex set of challenges when they transition to parenthood at an early age, they also report a socially engaged fatherhood. This constitutes a process of adjustment to fatherhood, and a transition to seeing fatherhood as an accomplishment, a source of pride and responsibility, and an opportunity to give and receive love (Arai, 2009; Ayoola et al, 2010; Elkington, 2017; SmithBattle et al, 2019). In this framework, the transition to fatherhood is identified as a reason for young men to reject earlier riskier behaviours in favour of deriving new meaning and purpose through fatherhood (Buston et al, 2012). In sum, young fatherhood is reframed as a potential opportunity for change for young men rather than a catastrophe (Duncan, 2007).

'Being there', father involvement and caring masculinities

The idea of 'being there', strongly accords with the social engagement framework. Indeed, explanations about how young fathers' identities and practices may transition through parenthood can be explained by increasingly sophisticated theoretical frameworks that capture men's growing commitment to, and participation in, family life and caregiving. The relatively recent and evolving international body of research that has been conducted with young fathers offers compelling evidence that despite the many systemic challenges they have to navigate, young fathers remain committed to their children and express a distinct desire to 'be there' for them (Neale and Tarrant, 2024). According to Randles (2020), 'being there' has become the prevailing script of responsible fatherhood and one that has an amorphous quality that is both mouldable and reflects capacity for change among men. The 'social engagement' framing of young fatherhood has therefore developed in parallel with a broader pattern of increasingly evidenced involvement of men in the nurturing and intimate aspects of fatherhood, theorised as involved or engaged fatherhood (for example, Dermott, 2008; Miller, 2010). Models of engaged fatherhood, which can encompass caring masculinities, are increasingly considered as catalysts for progress towards gender equality among couples, as men engage more in shared parenting to balance wage earning.

How far this ethos of engaged fatherhood, and what Boyer et al (2017) describe as a process of 're-gendering of care', is accepted and even realised among contemporary fathers, and is shaping their family practices is less understood and remains firmly at the centre of sustained academic interest and debate (for example, Dermott, 2008; Dermott and Miller, 2015; Tarrant, 2021). In 2012, Dowd, for example, argued that a recalibration towards equality among parents has not yet fully taken place, an argument to which recent data about father involvement and men's caregiving also attests, despite some gains (State of the World's Fathers, 2023). Women continue to do both paid work, as well as a 'second shift' (Hochschild, 1989) involving care for family and domestic labour. They also carry a mental load, which has been described as an 'invisible shift' (Occhiuto, 2021); a form of emotional labour that permeates nearly all aspects of an individual's life (Delaney et al 2023). Certainly, lack of supportive family policies combined with discrimination, both in terms of enabling women to work and men to parent, have been posited as explanations for the stall in the equality revolution (Dowd, 2012). Moreover, 'understanding of the factors, motivations, and institutions that facilitate and constrain this nascent "regendering of care" phenomenon amongst a growing number of men – in the context of stubborn gender inequalities of household care – remains partial' (Boyer et al 2017: 56).

More recent international studies of young fathers have begun to move away from the 'social problems' framing that has been applied to so many studies of teenage and young parenthood in favour of attention to how and to what extent young fathers align with the values of and embody caring masculinities (for example, Enderstein and Boonzaeir, 2015; Bhana and

Nkani, 2014; Johannson and Hammarén, 2014). This concept has been developed to capture and explain newer facets of contemporary masculinities (Wojnicka, 2021), theorising a radical shift among men from more traditional, hegemonic forms of masculinity (Connell, 1995) to a more optimistic text on masculinities and male identities (Johannson and Hammarén, 2014). Integrating a feminist ethic of care, caring masculinities capture how men's commitment to, and engagements in care work, of which fathering is just one example, help men to develop practices that embody caring and nurturing identities with transformative potential, especially in terms of progress towards gender equality (Hanlon, 2012; Elliot, 2015).

Applying the framework to their empirical study of young fathers in South Africa, Mvune and Bhana (2022: 1357) assert that 'caring masculinities open up the possibilities for understanding young fathers away from dominant stereotypes that position them as uncaring, irresponsible and reckless'. Highlighting the interrelationships between fathering and masculinities, they argue that caring masculinities are disruptive of normative assumptions about the irresponsibility of teenage boys, but are also simultaneously bound up with a continued adherence to traditional notions of masculinity associated with economic provision.

It is important to note here that existing research about fathers and the theorisations that are both applied and developed to explain their experiences are typically based on hegemonic fatherhoods, associated with father groups who are economically resourced, white, married and heterosexual (Strier and Perez-Vaisvidovsky, 2021; Tarrant, 2021; Gallais, 2023). Cautions have been raised that caring masculinities frameworks are rarely applied to empirical research involving low-income fathers (Tarrant, 2021) and working-class boys and men (Roberts and Elliott, 2020). The risk therein is that critical men and masculinities and fatherhood scholarship inadvertently contributes to and creates an impression that working-class and/or disadvantaged men are uncaring, and that social change and progress towards gender equality can only ever be seen as the preserve of middle-class/resourced men. The applications of caring masculinities through the social engagement framework are therefore pertinent, explaining the potential both for theoretical advance and recognition that all men have capacity to care, especially given prevailing societal conditions for this to flourish, as we shall argue.

The 'Following Young Fathers Further' research programme

In line with theoretical developments explaining shifts towards models of socially engaged fatherhood among young fathers, this chapter reports on analyses of qualitative data generated in interviews with a cohort of 34 British young fathers between January 2020 and January 2024. These interviews were conducted as part of the third funded phase of the FYFF research programme. In combination, the studies comprising the FYFF programme have established the first longitudinal evidence base about young fathers, as well as extended collaborative partnerships between young fathers, practitioners and policy makers over time for the purposes of enriching and enhancing professional practice and policy (Tarrant, 2023; Neale and Tarrant, 2024).

Since January 2020, the FYFF team has followed a total cohort of 44 young fathers over time. Nine of these participated in the linked Following Young Fathers (FYF) baseline study (Neale and Lau Clayton, 2012–2015) and have contributed to interviews as many as eight times. Ten of these are young fathers in Sweden. Elsewhere we have developed an international comparison of these data, demonstrating the shared commitments among both cohorts of young fathers to 'being there' for their children, demonstrating how the family-friendlier welfare system of Sweden more effectively supports young fathers to realise their ambitions for engaged fatherhood (Andreasson et al, 2022; Tarrant et al, 2022).

In this chapter, we focus in-depth on the British cohort of young fathers (n = 34). Exact figures are hard to provide here, given the changing dynamics of their circumstances over time, although indicative information about socioeconomic status, number of children and relationship status at the time of interview are provided in the empirical sections for some context. As a brief overview, the age range for the sample was 14–33 years old. Diverse and dynamic living arrangements were reported, including some living with their own parents while finishing school, others living alone or with new partners as own household parents, or with their partners and children.

Of the 34 young fathers interviewed, there was diversity in terms of the socioeconomic backgrounds of the participants. Highly paid, secure employment was more prevalent among the older cohort of fathers, whereas the younger fathers or those with longer histories of deprivation were more likely to be job seekers or in insecure employment that contributed to strained financial circumstances. It is also worth noting that those who have participated in the research programme for over a decade are no longer aged 25 and under (an age-based policy framing for young fatherhood), yet they carry their identities as young fathers with them as they adjust to parenting older children at a younger age compared to a wider national cohort of fathers.

Four sweeps of interviews were conducted with the participants between 2020 and 2023, although there was variation in the number of interviews in which participants were able to engage. The interviews tracked change and continuities in the parenting journeys of these young men, but were also thematically organised, exploring the impacts of the COVID-19 pandemic (wave 1), gender ideologies and co-parenting (wave 2), mental health (wave 2.1[1]), place/housing (wave 3), and leisure/friendships (wave 4). Of the 32 young fathers interviewed, there was diversity in terms of the socioeconomic backgrounds of the participants. During the interviews, participants were asked a set of core questions about their parenting experiences, including what might have changed or remained the same for those with whom we conducted follow-ups. We also introduced a new thematic focus for each interview. In the second wave of interviews, we asked the fathers explicit questions about their perspectives on gender equality and what they considered to be 'good' fatherhood in their view. We also asked about their fathering practices and parenting arrangements to explore similarities and differences between ideological perspectives about fatherhood and their practices of fathering. In another set of interviews, we explored their experiences of parental leave in the UK, including shared parental leave, as well as their engagements with the welfare system so we could explore their biographies in the context of both wider sociohistorical and policy processes (which included the COVID-19 pandemic in this study) and the exosystem through which young fathers navigate their parenting journeys (Deslauriers and Kiselica, 2022). This comprises macro-level processes associated with education, employment and training, housing and engagements with universal and specialist support services.

All interviews were audio recorded and transcribed verbatim, and the study received ethical approval from the Ethics Committee at the University of Lincoln. In this chapter, pseudonyms have been attributed to each participant to protect their identities and all identifiable material has been anonymised for the purposes of ensuring confidentiality both for the participants and those who were discussed in the narratives. The data presented in this chapter were analysed as part of the larger qualitative longitudinal dataset using framework analysis, a flexible and powerful method of analysis that enables the identification, description and interpretation of key patterns within and across cases, as well as thematic analysis (Goldsmith, 2021). We have also employed a diverse set of analytical tools to analyse the dataset, including pen portraits and descriptive cases, enabling us to derive meaningful insights in relation to key questions. In employing multiple analytical tools, we have systematically categorised and interpreted the data in a manner that has supported the development of overarching themes and created opportunities to make connections within cases and across the dataset. For example, each case for each participant contains anonymised transcripts, detailed fieldwork notes, descriptive cases or analytical narratives describing key elements of the interview, ordered by theme, framework grids that are organised and presented in two formats (one for each participant organised by themes down the column and interview waves across the rows and another for each theme organised by participants down the columns and waves across the rows) and pen portraits, comprising small paragraphs describing the key points for the participant at each wave of interviews to build a composite picture of change and continuity over time for each father. The data have also been analysed thematically and coded using NVivo.

Applying caring masculinities as a conceptual lens, we now move on to demonstrate tensions between the alignment of these young men's commitments to cultural expectations of engaged fatherhood and gender-equal parenting, and some of the challenges that impact on their realisation.

Articulations of 'good fatherhood' among young fathers

In line with previous studies conducted with low-income and teenage/young fathers (for example, Summers et al, 2006; Randles, 2020), the young men who participated in the FYFF study articulated a strong sense of obligation to their children and clarity about what it means to be a 'good' father. Expectations of good fatherhood and caring masculinities, which are transgressive of otherwise deep-rooted gender stereotypes, were recognised and aspired to among these young men, regardless of their age, socioeconomic circumstances or relationship status:

> Being a good dad is summat I'd dreamed of since I was a kid. My dad left me when I was a kid and I always wanted to be a good dad. (Jonny, FYFF wave 1, aged 21, low-income, separated, two children)

> What makes a good parent for me is finding that balance ... What makes a good parent is being there. Getting in touch with your child's feelings, talking to your children, not buying them everything, staying through love. (Raymond, FYFF wave 2, aged 22, low-income, in a relationship, four children)

Self-representations as 'caring fathers' among this cohort of young men, who dissociate themselves from stereotypical and deficit images (Johansson and Hammerén, 2014; Mvune and Bhana, 2022), indicate gradual shifts in the articulation of caring masculinities among this cohort of young fathers. However, what this meant in practice differed across the sample. Where Jonny presents a narrative of intergenerational change and a desire to do things differently from his own father, Raymond emphasises the emotional investments needed to sustain relationships of love, care and commitment to his children above and beyond financial provisioning.

While expressing shared attitudes about the importance of being there and caregiving as a core component of good fatherhood, the weight of these expectations was also interwoven with stigma associated with parenting at a young age and stereotypes of young fatherhood of which these young men are keenly aware. This was especially the case for those in low-income circumstances or who were transitioning to parenthood at a young age:

Most people probably expect, you know, in your late-20s, mid-30s, for you to settle down and start having kids and a family, 'cause by that time you've had loads of life experience and you've probably got a job and, you know, you're with someone, you've been with them for probably a couple of years. They probably look on us and think 'oh well, they're wasting their lives, 'cause now their whole life is just centred around looking after a child at such a young age and they're not gonna get to experience things properly'. But outside of that, young dads wise, people expect them to be there and at least try at a young age, but at the same time, most people probably also think that young dads, they probably don't care and they don't wanna try because, you know, teenagers, they'll sleep around, get a lass pregnant or something, and then they'll just leave. (Nathan, FYFF wave 2.1, aged 19, low-income, separated, one child)

I think having that ability to be a family man, you know, and to be there for your family when they need you, even if it's not just staying at home, you know, even if it's choosing to be a part-time worker rather than a full-time worker because you want to be there, you want to be around your children more often, that should be okay, you know, that should be an option, a fair choice for any father to make. (Jake, FYFF, wave 1, aged 27, low-income, in a relationship with co-parent, one child)

For young fathers like Nathan and Jake, there is a mismatch between dominant ideologies around caring masculinities and fatherhood, and the realities of achieving this in practice. Early on in their parenting journeys, young fathers are still in the process of working out what it means to be a man, especially in terms of gendered and age-related norms (see also Weber, 2020). Nineteen-year-old Nathan, who was also attending court to secure care arrangements for his daughter, particularly grapples with these expectations in a way that demonstrates the intersections of his identity both as a parent and as a young man. Highlighting how work and care are interwoven in expectations of engaged fatherhood, Jake's narrative reveals the limited options available to marginalised fathers in achieving a better work-care reconciliation. Although demonstrating the multiplicity of ways that men (and women) say they want to engage in parenting in more intensive ways as both caregivers and providers (see Gallais [2023] on shifts towards 'intensive fathering'), 'being there' as an economic provider and being simultaneously present for children is still out of reach for many fathers.

Most notably, the imperative to earn remains central to the narratives of both Nathan and Jake. It is worth highlighting here that of the 11 young fathers we interviewed who were over the age of 25, three were stay-at-home fathers and four had secured employment or a higher education degree, indicating that normative resources associated with good fatherhood are achievable, if protracted, for young fathers. The others, with less interpersonal and financial resources available to them, were struggling to secure stable employment following the COVID-19 pandemic. Achieving educational qualifications and employment security are therefore possible for young fathers, but can also remain fraught for those who are lower skilled, as we explore in more detail in the next section.

Imperatives to earn

Balancing earning with caring (and sometimes even learning, where dads are still in education; see Neale and Tarrant [2024]) remains central to how young fathers construct caring masculinities. The ability to provide financially for children has always been a pressing concern for all fathers. Not only are practices of 'caring' and 'earning' intertwined and central aspects of fathering identities, but being a financial provider is also intimately bound up with ideals relating to male identity (Neale and Davies, 2016). For young fathers, the ability to achieve good fatherhood is challenged by numerous structural constraints that impinge on their ability to become independent. In the UK, the balance of earning and caring for young people has been compounded by limited educational opportunities, inadequate training provision, insecure youth labour markets and reduced welfare entitlements associated with austerity (Neale and Tarrant, 2024), as well as age discriminatory social security rates and housing (Ladlow, 2021; Ladlow et al, 2024).

Despite these challenges, the young men nevertheless regard breadwinning as a 'taken-for-granted' aspect of their emerging adult status and identity (see also Glikman, 2004; Duncan et al, 2010; Negura and Deslauriers, 2010; Shirani, 2015; Weber, 2020). Reflective of a breadwinner ideology, young fathers aspire to provide both materially and financially for their children, while also investing in nurturance and care. Financial provisioning has long been a defining feature of fatherhood and male identities, although as noted earlier the balance of earning and caring between parents reflects a more fluid picture than these binaries might imply (Neale and Tarrant, 2024).

Nevertheless, state agencies were often complicit in enforcing the breadwinner ideology over the caring aspects of these young men's identities. In the drive to increase employment, men's citizenship as workers still tends to be prioritised over their caregiving responsibilities. This was especially the case for those who were unemployed or in semi-skilled, low-wage occupations, in some cases for many years. These young men often found themselves caught up in cycles of pressure to work that were enforced by external agencies and at odds with their intentions to be present parents. Aaron observes:

Recently, I haven't been able to, well, I've sort of put on hold looking for work until a certain part of court had gone through, but then as soon as that went through, and then the Job Centre was on me, and 'cause I've always been a worker, a lot of pressure did start coming down on me, 'cause I thought I need to get a job so she [daughter] can see that this is what we do when we get older, we work. So yeah, it did get pressured to work as well as look after her (Aaron, aged 33, FYFF wave 2, with mother of third child)

Aaron is one of the three longer-term stay-at-home fathers, a still rare yet increasing phenomenon (see, for example, Chesley, 2011; Solomon, 2017). As a primary caregiver, his role as a parent goes beyond 'being there', a terminology that typically implies a secondary parenting role in terms of availability and support for mothers as primary caregivers (Brooks and Hodkinson, 2020). All three of these young men felt that they were failing as fathers because they were unemployed and not contributing financially. Where a complex blend of factors across the trajectories of young fathers' parenting journeys may intersect to influence the equilibrium of their mental health, these participants attributed the escalation of their mental health problems predominantly to employment instability and economic disconnection (Ladlow et al, 2024). Sharing commonalities with others interviewed, Adam, who had been fired from one job because of depression and mental ill-health, lacked an element of choice in becoming a stay-at-home father. He reflects on how his perceived failure to provide financially led to a further downward spiral in his mental health:

I think it's important to work … to be a father figure for [my son] … I don't want my son to be on the dole. I want him to be able to provide for his family when he eventually has one. God forbid it'll be when I did, but hopefully like come 20, 25 years from now he'll have a family. And he'll be able to support them with a job. And he'll be able to look after them. I mean I don't want to be on the dole all my life doing nothing for no-one. I want to be able to help people … the way I can do that is by getting a job. (Adam, aged 26, FYFF wave 1, one child, in a relationship with mother of child, low-income)

As a guy you are kind of raised to have that feeling that you have to provide, and that kind of got ingrained to me personally, so right now, I don't feel really great. I sit at home, clean up and I know I'm being productive and helping, but like, I don't feel like I'm helping, I don't feel like I'm useful. It's, like I say, it's not a nice feeling. But I mean, there's a lot of people that would think it's fine 'cause I'm doing to the best of my ability what I can to get involved; keeping the house tidy and, you know, just getting involved with washing clothes and just keeping the house running, functional, but I don't know, it just doesn't, as a guy, as a father, I feel like I should be bringing home the money. You know what I mean? Financially supporting them, which I'm not at the moment. So it doesn't feel too great in that aspect, but I don't know, I'm doing me best. (Adam, aged 27, FYFF wave 2.1)

Adam's reflections demonstrate that gendered expectations for fathers to earn and provide, as well as to engage in domestic work and the caring and nurturing aspects of fatherhood, undermine his understanding own perceptions of the value of his vital contributions as a stay-at-home father. This has negative implications for his own sense of self-worth and wellbeing. Mirroring findings of unemployed men from nearly a century ago (Komarovsky, 2004a, b), the cultural imperative for provision is still keenly felt by fathers despite a growing cultural acceptance of caring masculinities. In the UK, only one in nine stay-at-home parents are fathers, so this remains a highly marginalised experience. While all of these young men are perhaps the most present in their family lives and were playing a vital role in supporting their children and partners to work, traditional societal norms about men's identities and their association with paid work loomed large over these young men, undermined their confidence in their commitments to engaging in caring masculinities, and represented an imbalance for them in terms of their contributions to family and employment.

Sustaining relationships with co-parents

Reflecting existing scholarship (for a review, see Neale and Tarrant, 2024), relationships with co-parents were also pivotal in realising the potential to re-gender care and the extent to which these young men were able to sustain a relationship with their children over time and perform caring masculinities. Of the 11 young fathers we interviewed who are now in their thirties, most were still living with and/or seeing their preteen/teenage children, even if they were not in a relationship with the mother of their child. For these young men, the prevalence of caring masculinities was reflected less in the hands-on and nurturing aspects of caregiving, and more in their efforts and capacity to maintain relationships with their co-parents, on which their engagements with their children were contingent. Dominic's longitudinal case illustrates this capacity effectively. First interviewed at the age of 15 and at the latest point at the age of 30, he has long described a tenuous and troubled relationship with his ex-partner, but also the tenacity with which he has maintained contact with his son, who is now a teenager himself:

Sometimes his mother will collect him in the morning, sometimes it will be afternoon. But roughly what came, 'cause we had a mediation contract signed up. And what it came to is like in a 14 week, in a 14-day period, it'd work out more or less seven days. So we're half, which I set out to have. She wanted it a lot more minimal and a lot more, you know, potentially having every other weekend, all weekends. But, I pushed for ... I want to be proactive in my son's life. And I wasn't happy with the way that her and her family looked after my son as well. So I were pushing for potentially more. (Dominic, aged 15, wave 1, FYF, separated, middle income)

It's been up and down over the years but hopefully it's evening out. Not in a bad way, but you can see light at the end of the tunnel in terms of he's getting, he'll be getting to the point where he'll be an adult shortly anyway, so it's, even when there's stuff bubbling away, I can see that there's only sort of, there's only a bit of time when we [referring to his co-parent] need to be forced to sort of work together really. If that makes sense? (Dominic, aged 31, wave 3, FYFF, single, high income, one child)

Dominic's longer-term engagement with his son over a 15-year period demonstrates the possibilities for young fathers to sustain their family participation over time even in the most challenging of circumstances. Where the relational troubles with his co-parent and the maternal family required external intervention at times, Dominic's determination to be there as a father meant that he sought an amicable relationship with his ex-partner and her family, exemplifying some progress towards gender equality in seeking to balance contact with his son more effectively across households.

The older fathers in the sample more generally recognised the need to sustain more amicable and positive relationships with the mother(s) of their children upon separation if they are to co-parent effectively and remain in contact with their children. As Dominic's case illustrates, these relationships are often worked out over time such that when their relationships with their co-parent are amicable, they are more likely to sustain contact with their children. When they are less amicable, young fathers' relationships with their children are at the greatest risk of becoming estranged. The experiences of these participants reflect the capacity of young fathers to prioritise their children and to navigate the complexities of their interpersonal relationships with their co-parent(s) in order to sustain their connection with their child (or children) over time. As a young father who has conceived children with multiple partners, typically a highly stigmatised set of circumstances, Trevor explains how he has managed to remain on good terms with one of his partners over an extended period, even describing her as like a family member:

Yeah so that's my eldest daughter's mum. We're at a point in life now where it's like well it's not even ... like what most parents are like. Like most separated parents still have like a bit a' tension and stuff like that. Like I would usually look at her like another family member now. It's, it sounds weird to say but it's, it is like that. Like it's someone that you are gonna argue with, obviously it's inevitable but at the same time like you're still gonna be in each other's life and you can't help it, so you've just got to learn how to get along. I think we do get along in a much better sense than we did when we were younger ... so yeah it's quite a good little co-parent relationship I'd say. (Trevor, aged 23, FYFF wave 1, low-income, separated, two children)

However, like Dominic, Trevor has been accessing mediation to support him in his relationship with the mother of his second child. For low-income young fathers, receipt of support from the courts is expensive and therefore not always accessible, creating financial barriers for those who might otherwise be a resource for their children:

With my second daughter I've attempted mediation a few times and separate mediation happened a few times. And then like unrealistic things were getting said that needed to happen. And even the mediator to a sense even kinda said to me, 'look you might as well just pursue court with this'. (Trevor, aged 24, FYFF wave 1, separated, two children)

What these examples demonstrate is that the dynamics of gendered relationships with co-parents are vital in shaping the parenting journeys of young fathers and their ability to be there for their children over time (see also Neale and Tarrant, 2024). This is especially pertinent for those in contexts of separation and re-partnering. Where Trevor demonstrates a commitment to his first child and recognises the importance of developing a positive relationship with his co-parent, he nevertheless continues to persevere with attempts to be there for his youngest daughter in a context where his relationship with his second co-parent is more tenuous and he is being advised to apply to court for support. In both examples, interpersonal and structural constraints interact to shape the extent to which these young men can align their own experiences of fathering with scripts of engaged fatherhood and caring masculinities.

However, as young men who are marginalised by their young age, gender, socio-socioeconomic and relationship status, their ideologically expressed intentions and aspirations to be there for children are inevitably structured by the dynamics of their interpersonal, shifting societal expectations, circumstances and processes, gendered expectations around work and care and the resources available to them to parent independently and with minimal state intervention.

Conclusion: Gradual progress towards socially engaged young fatherhood

This chapter contributes to a developing strand of analysis in young fatherhood research that critically engages with young fathers' narratives of engaged fatherhood and caring masculinities, and how these articulate with wider societal transformations, including the 'regendering of care' (for example, Enderstein and Boonzaier, 2015; Boyer et al, 2017; Beggs Weber, 2020). Through a focus on how young fathers in the UK narrate their perspectives of good fatherhood and seek to reconcile these in contexts of stigma, social deficit discourses and wider systemic expectations and constraints, we argue that there is some cause for optimism. These young fathers sustain self-representations as caring fathers over time and demonstrate commitment to what we conceptualise as *socially engaged fatherhood*. Apparent in their narratives of parenting and partnering, the findings suggest that young fathers recognise the value of adhering to an ethos of engagement in the lives of their children and co-parents even where these may be troubled, and indicate how caring dispositions are interwoven aspects of their identities, transitions and interpersonal relationships.

Nevertheless, the continued entanglements of work and care (Doucet, 2020), confirm that young fathers still see breadwinning and financial provisioning as a central aspect of 'care' for their children in ways that are reinforced in a dual-earner economy. For those with the interpersonal and material resources to balance work and care, young fathers still typically form an imperative to earn, but do so as an integral part of care and provisioning (Neale and Patrick, 2016; Doucet, 2020; Hughes and Tarrant, 2023). Their expressions and practices of caring and hegemonic masculinities therefore sit alongside one another (see also Edin and Nelson, 2013; Hunter et al, 2017; Neale and Tarrant, 2024), constructing hybrid paternal masculinities similar to those identified internationally (for example, Wang and Keizer, 2023). Tellingly, where young fathers occupy the most transgressive of gendered roles as primary caregivers and stay-at-home fathers, they consider themselves as failed fathers, suggesting that having the choice to balance work and care remains a preferred option for co-parenting and achieving equality in parenting.

Given the dynamics and diversity of young fathers' circumstances and the 'shaky ground' (SmithBattle et al, 2019) they navigate in order to establish themselves as parents, our findings therefore indicate that caring masculinities may be apparent, but are not always automatically emancipatory for these young men. Those with limited resources may have less capacity to augment dominant masculinities, especially where their young age, social stigma and socioeconomic disadvantage intersect to shape their experiences. Constructions of fatherhood and paternal masculinities must therefore be understood as shaped by, interacting with and sometimes undermined by wider contexts, processes and intersecting inequalities. Overall, we conclude that the new family dynamics that constitute socially engaged young fatherhoods and caring masculinities are both apparent and recognised by young fathers. However, individual shifts among individuals and couples are not enough on their own. Whether marginalised by age, ethnicity or other axes of difference, the re-gendering of care will only ever make partial progress if marginalised fathers are not supported to flourish by policies and wider systems. The risk remains that caring masculinities are seen only as the preserve of privileged fathers and those who have acquired or accrued greater resources to parent.

Acknowledgement
The research presented in this chapter was funded by the UKRI Future Leaders Fellowship scheme. Grant Ref: MR/S031723/1

Note
[1] We conducted some more in-depth interviews specifically on mental health with a small subsample of four young fathers who had expressed challenges with their emotional wellbeing in previous interviews. Mental health also remained a key theme across waves to track fluctuations among those who felt their mental health was less problematic in earlier waves.

References
Andreasson, J., Tarrant, A., Ladlow, L., Johansson, T. and Way, L. (2022) Perceptions of gender equality and engaged fatherhood among young fathers: parenthood and the welfare state in Sweden and the UK, *Families, Relationships and Societies*, 12(3): 323–340.

Arai, L. (2009) *Teenage Pregnancy: The Making and Unmaking of a Problem*. Bristol: Policy Press.

Ayoola, L., Gates, P. and Taylor, M. (2010) *Exploring the Needs and Experiences of Teenage Fathers in the City of Nottingham: Creating Families, Building Futures*. Nottingham: Leslie Ayoola Consultants and the City of Nottingham.

Berger, L. and Langton, C. (2011) Young disadvantaged men as fathers, *Annals of the American Academy of Political and Social Science*, 635(1): 56–75.

Bhana, D. and Nkani, N. (2014) When African teenagers become fathers: culture, materiality and masculinity, *Culture, Health & Sexuality*, 16(3/4): 337–350.

Boyer, K., Dermott, E., James, A. and MacLeavy, J. (2017) Regendering care in the aftermath of recession? *Dialogues in Human Geography*, 7(1): 56–73.

Brooks, R. and Hodkinson, P. (2020) *Sharing Care: Equal and Primary Carer Fathers and Early Years Parenting*, Bristol: Bristol University Press.

Buston, K., Parkes, A., Thomson, H., Wight, D. and Fenton, C. (2012) Parenting interventions for male young offenders: a review of the evidence on what works, *Journal of Adolescence*, 35(3): 731–742.

Chesley, N. (2011) Stay-at-home fathers and breadwinning mothers: gender, couple dynamics and social change, *Gender & Society*, 25(5): 642–664.

Connell, R. (1995) *Masculinities*, New York: Taylor & Francis.

Delaney, C. Bobek, A. and Clavero, S. (2023) 'It was too much for me': mental load, mothers and working from home during the COVID-19 pandemic, *Frontiers in Psychology*, 14.

Dermott, E. (2008) *Intimate Fatherhood: A Sociological Analysis*, Abingdon: Routledge.

Dermott, E. and Miller, T. (2015) More than the sum of its parts? Contemporary fatherhood policy, practice and discourse, *Families, Relationships and Societies*, 4(2): 183–195.

Deslauriers, J.-M. (2011) Becoming a young father: a decision or an ;accident?;, *International Journal of Adolescence and Youth*, 16(3), 289–308.

Deslauriers, J.-M. and Kiselica, M.S. (2022) An ecological approach to understanding the paternal commitments of young fathers: from the pregnancy test to the child's first birthday, *Child & Adolescent Social Work Journals*, https://doi.org/10.1007/s10560-022-00845-5

Doucet, A. (2020) Father involvement, care and breadwinning: genealogies of concepts and revisioned conceptual narratives, *Genealogy*, 4(1): 14.

Dowd, N.E. (2012) Fatherhood and equality: reconfiguring masculinities, *Suffolk University Law Review*, 45(4): 1047.

Duncan, S. (2007) What's the problem with teenage parents? And what's the problem with policy? *Critical Social Policy*, 27(3): 307–334.

Duncan, S., Edwards, R. and Alexander, C. (eds) (2010) *Teenage Parenthood: What's the Problem?* London: Tufnell Press.

Edin, K. and Nelson, T.J. (2013) *Doing the Best I Can: Fatherhood in the Inner City*. Berkeley: University of California Press.

Elkington, A. (2017) The everyday lives of young Maori fathers: an explorative study, *Journal of Indigenous Well-Being*, 2(3): 3–17.

Elliott, K. (2016) Caring masculinities: theorizing an emerging concept. *Men and Masculinities*, 19(3): 240–259.

Enderstein, A.M. and Boonazier, F. (2015) Narratives of young South African fathers: redefining masculinity through fatherhood, *Journal of Gender Studies*, 24(5): 512–527.

Gallais, C. (2023) *Fatherhood and Masculinities: Intersections of Care, Bodies and Race*. London: Palgrave Macmillan.

Glikman H. (2004) Low-income young fathers: contexts, connections and self, *Social Work*, 49(2): 195–206.

Glikman, H. (2004) Low-income young fathers: contexts, connections, and self, *Social Work*, 49(2): 195–206.

Goldsmith, L.J. (2021) Using framework analysis in applied qualitative research, *The Qualitative Report*, 26(6): 2061-2076. https://doi.org/10.46743/2160-3715/2021.5011

Hanlon, N. (2012) *Masculinities, Care and Equality: Identity and Nurture in Men's Lives.* London: Palgrave Macmillan/Springer Nature.

Hochschild, A. (1989) *The Second Shift: Working Families and the Revolution at Home*, New York: Penguin.

Hughes, K. and Tarrant, A. (2023) *Men, Families and Poverty: Tracing the Intergenerational Trajectories of Placed-Based Hardship.* London: Palgrave Macmillan.

Hunter, S.C., Riggs, D.W. and Augoustinos, M. (2017) Hegemonic masculinity versus a caring masculinity: Implications for understanding primary caregiving fathers, *Social and Personality Psychology Compass*, 11(3): e12307.

Johansson, T. and Hammarén, N. (2012) 'Imagine, just 16 years old and already a dad!' The construction of young fatherhood on the Internet, *International Journal of Adolescence and Youth*, 19(3): 366–381.

Johansson, T. and Hammarén, N. (2014) 'Imagine, just 16 years old and already a dad!' The construction of young fatherhood on the internet, *International Journal of Adolescence and Youth*, 19(3): 366–381.

Kiselica, M. (forthcoming) Moving beyond stigma: re-examining the lives of teenage fathers. In M. Lafrance, J. Deslauriers and G. Trembly (eds) *The Forgotten Realities of Men.* Vancouver: University of British Columbia Press.

Komarovsky, M. (2004a) *The Effect of Unemployment upon the Status of the Man in Fifty-Nine Families*, updated edn, M. Kimmel (ed). Lanham, MD: Rowman & Littlefield.

Komarovsky, M. (2004b) *The Unemployed Man and His Family: The Effect of Unemployment upon the Status of the Man in Fifty-Nine Families.* Lanham, MD: Rowman & Littlefield.

Ladlow, L. (2021) Housing young parents: a micro-dynamic study of the housing experiences and support needs of young mothers and fathers. PhD thesis, University of Leeds.

Ladlow, L., Neale, B. and Tarrant, A. (2024) Finding a place to parent: young fathers' housing needs and pathways. In B. Neale and A. Tarrant (eds) *The Dynamics of Young Fatherhood: Understanding the Parenting Journeys and Support Needs of Young Fathers.* Bristol: Policy Press.

Lemay C.A., Cashman S.B., Elfenbein D.S. and Felice M.E. (2010) A qualitative study of the meaning of fatherhood among young urban fathers, *Public Health Nursing*, 27(3): 221–231.

Lewin, A., Mitchell, S.J., Waters, D., Hodgkinson, S., Southammakosane, C. and Gilmore, J. (2015) The protective effects of father involvement for infants of teen mothers with depressive symptoms, *Maternal Child Health*, 19: 1016–1023.

Miller, T. (2010) *Making Sense of Fatherhood: Gender, Caring and Work*, Cambridge: Cambridge University Press.

Mvune, N. and Bhana, D. (2022) Caring masculinities? Teenage fathers in South Africa, *Journal of Family Studies*, 29(3): 1346–1361.

Neale, B. (2016) Editorial introduction: Young fatherhood: lived experiences and policy challenges, *Social Policy and Society*, 15(1): 75–83.

Neale, B. and Davies, L. (2016) Becoming a young breadwinner? The education, employment and training trajectories of young fathers, *Social Policy and Society*, 15(1): 85–98.

Neale, B. and Patrick, R. (2016), *Engaged Young Fathers? Gender, Parenthood and the Dynamics of Relationships*, Following Young Fathers, Working Paper Series No 1. Available from: https://followingfathers.leeds.ac.uk/wp-content/uploads/sites/79/2015/10/FYF-Working-Paper-Engaged-young-fathers.pdf

Neale, B. and Tarrant, A. (2024) *The Dynamics of Young Fatherhood: Understanding the Parenting Journeys and Support Needs of Young Fathers*. Bristol: Policy Press.

Negura, L. and Deslauriers, J. (2010) Work and lifestyle: social representations among young fathers, *British Journal of Social Work*, 40(8): 2652–2668.

Occhiuto, A.M. (2021) The invisible shift: the mental load of motherhood. Master's thesis, Concordia University Montréal, Québec, Canada.

Parikh, S. (2009) Validating reciprocity: supporting young fathers' continued involvement with their children, *Families in Society: The Journal of Contemporary Social Services*, 90(3): 261–270.

Pirog, M., Jung, H. and Lee, D. (2018) The changing face of teenage parenthood in the United States: evidence from NLSY79 and NLSY97, *Child and Youth Care Forum*, 47(3): 317–342.

Randles, J. (2020) The means to and meaning of 'being there' in responsible fatherhood programming with low-income fathers, *Family Relations*, 69(1): 7–20.

Roberts, S. and Elliott, C. (2020) Challenging dominant representations of marginalized boys and men in critical studies on men and masculinities, *Boyhood Studies*, 13(2): 87–104.

Shirani, F. (2015) 'I'm bringing back a dead art': continuity and change in the lives of young fathers, *Families, Relationships & Societies*, 4(2): 253–266.

Smart, C. and Neale, B. (1999) 'I hadn't really thought about it': new identities/new fatherhoods. In J. Seymour and P. Bagguley (eds) *Relating Intimacies: Power and Resistance*. London: Springer, pp 118–141.

SmithBattle L., Phengnum W., Shagavah A.W. and Okawa S. (2019) Fathering on tenuous ground: a qualitative meta-synthesis on teen fathering, *MCN: The American Journal of Maternal/Child Nursing*, 44(4): 186–194.

Solomon, C.R. (2017) *The Lives of Stay-at-Home Fathers: Masculniity, Carework and Fatherhood in the United States*. Leeds: Emerald Publishing.

State of the World's Fathers (2023) Centering Care in a World in Crisis, Equimundo/MenCare report. Available from: https://www.equimundo.org/wp-content/uploads/2023/07/State-of-the-Worlds-Fathers-2023.pdf

Strier, R. and Perez-Vaisvidovsky, N. (2021) Intersectionality and fatherhood: theorizing non-hegemonic fatherhoods, *Journal of Family Theory & Review*, 13(3): 334–346.

Summers, J.A., Boiler, K., Schiffman, R.F. and Raikes, H.H. (2006) The meaning of 'good fatherhood': low-income fathers' social constructions of their roles, *Parenting*, 6(2-3): 145–165.

Tarrant, A. (2021) *Fathering and Poverty: Uncovering Men's Participation in Low-Income Family Life*. Bristol: Policy Press.

Tarrant, A. (2023) Instigating father-inclusive practice interventions with young fathers and multi-agency professionals: the transformative potential of qualitative longitudinal and co-creative methodologies, *Families, Relationships and Societies*, 1–19.

Tarrant, A., Ladlow, L., Johansson, T., Andreasson, J. and Way, L. (2022) The impacts of the COVID-19 pandemic and lockdown policies on young fathers: comparative insights from the UK and Sweden, *Social Policy and Society*, 1–11.

Townsend, N. (2002) *The Package Deal: Marriage, Work and Fatherhood in Men's Lives*. Philadelphia: Temple University Press.

Uengwongsapat, C., Kantaruska, K., Klunkkin, A. and Sansiriphun, N. (2018) Growing into teen fatherhood: a grounded theory study, *International Nursing Review*, 65: 244–253.

Wang, L. and Keizer, R. (2024) 'I am a traditional but caring father': narrative of paternal masculinity in urban Chinese families, *Journal of Gender Studies*, 1–16.

Weber, J.B. (2020) Being there (or not): teen dads, gendered age, and negotiating the absent-father discourse, *Men and Masculinities*, 23(1): 42–64.

Wojnicka, K. (2021) Men and masculinities in times of crisis: between care and protection, *NORMA*, 16(1): 1–5.

11

Gendered framings of responsibility for care and the availability of leave policies for fathers from a global perspective

Alison Koslowski

Introduction

Employment-based parenting leave policies allow for working fathers (and mothers) to spend time looking after infants safe in the knowledge that their employment is protected. These policies are widely available in countries with developed formal economies (Addati, Cattaneo and Pozzan, 2022). In many cases, they also offer financial support during this period of leave, though there is wide variation in the generosity of this replacement income. In some countries, parenting leave policies may also provide support for self-employed, unemployed and other non-employed parents, such as students or recently arrived immigrants (Blum et al, 2023).

Parenting leave is a term that is increasingly being used as an umbrella term for the range of leave policies available to parents (for example, Dobrotić, Blum and Koslowski, 2022). This range includes maternity leave, paternity leave, parental leave, birth leave, pregnancy leave and primary carer leave. The nomenclature of leave policies is evolving (see Blum et al, 2023). Many parents (and in particular fathers) also use annual leave entitlements to care for infants (for example, Koslowski and Kadar-Satat, 2019, Sant, 2023), but this is not considered as a distinct parenting leave in most leave policy scholarship.

Parenting leaves may serve multiple aims and functions (as discussed in Koslowski and O'Brien, 2022), and increasing fathers' informal caring, thus shifting cultural understandings of responsibilities for care for infants, can be one of these aims. Indeed, leave policies, when purposefully designed and implemented, are perhaps some of the most effective policies when it comes to supporting men's caregiving and promoting gender equality in this sphere. However, leave policies can also be designed in such a way that make it very unlikely that fathers can participate meaningfully in infant care (Wright and Brighouse, 2008; Koslowski, 2021). Leave policies are empirical representations of a country's care ideology – crystallised gendered understandings of whether only mothers or also fathers – should be supported with caring for infants. They also tell us about the framing of individual versus state responsibility for the care of children, and of responsibility for gender equality. As such, leave policies act as a lens through which to look at care and gender equality in a given country context.

Drawing upon a selection of countries across the world (Australia, Chile, Japan, South Africa, Sweden and the US), this chapter considers how their various approaches to leave policy constructions reflect different gendered framings of responsibility for care of infants. How do policies enable or constrain forms of caring from fathers, or the care of some fathers and not others? Data on leave policies are available from *The International Review of Leave Policies and Research 2023*, which collects information annually about the leave policies available to parents across 50 countries (Blum et al, 2023). This chapter describes the variation in policies available to fathers in these six country cases in 2023 and uses this information to consider the various conceptualisations of care which underpin the different expectations of paternal caretaking. These six country cases are chosen as illustrations of leave policies across the continents, though they are not necessarily typical representatives of the other countries in their regions. They are chosen as examples of very different leave policy system designs.

Ideas on who should care for infants and young children and leave policy design

In a global policy context, it is easier to achieve consensus on supporting mothers and babies than it is to achieve consensus on supporting fathers to care for their infants (O'Brien and Uzunalioglu, 2022). The norm of maternalism remains culturally dominant. Indeed, provision of care is extremely socially stratified by gender; overall, women are doing much more caring than men, especially for infants (for example, EIGE, 2022). This results in a far greater emphasis from international organisations, such as the International Labour Organization (ILO), the World Health Organization (WHO) and the United Nations (UN), on the policy logics behind countries implementing leave for mothers (including the health and welfare of mothers and babies, and supporting female labour market participation). Those who also seek to support paternal informal caring as a necessary partner to female labour market participation are still deemed as too radical for anything approaching an international consensus.

Attitudes towards who should be looking after infants are certainly changing in some communities. Younger men are expressing a desire to spend more time caring for their infants, and younger women seek to share the caring more evenly with their partners than was the case in the past (for example, Gerson, 2011). Mencare is an example of an international organisation that 'believe[s] that true equality between men and women will not be reached until men and boys take on 50 per cent of the caregiving and domestic work'.[1] This implies a more equal sharing of care for infants and young children – that this is not primarily women's work. There are an increasing number of countries with parenting leave systems set up to support this approach: the Nordic countries can be seen as the pioneers in this respect (for example, Eydal and Rostgaard, 2016).

In some countries, policies that have been designed to increase fathers' role in caring for infants have led to changes in behaviour (see Chapter 12 in this volume). Key aspects which increase leave taking by fathers include high-income replacement as well as leave to which only fathers are entitled and which cannot be transferred to another carer (usually the mother) (Eydal et al, 2015). An individual and nontransferable entitlement to leave is considered the gold standard in terms of encouraging take-up by fathers (Kvande, 2022). In cases where fathers do not have equal entitlement (as mothers) to leave, they are unlikely to care as much for infants as mothers do (Koslowski, 2021).

Policy reviews aiming to change the policy aims and design of parenting leave systems can become ideologically charged and reduced to becoming forums where mothers and fathers are often pitted against one another. The assumption can be that any new resource given to fathers is likely to pose a threat to the resource given to mothers. This fear has blocked attempts at reform of the parenting leave system in the UK (Moss and O'Brien, 2019). Recent reforms in Spain see the same 'birth leave' being granted to all parents – indeed, compulsory for all parents – but relatively short in duration. Protection for mothers has not been a priority and so much of the leave taken by Spanish women remains unpaid (Meil et al, 2022; Meil, Escebedo and Lapuerta, 2023).

In summary, there is a tension between those who believe that we must change the structures of support to allow for equal sharing (for example, offer the same or very similar parental leave to both parents) and those who believe this is a poor use of resources, as in practice mothers will continue to do the majority of infant care. Some believe that care norms are socially constructed and if we change the policy, social change (which they perceive as desirable) will follow. Others have a more essentialist view of infant care – that it is the realm of women. So, how does this play out on the global stage? In the next section, we travel around the continents to see some of the varying leave systems and their accessibility – or lack of – to fathers.

The availability of leave policies to fathers from a global perspective

This section provides empirical examples of the leave potentially available for fathers in six countries in 2023: Australia, Chile, Japan, South Africa,

Sweden and the US. This information on leave policies is open access and available from *The International Review of Leave Policies and Research 2023* (Blum et al, 2023). The following accounts draw on the relevant country notes in the review, which are authored by country experts.

The parenting leave systems described here are the statutory systems, that is, the baseline required by legislation in a given country. It might be that some employers offer more generous options to 'top up' the statutory provision, both in terms of duration and payment, or that there are collective agreements which also result in augmented provision. There are different aspects of leave policy to consider, such as benefit scope and implementation. In addition, for a full picture of accessibility to leave, it is essential to also consider those who are not eligible to the baseline statutory provision.

Not all fathers in a country will be eligible for the statutory leave that is in principle available to fathers. Scholars are increasingly considering the inclusiveness of access to parenting leave policies (Blum and Dobrotić, 2021). Eligibility to leave is configured by an entitlement principle, which is usually employment-based, citizenship-based and/or in some cases family status-based (see Dobrotić and Blum, 2020; EIGE, 2020). In the event that the entitlement to leave is solely employment-based, this would mean that access to leave is derived through a father's employment status – most frequently that he is employed. Even if he meets this entitlement principle, he may also need to meet further eligibility criteria, such as having worked for the employer for a period of time. The more stringent the eligibility criteria, the fewer fathers will have access to leave, and the greater the social inequalities in this access are likely to be (Dobrotić, Blum and Koslowski, 2022).

In addition to annual leave, the two types of parenting leave most commonly available to fathers are paternity leave and parental leave. Paternity leave is generally a shorter leave available to the nonbirth parents for the first days and weeks following the birth of a child. Parental leave is typically available during the first year of an infant's life and is equally available to both parents, but in some countries, it may be available throughout childhood. The leave names may be directly translated from the relevant languages to paternity and/or parental leave, or they may, for example, be couched in gender-neutral terms. Relatedly, as a country recognises LGBT parenting in legal frameworks, this leave is then usually also available to parents regardless of sex or gender.

In the follow subsections, the parenting leave available to fathers is described and the eligibility criteria are noted. Following the template for the standardised country note in *The International Review of Leave Policies and Research 2023* for each country, the nomenclature for available leave policies is presented, followed by the scope of the benefit (payment amount and duration) and whether leave is an individual or transferable entitlement. The eligibility criteria are noted, including whether leave is available to

Table 11.1: Labour force participation rates for women and mothers

Country (2023)	Labour force participation rate, female (% of female population aged 15+)	Maternal employment rate, 2021 (OECD)
Australia	62	72.2
Chile	52	59.4
Japan	55	74.8
South Africa	52	n/a
Sweden	63	82.9
US	57	67.1

Source: World Bank (https://data.worldbank.org/indicator/SL.TLF.CACT.FE.ZS), OECD (https://web-archive.oecd.org/temp/2024-06-21/69263-database.htm#public_policy)

the employed and self-employed. Where available, other features of the country's leave system (including access to carer's leave) are mentioned. In addition, the labour force participation rate for the female population published by the World Bank (for all six countries) and the maternal employment rate published by the Organisation for Economic Co-operation and Development (OECD) (not available for South Africa) are presented for context in Table 11.1. The OECD figures reflect different norms for maternal employment, ranging from 59.4 per cent in Chile to 82.9 per cent in Sweden. Thus, we might expect explicitly gendered leave policy systems which support male breadwinning and female caring to a greater extent in those countries with lower levels of maternal employment.

Consolidating fathers' secondary care role: Australia[2]

> Short secondary carer leaves set normative standards of fathers as 'supporters' rather than recognising substantive involvement in care.
> Baird, Hamilton and Constantin, 2021: 562

In Australian national legislation, there is no separate statutory entitlement to 'maternity' or 'paternity' leave. If employed, both parents have access to the unpaid parental leave provisions of the Fair Work Act 2009. The Australian parenting leave system operates in gender-neutral terms, but it also legislates an explicit 'primary' and 'secondary' carer model. This means that in practice, fathers are overwhelmingly conceived as the secondary carers (Baird et al, 2021).

Each eligible employed parent is entitled to 12 months' unpaid parental leave, which is job-protected in many cases. Same-sex relationships are recognised by the legislation. This is an individual entitlement, but for the most part (with the exception of eight weeks in the first year of a baby's life) cannot be taken by parents simultaneously. If both parents are entitled to this leave, they could take 12 months sequentially. This unpaid leave is transferable (subject to employer agreement). In all countries, fathers are very unlikely to take unpaid parental leave, and Australia is no exception.

In terms of eligibility for unpaid parental leave, only employed workers (including hourly paid employees) are covered by the legislation, not the self-employed or the unemployed. Leave is only available to employees with 12 months' continuous service with the same employer immediately prior to the expected date of birth. If a fixed-term contract ends while they are on leave, then the employer is not required to extend the contract period.

Leave and payment while on leave are dealt with separately, in legislative terms. Since July 2023, parents have access to 20 weeks of payment based on the national minimum wage. For couples (including same-sex couples), two weeks is reserved for each parent, with the remaining 16 weeks to share as they choose. Only two weeks of this paid leave can be taken concurrently. To be eligible, the primary carer (usually the mother) must be resident in Australia and meet the requirements of a work test, which includes both employees and self-employed workers. The same criteria apply for fathers' or partners' eligibility to the two weeks' Dad and Partner Pay. Pay is restricted to individuals with a taxable income below a certain threshold. The other leave potentially available to fathers is ten days per year paid personal leave, which covers both personal illness and family illness.

Employers may and do often supplement this baseline provision. Employer-paid parental leave, which is sometimes specified as paternity or secondary carer leave, is available via some collective agreements and company policies, and these provisions are usually at the level of full replacement salary.

In summary, while it is technically possible for fathers to take on the role of primary carer, this means by definition that the mother will not be able take on this role. If a couple wants to share the caring more evenly, this will be at their own expense.

Fathers as emergency carers: Chile

In Chile,[3] employed fathers are entitled to five working days of paternity leave and it is obligatory to take the whole period, though they can distribute the days over the first month following the birth. Obligatory leave is particularly common internationally for mothers, but increasingly also for fathers: the compulsory aspect is seen as a protective factor towards parents from workplace norms which might discourage leave taking. The paternity leave is set at 100 per cent of earnings, which is paid by the employer.

There is no parental leave entitlement in Chile. A period of maternity leave is potentially transferable to the father, though this happens very rarely (less than 0.2 per cent of leave cases). This low transfer rate may be linked to fathers not having the same legal job protections as mothers. Maternal jurisdiction lasts two years, while paternal immunity is only double the time they took the leave. In addition, every father (and mother) is entitled to paid leave in the case of serious illness of a child under the age of one year, though the father can take the leave only if the mother allows it. After the age of one, this leave is primarily for working mothers and can be transferred to the father. This system of insurance for the purpose of caring for a child with a serious illness is well developed (see endnote 3 for more information). In addition, all workers are entitled to ten days per year to care for a disabled person for whom they are responsible, though they are expected to make up the time. Again, the presumption is that this is primarily for women.

From the way in which the legislation is framed, it is clear that the father is considered as the emergency back-up in the case of catastrophic situations, such as the death of the mother.

All employees are eligible for paternity leave if they have a contract. The contract can be permanent or fixed term, which is a difference compared to maternity leave, where a fixed-term contract implies more stringent eligibility criteria. The self-employed are not eligible. In the (presumably rare) case that a father is deprived of his parental rights, he is no longer eligible for either paternity or transferable maternity leave. Same-sex couples are not recognised in Chilean law.

The Chilean case brings three aspects of note to our attention: first, it demonstrates the notion of compulsory leave, even if for a very short period; second, it showcases the notion of fathers as back-up carers in extremis; and, third, it is a country where there is differential labour law applied to men and women in terms of job protection while on leave.

Supportive policies for fathers, but in an unsupportive context: Japan

Eligible fathers in Japan[4] are entitled to 'Childcare Leave at Birth' of four weeks, which can be taken in two time periods during the first eight weeks after the birth. This leave is paid at a rate of 67 per cent of daily earnings, up to an upper limit of around €97 per day (the minimum wage would be around €50 per day, subject to regional variation). In addition, fathers have an individual, nontransferable entitlement to paid parental leave until a child is 12 months old. In the event that both parents take some of the leave, the leave can be extended until the child is 14 months old. Both parents can take leave at the same time, with both receiving benefit payments as eligible. In practice, if both parents take leave, it can mean a substantial drop in household income during this period (Nakazato, 2023).

Eligibility is somewhat restricted (similar criteria apply to both paternity and parental leave). Same-sex couples are not eligible. Self-employed and unemployed parents are not eligible. Eligibility is linked to employment status only, not citizenship or residency status. Leave is also unavailable to certain categories of employed workers, who must have been employed for at least a year. Those employed on a day-to-day basis are not eligible. Those on a fixed-term contract may not be eligible. Eligibility to benefit also depends on 12 months' contributions to employment insurance.

One aspect of the Japanese approach is that there is the flexibility for fathers to continue to work up to 10 days (80 hours) per month while on leave and still receive the benefit, though the payment is then reduced accordingly.

Japan has enacted the Act on the Advancement of Measures to Support Raising the Next Generation of Children. As a result, there are various incentives for employers to promote parental leave, though arguably with an emphasis on female leave taking. The Japanese government has created certification marks for employers to promote leave use by both mothers and fathers, which lead to preferential tax treatment. Achieving a leave uptake rate of 13 per cent or more among male employees whose partner has given birth is awarded a special certificate, which comes with further benefits. Large employers (those with more than 1,000 workers) are obliged to publicly announce on an annual basis the status of take-up of parental leave by their employees.

Fathers (and mothers) also potentially have access to short-term (five days per year per child under the age of six) unpaid family care leave. There is also longer-term paid family leave available in the case of serious illness or disability of a family member.

While designed in gender-neutral terms, Japan has not seen a substantial take-up of leave by fathers, as had been hoped for by policy reformers. Scholars argue that this is in part linked to the difficulties for parents to find suitable childcare places following the leave period, which cements mothers' role as primary home carers (Nakazato, 2023).

The Japanese case highlights that even following reforms, conditions (such as being eligible in the first place, the level of pay, and an integrated leave and Early Childhood Education and Care [ECEC] systems) have to be right for fathers to be able to realise their entitlements. Other cultural factors may also be relevant, such as a long working hours corporate culture (Boling, 2015). Another aspect of the Japanese case is the possibility to work while being on leave, which is also a feature in systems in some other countries.

Challenges in a context of informal employment: South Africa

In South Africa,[5] currently there is no designated paternity leave, but eligible employees (who are parents irrespective of sex, but excluding biological mothers) are entitled to ten calendar days of parental leave commencing on the day that the child is born. These days are paid at a rate of 66 per cent of earnings, as legislated by the Unemployment Insurance Act. Eligible mothers are entitled to four months' unpaid maternity leave, but they may be eligible for benefits from the Unemployment Insurance Fund. Some employers offer more than this baseline. Legislation may be about to change as a court ruling[6] in October 2023 decreed that new parents can share the four months of maternity leave. Policy makers must refine and develop the law in line with the ruling by October 2025.

To be eligible for parental leave, the individual has to have been employed for 13 weeks. The self-employed are not covered. In South Africa, around 34 per cent of workers are in the informal sector (ILO, 2023). Adoption leave of ten weeks (unpaid) is available for one member of an adopting couple, including same-sex couples. Surrogacy is supported.

In addition to these policies, family responsibility paid leave is three days per year (five days in the public sector). An employee must work four days per week to qualify and have been employed for at least four months by the same employer.

While eligibility criteria for the employed are not too restrictive, the South African case reminds us of the particular challenges in supporting parents who are not engaged in the formal sector. Policies can be in place and yet not be available to many in the population.

Supporting fathers as equal carers: Sweden

Many books have been written about Swedish fathers and fatherhood (for example, Haas, 1992; Hobson, 2002). Sweden[7] was the first country to introduce an individual entitlement to parental leave for fathers in 1974. It is one of the few countries in the world where it is not unusual to see a man pushing a baby in a pram on a weekday mid-morning. While mothers still take more leave days to care for infants, the policy and practice of leave taking in Sweden certainly supports shared parenting between men and women. Fathers have access to ten days of 'temporary leave in connection with a child's birth or adoption', which is the full label for what used to be considered as paternity leave. This is designed to be used for the other parent to attend delivery, to care for older siblings while the mother is in the hospital, and to participate in childcare when the mother comes home. Leave is paid at a minimum of 77.6 per cent of earnings (up to an upper limit, but often topped up due to collective agreements to close to 100 per cent of wages). Leave is increased in the event of multiple births.

In addition, fathers have access to parental leave until the child reaches 18 months of age. Parents with joint custody are eligible for 240 days of parental leave benefit each; some days may be transferred between them, while others are nontransferable. Both parents can take up to 30 days of paid leave at the same time. Men tend to take leave when the babies are aged one and two. Fathers take around 30 per cent of leave days. A total of 20 per cent of couples share leave equally during the child's first 24 months. Approximately 77 per cent of eligible persons took paternity leave in 2022.

So, fathers are not cast as secondary carers in Sweden, though there is the flexibility for this to become the role in the event that this is the couple's preference. There is excellent parenting leave data available in Sweden, and scholarship on the subject is correspondingly advanced. As such, we know that fathers with higher formal education take more parental leave, as do fathers whose partners have higher levels of formal education, with 28 per cent of tertiary-educated parents sharing leave equally in 2020 (Duvander and Lögren, 2023: 548). Fathers in the private sector are less likely to take leave, as are self-employed fathers (Fahlén and Duvander, 2023).

Eligibility criteria mean that many fathers are included. All employees are eligible to paternity leave, with no qualifying period. However, there is a minimum income threshold (which is the same as the threshold for sickness benefits). Parental leave eligibility is both residency and employment-based. All parents are entitled to either a flat rate or an income-related rate for those who qualify. The self-employed qualify via social security contributions. Same-sex parents have the same rights as different sex parents: rights to leave and benefits are based on custody.

In addition, temporary leave is available for 120 days per year per child for children under 15 years as a family entitlement. For terminally ill children, there is no limit and both parents can take leave at the same time.

In short, Sweden gives an example of how parenting leave can support equal sharing of care for infants by two parents for those who want to parent in this way.

Intersectional inequalities in corporate based leave initiatives: the US

The US[8] is remarkable in that it does not provide a statutory right to any of the types of leave mentioned so far at the federal level (see Kaufman, 2020). Furthermore, it is unusual from an international comparative perspective in that maternity is often considered as a short-term disability – and is covered under disability insurance categories. The only relevant legislation at federal level is the Family and Medical Leave Act (FMLA) of 1993, which provides unpaid leave for a variety of reasons including childbirth or the care of a newborn child up to the age of 12 months. The FMLA provides up to 12 weeks in a 12-month period and is an individual entitlement (for those who are eligible). However, in recent years, 12 states, the District of Columbia and Puerto Rico have adopted paid leave insurance for pregnancy and/or family caregiving, and all leave rights are granted as individual entitlements. Some cities have also regulated for their public sector workers.

In addition, some employers have their own schemes. Corporate schemes can match statutory schemes found in other countries (a well-known example is the company Netflix, which offers a year of paid parental leave to all salaried employees, irrespective of their gender or tenure). In March 2022, estimates were that 25 per cent of civilian workers had some access to paid family leave and 90 per cent to some unpaid family leave via one scheme or another (Bureau of Labor Statistics, 2022). However, estimates suggest that only 4–6 per cent of fathers take more than two weeks of paternity leave (Petts, Knoester and Li, 2020).

It should be noted that the policies that are available are often gender-neutral and on an individual entitlement basis, perhaps reflecting a particular legal framework relating to matters regarding gender equality discrimination. In addition, the US is an example of how policy can develop as a corporate rather than a state initiative, with the ensuing inequalities of access.

Supported fathers and unsupported fathers in a global context: when there are different ideas of who should be supported

A whistlestop tour around the world reveals quite some difference in policy understandings of a father's role in the care of infants. One way to compare across countries is to consider the extent to which parenting leave is compensated in a way that is related to wages or not, and to highlight the gender gap in this type of leave (for example, Ray, Gornick and Schmitt, 2010; Koslowski, 2021). The term 'well paid' here is certainly worthy of discussion. The definition of well-paid leave used in Table 11.2 is 66 per cent of earnings or more (or a flat rate of more than €1,000 per month), but 66 per cent of earnings, especially in the case of a upper limit, or ceiling, might still be a sufficient disincentive to not take leave (for example, Nakazato, 2023). The 66 per cent threshold has been used in in the past by the European Commission, which is why it was adopted by the Leave Review editors in the comparative tables.

All the well-paid leave available shown in Table 11.2 is subject to a ceiling cap on payment. See individual country notes in the Leave Review for more detail.

Table 11.2 shows the two aspects of leave known to be most pertinent to father uptake: whether leave is well paid and whether it is an individual entitlement. We see that Australia and the US do not provide parents (mothers or fathers) with well-paid leave. South Africa provides a very short period of well-paid leave to fathers, but not to mothers. Chile is an example of a country which chooses to support mothers relatively generously, but not fathers. Japan looks exemplary in terms of its gender-equal offer to mothers and fathers, but we know that fathers barely use this leave, which perhaps throws into question whether the 66 per cent threshold can be

Table 11.2: Total amount of statutory 'well-paid' leave available to parents in the first 18 months of a child's life: April 2023

Country (2023)	Well-paid leave as family entitlement	Period of 'father-only' well-paid leave	Period of 'mother-only' well-paid leave (months)
Australia	0	0	0
Chile	0	5 days	5.5
Japan	0	6 months	6
South Africa	0	10 days	0
Sweden	9.8 months	3.3 months	3
US	0	0	0

Source: adapted from https://www.leavenetwork.org/fileadmin/user_upload/k_leavenetwork/annual_reviews/2023/3.8._Wellpaid_Leave.pdf

considered well paid, especially as there is also an upper limit to payments. This leaves Sweden, which has well-paid leave and equally available individual entitlements for mothers and fathers. Sweden also has a long period of transferable entitlement, which is mostly used by mothers, but can also be used by fathers.

The range of attitudes towards fathers is from near-parity (Sweden) to fathers being a worst-case scenario emergency back-up (Chile). In the middle we have the supposedly gender-neutral primary carer framework in Australia, which does provide some optionality, but on the whole reinforces the distinct role norms for mothers and fathers, and does not provide wage replacement. The US is an outlier with no dedicated paid maternity or paternity leave legislation at the federal level; parenting is treated as largely a private affair.

In three of the case studies (Australia, Chile and South Africa), the legislation reflects and reinforces the strong gender norms of maternalism, with the notion of father as a back-up carer. Japan and Sweden have legislation that in principle should support the notion of more equal sharing, though in practice, this has so far only been achieved in Sweden. This highlights that parenting leave is only part of the overall parenting support system, which also needs to be integrated into well-functioning formal early childhood education and care. In the US, both mothers and fathers are largely left to fend for themselves.

The different cases provide an insight into the toolkit of policy design features at a leave policy maker's disposal. For example, the notion of compulsory leave is an interesting one. We see it in Chile. What is the purpose of making such a short period of leave obligatory? Japan introduces the concept of certification of companies which can demonstrate a sufficient level of take-up of leave, leading to corporate tax breaks. Another aspect of the Japanese design is the possibility to take leave flexibly – almost on a part-time basis, which is seen in other systems as a way to promote take-up of leave by fathers.

We can already see from this limited selection that the eligibility base for leave can be more or less inclusive of fathers across a given population. Employment eligibility criteria range from leave being a first day right (from the very first day of employment) to parents requiring a 12-month period with the same employer prior to leave before they become eligible. Most examples in this chapter link entitlement to employment rather than residency, though Sweden requires both, which in practice broadens the eligibility base. In addition, LGBT parenting rights vary hugely across countries. In some countries, the nonbirth parent can legally only be a father, and this is echoed in the leave entitlement, while in others, the definitions of a legal parent are more inclusive, and the leave legislation expands to explicitly include LGBT parents.

Conclusions

The focus of this book is the caring by fathers in a global context: practices, policies and ideologies. In this chapter, looking at the policy structures and, where available, leave uptake statistics gives us some insight into all three aspects. This chapter has considered the situation in Australia, Chile, Japan, South Africa, Sweden and the US. We can see that the gendered framings of responsibility for care and the availability of leave policies for fathers can be configured quite differently from a global perspective. Policies clearly enable or constrain caring by fathers. They also promote the caring of some fathers over other fathers. The implications of the different systems for fathers' care are considerable. As other studies have found (for example, Ray et al, 2010; Bünning and Pollmann-Schult, 2016; Kvande, 2022), there is a correlation between father's use of leave and whether leave is well remunerated (around 100 per cent wage replacement rate), as well as whether it is earmarked for fathers. Countries which do not provide well-paid leave, even if they also offer leave to fathers, tend to rely on mothers to do most of the care for infants. Similarly, countries providing much less leave provision for fathers as compared to mothers as part of the way in which leave policies are structured do not see many fathers taking leave.

Acknowledgements

I gratefully acknowledge the work of the county note authors without which this chapter would have been so much more difficult to write.

Notes

[1] https://www.mencare.org/what-we-do/advocacy/paid-parental-leave/
[2] For more information, see Baird, Baxter and Hamilton, 2023.

3   For more information, see Bosch, 2023.
4   For more information, see Nakazato, Takezawa and Nishimura, 2023.
5   For more information, see Jaga and Farista, 2023.
6   *Van Wyk and Others v Minister of Employment and Labour* (2022-017842) [2023] ZAGPJHC 1213; [2024] 1 BLLR 93 (GJ); (2024) 45 ILJ 194 (GJ); 2024 (1) SA 545 (GJ) (25 October 2023).
7   For more information, see Duvander and Löfgren, 2023.
8   For more information, see Engeman et al, 2023.

References

Addati, L., Cattaneo, U. and Pozzan, E. (2022) *Care at Work: Investing in Care Leave and Services for a More Gender Equal World of Work*. Geneva: International Labour Organization.

Baird, M., Baxter, J.A. and Hamilton, M. (2023) 'Australia country note', in S. Blum, I. Dobrotić, G. Kaufman, A. Koslowski and P. Moss (eds) *19th International Review of Leave Policies and Related Research 2023*. Available from: https://www.leavenetwork.org/fileadmin/user_upload/k_leave network/annual_reviews/2023/Blum_etal_LPRN_full_report_2023.pdf

Baird, M., Hamilton, M. and Constantin, A. (2021) 'Gender equality and paid parental leave in Australia: a decade of giant leaps or baby steps?', *Journal of Industrial Relations*, 63(4), 546–567.

Blum, S. and Dobrotić, I. (2021) 'The inclusiveness of social rights: the case of leave policies', *Social Inclusion*, 9(2), 222–226. https://doi.org/10.17645/si.v9i2.4523

Blum, S., Dobrotić, I., Kaufman, G., Koslowski, A. and Moss, P. (eds) (2023) *19th International Review of Leave Policies and Related Research 2023*. Available from: https://www.leavenetwork.org/fileadmin/user_upload/k_leavenetw ork/annual_reviews/2023/Blum_etal_LPRN_full_report_2023.pdf

Boling, P. (2015) *The Politics of Work and Family Policies: Comparing Japan, France, Germany and the United States*. Cambridge: Cambridge University Press.

Bosch, M.J. (2023) 'Chile country note', in S. Blum, I. Dobrotić, G. Kaufman, A. Koslowski and P. Moss (eds) *19th International Review of Leave Policies and Related Research 2023*. Available from: https://www.leavenetw ork.org/fileadmin/user_upload/k_leavenetwork/annual_reviews/2023/Blum_etal_LPRN_full_report_2023.pdf

Bureau of Labor Statistics (2022) *Employee Benefits in the United States*. Available from: https://www.bls.gov/ebs/latest-numbers.htm

Bünning, M. and Pollmann-Schult, M. (2016) 'Family policies and fathers' working hours: cross-national differences in the paternal labour supply', *Work, Employment & Society*, 30(2), 256–274.

Dobrotić, I. and Blum, S. (2020) 'Inclusiveness of parental-leave benefits in twenty-one European countries: measuring social and gender inequalities in leave eligibility', *Social Politics: International Studies in Gender, State and Society*, 27(3), 588–614.

Dobrotić, I., Blum, S. and Koslowski, A. (eds) (2022) *Research Handbook on Leave Policy*. Cheltenham: Edward Elgar.

Duvander, A.-Z. and Löfgren, N. (2023) 'Sweden country note', in S. Blum, I. Dobrotić, G. Kaufman, A. Koslowski and P. Moss (eds) *19th International Review of Leave Policies and Related Research 2023*. Available from: https://www.leavenetwork.org/fileadmin/user_upload/k_leavenetwork/annual_reviews/2023/Blum_etal_LPRN_full_report_2023.pdf

EIGE (European Institute for Gender Equality) (2020) *Eligibility for Parental Leave in EU States*. Publications Office of the European Union. doi:10.2839/919049

EIGE (2022) *Gender Equality Index 2022: The COVID-19 pandemic and care*, Luxembourg: Publication Office of the European Union. Available from: https://eige.europa.eu/sites/default/files/documents/gender_equality_index_2022_corr.pdf

Engeman, C. Petts, R.J. Gatenio Gabel, S. and Kaufman, G. (2023) 'US country note', in S. Blum, I. Dobrotić, G. Kaufman, A. Koslowski and P. Moss (eds) *19th International Review of Leave Policies and Related Research 2023*. Available at: https://www.leavenetwork.org/fileadmin/user_upload/k_leavenetwork/annual_reviews/2023/Blum_etal_LPRN_full_report_2023.pdf

Eydal, G. and Rostgaard, T. (eds) (2016), *Fatherhood in the Nordic Welfare States: Comparing Care Policies and Practice*. Bristol: Bristol University Press.

Eydal G.B., Gíslason, I.V., Rostgaard, T., Brandth, B., Duvander, A.-Z. and Lammi-Taskula, J. (2015) 'Trends in parental leave in the Nordic countries: has the forward march of gender equality halted?', *Community, Work & Family*, 18(2), 167–181.

Fahlén, S. and Duvander, A.-Z. (2023) *Fathers Who Do Not Use Parental Leave: A Register-Based Analysis of Swedish Fathers to Children Born Between 1994 and 2017*. ISF Rapport 2023:1WP. Available from: https://isf.se/publikationer/rapporter/2023/2023-04-04-fathers-who-do-not-use-parental-leave

Gerson, K. (2011) *The Unfinished Revolution*. Oxford: Oxford University Press.

Haas, L. (1992) *Equal Parenthood and Social Policy*. New York: SUNY Press.

Hobson, B. (2002) *Making Men into Fathers: Men, Masculinities and the Social Politics of Fatherhood*. Cambridge: Cambridge University Press.

ILO (International Labour Organization) (2023) Statistics on the informal economy. Available from: https://ilostat.ilo.org/topics/informality/

Jaga, A. and Farista, F. (2023) 'South Africa country note', in S. Blum, I. Dobrotić, G. Kaufman, A. Koslowski and P. Moss (eds) *19th International Review of Leave Policies and Related Research 2023*. Available from: https://www.leavenetwork.org/fileadmin/user_upload/k_leavenetwork/annual_reviews/2023/Blum_etal_LPRN_full_report_2023.pdf

Kaufman, G. (2020) *Fixing Parental Leave: The Six Month Solution*. New York: New York University Press.

Koslowski, A. (2021) 'Capturing the gender gap in the scope of parenting related leave policies across nations', *Social Inclusion*, 9(2), 250–261.

Koslowski, A. and Kadar-Satat, G. (2019) 'Fathers at work: explaining the gaps between entitlement to leave policies and uptake', *Community, Work and Family*, 22(2), 129–145. https://doi.org/10.1080/13668803.2018.1428174

Koslowski A. and O'Brien M. (2022) 'Fathers and family leave policies: what public policy can do to support families', in M. Grau. M. las Heras Maestro and H. Riley Bowles (eds) *Engaged Fatherhood for Men, Families and Gender Equality: Contributions to Management Science*. Cham: Springer, pp 141–152. https://doi.org/10.1007/978-3-030-75645-1_7

Kvande, E. (2022) 'Individual parental leave for fathers: promoting gender equality in Norway', in M. Grau. M. las Heras Maestro and H. Riley Bowles (eds) *Engaged Fatherhood for Men, Families and Gender Equality: Contributions to Management Science*. Cham: Springer, pp 153–163. https://doi.org/10.1007/978-3-030-75645-1_8

Meil, G., Escebedo, A. and Lapuerta, I. (2023) 'Spain country note' in S. Blum, I. Dobrotić, G. Kaufman, A. Koslowski and P. Moss (eds) *19th International Review of Leave Policies and Related Research 2023*. Available from: https://www.leavenetwork.org/fileadmin/user_upload/k_leave network/annual_reviews/2023/Blum_etal_LPRN_full_report_2023.pdf

Meil, G. Wall, K. Atalaia, S. and Escebedo, A. (2022) 'Trends towards de-gendering leave use in Spain and Portugal', in I. Dobrotić, S. Blum and A. Koslowski (eds) *Research Handbook on Leave Policy*. Cheltenham: Edward Elgar, pp 218–230.

MenCare (n.d.) The MenCare Parental Leave Platform. Available from: https://www.mencare.org/resources/the-mencare-parental-leave-platform/

Moss, P. and O'Brien, M. (2019) 'United Kingdom: leave policy and an attempt to take a new path', in P. Moss, A.-Z. Duvander and A. Koslowski (eds) *Parental Leave and Beyond*. Bristol: Policy Press.

Nakazato, H. (2023) 'Has 'Nordic turn' in Japan crystalized? Politics of promoting parental leave take-up among fathers and the divergence from the Nordic system', *Journal of Family Studies*, 29(6), 2615–2630. https://doi.org/10.1080/13229400.2023.2179533

Nakazato, H. Takezawa, J. and Nishimura, J. (2023) 'Japan country note', in S. Blum, I. Dobrotić, G. Kaufman, A. Koslowski and P. Moss (eds) *19th International Review of Leave Policies and Related Research 2023*. DOI: 10.25365/phaidra.431. Available from: https://www.leavenetwork.org/fileadmin/user_upload/k_leavenetwork/annual_reviews/2023/Blum_etal_LPRN_full_report_2023.pdf

Petts, R.J., Knoester, C. and Li, Q. (2020) 'Paid paternity leave-taking in the US', *Community, Work & Family*, 23(2), 162–183.

Ray, R., Gornick, J. and Schmitt, J. (2010) 'Who cares? Assessing generosity and gender equality in parental leave policy designs in 21 countries', *Journal of European Social Policy*, 20(3), 196–216.

Sant, R. (2023) *Parental Rights Survey 2019 Survey Report*. Brighton: Institute for Employment Studies. Available from: https://www.employment-studies.co.uk/resource/parental-rights-survey-2019

Wright, E.O. and Brighouse, H. (2008) 'Strong gender egalitarianism', *Politics & Society*, 36(3), 360–372.

12

Gender role attitudes, perceptions of parenthood and father's parental leave use in Finland

Miia Saarikallio-Torp, Johanna Lammi-Taskula, Anneli Miettinen, Johanna Närvi and Ella Sihvonen

Introduction

In this chapter, we examine how attitudinal factors are connected to fathers' use of parental leave that can facilitate their role as a caring parent. Plenty of research has been conducted on how fathers' participation in childcare and the use of parental leave are determined by various individual, organisational and societal-level factors, but literature on how attitudes and beliefs about gender roles, fatherhood and parenting shape fathers' involvement – and especially parental leave use – is scarce. Understanding the complexities, barriers and facilitators to fathers' parental leave uptake is important in promoting fathers' involvement in childcare.

Aiming at promoting gender equality, the Nordic countries, including Finland, have been pioneers in designing parental leave to support each parent's participation in working life and childcare, first by providing paid leave that parents could freely share between them and later by implementing an earmarked parental leave for fathers – that is, the father's quota (Eydal et al, 2015; Eydal and Rostgaard, 2016; Koslowski, Chapter 11, this volume). Research on the father's quota has shown that it has indeed had an impact on the gendered division of parental leave and men's engagement in childcare (Duvander et al, 2019; Patnaik, 2019; Canaan et al, 2022). However, mothers still use the bulk of parental leave even in the Nordic countries. In Finland, father's quota was introduced later than in the other Nordic countries (Lammi-Taskula, 2022), and the share of leave taken by fathers is lower than in the other Nordic countries (Duvander et al, 2019; Saarikallio-Torp and Miettinen, 2021).

Although mothers still use the majority of parental leave, fatherhood has changed profoundly in many countries, including Finland, and fathers are willing to take more caring and nurturing roles in their children's lives (for example, Eerola et al, 2019; Eerola, Mustosmäki and Pirskanen, Chapter 8, this volume). The contemporary ideals of fatherhood challenge traditional gender norms and promote a more egalitarian division of labour within households in terms of domestic tasks as well as childcare; fathers are seen not only as providers but also as nurturers (Miller, 2010; McGill, 2014). This transition is reinforced by evolving societal norms and cultural shifts emphasising the importance of paternal involvement in childcare and its benefits for the child's wellbeing (Doucet, 2006; Miller, 2010). In parallel to changes in fatherhood, parenthood more generally has seen a change towards 'intensive parenting', which refers to a child-centred approach characterised by expert guidance, emotional involvement and labour-intensive care (Hays, 1996).

In this chapter, we examine whether and how fathers' attitudes towards gender roles and perceptions of fatherhood as well as the cultural ideology of intensive parenting are related to their use of parental leave. Rather than understanding being on parental leave as a synonym for caring fatherhood – which entails not just involvement in care tasks but a more general 'habit of mind' and taking responsibility for the child's wellbeing (see Doucet, Chapter 2, this volume) – we are interested in how different ideals of care are reflected in the take-up of parental leave. We use a survey conducted in 2022 among Finnish parents with small children, and distinguish between three types of parental leave (birth-related leave, father's quota and shared parental leave) to examine if attitudes are differently associated with fathers' use of leave depending on their design. While this distinction reflects the development of parental leave schemes in Finland over time, each leave type also embodies different views on fatherhood and the father's role in childcare. Gender egalitarian attitudes are likely to increase fathers' use of parental leave, but the association may be weaker for earmarked leave. The use of freely shared parental leave may require negotiations between the parents as well as attitudes that strongly support the equal participation of fathers. Adherence to the ideal of intensive parenting could increase fathers' parental leave use. However, the concept of intensive parenting was first developed to reflect expectations towards mothers (for example, Hays, 1996; Lee et al, 2014) and it is not clear to what extent these demands apply to fathers. Finland provides an interesting context for this study, as the country ranks high in gender equality, and family policies support the dual-earner family model. Yet, the division of childcare is still gendered.

Changing fatherhood: gender equal, caring and intensive?

During the past few decades, the conceptions and norms of masculinity and fatherhood in Western societies have been expanded. The contemporary understanding of fatherhood has meant a shift away from the traditional and previously hegemonic forms of masculinity and fatherhood towards caring masculinity (see Tarrant et al, Chapter 10, this volume). This change has been characterised by an increase in fathers' involvement in care and family life. While traditionally breadwinning has been fundamental for fathering identity as a form of providing care, fathers are now increasingly seen as involved and engaged in co-parenting, capable of nurturing and participating in childcare, and appreciating family time, emotional availability and the father–child relationship (Gerson, 2010; Miller, 2011; McGill, 2014; Eerola and Mykkänen, 2015; Hunter et al, 2017).

The development of caring masculinities has been identified as a question of men's empowerment, enabling men to develop nurturing identities and experience the benefits of father–child bonding, affection and giving care, but also as a question of gender equality, when care work is understood as a necessity that has to be done by someone (Elliot, 2016). Caring fatherhood would thus mean adopting caring activities or tasks – including but not limited to taking parental leave – and possibly also changing the identities and mindsets involving responsibilities and responsiveness to the needs of the child (see Doucet, Chapter 2, this volume).

Attitudes concerning parenting and gender are found to be more egalitarian in the Nordic countries than elsewhere (Salin et al, 2018). However, some scholars have argued that the development of egalitarian gender roles has slowed down or reached a point of 'stalled gender revolution' even in countries like Finland, where gender equality is believed to have reached high levels and governments have implemented parental leave reforms encouraging fathers to take a more active role in childcare (for example, Begall et al, 2023; Knight and Brinton, 2017). This is reflected in the division of unpaid work between men and women, as mothers continue to carry the main responsibility for childcare while also being engaged in paid work.

Instead of a fundamental change towards gender equality in parenthood, the ideas around caring masculinity have broadened the scope of hegemonic masculinity, meaning that fathers are now expected to be involved and nurturing in addition to providing for the family (Hunter et al, 2017; Peukert, 2019; see also Shirani et al, 2011; Tarrant et al, Chapter 10, this volume). Therefore, attitudes on gender roles and parenting can be seen as multidimensional. Rather than forming a single continuum with traditionalism (man as the breadwinner, woman as the carer) at one end and egalitarianism (dual earner/dual carer) at the other, traditional views on breadwinning may coexist with views that consider caregiving as central to fatherhood (Wall and O'Brien, 2017; Knight and Brinton, 2017).

In Finland, for example, parents' cultural narratives have emphasised 'decent fatherhood', characterised by family-oriented, participatory paternal responsibilities and male nurturance, but still divergent parental gender roles. However, these understandings coexisted with more gender equally oriented narratives, including comprehensive paternal responsibility and equal parental gender roles, as well as persisting narratives of the traditionally masculine father (Eerola and Mykkänen, 2015).

Besides the evolving gender roles in parenting, there have also been shifts in terms of what constitutes culturally desirable parenting. Expectations now lean towards intensive parenting, which requires significant emotional, financial and laborious investment in expert-guided parenting practices (Hays, 1996; Faircloth, 2014). This kind of parenting is characterised by a continuous awareness of the potential risk of wrongdoing from the moment of conception (Lee et al, 2014; Roman, 2014; Macvarish, 2018).

Although intensive parenting appears gender-neutral, most scholars agree that its demands primarily target mothers (for example, Daly, 2013; Sihvonen, 2023). However, it is crucial to consider the extent to which these demands extend to fathers, who certainly have not been immune to these cultural changes (Dermott, 2008; Miller, 2011). According to Wall and O'Brien (2017), gender-equal parenting and involved fatherhood should be conceptualised as different dimensions, and the same seems to apply to intensive fathering and equal parenting (for example, Shirani et al, 2011; Faircloth, 2023).

Evidence on the role of parents' gender ideologies for the fathers' involvement in the family suggests that egalitarian attitudes and perceptions of fathers as carers promote fathers' participation in childcare (for example, Gaunt, 2006). Men with more egalitarian gender role attitudes have been found to be more involved both in housework and childcare, especially in basic childcare and indirect care activities such as arranging doctor's appointments. The association was weaker for recreational (playing, drawing and so on) and physical and logistical tasks (bathing the child, driving the child to daycare/school and so on) (Evertsson, 2014; Keizer, 2015; Streckenbach el al, 2022).

Fathering ideals can also moderate the relationship between paid work and fathers' involvement. There seems to be a trade-off between time spent at work and with family for fathers holding traditional fathering attitudes. Such a trade-off is weaker among fathers who embrace their roles as caregivers despite the hours spent at work (McGill, 2014).

To our knowledge, there are only a few studies that examine the role of attitudes in fathers' parental leave use. In the Finnish context, Lammi-Taskula (2008) found that when fathers were critical towards the mother's primacy as the carer and the idea of the father as the main provider, they were more likely to share parental leave with the child's mother. In Sweden, Duvander (2014) found that men's strong egalitarian attitudes were positively connected to their parental leave use, but not to the length of the leave. Using US data, Petts and Knoester (2018) found that attitudes shape the relationship between fathers' parental leave taking and their involvement. Furthermore, attitudes were also found to explain the relationship between leave length and engagement.

Childcare policies in Finland

Finland is a Nordic welfare state with a longstanding policy goal of supporting gender equal parenthood. Mothers' employment rate is high, except for mothers of children under the age of three, and fathers have substantially increased their time spent on childcare over the past few decades (Miettinen and Rotkirch, 2012). Early childhood education and care services are provided to all children below school age (under seven years of age), and these services are substantially subsidised through public funding, ensuring accessibility for all families regardless of income. During the last 20 years, the parental leave reforms in Finland have concentrated on encouraging fathers' parental leave use and increasing mothers' labour market participation. The Finnish parental leave scheme promotes a dual-earner/dual-carer family model and creates good possibilities for fathers to participate in childcare during the child's first years by providing them with a nontransferable parental leave quota (Lammi-Taskula et al, 2023).

While fathers of young children in Finland are willing to participate in childcare (Eerola and Mykkänen, 2015; Lammi-Taskula, 2017), the Finnish childcare policy includes elements that reproduce the primacy of the mother by supporting a longer child home care with a cash-for-care (home care allowance) system (Alasuutari et al, 2022). Thus, one of the main obstacles for fathers' take-up of leave is a longer leave period taken by the mother (Saarikallio-Torp et al, 2024).

Before the latest parental leave reform in 2022 and during our data collection, the Finnish parental leave scheme emphasised the parents' freedom of choice, although it also included the father's quota. As the parents who responded to the survey had used parental leave before the 2022 reform, the description given here applies to the old parental leave scheme. The scheme consisted of maternity leave (17.5 weeks), father's birth-related leave (three weeks) and shared parental leave (26 weeks), which parents were able to share between them as they wished. In addition to the birth-related leave, fathers were entitled to a father's quota, which they were able to use after the shared parental leave period. Altogether, the length of leave designated to fathers was nine weeks (including the birth-related leave). While the take-up of the birth-related leave has been very popular and the take-up of the quota leave has gradually increased, especially among highly educated fathers and fathers employed in white-collar jobs, the shared parental leave has been used mainly by mothers (Saarikallio-Torp and Miettinen, 2021). Furthermore, as shared parental leave is generally understood as the mother's entitlement, dividing it between the parents means that the mother needs to give up part of the leave for the father to use.

Data and methods

The data used in this study are based on Parental Leave Survey 2022, collected in May 2022 by the Social Insurance Institution of Finland (Kela) and the Finnish Institute for Health and Welfare (THL). The survey was targeted at mothers and fathers of children aged one to two, and simple random samples of 7,000 fathers and 5,050 mothers were obtained from the parental allowance registers of Kela. The invitation to the online survey was sent to the study population by email. The data were weighted by the age of the child and parents, parents' number of children and the geographical area to better match the target population (see Kinnunen et al, 2024). In this study, we employ the data on fathers (n = 1,524). As the sample was drawn from the benefit registers, the data include fathers who have received at least one day of parental allowance, thus excluding fathers who used no leave at all (about one quarter of all fathers; see Saarikallio-Torp and Miettinen, 2021).

To examine the role of attitudes, we named the variables measuring gender role attitudes and perceptions of parenting as 'caring father', 'traditional father' and 'intensive parenting'. The measurement for the *caring father* is based on the item 'Fathers are just as capable as mothers of taking care of a small child'. The measure for *traditional father* is based on three items: 'Mothers of small children should stay at home and take care of the child', 'Even if a woman works, the man should be the primary earner for the household' and 'Caring for a small child is primarily the mother's responsibility, even if the father is involved in the child's care' (Cronbach's alpha 0.78). Items were modified from national parental leave surveys and international value surveys (see Takala, 2005; International Social Survey Programme 2012; Salmi and Närvi, 2017; European Values Study 2017). The measurement of *intensive parenting* is based on three items (see Gauthier et al, 2021): 'Children's needs should come before those of their parents', 'Good parents should be aware of what experts say and write about the development of children' and 'Parents should always be available to their children' (Cronbach's alpha 0.49). The respondents were asked to evaluate the statements with a five-point Likert scale: 1 = strongly disagree, 5 = strongly agree. The items in different dimensions were averaged into a scale where higher scores (ranging from 1 to 5) refer to either a more caring role in fathering (caring father), more intensive parenting perceptions (intensive parenting) or more traditional gender role attitudes (traditional father). As control variables, we used the father's age, number of children, education and income, as well as occupational level and weekly working hours. In the analysis, we also included information on the partner's (mother's) educational level and her employment status before the child was born. To match the Finnish educational system, we distinguish three educational groups: upper secondary-level vocational education or lower, tertiary degree in applied sciences, and tertiary degree (academic).

The control variables were chosen based on previous literature on factors associated with fathers' parental leave use.

We use multinomial regression analysis to investigate how attitudinal dimensions are associated with fathers' parental leave use. Fathers were divided into three groups: fathers who (a) only used birth-related leave (n = 293, the reference category), (b) used earmarked father's quota leave (n = 1,021), and (c) used shared parental leave (n = 199). We hypothesise that fathers endorsing caring father attitudes use more parental leave than other fathers. We further hypothesise that in order to reinforce their masculinity and roles as breadwinners, fathers holding traditional gender role attitudes use less parental leave. We assume that the institutional framework plays a strong role; we expect different patterns regarding the use of father's quota leave and shared parental leave. We assume that as the use of the father's quota has become more popular, it is less likely to challenge traditional gender roles in the family. Consequently, we expect that fathers' attitudes are less salient in explaining the differences in father's quota use. In contrast, as shared parental leave continues to be used mainly by mothers, fathers' caring and nontraditional attitudes are expected to be positively related to their use of shared parental leave. Due to a lack of previous studies on intensive parenting among fathers, we withdraw from setting a clear hypothesis for this dimension. In the regression analysis, the three dimensions of attitudes were added to the model step by step; first introducing the caring father dimension, then the intensive parenting dimension, and finally the traditional father dimension.

Results

Descriptive results

We start by showing descriptive information on our study population (Table 12.1). Table 12.1 also shows the mean values of the attitudinal dimensions and their means in the categories of the background variables. On average, 60 per cent of fathers in our sample had used the father's quota and 12 per cent had used shared parental leave. The share of fathers using parental leave in the study sample was somewhat higher compared to national parental allowance statistics (for example, Saarikallio-Torp and Miettinen, 2021), mainly because the sample excluded fathers who did not use any leave. Pearson's correlation coefficient was adopted to test the relationship between attitudinal dimensions. The analysis revealed only a weak correlation between the caring father and intensive parenting dimensions ($r_p = 0.099$, $p < 0.001$) and only a slight correlation between caring father and traditional father, though negative ($r_p = -0.408$, $p < 0.001$). Regarding the dimensions of traditional father and intensive parenting, the correlation coefficient was 0.075 ($p = 0.004$). The weak correlations between the parenting dimensions

Table 12.1: The characteristics of fathers included in the analysis and the mean values and standard deviations for attitudinal dimensions by background variables

	% (N)	Caring father Mean (SD)	Traditional father Mean (SD)	Intensive parenting Mean (SD)
All fathers		3.91 (0.85)	2.42 (1.07)	4.01 (0.64)
Father's education level				
Vocational or lower	39.6 (602)	3.65 (0.86)	2.65 (1.10)	4.04 (0.64)
Tertiary degree in applied sciences	31.1 (473)	3.93 (0.88)	2.44 (1.01)	4.06 (0.61)
Tertiary degree (academic)	29.4 (447)	3.85 (0.82)	2.09 (0.99)	3.94 (0.66)
Father's income (net, month)				
€0–1,500	7.3 (110)	3.12 (0.94)	2.66 (1.11)	4.12 (0.63)
€1,501–2,000	14.5 (226)	4.11 (0.79)	2.40 (1.06)	4.05 (0.64)
€2,001–2,500	29.3 (443)	3.95 (0.88)	2.45 (1.07)	4.08 (0.58)
€2,501–3,000	22.7 (342)	3.83 (0.84)	2.37 (1.04)	4.01 (0.64)
> €3,000	25.8 (389)	3.84 (0.81)	2.36 (1.07)	3.90 (0.68)
Father's occupational level				
Managerial position and upper white collar	34.3 (519)	3.87 (0.85)	2.20 (0.99)	3.97 (0.64)
Lower white collar and blue-collar	59.4 (898)	3.95 (0.85)	2.51 (1.08)	4.04 (0.64)
Self employed/Other	6.3 (95)	3.80 (0.85)	2.84 (1.08)	3.96 (0.59)
Father's weekly working hours				
Regular (or short) hours	74.3 (1,072)	3.94 (0.85)	2.33 (1.03)	4.03 (0.62)
Long hours (> 40 hrs/wk)	25.7 (370)	3.81 (0.88)	2.64 (1.09)	3.96 (0.67)
Spouse's education level				
Vocational or lower	32.4 (488)	3.92 (0.88)	2.75 (1.12)	4.04 (0.66)
University degree of applied sciences	33.6 (506)	3.93 (0.85)	2.50 (1.03)	4.02 (0.63)
University degree (academic)	34.0 (511)	3.90 (0.83)	2.02 (0.91)	3.98 (0.63)
Spouse's employment status (before childbirth)				
Employed/entrepreneur	80.1 (1,205)	3.92 (0.84)	2.31 (1.01)	4.01 (0.63)
Studying/taking care of child/unemployed	19.9 (300)	3.88 (0.89)	2.87 (1.15)	4.01 (0.67)

Source: Parental Leave Survey 2022, authors' own calculations

allow us to include all three dimensions into a single regression equation. Furthermore, it also justifies interpreting them as capturing different attitudinal dimensions.

Associations between attitudes and father's parental leave use

Next, we show the results from the multinomial regression analysis examining the associations between attitudinal and parenting dimensions and fathers' use of parental leave while controlling for the background variables (Table 12.2). Results from Model I, where we included only the caring father dimension (and controls) to the regression equation, show that fathers with caring attitudes were more likely to use shared parental leave when controlling for the socioeconomic factors. However, the caring father dimension was not associated with father's quota use.

The intensive parenting dimension was not associated with father's parental leave use, not the designated quota leave or shared parental leave (Model II). In addition, adding the dimension to the model does not change the result for the caring dimension. Given that the variation in the mean values in this dimension by categories of the background variables was small (see Table 12.1 on descriptive statistics), it seems that fathers in Finland might not respond to the requirements of intensive parenting or that these demands do not distinguish fathers in terms of their parental leave take-up. It is also important to note that the items used in constructing the indicator of intensive parenting did not specify which parent was being referred to. Thus, fathers may have thought that the statements reflected parenting pressures on both parents or mothers specifically rather than solely on themselves.

Moving on to traditional father attitudes (Model III), the results are in line with what we hypothesised: there was no statistically significant association between traditional gender role attitudes and father's quota use (the socioeconomic background factors controlled for). However, a father's traditional attitudes about gender roles have a strong and negative association with shared parental leave use. Thus, father's traditional attitudes do not prevent father's quota use, but do so for the shared parental leave.

Fathers in managerial or upper white-collar positions being less likely to use shared parental leave suggests that the division of the leave between parents may depend more on pragmatic factors, such as employment situation, than on the father's caring attitudes. The result of the spouse's employment increasing the father's use of shared parental leave further confirms this interpretation. Furthermore, fathers with less educated partners were less likely to use the father's quota, suggesting that the mother's low education and weak labour market prospects are stronger determinants of whether the father uses his earmarked leave than his breadwinning ideology. On the other hand, fathers' traditional attitudes were negatively associated with using shared

Table 12.2: The results from the multinomial logistic regression (odds ratios and their statistical significance) (reference category = father has used only birth-related leave)

	Model I		Model II		Model III	
	Father's quota	Shared parental leave	Father's quota	Shared parental leave	Father's quota	Shared parental leave
Caring father	1.09	1.44**	1.10	1.44**	1.06	1.13
Intensive parenting			0.99	0.96	1.01	1.05
Traditional father					0.92	0.53***
Father's education level						
Vocational or lower	0.77	1.16	0.78	1.17	0.78	1.16
Tertiary degree in applied sciences	ref.		ref.			
Tertiary degree (academic)	0.85	1.17	0.85	1.16	0.84	1.05
Father's income						
I	0.58	0.67	0.57	0.65	0.57	0.71
II	0.83	0.71	0.82	0.70	0.80	0.66
III	ref.		ref.			
IV	0.82	0.95	0.82	0.95	0.82	0.95
V	0.86	0.88	0.85	0.87	0.87	0.93
Father's occupational level						
Managerial position and upper white collar	0.90	0.60*	0.90	0.60*	0.89	0.55*
Lower white collar and blue collar	ref.		ref.			
Self-employed/Other	0.69	0.47	0.69	0.47	0.70	0.50
Father's weekly working hours						
Normal hours	ref.		ref.			
Long hours (> 40 hrs/wk)	0.95	0.63	0.95	0.63	0.96	0.67
Spouse's education level						
Vocational or lower	0.68*	0.59	0.69*	0.59	0.70*	0.65
University degree of applied sciences	ref.		ref.			
University degree (academic)	1.51	4.19***	1.51	4.19***	1.47	3.57***
Spouse's employment status (before childbirth)						
Employed	1.62**	2.08*	1.60**	2.05*	1.55*	1.68
Student/unemployed/at home	ref.		ref.			

Notes: Model also included demographic controls: father's age and number of children.
   *** $p < 0.001$; ** $p < 0.01$; * $p < 0.05$.
Source: Parental Leave Survey 2022, authors' own calculations

parental leave, which suggests that traditional views on the division of paid and unpaid work in the family effectively bars fathers' use of shared leave.

The demographic factors and father's socioeconomic background had only a limited role in explaining the differences in fathers' parental leave use. In particular, fathers' educational attainment, income or working hours were not associated with the use of parental leave. Thus, fathers' caring and traditional attitudes were associated with their parental leave use regardless of educational attainment or income level.

In contrast, mother's socioeconomic background, education and employment status had a strong relevance to fathers' parental leave use. Fathers with low-educated spouses were less likely to use the father's quota and less likely to use shared parental leave, although the latter association did not reach statistical significance, whereas fathers with highly educated spouses were more likely to use shared parental leave. In addition, if the mother was employed (before childbirth), the father was more likely to use parental leave; either quota or shared leave. However, this association turned statistically insignificant once the traditional father dimension was added to the model. Interestingly, even though the mother's education is strongly linked to fathers' parental leave use, his attitudes continue to matter. Notably, father's traditional attitudes seem to hinder using shared parental leave, even in families where the mother is highly educated.

All in all, fathers' attitudes – being caring, praising intensive parenting or having traditional perceptions of gender roles – were not associated with the use of the father's quota: regardless of their attitudes towards gender roles, fathers use the quota just as often. Furthermore, caring attitudes increase the likelihood of fathers using shared parental leave. However, traditional gender role attitudes seem to overrun the caring attitudes, as the association between the caring dimension and fathers' parental leave use disappeared when we added the traditional father dimension to the model (see Table 12.2).

Conclusions

The focus of this chapter has been to examine the relationship between attitudinal factors and fathers' involvement in childcare measured with their parental leave use in Finland. The research holds significant value because there is only little prior empirical evidence on how attitudinal factors influence the division of parental leave in particular. Although Finland represents a rather egalitarian country where family policies support the dual-earner/dual-carer model, the division of childcare still remains gendered. Our results also have broader relevance regarding the limited success of the introduction of nontransferable parental leave quotas for fathers in terms of transforming the gendered division of childcare more profoundly.

We have sought to find out to what extent gender role attitudes and perceptions of parenthood are linked to fathers' use of parental leave, and whether the relationship is different when looking at different types of parental leave. Different leave types also have different policy goals: birth-related leave is used simultaneously with the mother, often soon after childbirth, and it aims at providing a helping hand for mothers, whereas shared parental leave and the nonsharable father's quota enable fathers to take the primary responsibility of childcare – and mothers to return to work. The Nordic countries are pioneers in developing parental leave schemes promoting fathers' participation in childcare. In Finland, mothers still use the bulk of leave, even though fathers have gradually increased their take-up of parental leave. However, this development applies mostly to the father's quota, and the share of fathers using shared parental leave has remained unchanged (Saarikallio-Torp and Miettinen, 2021). In addition, while intensive parenting is well studied in mothers, primarily through qualitative research, there are only a few existing quantitative studies on the topic, particularly in relation to fatherhood. To address this gap in research, we investigated whether intensive parenting ideals are linked to fathers' use of parental leave.

We found that, indeed, attitudes matter. Our results show that, in addition to socioeconomic characteristics, fathers' caring and gender role attitudes are also relevant determinants of their parental leave use: caring attitudes increase fathers' shared parental leave use, while traditional gender role attitudes decrease it. Moreover, our results show that the relationship between attitudes and fathers' parental leave use varies between different types of leave.

Furthermore, we found that neither caring nor traditional attitudes on gender roles were associated with the use of father's quota. Thus, fathers' traditional views on gender roles do not prevent them from using the quota leave. It is possible that as more fathers are using the quota (Saarikallio-Torp and Miettinen, 2021; Carnicelli, 2024), it has become a more normative part of fatherhood and therefore used regardless of gender role attitudes. The use-it-or-lose-it nature of the quota supports fathers' participation in childcare – perhaps also because it does not 'threaten' mothers' role as the primary carer. It seems that using father's quota does not compromise fathers' role as the main breadwinner, also making it more attractive to fathers who hold traditional attitudes. Thus, the institutional framework matters for fathers' parental leave beyond attitudinal factors. The designated quota leave has been found to be an effective way to encourage fathers to use parental leave in other countries (Kluve and Tamm, 2013; Duvander et al, 2019; Patnaik, 2019). Based on our results, we can therefore speculate that fatherhood and gender role attitudes also have a less pronounced role in the use of father's quota in other countries that have introduced similar leave policies.

When looking at fathers' use of shared parental leave, we found that fathers' traditional views on gender roles decrease their use of the leave. By contrast, fathers' caring attitudes did not predict their use of shared parental leave once the traditional attitudes were taken into account. This suggests that fathers' readiness to care may not be enough for them to use leave longer than their earmarked quota if they still consider themselves as the primary breadwinners in the family (see Duvander, 2014). The fact that the vast majority of shared parental leave users are mothers might be reflected in the results; mothers' priority as caregivers overrides fathers' caring attitudes, and the institutional design of parental leave enables mothers to take most of the leave available. This has also been evident when asking fathers about the obstacles of parental leave use. In a recent Finnish study, the most important reason for fathers not taking leave was that the mother was at home taking care of the child (Saarikallio-Torp et al, 2024). Thus, rather than acting as gatekeepers (Allen and Hawking 1999), mothers end up using long leave periods due to both structural and cultural realities, especially among families from the lower socioeconomic strata (see also Cannito, 2020). Furthermore, the sharable leave often requires explicit negotiations between the parents if the father wants to use it.

Regarding the results on intensive parenting, it appears that this dimension was not a significant predictor of fathers' use of parental leave (see also Faircloth, 2021). However, the current intensity measures might lack robustness, as most of the previous studies have concentrated on mothers. It is possible that fathers are also somewhat shielded from the demands of intensive parenting culture (see also Shirani et al, 2011; Faircloth, 2021) or that they expect the ideal of intensive parenting to be actualised by the child's mother. Further research is needed to study intensive fathering.

The current research has some limitations. First, because of the cross-sectional data and the fact that attitudes were measured after the child was born and, in many cases, when the father had already used at least some part of parental leave, we cannot make any causal interpretations. Thus, future research should shed light on the possible causal associations with longitudinal data. Furthermore, further research could explore how both parents' attitudes on gender roles and parenting are connected to parental leave use. Despite its limitations, this study adds to our understanding of the role the attitudinal factors have on fathers' parental leave use. Our results also highlight the previous finding that attitudes should be looked at from a multidimensional perspective, as gender role ideologies are a complex, nuanced and multidimensional construct (see, for example, Düval, 2023; Raz-Yurovitch and Okun, 2024), making them challenging to measure.

It is important to acknowledge that fathers can be caring fathers without using parental leave, as, for example, obstacles related to working life might hinder their leave take-up (Haas and Hwang, 2019). Fathers can also take leave without becoming caring fathers if caring identity is understood as not just involvement in care tasks, but also a more general 'habit of mind' and taking responsibility for the child's overall wellbeing (see Doucet, Chapter 2, this volume). However, we argue that fathers' leave use can be considered a sign of willingness to take responsibility and to be available for as well as to engage in interaction with the child, at the expense of paid work. Being on parental leave could also open up possibilities for fathers to become more caring and nurturing. Furthermore, fathers can also stay at home taking care of the child without formally taking parental leave, for example, during annual holidays (see Carnicelli et al, 2024).

All in all, attitudes and beliefs about gender roles and fathers' perceptions about parenting seem to play an important role in fathers' parental leave use. Even in the relatively gender-equal Nordic countries, the gendered nature of childcare is deeply embedded in cultural perceptions of parenthood, and our study shows that, at least in Finland, fathers' traditional gender role attitudes especially seem to be clearly linked to fathers' parental leave use. Given that this holds true particularly for leave other than the father's quota, we can expect a similar trend in other countries that leave most of the parental leave to be freely shared between the parents. Despite the fact that a growing number of fathers take an involved role in childcare, as long as the traditional role of men as main providers in the family remains strong, the caring father attitudes are unlikely to break the deeply rooted gendered nature of childcare.

Funding

The research was supported by a grant from the Finnish Work Environment Fund.

References

Alasuutari, M., Lammi-Taskula, J., Repo, K., Karila, K., Närvi, J. and Eerola, P. (2022) 'Lastenhoidon ja varhaiskasvatuksen ratkaisujen tarkastelun lähtökohtia' [Starting points for examining childcare and early childhood education and care solutions], in P. Eerola, K. Repo, M. Alasuutari, K. Karila and J. Lammi-Taskula (eds) *Lastenhoidon ja varhaiskasvatuksen monet polut: Lasten, perheiden ja politiikan näkökulma* [*The many paths of childcare and early childhood education and care: perspectives of children, families, and policy*]. Helsinki: Gaudeamus, pp 7–28.

Allen, S. M. and Hawkins, A. J. (1999) 'Maternal gatekeeping: mothers' beliefs and behaviors that inhibit greater father involvement in family work', *Journal of Marriage and the Family*, 61, 199–212.

Begall, K., Grunow, D. and Buchler, S. (2023) 'Multidimensional gender ideologies across Europe: evidence from 36 countries', *Gender & Society*, 37(2), 177–207.

Canaan, S., Lassen, A. S., Rosenbaum, P. and Steingrimsdottir, H. (2022) 'Maternity leave and paternity leave: evidence on the economic impact of legislative changes in high income countries', IZA Discussion Paper DP No. 15129.

Cannito, M. (2020) 'The influence of partners on fathers' decision-making about parental leave in Italy: rethinking maternal gatekeeping', *Current Sociology Review*, 68(6), 832–849.

Carnicelli, L. (2024) 'Studies on labor force participation and paternity leave reforms', PhD thesis, University of Helsinki, Dissertationes Universitatis Helsingiensis 10/2024.

Carnicelli, L., Miettinen, A., Ravaska, T., Räsänen, T. and Saarikallio-Torp, M. (2024) 'Impacts of a paternity leave reform: exploring seasonality and heterogeneity in fathers' take-up of parental leave'. Working Paper 191, Helsinki Social Insurance Institution.

Daly, M. (2013) 'Parenting support: another gender-related policy illusion in Europe?', *Women's Studies International Forum*, 41, 223–230.

Dermott, E. (2008) *Intimate Fatherhood: A Sociological Analysis*. Abingdon: Routledge.

Doucet, A. (2006) *Do Men Mother? Fathering, Care, and Domestic Responsibility*. Toronto: University of Toronto Press.

Duvander, A.-Z. (2014) 'How long should parental leave be? Attitudes to gender equality, family, and work as determinants of women's and men's parental leave in Sweden', *Journal of Family Issues*, 35(7), 909–926.

Duvander, A.-Z., Eydal, G., Brandth, B., Gislason, I., Lammi-Taskula, J. and Rostgaard, T. (2019) 'Gender equality: parental leave design and evaluating its effects on fathers' participation', in P. Moss, A. Duvander and A. Koslowski (eds) *Parental Leave and Beyond: Recent International Development, Current Issues and Future Directions*. Bristol: Policy Press, pp 187–204.

Düval, S. (2023) 'Do men and women really have different gender role attitudes? Experimental insight on gender-specific attitudes toward paid and unpaid work in Germany', *Social Science Research*, 112, 102804.

Eerola, P. and Mykkänen, J. (2015) 'Paternal masculinities in early fatherhood: dominant and counter narratives by Finnish first-time fathers', *Journal of Family Issues*, 36, 1674–1701.

Eerola, P., Lammi-Taskula, J. O'Brien, M., Hietamäki, J. and Räikkönen, E. (2019) 'Fathers' leave take-up in Finland: motivations and barriers in a complex Nordic leave scheme', *SAGE Open*, 9(4), 1–14.

Elliott, K. (2016) 'Caring masculinities: theorizing an emerging concept', *Men and Masculinities*, 19(3), 240–259.

European Values Study (2017) *Integrated Dataset (EVS 2017)*. GESIS, Cologne.

Evertsson, M. (2014) 'Gender ideology and the sharing of housework and child care in Sweden', *Journal of Family Issues*, 35(7), 927–949.

Eydal, G. and Rostgaard, T. (2016) *Fatherhood in the Nordic Welfare States. Comparing Care Policies and Practice*. Bristol: Policy Press.

Eydal, G., Gíslason, I., Rostgaard, T., Brandth, B., Duvander, A. and Lammi-Taskula, J. (2015) 'Trends in parental leave in the Nordic countries: has the forward march of gender equality halted?', *Community, Work & Family*, 18(2), 167–181.

Faircloth, C. (2014) 'Intensive parenting and the expansion of parenting', in E. Lee, J. Bristow, C. Faircloth and J. Macvarish (eds) *Parenting Culture Studies*. Basingstoke: Palgrave Macmillan, pp 25–50.

Faircloth, C. (2021) 'When equal partners become unequal parents: couple relationships and intensive parenting culture', *Families, Relationships and Societies*, 10(2), 231–248.

Faircloth, C. (2023) 'Intensive fatherhood? The (un)involved dad', in E. Lee, J. Bristow and J. Macvarish (eds) *Parenting Culture Studies*. Basingstoke: Palgrave Macmillan, pp 184–199.

Gaunt, R. (2006)' Biological essentialism, gender ideologies, and role attitudes: what determines parents' involvement in child care', *Sex Roles*, 55, 523–533.

Gauthier, A. H., Bryson, C., Fadel, L., Haux, T., Koops, J. and Mynarska, M. (2021) 'Exploring the concept of intensive parenting in a three-country study', *Demographic Research*, 44, 333–348.

Gerson, K. (2010) *The Unfinished Revolution: How a New Generation is Reshaping Work, Family, and Gender in America*. New York: Oxford University Press.

Haas, L. and Hwang, P. (2019) 'Workplace support and European fathers' use of state policies promoting shared childcare', *Community, Work & Family*, 22(1), 1–22.

Hays, S. (1996) *The Cultural Contradictions of Motherhood*. New Haven: Yale University Press.

Hunter, S. C., Riggs, D. W. and Augoustinos, M. (2017) 'Hegemonic masculinity versus a caring masculinity: implications for understanding primary caregiving fathers', *Social and Personality Psychology Compass*. 11, e12307.

International Social Survey Programme (2012) *Family and Changing Gender Roles IV – ISSP 2012*. GESIS Data Archive, Cologne.

Keizer, R. (2015) 'Which men become involved fathers? The impact of men's own attitudes on paternal involvement in the Netherlands', *International Review of Sociology*, 25(3), 359–372.

Kinnunen, A., Lammi-Taskula, J., Miettinen, A., Närvi, J. and Saarikallio-Torp, M. (eds) (2024) Perhevapaat ja työn ja perheen yhteensovittaminen muuttuvassa työelämässä [Family leaves and the reconciliation of employment and family life in a changing working life], Studies in social security and health 165. Helsinki: Social Insurance Institution of Finland.

Kluve J. and Tamm M. (2013) 'Parental leave regulations, mother's labor force attachment and fathers' childcare involvement: evidence from a natural experiment', *Journal of Population Economics*, 26, 983–1005.

Knight, C. R. and Brinton, M. C. (2017) 'One egalitarianism or several? Two decades of gender-role attitude change in Europe', *American Journal of Sociology*, 122(5), 1485–1532.

Lammi-Taskula, J. (2008) 'Doing fatherhood: understanding the gendered use of parental leave in Finland', *Fathering: A Journal of Theory, Research, and Practice about Men as Fathers*, 6, 133–148.

Lammi-Taskula, J. (2017) 'Fathers on leave alone in Finland: negotiations and lived experiences', in M. O'Brien and K. Wall (eds) *Comparative Perspectives on Work-Life Balance and Gender Equality: Fathers on Leave Alone*. London: Springer Open, pp 89–106.

Lammi-Taskula, J. (ed.) (2022) 'Young parents on parental leave in the Nordic countries', Discussion Paper 13/2022, Helsinki: THL. Available from: http://urn.fi/URN:ISBN:978-952-343-849-1

Lammi-Taskula, J., Miettinen, A. and Närvi, J. (2023) 'Finland country note', in S. Blum, I. Dobrotić, G. Kaufman, A. Koslowski and P. Moss (eds) *International Review of Leave Policies and Research 2023*. Available from: https://www.leavenetwork.org/annual-review-reports/

Lee, E., Bristow, J., Faircloth, C. and Macvarish, J. (eds) (2014) *Parenting Culture Studies*. Basingstoke: Palgrave Macmillan.

Macvarish, J. (2018) *Neuroparenting: The Expert Invasion of Family Life*. London: Palgrave Macmillan.

McGill, B. S. (2014) 'Navigating new norms of involved fatherhood: employment, fathering attitudes, and father involvement', *Journal of Family Issues*, 35(8), 1089–1106.

Miettinen, A. and Rotkirch, A. (2012) *Yhteistä aikaa etsimässä. Lapsiperheiden ajankäyttö 2000-luvulla* [Looking for family time. Families' time use in the 2000s], Väestöntutkimuslaitos Katsauksia E42/2012. Helsinki: Väestöliitto.

Miller, T. (2010) *Making Sense of Fatherhood: Gender, Caring and Work*. Cambridge: Cambridge University Press.

Miller, T. (2011) 'Falling back into gender? Men's narratives and practices around first-time fatherhood', *Sociology*, 45(6), 1094–1109.

Patnaik, A. (2019) 'Reserving time for Daddy: The consequences of fathers' quotas', *Journal of Labor Economics*, 37(4), 1009–1059.

Petts, R. J. and Knoester, C. (2018) 'Paternity leave-taking and father engagement', *Journal of Marriage and Family*, 80, 1144–1162.

Peukert A. (2019) '"Little children are not for dad's?" Challenging and undoing hegemonic masculinity', *Gender, Work & Organization*, 26, 1451–1466.

Raz-Yurovich, L. and Okun, B. S. (2024) 'Are highly educated partners really more gender egalitarian? A couple-level analysis of social class differentials in attitudes and behaviors', *Demographic Research*, 50(34), 1005–1038.

Roman, C. (2014) 'Children and risk: a qualitative study on Swedish IT specialists' transition to parenthood', *Families, Relationships and Societies*, 3(3), 443–457.

Saarikallio-Torp. M., Lammi-Taskula. J., Kinnunen, A., Miettinen, A. and Närvi, J. (2024) 'Perhevapaiden sukupuolistuneita ratkaisuja ja perinteisen työnjaon murtumia' [Gendered solutions in family leaves and fractures in the traditional division of labour], in A. Kinnunen, J. Lammi-Taskula, A. Miettinen, J. Närvi and M. Saarikallio-Torp (eds) *Perhevapaat ja työn ja perheen yhteensovittaminen muuttuvassa työelämässä* [Family leaves and the reconciliation of employment and family life in a changing working life], Studies in social security and health 165. Helsinki: Social Insurance Institution of Finland.

Saarikallio-Torp, M. and Miettinen, A. (2021) 'Family leaves for fathers: non-users as a test for parental leave reforms', *Journal of European Social Policy*, 31(2), 161–174.

Salin, M., Ylikännö, M. and Hakovirta, M. (2018) 'How to divide paid work and unpaid care between parents? Comparison of attitudes in 22 Western countries', *Social Sciences*, 7(10), 1–20.

Salmi, M. and Närvi, J. (eds) (2017) Perhevapaat, talouskriisi ja sukupuolten tasa-arvo [Parental leaves, economic crisis and gender equality]. Helsinki: Terveyden ja hyvinvoinnin laitos.

Shirani, F., Henwood, K. and Coltart C. (2011) 'Meeting the challenges of intensive parenting culture: gender, risk management and the moral parent', *Sociology*, 46(1), 25-40.

Sihvonen, E. (2023) '"They are alone in their parenthood": parenting support and (re)building community', *Sociological Research Online*, 28(3), 644–661.

Streckenbach, L. A., Castiglioni, L. and Schober, P. S. (2022) 'Paid parental leave and fathers' involvement capturing fathers' gender beliefs and fathering perceptions', *Families, Relationships and Societies*, 11(3), 409–427.

Takala, P. (2005) 'Uuden isyysvapaan ja isän muiden perhevapaiden käyttö' [Use of the new paternity leave and other family leave schemes for fathers]. Social security and health research: working paper 43, Helsinki: Kela.

Wall, K. and O'Brien, M. (2017) 'Discussion and conclusions', in M. O'Brien and K. Wall (eds) *Comparative Perspectives on Work-Life Balance and Gender Equality: Fathers on Leave Alone*. London: Springer Open, pp 257–266.

PART IV

Minoritised fathers and care

13

Syrian refugee dads in the UK: gendered practices of 'involvement'

Tina Miller and Esther Dermott

> If a man doesn't work, his life would be hard.
> Mustafa, father of three children

Introduction

The qualitative study drawn upon in this chapter focuses on Syrian refugee fathers and unfolding accounts of their experiences as they navigate fathering and masculine tropes in new cultural landscapes. By taking this temporally sensitive approach, we examine what is highlighted and/or unsettled by a focus on the experiences of minoritised fathers and practices of familial caring and protection. As such, the chapter goes beyond the aim of simply filling a knowledge gap or building a more complete picture of this group of fathers and prompts us to take a more critical stance in relation to earlier research on involved fatherhood, including particular forms of involvement being taken to indicate a progressive shift towards more equal parenting activities of men and women.

In the following sections we draw upon qualitative data collected during a year of repeat interviews which commenced in 2019, together with data collected in an (ongoing) postpandemic interview phase. Using these materials, we highlight how economic provisioning is not only central in the fathers' accounts but is also uncomplicated by other, Western-influenced tropes of types of father involvement and 'work-family balance' ideals. The examination of daily practices and 'felt' responsibilities enacted and described in the interviews prompts us to think about the relationship between activities and identities, and the adequacy of our existing theoretical tools used to conceptualise shifts in behaviour and long-term transformations in relation to fathering. It poses the following overarching question: have we overly focused on fatherhood as a single, transformative trajectory of development, when might it be the multiplicity of fatherhood that is in fact the character of 21st-century fatherhood?

Background

The war in Syria began in 2011 and led to an unprecedented increase in people seeking refuge – the United Nations (UN) estimates over four million individuals – many of whom turned to Western Europe, including the UK (UNHCR, 2021; Volk and Inhorn, 2021). Across different European countries, Syrian men and their families have been 'resettled', through a range of organised schemes (for example, the Vulnerable Persons Resettlement Scheme [VPRS] in the UK) (Home Office, 2017; McGuinness, 2017), or following arrival into counties through unofficial routes, in order to seek asylum (Turner, 2015). A key aim for many of the men who arrived was to bring their family to 'safety' and away from war zones and overcrowded refugee camps in neighbouring countries (Dermott and Miller, 2022; see also Bergnehr, Chapter 15, this volume). Once given permission to stay ('the right to remain') in the UK, families then encounter different settlement and 'integration' processes as they seek to re-establish family lives in changed geographical and cultural contexts. However, previous research that has documented aspects of refugee 'integration' as part of a minoritised group has tended to focus on individual refugees or on mothers who are often regarded as primary and/or more vulnerable actors in family lives while fathers continue to be viewed with suspicion or negatively (Wray, 2015; Inhorn and Volk, 2021).

In the Global North, scholarship has invoked factors such as essentialism, gendered histories, structural factors and power as explanatory factors in the everyday organisation of caring and paid work in families. These factors contribute to practices and responsibilities that are often cast as binary and unequal (Miller, 2011, 2017; 2023; Grunow and Evertsson, 2019). The resulting research has focused on the historical separating out of 'caring' and 'breadwinning', as 'binary oppositions' (Doucet, 2020; see also Doucet, Chapter 2, this volume) with associated gendered positions further aligned to binary spaces of 'public' and 'private' in which particular practices of caring and paid work have been assumed (Ribbens and Edwards, 1998). In many respects, the research on fatherhood that has grown rapidly over the past few years has often sought to examine and disrupt these binary positions advocating for structural changes (for example, policies) to enable men's greater involvement in caring, as a distinct activity and in contrast to traditional, economic 'breadwinning' (see Twamley et al, Chapter 1, this volume). This has arisen alongside more nuanced and critical theorisations of masculinities as hierarchical and plural, but also fluid and caring (Connell and Messerschmidt, 2005; Elliot, 2016; Johansson 2023). Changes to fatherhood have been identified at the level of practise and discourse (Brooks and Hodkinson, 2021, Dermott 2008), even if this is not at the rate or as widespread as was previously anticipated by many, and with an acknowledgement that dominant narratives and counternarratives may coexist (Eerola and Mykkänen, 2015).

Momentum towards the more involved, caring and hands-on father, whose visibility is now commonplace in once largely maternal spaces, has also been taken to signal ideals and confirmation of the 'good father' (Dermott and Miller, 2015). Similarly, in countries where practices denoting the more involved, 'caring' father are more established and normative (for example, in the Nordic countries), these are often referred to by those in other countries to indicate greater gender equality. Indeed, the Swedish state has itself promoted the 'Swedish Dad' as a model of good fatherhood that other countries could adopt (Goedecke and Klinth, 2021). However, ideals of the 'good father' (acknowledging that such conceptualisations themselves may not be made in this way) are clearly not universally experienced or similarly expressed. And so being a 'good father' will be understood and practised in different ways globally, and this was illustrated among the Syrian fathers in our study.

Study design

The refugee men focused on in this chapter comprise a group of Syrian dads in the UK who have been forcibly displaced by war. The data which has informed our arguments arise from a qualitative study conducted in the UK, with a parallel study conducted in Sweden,[1] which was designed to explore Syrian refugee men's experiences of being a father and a refugee. The study design sought to prioritise and explore men's fatherhood identity and fathering practices when also identified as being a minoritised group – in this case, being a refugee who has fled war in Syria. The study commenced in 2018 once university ethics approval had been received and involved recruiting Syrian refugee fathers who have been granted initial 'permission to remain' in the UK having arrived either through the 'Syrian Vulnerable Persons Resettlement Programme (VPRP)'[2] and interviewing them on at least two occasions over a period of up to 18 months. The research recognised migration as an ongoing process, with the initial period being captured through interviews as these men navigated new lives in the UK for themselves and their families. In 2024 an additional application was made to the university research ethics committee[3] to undertake a further (postpandemic) round of interviews with the fathers, and this extended phase of the research is ongoing. In the UK (and Sweden) ten fathers were recruited and interviews conducted primarily with the father, but at times other members of the family joined in the interviews, which have all been conducted in the homes of the participants. At the time of the first interview, the fathers had between one and four children, aged between three months and 16 years. The interviews were conducted in researcher pairs, comprising a member of the team for whom English (or Swedish) was a first language and a Syrian research assistant (both also originally refugees), who had Arabic as a first language and fluency in English (or Swedish). This chapter is based on the UK data only and all names have been changed to pseudonyms.

A thematic analysis of the interview transcripts was undertaken independently by team members following the first interviews and then shared in team data analysis meetings (in the UK and Sweden). Themes that were identified included perceived changed responsibilities and practices, economic provision and family/individual wellbeing. In the UK context, experiences of navigating complex and, to the participants, overly bureaucratised systems of welfare and other forms of statutory support were experienced as draining and demoralising (for more details, see Dermott and Miller, 2022).

Other themes identified, focused on the men's individual experiences as fathers and finding themselves in situations over which they felt they had little control. This included taking on practices and responsibilities related to caring that had previously been clearly demarcated as 'women's work' in Syria. So, while the men were wearily thankful that they had got their family out of a war zone and to safety, the absence of familiar, cultural reference points in their new everyday practices was experienced as unsettling and dispiriting. Now it was the men's vulnerability that became apparent, as other family members settled more quickly into school and language-learning activities.

Findings

Navigating new contexts

Several themes related to how the men navigated family life in a new cultural context emerged in the data analysis. Factors included interactions with what were experienced as unnecessarily bureaucratic systems linked to accessing welfare, jobseeker assistance, schools, health and other services (Dermott and Miller, 2022). The structural and bureaucratic features of the UK also patterned life in the home, which sat in contrast to how lives had been lived in Syria. The less temperate climate, numerous appointments and different employment opportunities limited possibilities for them to socialise, especially outside the home, which had been an important aspect of their male and extended family relationships in Syria. As Adnan explains:

> But the traditions are different. There I would go and see my friends, I would have good time with my friends. My friends would visit me. I go out and work. There, you can work at anything you want in Syria. But here is not like Syria. You cannot work any jobs you want ... Yes. I used to work as a blacksmith, as a carpenter. I used to

work at everything. But I cannot do this here. Here you cannot do this. Everything needs a certificate. It is different. (Adnan, father of three children)

Basel too invokes cultural differences and the more individualised and nuclear organisation of family lives in the UK: 'I miss some friends, family, neighbourhood, yeah. You can sit outside your house and with your neighbours that is like a common thing. Here it's like everyone is like more isolated' (Basel, father of one child).

Perceptions of cultural differences and how lives are lived between 'English people' and Syrian families is nostalgically described by Yasser in the following extract:

So they, the English people they go to work, they come back home and they go to bed, what we are used to is finishing work and then visiting our relatives, our friends, our aunts and brothers. So that's different for us ... In Syria the shops, the people, you can see them on the street at midnight, because you do your shopping and see friends and go out, but here everything closes at five. (Yasser, father of three children)

It is also important to note the effect of protracted refugee journeys to safety. These had implications for the fathers' sense of their identity and their 'breadwinner' status. Regardless of whether the men had arrived in the UK (or Sweden) via official routes (for example, the VPRS in the UK) or through unofficial routes, they had often spent many months or even years in refugee camps in countries bordering Syria. This period of effective limbo, in refugee camps or temporary housing between the home and (potential) host country, began the process for some of undermining and/or eroding their sense of agency as head of household and provider, as Khaled explains in the following exchange:

Tina: So your days here are very different to when you were in Syria?

Khaled: Not just in Syria. In Syria, in Lebanon, in Saudi Arabia and in this region. I left Syria in 2011. And the application [to the UN] took me around four years. I applied in early 2011 ... finding a job was hard in Beirut because there was a lot of Syrian people trying to find a job there. Half of Syria migrated to Lebanon ... First of all, the UN used to support us ... After three years they stopped supporting us. So, I started working. I would work a day and some days I couldn't find a job but thank God we managed. I used to work in construction. Life was very hard ... our situation was so miserable that we needed to leave as soon as possible. You know, where we come from, it's the man's responsibility to provide for his family.

(Khaled, father of two children)

The difficulties around securing paid work became a recurring theme across the interviews as the importance of the breadwinner role to the father's identity and wellbeing became apparent.

Restrictions on breadwinning

The primary aim of all the men once their families had also reached the UK (through family unification if the men had travelled ahead) was to secure employment and to provide economically for them. They were proud of their work histories and accomplishments in Syria ('I'd just graduated as a teacher in Idlib', Mustafa), whatever their previous employment status. Their expectation of a continued work trajectory fits with Lund Mortensen's ethnographic work conducted with young Syrian men in exile in Amman, which reports 'a gendered notion of "the Arab way"', which reflects life stages of 'a job, a house and a family' as milestones to be achieved in early adulthood, with an 'orientation toward the position of responsible family breadwinner' (Mortensen, 2021: 139).

However, regaining their 'breadwinner' role turned out to be more difficult than they had anticipated (see Wu and Del Rey Poveda, Chapter 14, this volume). Barriers to securing employment were multiple. For some fathers, lacking language proficiency was a problem and resulted in hostile communications; 'go and work with the Arabs', one man was told. For others, a lack of recognition of Syrian qualifications caused problems, whether these would have provided for access to specific careers (for example, a teaching qualification) or more generally would have increased employment opportunities (for example, a driving licence). Even when qualifications appeared similar, the requirements of the job in the UK could be found to be different from experiences in Syria, as Basel, a pharmacist, describes:

> My background is a pharmacist, back home in Syria. I have my own pharmacy and when I went to Jordan [as a refugee] I found a job as a pharmacist assistant at the beginning ... Here [the UK] I've been working in a pharmacy for three months, but I didn't like it. In Syria, to be a pharmacist itself, it's more creative than here, because we can make and we can produce some medicines ourselves. We can make like creams, we can make like many stuff at the pharmacy. But here

> you are stuck with a system, only work that the computer tells you ... I hate it. I hated it. (Basel, father of one child)

Navigating the bureaucracy around employment requirements and regulations was also challenging, partly due to not having the necessary language skills but also due to the high level of bureaucracy in the UK system, as Basel also notes:

> You feel like to do something here takes like a longer time, I don't know, is it bureaucratic or ... that's how I feel like at the beginning, because you wait like a letter from this institute, or this, for example like HMRC, or whatever, everything is by letters. (Basel, father of one child)

For other fathers, being in receipt of the welfare benefit 'Universal Credit', which is a payment to help with living costs requires people who are unemployed to attend regular (often weekly) appointments at the Job Centre in order to demonstrate that they are seeking employment. Additionally, in those families who were accepted into the UK under the VPRS, the fathers were often occupied chaperoning the family member(s) to the hospital/other appointments associated with the vulnerability (for example, hospital and other professional service appointments) which were often time-intensive and involved large amounts of paperwork.

The combination of domestic responsibilities and barriers to paid work meant that most of the fathers were mainly at home. Not being able to provide economically for their family was unexpected and in marked contrast to their previous life in Syria, in which employment had been a key part, and their working histories, which had begun as young adults or even earlier when family circumstances demanded: 'My father passed away when I was nine years old. My family stopped sending me to school and I started working and giving what I earn to my mother' (Khaled). Fathers found this significant change in circumstances hard to tolerate.

Caring in the home

Being at home was experienced as demoralising for the Syrian fathers' already threatened sense of masculinity. While being at home clearly involved 'being there' in a physical, domestic and caring space and temporal way, it was not experienced or narrated in ways that denote 'involved fatherhood' as conceptualised and theorised in Western research (see Doucet, Chapter 2, this volume). For the refugee fathers, not working and not having other social spaces in which to easily socialise with other men meant that being physically in the home was experienced as emasculating and mentally detrimental. It challenged the men's previous experiences of successful breadwinning masculinity, where economic provision was primary and culturally normative. Even so, in their new circumstances with extended time at home, the men demonstrate capacities to enact caring practices and, viewed through a particular lens which foregrounds actions, could easily be interpreted as evidence of change and even cultural transformation. However, we would caution against this overly straightforward analysis or narrative.

Through descriptions of daily practices and aspects of family living witnessed in the homes during the interviews, it became clear that the men were helping in new and different ways compared to how family life had been organised in Syria. This included involvement in household and childcare practices, and being there physically. Cultural differences in household responsibilities between Syria and the UK were regularly pointed out, as in the following comment from Khalil:

> In Syria it's much easier we feel more at ease in Syria, because the husband, the man would go out and make money and that's his responsibility and the woman would stay at home, cook for the children, wake up her children and send them to school, she doesn't have to take them to school [as in the UK]. Then she'll have free time to cook, to work in the house and then the husband comes back in the evening and eats, so life is more simple. (Khalil, father of three children)

In the following exchange, Adnan and his wife (who have three sons) also reflect on the differences in how domestic work is managed. In doing so, they reflect on what they have observed about the way of life in England ('Here the man is for the kitchen') and imply gendered differences in practices and arenas. These are rejected by Adnan, who wants to work again:

Wife: I'm the one cooking. He helps me sometimes when I'm in a hurry.
Adnan: This is the woman's job. The kitchen is the woman's work. It's not the man's job to cook. But I want to work.
Wife: It is not the same in England. Here the man is for the kitchen. Women are working outside.
Adnan: Here I cannot work. If there was work, I would go out and work but there is no work. Work would fill my time and entertain me. But now because of the lack of work I have a mental illness.

In the following extract, Basel talks about different, shared household practices in his new home in southern England facilitated by his changed working pattern as he is now studying:

Um, with the household we share our work here, we help each other. In Syria I used to work all the time and come back home just to rest. Here we both go to study [language classes] and when we come back, we both help each other out. (Basel, father of one daughter)

What these and other examples highlighted was the men's capacities to undertake household chores and to care for their children. However, the fathers were keen to explain that even though they felt forced by circumstance to engage in these practices, they were not doing 'women's work'. Nor were they adapting to Western practices of involved fatherhood, but rather they were filling in time resulting from a different way of living in the UK and not being able to (yet) find work outside the home. Even so, normative expectations in Syria that men should work and provide was continually invoked by the fathers and illustrated through references to their past hard work and economic provision ('I was a businessman, I was doing business in Lebanon. In Lebanon I was a pharmaceutical representative. I was doing business between Syria and Lebanon', Adnan, father of three children). For the men, living according to culturally normative expressions of hardworking Syrian masculinities in a new cultural landscape was challenging.

Mustafa, a father of three, had arrived in the UK under the VPRS scheme (Home Office 2017), having fled Syria and then had spent six years in Lebanon refugee camps/other accommodation. His eldest child has a serious medical condition requiring regular hospital visits and stem cell treatment. These require Mustafa to take his child to weekly appointments and to stay with her during longer hospital stays. In many ways the practices he performs place him as her main carer in these exceptional medical circumstances. Even though he feels secure in the economic support his family receive through various welfare (Universal Credit) and carer benefits, Mustafa misses working outside the home and his time-intensive caring role does not compensate for this. As he explains in the following extract:

Mustafa: But I think that when you work, you improve your relationship with people, you improve your language, you fill your time, and you gain experience. All these things would benefit me for the future … And at the same time, we're not used to this. Not in Syria, and not in Lebanon, in which I lived for six years. We're not used to sitting at home and receiving a 'salary' [benefits] without working. We're not used to this, and we very quickly get annoyed and bored of it. We're used to working for money. We don't like to be a burden on anybody. A man is supposed to work and provide for his house and his family. I lived for six years in Lebanon, during this time I was able to provide

	the rent, and provide food on the table, and provide my daughter's treatment, all because of my work.
Tina:	It would be nice for you [to work], if that is what you want to do.
Mustafa:	Of course. We're not used to sitting at home at all. I usually wake up early. I wake at around six in the morning. I look around and think of something to do, but I find that I cannot do anything. I go out for a walk sometimes, but I don't do much. It's boring. It's depressing … If a man doesn't work, his life would be hard. In Lebanon, I worked in construction. I used to do everything that has to do with construction, from concrete, to woodwork, to heavy lifting. I would do anything but not stop working. Some days I would do double shifts, one in the morning and one in the afternoon.

A further 'emasculating' structure invoked by the fathers, including Mustafa in the previous extract, is their dependence on the state. The state is a provider through financial support (Universal Credit), but is also perceived as being overly involved in their lives and particularly the lives of their children. The state is seen as overriding aspects of their paternal agency and undermining their position as the head of the household. This further highlights how normative practices of paternal caring as economic provision in Syria has been dislodged through enforced mobility and migration. Not only do some of the fathers feel a 'burden' and 'depressed' by finding themselves in these circumstances, but their fathering practices can also be held to account, as Mustafa explains:

> Here even the government takes care of the children. If there was a problem at School they call you to come in. If my daughter had an appointment, they call you … [in Syria] if you didn't take your child to school or your daughter to the hospital, no one would call you. (Mustafa, father of three children)

Even so, men's capacity to care – and to recognise the work of caring – is demonstrated in several of the interviews and highlighted in the following extract by Mohammad, who is experiencing caring responsibilities in new and culturally different, ways. Mohammad is a single parent as his wife died before being able to join him in the UK as the family awaited permission for family reunification to be granted. He has three children and also cares for his mother, who eventually travelled to the UK with his three children and has since been diagnosed with cancer. In the following extract, he describes how his time is taken up with new responsibilities caring for his children:

No, it's totally different here ... here you are more responsible, you have a lot more responsibility ... My life is about taking the children to school and bringing them back home and take my mum to the hospital, bring her back from the hospital, take her to the GP ... Life here is more difficult, you have more responsibilities ... The work, the house, the children, so much ... But it's better than how it was back home. Yeah, it's better than Syria. At least there is safety. (Mohammad, father of three children)

When Mohammad was re-interviewed four years later in 2024 in a new phase of interviews (see Wissö and Miller, forthcoming 2025), it was apparent that he continued to feel conflicted by the everyday responsibilities he performed. In the following extract, he describes himself doing both mothering and fathering, and still struggling to achieve a sense of a masculine self as a provider as he has to undertake activities that he continues to regard as being the 'mother's role', which should, he thinks, properly sit with a woman:

Because the children are a big responsibility like when they finish their schools, who is going to pick them up, who is going to cook for them, who is going to take them to the park, or buy them stuff and care for them and cook for them. I told the job centre if you want to hire someone to take care of my children, I will work, but the children themselves are full-time work. And you know that when your children are young, you know how big the responsibility is. (Mohammad, father of three children)

The two extracts from interviews with Mohammad undertaken four years apart remind us not only of positionality and how we might 'read' behaviours through a particular cultural lens, but also of the importance of adding time into projects which can trace mobilities and unfolding experiences of relocation. Time has passed for Mohammad and his children, who are now teenagers with career aspirations, which includes becoming a vet for the eldest child. But for Mohammad, the inability to perform a culturally recognisable role as the family breadwinner continues to be lamented.

Nature and understanding of practices

These Syrian men take on a range of activities which are viewed collectively as key aspects of caring fatherhood (Miller, 2011; Brandth and Kvande, 2018). This includes taking children to school and other appointments, but also doing the home-based work of care that is indirect but often as core and underappreciated, such as shopping, cooking and being around the house when children return from school. In addition, they often take on the 'management' activities associated with health and education that have been flagged as the invisible parenting work more often carried out by mothers. However, they undertake these activities either reluctantly, as an unfortunate (hopefully temporary) circumstance, and often with sadness, as a reflection of their inability to enact the form of caring fatherhood – that is, providing financially – which they see as central. If further evidence were needed, this highlights again the importance of not only capturing actions but also providing a contextual understanding of those actions. It is important not to dismiss the fact that these men are currently engaged in a range of significant parenting activities while understanding their frustrations in having to do so. As such, it highlights a key tension with some simplistic binaries both in capturing practice and also theoretically.

Scholarly developments that have shifted theorisations of fatherhood have often focused on binary categories in order to map activities in these areas – especially how these relate to gender equality and power – even though binary oppositions have acknowledged limitations in capturing the messy lived reality and dynamic nature of caring lives. Doucet has noted 'that an approach to concepts that connect or entangle caring and breadwinning recognizes that people are care providers, care receivers, financial providers, and financial receivers in varied and multiple ways across time' (2020: 1) may be beneficial in better thinking about care. Certainly, a recognition of *entanglements* and temporality is helpful when analysing the descriptions of the daily practices that the Syrian fathers share. This helps to highlight men's engagement in a range of caring activities, while the men narratively distance themselves from this temporary period of being entangled in 'women's work'. However, it is also the case that what they yearn for is a return to their breadwinner role to anchor them in the upheaval they have experienced. But for now, they view the binary world of complementary and distinct roles for fathers and mothers as currently unattainable, but preferable.

Facilitating involved fatherhood

Maintaining and being able to narrate a recognisable self as having agency as a ('good') provider (and thus father) is clearly difficult for these men as their lives are managed in new cultural circumstances that are not of their choosing. Across the data there are examples of the men narratively invoking their past selves as good providers in their descriptions of their lives in Syria. Indeed, making sense of upheaval and re-establishing a recognisable worker self and identity might be a prerequisite to thinking about new ('involved' and home-based) practices as anything more than circumstantial. This raises an important question about the conditions that may facilitate and enable 'involved' and 'intimate' fatherhood in ways described in Western research over the past 25 years (Dermott and Miller, 2015). There is a need to distinguish between men's capacities to care (which these men demonstrate in a variety of ways) and their intentions to actively participate in caring for their children in ways which coincide with ideas of changing fatherhood (Ivanova, Chapter 5, this volume).

We suggest that, in turn, this provides a challenge to how we conceptualise and reconfigure thinking about the blockers to change. Often recent research from Western Europe has framed limitations to greater father involvement and engagement as limited not by fathers' sentiments and preferences, but rather by outdated social policies (such as leave entitlements that position fathers as additional rather than central) or social expectations and strong maternal gatekeeping that exclude or downplay fathers' involvement in key aspects of their children's lives. This research brings back into focus the importance of fathers' own orientation and priorities. As such, the implication for policy that emerges here is that initiatives which are imposed without being based on an underlying need may be practised for a time, but ultimately resisted. The men interviewed for this research had clear ideas about masculinity and fatherhood that have been lived in Syria: when these met 'opportunities' in the UK to do fathering differently, they were rejected because they were fundamentally at odds with the existing cultural values.

Rather, and complementing Johansson and Andreasson's (2017) conceptualisation of fathering practices as being in transition in transnational families, it is important to remind ourselves how the role of place and physical location influences how practices are seen as in contradiction to majority cultural expectations. The Syrian men who have been quoted throughout this chapter asserted strongly that their value and preferred practices of fathering had not altered, but that their physical displacement had imposed a different lens through which they were viewed. We would add that this adds a new dimension to the way in which academic researchers consider the limits to 'jolts' that may prompt a rethinking of expectations and practices of fatherhood. As with other examples, such as the impact of involuntary unemployment in the context of a recession (see Boyer et al, 2017) or the different requirements for care and work during the COVID-19 pandemic (see Ruxton and Burrell, 2022), points of transition are not necessarily transformative in the longer term. The process of migration, as in other spheres of activity, necessitates a reflexivity around previously taken-for-granted practices, but not necessarily with a singular response.

Conclusion

Focusing on the everyday experiences of individuals in groups identified as 'minoritised' is increasingly necessary as different forms of mobilities and migration are undertaken as a consequence of global uncertainty, incursions and climatic crisis. In this chapter we have drawn on the accounts of a group of fathers originally from Syria who through forced migration were living in England, and how these challenge a narrative in fatherhood research which has become dominant in recent decades – namely, that culturally recognisable ideas of 'involved' (or intimate or intensive) fatherhood have widened and deepened their reach to become the default.

The experiences and views captured in this study do not provide evidence of a neatly evolving 'progressive' and more equal relationship between mothers and fathers. Our Western conceptualisations of the 'good' involved father being a significant caring actor in the domestic sphere (as well as in paid work) did not fit with what we found in the men's accounts of navigating new family lives in the UK. Rather, even though their activities and time spent in the home replicated Western ideals and practises of the 'involved' father, they sought to distance themselves from such constructions. The fathers wanted their culturally familiar 'breadwinner' role back. Their accounts highlight the importance of care with the language of 'transformation' and, we suggest, that transitions better capture the changes these fathers have experienced and navigate.

By focusing on a particular group of minoritised fathers, through a period of forced displacement, we have offered further insights into the relationship between fatherhood and masculinity, and expectations regarding male parenting. These insights not only challenge singular and simultaneously generalised notions of the male refugee and migratory experiences, but also highlight the limitations of drawing our ideas of changing fatherhood drawn from perspectives only or largely developed from scholarship in Western Europe and North America, and the value of more genuinely global perspectives. We hope that this discussion not only offers insights into the views of a particular group of fathers during a difficult period in their lives, but also poses some challenging questions to current and new research in the field of fatherhood and suggests how they need to be included in future conceptualisations of fatherhood.

Notes

[1] Our research colleague in Sweden is Professor Therese Wissö, who is based at Gothenburg University. The study was funded by the British Academy (SRG18R1\180586).

[2] The 'Syrian Vulnerable Persons Resettlement Programme' (VPRP) was introduced in the UK in 2014. It was renamed and expanded in 2015, becoming the 'Syrian Resettlement Programme' (SRP).

[3] UREC Registration Number: 181257 (Oxford Brookes University).

References

Boyer, K., Dermott, E., James, A. and MacLeavy, J. (2017) Regendering care in the aftermath of recession, *Dialogues in Human Geography*, 7(1): 56–73.

Brandth, B. and Kvande, E. (2018). Masculinity and fathering alone during parental leave. *Men and Masculinities*, 21(1): 72–90.

Brooks, R. and Hodkinson, P. (2021) *Sharing Care: Equal and Primary Carer Fathers and Early Years Parenting*. Bristol: Bristol University Press.

Connell, R.W. and Messerschmidt, J.W. (2005) Hegemonic masculinity: rethinking the concept, *Gender & Society*, 19(6): 829–859.

Dermott, E. (2008) *Intimate Fatherhood*. Abingdon: Routledge

Dermott, E. and Miller, T. (2015) More than the sum of its parts? *Families, Relationships and Societies*, 4(2): 183–195.

Dermott, E. and Miller, T. (2022) Being a father and a refugee: new social worlds of welfare and integration. In A. Tarrant, L. Ladlow and L. Way (eds) *Men and Welfare*. London: Routledge, pp 87–100.

Doucet, A. (2020) Father involvement, care, and breadwinning: Genealogies of concepts and revisioned conceptual narratives. *Genealogy*, 4(1): 1–17.

Eerola, P. and Mykkänen, J. (2015) Paternal masculinities in early fatherhood: dominant and counter narratives by Finnish first-time fathers. *Journal of Family Issues*, 36(12): 1674–1701.

Elliott, K. (2016) Caring masculinities: theorizing an emerging concept. *Men and Masculinities*, 19(3): 240–259.

Goedecke, K. and Klinth, R. (2021) Selling Swedish fathers: on fatherhood, gender equality and Swedishness in strategic communication by the Swedish Institute, 1968–2015. *NORA: Nordic Journal of Feminist and Gender Research*, 29(4): 261–274.

Grunow, D. and Evertsson, M. (eds) (2019) *New Parents in Europe: Work-Care Practices, Gender Norms and Family Policies*. Cheltenham: Edward Elgar.

Home Office (2017) *Syrian Vulnerable Persons Resettlement Scheme (VPRS): Guidance for Local Authorities and Partners*. Available from: https://assets.publishing.service.gov.uk/government/ uploads/system/uploads/attachment_data/file/631 369/170711_Syrian_Resettlement_

Inhorn, M. and Volk, L. (eds) (2021) *Un-settling Middle Eastern Refugees: Regimes of Exclusion and Inclusion in the Middle East, Europe, and North America*. Oxford: Berghahn Books.

Johannsson, T. (2023) Theorising fatherhood: challenges and suggestions. *Families, Relationships and Societies*, 12(1): 49–59.

Johansson, T. and Andreasson, J. (2017) Transnational fatherhood. In T. Johansson and J. Andreasson (eds) *Fatherhood in Transition: Masculinity, Identity and Everyday Life*. London: Palgrave Macmillan, pp 163–183.

McGuinness, T. (2017). *Briefing Paper: The UK Response to the Syrian Refugee Crisis*. House of Commons Library. Available from:https://researchbriefings.parliament.uk/ResearchBriefing/Summary/SN06805

Miller, T. (2011) Falling back into gender? Men's narratives and practices around first-time fatherhood. *Sociology*, 45(6): 1094–1109.

Miller, T. (2017) *Making Sense of Parenthood*. Cambridge: Cambridge University Press.

Miller, T. (2023) *Motherhood: Contemporary Experiences and Generational Change*. Cambridge: Cambridge University Press.

Mortensen, E.L. (2021). Reimagining 'the Arab way' in exile: futures 'off line' among Syrian men in Amman. In M.C. Inhorn and L. Volk (eds) *Un-settling Middle Eastern Refugees: Regimes of Exclusion and Inclusion in the Middle East, Europe, and North America*. Oxford: Berghahn Books, pp 134–146.

Ribbens, J. and Edwards, R. (eds) (1998) *Feminist Dilemmas in Qualitative Research*. London: Sage.

Ruxton, S. and Burrell, S. (2022) Men, work and care in the UK in the wake of COVID-19. In A. Tarrant, L. Ladlow and L. Way (eds) *Men and Welfare*. London: Routledge, pp 46–59.

Turner, L. (2015) On encampment and gendered vulnerabilities: a critical analysis of the UK's vulnerable persons relocation scheme for Syrian refuges. *Oxford Monitor of Forced Migration*, 52(2): 21–25.

UNHCR (United Nations High Commissioner for Refugees) (2021) *Asylum in the UK*. Available from: www.unhcr.org/uk/asylum-in-the-uk.html

Volk, L. and Inhorn, M. 2021. Introduction: un-settling Middle Eastern refugees. In M.C. Inhorn and L. Volk (eds) *Un-settling Middle Eastern Refugees: Regimes of Exclusion and Inclusion in the Middle East, Europe, and North America*. Oxford: Berghahn Books, pp 1–22.

Wissö, T. and Miller, T. (forthcoming 2025) How is fatherhood experienced during times of crises? A comparison of fathering in Sweden and the UK following experiences of forced displacement and the COVID-19 pandemic. In T. Miller, L. Plantin and A. Westerling (eds) *Doing Fatherhood: Navigating contemporary practices of involvement*. Bristol: Bristol University Press.

Wray, H. (2015). 'A thing apart': controlling male family migration to the United Kingdom, *Men and Masculinities*, 18(4): 424–447.

14

Reconstruction of fatherhood in a strange land: exploring fathering practices of Chinese migrants in Spain

Mengyao Wu and Alberto Del Rey Poveda

Introduction

Despite the emerging 'new image' of fatherhood and the increased involvement of fathers in childrearing over the past few decades, traditional gendered care regimes remain prevalent in most segments of society (Kilkey, Plomien and Perrons, 2014). Economic provision for family wellbeing is considered to be at the core of fathering (Aure, 2018; Fiałkowska, 2019b), whereas hands-on childcare activities are traditionally performed by women (Kang, 2012; Wang and Keizer, 2024). These gendered family roles are largely culturally and economically constructed, as in some countries, traditional patriarchal norms often persist over time, and dual-career families in which women and men earn roughly the same amount of money are still extremely atypical (Hondagneu-Sotelo and Messner, 2000). Thus, gendered power relations remain unequal in the household domain (Fiałkowska, 2019a; Cerchiaro, 2023).

Despite the persistence of cultural gendered ideologies around parenthood, the increase of migration complicates these processes. As a complex transition, migration can serve as a transformative process reshaping gender roles and caregiving responsibilities within migrant families (Hibbins, 2005; Lee, 2021; Yuan and Zhang, 2023). On the one hand, structural challenges that migrant fathers face when moving to a new country, such as unemployment or underemployment, can severely limit their ability to fulfil their traditional breadwinner role (Locke, 2017; Gentles-Gibbs and Gibbs, 2020), contributing to a reshaping of fathers' perceptions of their parental responsibilities. On the other hand, changes in contextual factors, such as the absence of a kinship network and the increase in women's labour force participation following migration, tend to create increasing childcare demands for fathers to become more actively involved in parenting (Belsky and Jain, 1997; Schoppe-Sullivan and Fagan, 2020). These changes complicate the context in which family life takes place for these fathers, leading to a reconfiguration of the fathering role in a new social context (Strier and Roer-Strier, 2005; Kealy and Devaney, 2023). While migration is a major life event that challenges both men's and women's family roles, existing studies on migration and parenting have focused primarily on mothers' experiences (Duncan et al, 2003; Bruhn and Oliveira, 2022). Yet, fatherhood also profoundly shapes the lives of men (Eggebeen and Knoester, 2001), and migrant men's experiences of negotiating caring responsibilities and their ideals of fatherhood may differ from those of women owing to the societal expectations, values and meanings attached to paternal masculinity.

This chapter explores paternal involvement, fathering practices, and father-child relationships among Chinese migrant families in Spain. By 2022, the number of Chinese immigrants in Spain had reached 193,046, making them the largest Asian community in the country (INE, 2022). More importantly, Chinese migration to Spain is characterised by a prevalent family migration pattern that involves young children (Sáiz López, 2011). These two countries hold significant differences in notions of fatherhood, with the Chinese ideal of fatherhood strongly influenced by the powerful notions of Confucianism (Wang and Keizer, 2024) and thus firmly embedded in patriarchal norms (Cao and Lin, 2019), while gender roles in Spain are gradually becoming more liberal (Escobedo and Wall, 2015). Thus, migration from China to Spain provides a unique opportunity to compare and observe if and how migration redefines Chinese fathers' involvement with children in a new social context. Based on 15 in-depth interviews conducted between 2020 and 2021, our results indicate that Chinese fathers in Spain experience migration as a major change in their lives as men and fathers, and report becoming more involved and responsive to their children. This chapter highlights changes in the contextual factors following migration that affect fathering practices and underlines the importance of socioeconomic circumstances in shaping men's perceptions of fathering, which may provide new insights into the complexities of constructing fatherhood among migrant fathers in new settlement destinations.

Fathers in the context of migration: socioeconomic challenges and changing family roles

While perceptions of fatherhood are socially constructed, and fathers' involvement with their children varies greatly across cultural groups (Mogro-Wilson, Rojas and Haynes, 2016), the increase of migration of men and families has always been viewed as an opportunity to redefine traditional family roles (Miller and Maiter, 2008). One of the most significant challenges migrant parents face when settling in a new country is the loss of childcare support (Lie, 2010; Fiałkowska, 2019a). This is especially true for those from collectivist, family-oriented cultures such as China, where childcare responsibilities are traditionally shared within the extended family by grandparents and other relatives (Qin, 2009; Wang, 2020). In Chinese society, the dominant pattern of parenting remains contextualised by the traditional division of labour, where the role of men in the family primarily involves providing financial support and physical protection for women and children (Wang and Keizer, 2024), while the daily care of children is mostly provided by mothers and supported by extended family members, especially paternal grandparents, as it is seen as support for the continuation of their son's lineage (Murphy, Tao and Lu, 2011). Yet, in the absence of an extended family support network, childcare responsibilities often fall solely on the parents, forcing migrant fathers to adjust to their new roles in the context of migration (Belsky and Jain, 1997) and adopt new fathering practices that cross the perceived gendered boundaries of male and female roles in the home (Onyeze-Joe, O'Neill and Godin, 2022). Furthermore, the host country's environment plays a vital role in shaping perceptions of migrant fathers' involvement in caregiving work (Kilkey, Plomien and Perrons, 2014). Being exposed to a society with more generous family-friendly policies (Moreno-Mínguez, Romero-Balsas and Laß, 2022) or a culture of involved fatherhood (Żadkowska, Kosakowska-Berezecka and Szlendak, 2020), migrant men may be more likely to embrace an active, involved and nurturing ideal of fatherhood (Strier and Roer-Strier, 2005). Previous research on Estonian men working in Finland, for example, found that working in various sociopolitical contexts allowed migrant fathers to reinterpret previous definitions of fatherhood in order to adapt to new cultural norms (Telve, 2018). These new cultural circumstances can have a positive impact on the practices of migrant fathers, as they gradually adapt to the host country context by developing more emotionally close relationships with their children.

Migration is a gendered process that may affect the experiences of the men and women involved differently (Choi, 2018). After migration, women face increased labour force participation and spend more time working outside the home due to financial obligations to their households and families back home (León-Pérez, Richards and Non, 2021; Schieckoff, 2023). Women's additional responsibilities in paid work often cause a shift in male migrants' gendered expectations, creating both an opportunity and a demand for fathers to become more actively involved in parenting (Formoso et al, 2007; Wang and Keizer, 2024). At this point, involved fathering is motivated by the need to shape family life and respond to the changing needs of the family (Perrons, Plomien and Kilkey, 2010). In addition, women's contributions to household income can bring about changes in traditional gender norms (Hondagneu-Sotelo and Messner, 2000), as men tend to face unexpected challenges after migration, such as language barriers (Datta et al, 2009), unemployment (Xhaho, Bailey and Çaro, 2022), perceived discrimination

(Qin, 2009) and limited opportunities (Bond, 2019), which become an additional source of stress (Bergnehr, 2022). These structural constraints make the traditional role of fathers as economic providers more difficult, potentially encouraging migrant fathers to seek new fathering practices and redefine fatherhood in a new society (Brannen et al, 2014).

The Chinese community in Spain: the dual-earner family model and the high prevalence of self-employment

Since the 1980s, Spain has witnessed a growing number of Chinese migrants (Robles-Llana, 2018), who tend to migrate as families with young children (Wu and Del Rey Poveda, 2024). According to the Spanish National Institute of Statistics, by 2019, the Chinese had become the largest Asian community and the second-largest non-European Union community in Spain (INE, 2022). Most Chinese migrate to Spain for economic reasons, in search of better opportunities. Notably, like other destination countries (Ceccagno, 2007; Coe and Pauli, 2020; Liu, Liang and Chunyu, 2021), one of the characteristics of Chinese migrants in Spain is the high rate of self-employment in family-owned businesses (Beltrán Antolín, 2002), as it is seen as a strategy for upward mobility and a better life in the destination country (Sanders and Nee, 1996). Since the 1980s, the number of businesses in the service sector, including grocery stores, restaurants and retail shops, has increased (Nieto, 2003). By the end of 2023, approximately 55.2 per cent of all Chinese workers were engaged in entrepreneurial activities, making them the second-largest group of migrant entrepreneurs in the country. These Chinese-owned businesses typically rely on cheap and flexible kinship labour, with all family members involved in the business and working intensively to reduce costs (Ceccagno, 2007; Sáiz López, 2012). Therefore, it is important to note the active labour force participation of Chinese women in Spain, with Chinese mothers always integrating into family businesses immediately after migration, and expected to be actively engaged in market work as their spouses (Sáiz López, 2011). According to the Ministry of Integration, Social Security and Migration, women account for 48.5 per cent (31,068) of all Chinese self-employed workers in Spain, which is higher than their counterparts from other migrant groups. As a result, self-employed Chinese migrant families typically have a dual-earner family model, with women assuming demanding work responsibilities, which may make it challenging for Chinese parents to balance work and parenting.

Alternatively, such work arrangements are quite informal and more flexible than those for employed workers, as working hours are always negotiated between the parents (Ceccagno, 2007; Lamas-Abraira, 2021). Previous research indicates that self-employed migrants can more easily reconcile family and work commitments given the flexibility and autonomy of their working conditions (Hundley, 2000; Bernard, 2001), which may facilitate their rescheduling and allow parents to switch between paid and unpaid activities throughout the day in a way that is impossible for employees (Craig, Powell and Cortis, 2012). In this context, the self-employment activities of Chinese parents provide a compelling case for examining how migrant men adapt their fathering roles to new circumstances. Thus, in this chapter, we aim to explore whether and to what extent Chinese migrant fathering is being redefined in a new context, considering both more flexible working hours and increased female labour force participation, which may provide new insights into the impact of work and migration on men's fathering experiences. In the following section, we describe the data and sample that form the basis of our empirical analysis. Findings are then presented and analysed. Lastly, we will conclude with the main implications of our findings for future research.

Data and methods

This analysis is based on research data generated as part of a larger project on the family life of Chinese migrant families in Spain. The fieldwork was conducted between 2020 and 2021 in the three largest Chinese districts in Spain, where most Chinese migrant families are concentrated: Usera (Madrid), El Fort Pienc (Barcelona) and La Roqueta (Valencia). Participants were recruited using a purposive sampling technique through personal visits by the researcher to Chinese businesses. The interview questions focused on participants' actual involvement in daily childcare responsibilities and the challenges they faced as fathers in a new country, which allowed us to explore their lived fathering experiences from a micro-perspective. To be eligible for the present study, participants had to be Chinese-born men aged 18 or older, and a father to at least one child. Ultimately, 15 participants were interviewed for the study. Both sampling and interviews were conducted by the first author, a Chinese immigrant scholar and trained sociologist. Their shared cultural background and immigrant status enhanced the rapport, facilitated access to the participants and interpretation of the contextualisation of the findings. The study was approved by the Research Ethics Committee of the University of Salamanca (registration no. 1154). Participation was voluntary, and participants were informed of their right to withdraw at any time for any reason. The interviews lasted between 45 minutes and one hour, were conducted in the participants' mother tongue (Mandarin) and were tape-recorded with prior consent. To protect the participants' identities, only pseudonyms are used.

To explore fathers' views on their parenting experiences from a holistic perspective, we used a thematic narrative analysis method (Riessman, 2008), whereby the themes were determined by the data and the produced themes were then critically interpreted through the lens of narrative inquiry. This helps researchers explore agency, development and change (Bergnehr, 2022) focusing on the stories informants told about changes in their everyday lives, new paternal roles and responsibilities, the availability of resources to facilitate adjustment, and coping strategies. The qualitative software ATLAS.ti was used for analysis. The analytical process consisted of close readings of the translated transcripts to assign the key theme regarding the contextual factors that influenced fathering experiences to the segments of transcripts. Then, we looked for the link between the coded segments using two main subthemes that highlighted the contextual factors that lead to changes in men's fathering roles in the context of migration.

Table 14.1 presents the demographic characteristics of the participants. We conducted semi-structured interviews with 15 male participants aged between 28 and 42, with an average age of 34.8. All had migrated to Spain for economic reasons and were self-employed entrepreneurs running their family businesses in the service sector, such as wholesale and retail stores, grocery stores, and restaurants. The participants' length of stay in Spain ranged from five years to more than 20 years. Most of them were first-generation immigrants who had migrated to Spain in the 2000s, and four

Table 14.1: Demographic characteristics of respondents (N = 15)

Characteristic	N (%)
Age (mean)	34.8
Duration of residence in years	
< 10 years	2 (13.3%)
10–15 years	3 (20%)
> 15 years	10 (66.7%)
Education	
Did not complete any schooling	3 (20%)
Primary school	4 (26.7%)
Junior high school	8 (53.3%)
Provinces of origin in China	
Zhejiang	9 (60%)
Fujian	2 (13.3%)
Others	4 (26.7%)
Number of children	
1	2 (13.3%)
2	6 (40%)
3 or more	7 (46.7%)

were 1.5-generation immigrants who had reunited with their parents in Spain since early childhood. All participants had between one and four children, with seven of them having children under the age of three at the time of the interviews. The participants had a relatively low level of education, with eight having completed secondary school and four having completed primary school; three had not finished any kind of school. Most interviewees reported a low-medium family income of approximately €21,600 per year. The majority of the participants had no extended family in close proximity; only three had parents living with them in Spain.

Findings and discussion

Using a critical lens, three key themes emerged from the data: (1) increased labour force participation among women; (2) loss of extended family support; and (3) improved fathering capacity enabled by the flexibility of self-employment. In what follows, we present migrant men's fathering narratives to illuminate how their ways of being a father change as they move to a new context, how their new fathering practices result in a more intimate father-child relationship, and how they perceive their changing fathering roles as they adjust to the challenges of migration in the new country.

Fathering challenges following migration: increased labour force participation among women and lack of family support

For most participants, moving to a new country represented a radical change in their family life. When asked about changes within their families that occurred after migration, the increase in women's labour force participation was significant because of the long working hours and demanding workload of Chinese family businesses. Notably, previous research has found that economic strain remains one of the most pressing concerns for Chinese families after starting a family business, as remittances are an important resource for paying off emigration debts and supporting the wellbeing of family members back home (Wu and Del Rey Poveda, 2024). In this context, both men and women must work to support the household economy, and women's labour force participation becomes more critical for the functioning of the family business. In a self-employed Chinese workshop, men are typically responsible for purchasing and accounting, while women are involved in cashiering and serving customers, which helps reduce business costs. This was the case for Xiong, a 31-year-old father of two. Before migrating to Spain, Xiong's wife was a stay-at-home mother in their hometown. Having started their own bazaar business in Barcelona after borrowing some money from relatives, Xiong's wife and two children joined him in Spain. To cut costs, both worked in their business under an alternative work arrangement. When asked about the reasons for the new arrangement, Xiong said: 'Our primary task is to pay off the migration debt; if she [my wife] stays at home with the children, then how can we afford the high cost of the whole family?'

While women's participation in family enterprises can alleviate the pressure on fathers to be the sole breadwinner, the dual-earner family model of Chinese families makes parenting particularly challenging, as balancing childcare needs with demanding working hours requires time, energy and financial resources. Faced with increased care responsibilities, most participants reported becoming more involved in their young children's daily lives and engaging in hands-on fathering activities. Xiong, for example, positioned himself as an 'involved father' by taking on alternate caregiving responsibilities and sharing childcare duties more equally with his wife than he had in his home country:

> Because my wife usually has to work in the shop and doesn't have time to take care of our children all the time, we have to take turns. In the morning, I go to work in the shop, and my wife takes our children to school. Then we work together until noon, after which I pick up the children from school, and my wife stays with our business. After the children have finished lunch, I come back and let her go home to have lunch; then we alternate shifts like this until 10 pm.

Xiong's statement in response to his wife's increasing involvement in the family business, 'I have to take more responsibility for childcare', indicates a deep sense of responsibility as a father, suggesting that women's active participation in paid work not only reshapes power relations within the household (Hondagneu-Sotelo and Messner, 2000) but, more importantly, also leads to a shift away from traditional perceptions of paternal responsibilities.

In addition to women's participation in the labour market, the loss of family support becomes a problematic aspect that reshapes the way in which the ideology of fatherhood is enacted after migration. In particular, Chinese society is characterised by strong social norms of family solidarity, where grandparents and other relatives are important sources of support in families, and it is common for grandparents to be involved in childcare, which is even seen as a normative responsibility towards family members (Qi, 2018). Traditionally, the responsibility for childcare falls first on the mother, then on the grandparents and finally on the father (Wang and Keizer, 2024). However, migration reduces the availability of physical family support (Critelli et al, 2021). For example, Han, a young father of a girl, explained the difficulties faced by migrant fathers in coping with the lack of family support:

> It is really hard for us to take care of a child in a foreign country without family support. In China, grandparents often take care of their

grandchildren, so fathers usually do not have to worry about childcare. But here [in Spain], there's no one to help us; we [my wife and I] are struggling on our own.

As our evidence shows, while migrant fathers once relied on extended networks for support prior to migration, most participants did not have parents in the host country to provide childcare support, and they felt that the loss of physical support triggered a radical change in their daily lives. Some expressed difficulty in adjusting to their new environment without this support. Han's narrative highlights the key factor of extended family support in Chinese fatherhood culture and illustrates how men's practice of fatherhood is constantly evolving based on social contexts to meet the needs of children. In the absence of family support in the host country, Chinese fathers perceive their caregiving role as essential to the functioning of family life; thus, they become more involved and responsive to their children. When describing his increased paternal involvement in everyday life, Han said: 'If I don't take care of the child, who will? It's a man's responsibility to care for and protect family members, especially in a new country with challenges. It's not about a man's or a woman's work – it's about the family's needs.'

While traditional Chinese fatherhood is characterised by a strong patriarchal norm in which the father's obligation is mainly to provide materially for the children, with rare involvement in everyday childcare (Liu et al, 2021), Xiong's narrative illustrates that perceptions of fatherhood are embedded in a broader social context and that the new challenges they face in the host society gradually change the prevailing expectations of fatherhood within the household domain, leading migrant fathers to participate in routine care activities traditionally considered the domain of women (see Doucet, Chapter 2, this volume). At this point, the absence of an extended family support network increases the father's responsibilities, and the role of a caregiver becomes a central component of good fatherhood.

Yet, many participants reported that managing their new roles as involved fathers in the context of migration has also been a major source of pressure and reported greater difficulties with dealing with caregiving duties even for the first time. Forty-two-year-old Jun described how becoming a father in Spain changed his life and how he had to quickly adjust to this new and demanding role:

In my home country, when my eldest son was born, it was my wife and my mother who took care of him, and I didn't need to worry. But it's different here; I have to discuss and coordinate with my wife. I remember that at the beginning, I wasn't used to it. When my wife wasn't at home, I didn't even know how to prepare meals, and everything was a learning process for me.

Jun's statement indicates that men who did not participate extensively in the home sphere before migration used China as their frame of reference to evaluate their new challenges with reconciling demands from the family spheres, and some came to view their new fathering roles as stressful and challenging in this new cultural context. At this point, new circumstances following migration led to transformations in gender relations between mothers and fathers, resulting in a renegotiation of their relationship in a more progressive way (Twamley et al, Chapter 1, this volume). These accounts suggest that migration plays a significant role in challenging traditional gender roles within the domestic domain and reshaping fathering in the migrant context.

New opportunities after migration: self-employed work arrangement and increasing fathering ability

The employment situation of migrant fathers plays a central role in shaping their ability to fulfil their fathering roles (Este and Tachble, 2009). Compared to those migrant fathers who face unemployment, which challenges their ability to provide materially for their children (Bergnehr, 2022), the dominant Chinese self-employment regime not only adapts to the hegemonic masculine identity of men as providers and breadwinners in the family (Miller, 2011), but also provides migrant fathers with greater flexibility and better working conditions to adapt their work efforts to the needs of their children. This is reflected in the story of Hui, who ran a wholesale business with his wife after working in a relative's workshop for two years. Reflecting on his own experience as a father and entrepreneur and his past as an employee, he said:

> Being a family business owner is obviously more flexible. If there's a time conflict, we [my wife and I] can discuss it and find a solution together. Oftentimes, we can also bring the children to the shop to look after them. It's quite different from when we used to work for someone else because, as an employee, you don't have many options when it comes to looking after the children.

A previous study on Chinese self-employment found that one of the main advantages of Chinese workshops is their flexibility (Ceccagno, 2007), with self-employed fathers frequently bringing their children to work with them, making it easier to combine work and childcare. In this regard, Hui's experience demonstrates that Chinese family businesses allow fathers to spend more time with their children and improve their ability to be involved fathers. Moreover, these changes challenge fathers' perceptions of fatherhood, with some participants expressing a growing awareness that fatherhood responsibilities extend beyond financial to physical and emotional responsibilities. As Hui explained:

> Since I moved to Spain, I've changed a lot as a father. Before, I used to work outside all day and hardly had time to be with them [my two children] because when I came home, they were almost asleep. But now I find that I'm closer to them and I'm more involved in their lives; every time I took them to school or back to school, we had a chat, and they always told me what they were going to do today or what happened today. Although at first I was 'forced' to do the caring task, which was difficult for me, now I find that it's not so difficult, and I've actually really enjoyed spending time with my children.

Hui's narrative was echoed by other participants, suggesting that the changes fathers experience in the host society gradually alter the prevailing gender role expectations within the household, where the notion of good fathering is not defined solely in terms of career success or the ability to provide financial support for the family. Instead, fathers begin to take on a more involved role and become more concerned with maintaining a strong relationship with their children. Accordingly, the participants reported increased paternal involvement in physical caregiving activities and became more active and emotionally involved in caring for their children. These fathers engage in caregiving tasks on a daily basis, such as picking up children and preparing meals, which then begins to become an integral part of their daily routine.

Conclusion

Using a qualitative approach, this chapter explored Chinese migrant fathers' narratives of the changes in family life that redefine and shape fatherhood in a new sociocultural context. Specifically, the findings suggest that, first, fathers perceive women's more prominent role in paid work and the lack of family support following migration as significant challenges, encouraging them to accept their new role as more involved fathers. Second, consistent with findings from previous research on self-employed parents (Matysiak and Mynarska, 2020), self-employment among Chinese migrant families provides fathers with more flexibility and autonomy to take an active role in fathering practices, resulting in a shift towards a 'new fatherhood' model as both provider and caregiver. Third, in the face of increased care responsibilities, while some fathers embrace new fathering roles and begin to develop emotionally close father-child relationships, others find their changing roles particularly stressful and come to view their dual responsibilities as a burden. Furthermore, it is crucial to note that despite fathers' increased involvement in childcare, some participants acknowledged that their changing fathering activities were primarily driven by the changing demands of domestic settlement in the host society, given mothers' limited time availability and fathers' sense of obligation to take responsibility for the family, where they felt they had 'no choice' but to take on the primary caregiving role for the wellbeing of their children. Therefore, dominant ideologies of gender and family are challenged but not sufficiently transformed, with fathers' caregiving practices still seen as secondary to their breadwinning role. This is consistent with research on migrant fatherhood among other migrant groups (Perrons, Plomien and Kilkey, 2010; Kang, 2012).

This study contributes to the existing literature on migrants and parenthood in several ways. First, previous research on migrant parenthood has focused primarily on the experiences of mothers. The narratives of men in this chapter provide a more complete picture of the challenges that migrant parents face in a new environment, highlighting distinctive experiences for fathers as they adjust and adapt to their host country. Second, this study goes beyond the traditional emphasis on unemployed migrant fathers' economic inability to fulfil their fathering aspirations by focusing on the flexibility offered by self-employment in Chinese families, which provides valuable insights into the importance of employment characteristics in the way in which men perform their paternal duties. Finally, although the challenges faced by Chinese immigrant families have been acknowledged (Sáiz López, 2011; Wu and Del Rey Poveda, 2024), research on paternal involvement in Chinese families has yet to be fully explored. This study is among the first to address these issues. Our findings have important implications for policy makers in developing comprehensive family-friendly policies to support men's transition to fatherhood in Chinese communities in immigrant-receiving countries. For example, more support from social workers and other professionals would be a valuable resource to help fathers engage in caregiving activities within the family.

Despite the study's strengths, several limitations should be considered. The most significant limitation is that this study focused primarily on low-income parents with limited education. Due to the sampling strategy, our sample does not reflect socioeconomic diversity, and therefore some voices are not captured in this chapter, including those migrants who may only be visible to researchers through their engagement with services. Thus, the findings may not be generalisable to all Chinese families in Spain, as middle-class fathers may have greater access to family support and financial resources, providing them with more opportunities to perform fathering activities in different ways. The potential influence of migration on high-skilled men's fathering experiences warrants further scholarly attention. However, our empirical findings regarding the spatial and temporal dimensions should be relevant to any future research on entrepreneurship and fathering among high-skilled immigrants. Lastly, not all host countries are alike, and it is crucial to recognise the heterogeneity of policies, constraints and opportunities in different destination countries.

References

Aure, M. (2018) 'Mobile fathering: absence and presence of fathers in the petroleum sector in Norway', *Gender, Place and Culture*, 25(8), 1225–1240. DOI: 10.1080/0966369X.2018.1462769

Belsky, J. and Jain, A. (1997) 'Fathering and acculturation: Immigrant Indian families with young children', *Journal of Marriage and Family*, 59(4), 873–883.

Beltrán Antolín, J. (2002) 'Asian immigrants in Spain: an overview', *Asian and Pacific Migration Journal*, 11(4), 485–504. DOI: 10.1177/011719680201100407

Bergnehr, D. (2022) 'Adapted fathering for new times: refugee men's narratives on caring for home and children', *Journal of Family Studies*, 28(3), 934–949. DOI: 10.1080/13229400.2020.1769708

Bernard, R.B. (2001) 'Married Chinese women's labor force and self-employment participation in the United States in 1990: a new look from ethnic subgroup perspectives', *Asian and Pacific Migration Journal*, 10(1), 169–198. DOI: 10.1177/011719680101000109

Bond, S. (2019) 'The essential role of the father: fostering a father-inclusive practice approach with immigrant and refugee families', *Journal of Family Social Work*, 22(1), 101–123. DOI: 10.1080/10522158.2019.1546965

Brannen, J. et al (2014) 'Fatherhood and transmission in the context of migration: an Irish and a Polish case', *International Migration*, 52(1), 165–177. DOI: 10.1111/imig.12067

Bruhn, S. and Oliveira, G. (2022) 'Multidirectional carework across borders: Latina immigrant women negotiating motherhood and daughterhood', *Journal of Marriage and Family*, 84(3), 691–712. DOI: 10.1111/jomf.12814

Cao, S. and Lin, X. (2019) 'Masculinizing fatherhood: negotiation of Yang and Jiao among young fathers in China', *Journal of Gender Studies*, 28(8), 937–947. DOI: 10.1080/09589236.2019.1625312

Ceccagno, A. (2007) 'Compressing personal time: ethnicity and gender within a Chinese niche in Italy', *Journal of Ethnic and Migration Studies*, 33(4), 635–654. DOI: 10.1080/13691830701265495

Cerchiaro, F. (2023) 'From son to father: memory, fatherhood and migration in the life stories of Muslim men married outside their religious group in Belgium and Italy', *NORMA: International Journal for Masculinity Studies*. DOI: 10.1080/18902138.2023.2251345

Choi, S.Y.P. (2018) 'Migration, masculinity, and family', *Journal of Ethnic and Migration Studies*, 1. DOI: 10.1080/1369183X.2018.1427562

Coe, C. and Pauli, J. (2020) 'Migration and social class in Africa: class-making projects in translocal social fields', *Africa Today*, 66(3/4), 3–19.

Craig, L., Powell, A. and Cortis, N. (2012) 'Self-employment, work-family time and the gender division of labour', *Work, Employment and Society*, 26(5), 716–734. DOI: 10.1177/0950017012451642

Critelli, F. M. et al (2021) 'Labor migration and its impact on families in Kyrgyzstan: a qualitative study', *Journal of International Migration and Integration*, 22(3), 907–928. DOI: 10.1007/s12134-020-00781-2

Datta, K. et al (2009) 'Men on the move: narratives of migration and work among low-paid migrant men in London', *Social and Cultural Geography*, 10(8), 853–873. DOI: 10.1080/14649360903305809

Duncan, S. et al (2003) 'Motherhood, paid work and partnering: values and theories', *Work, Employment and Society*, 17(2), 309–330. DOI: 10.1177/0950017003017002005

Eggebeen, D.J. and Knoester, C. (2001) 'Does fatherhood matter for men?', *Journal of Marriage and Family*, 63(2), 381–393. DOI: 10.1111/j.1741-3737.2001.00381.x

Escobedo, A. and Wall, K. (2015) 'Leave policies in Southern Europe: continuities and changes', *Community, Work and Family*, 18(2), 218–235. DOI: 10.1080/13668803.2015.1024822

Este, D.C. and Tachble, A.A. (2009) 'The perceptions and experiences of russian immigrant and sudanese refugee men as fathers in an urban center in Canada', *Annals of the American Academy of Political and Social Science*, 624(1), 139–155. DOI: 10.1177/0002716209334470

Fiałkowska, K. (2019a) 'Negotiating masculinities: Polish male migrants in the UK –insights from an intersectional perspective', *NORMA*, 14(2), 112–127. DOI: 10.1080/18902138.2018.1533270

Fiałkowska, K. (2019b) 'Remote fatherhood and visiting husbands: seasonal migration and men's position within families', *Comparative Migration Studies*, 7(1). DOI: 10.1186/s40878-018-0106-2

Formoso, D. *et al* (2007) 'Interparental relations, maternal employment, and fathering in Mexican American families', *Journal of Marriage and Family*, 69(1), 26–39. DOI: 10.1111/j.1741-3737.2006.00341.x

Gentles-Gibbs, N. and Gibbs, L. (2020) 'Social work practice with West Indian migrant fathers', *Journal of Ethnic and Cultural Diversity in Social Work*, 29(1–3), 80–94. DOI: 10.1080/15313204.2017.1416322

Hibbins, R. (2005) 'Migration and gender identity among Chinese skilled male migrants to Australia', *Geoforum*, 36, 167–180. DOI: 10.1016/j.geoforum.2003.10.003

Hondagneu-Sotelo, P. and Messner, M.A. (2000) 'Gender displays and men's power: the "new man" and the Mexican immigrant man', in H. Brod and M. Kaufman (eds) *Theorizing Masculinities*. London: Sage, pp 200–218.

Hundley, G. (2000) 'Male/female earnings differences in self-employment: the effects of marriage, children, and the household division of labor', *Industrial and Labor Relations Review*, 54(1), 95–114.

Kang, Y. (2012) 'Any one parent will do: negotiations of fatherhood among South Korean "wild geese" fathers in Singapore', *Journal of Korean Studies*, 17(2), 269–297. DOI: https://doi.org/10.1353/jks.2012.0018

Kealy, C. and Devaney, C. (2023) 'Culture and parenting: Polish migrant parents' perspectives on how culture shapes their parenting in a culturally diverse Irish neighbourhood', *Journal of Family Studies*, 1–19. DOI: 10.1080/13229400.2023.2216184

Kilkey, M., Plomien, A. and Perrons, D. (2014) 'Migrant men's fathering narratives, practices and projects in national and transnational spaces: recent Polish male migrants to London', *International Migration*, 52(1), 178–191. DOI: 10.1111/imig.12046

Lamas-Abraira, L. (2021) *Chinese Transnational Families: Care Circulation and Children's Life Paths*. Abingdon: Routledge.

Lee, S.H. (2021) '"I am still close to my child": middle-class Korean wild geese fathers' responsible and intimate fatherhood in a transnational context', *Journal of Ethnic and Migration Studies*, 47(9), 2161–2178. DOI: 10.1080/1369183X.2019.1573662

León-Pérez, G., Richards, C. and Non, A.L. (2021) 'Precarious work and parenting stress among Mexican immigrant women in the United States', *Journal of Marriage and Family*, 83(3), 881–897. DOI: 10.1111/jomf.12761

Lie, M.L.S. (2010) 'Across the oceans: childcare and grandparenting in UK Chinese and Bangladeshi households', *Journal of Ethnic and Migration Studies*, 36(9), 1425–1443. DOI: 10.1080/1369183X.2010.491746

Liu, H., Liang, Z. and Chunyu, M. (2021) 'Chinese immigrant entrepreneurship in the United States: temporal and spatial dimensions', *Journal of Ethnic and Migration Studies*, 49(11), 2855–2876. DOI: 10.1080/1369183X.2021.2007063

Liu, Y. et al (2021) 'Influence of father involvement, fathering practices and father-child relationships on children in Mainland China', *Journal of Child and Family Studies*, 30(8), 1858–1870. DOI: 10.1007/s10826-021-01986-4

Locke, C. (2017) 'Do male migrants "care"? How migration is reshaping the gender ethics of care', *Ethics and Social Welfare*, 11(3), 277–295. DOI: 10.1080/17496535.2017.1300305

Matysiak, A. and Mynarska, M. (2020) 'Self-employment as a work-and-family reconciliation strategy? Evidence from Poland', *Advances in Life Course Research*, 45. DOI: 10.1016/j.alcr.2020.100329

Miller, T. (2011) 'Falling back into gender? Men's narratives and practices around first-time fatherhood', *Sociology*, 45(6), 1094–1109. DOI: 10.1177/0038038511419180

Miller, W. and Maiter, S. (2008) 'Fatherhood and culture: moving beyond stereotypical understandings', *Journal of Ethnic and Cultural Diversity in Social Work*, 17(3), 279–300. DOI: 10.1080/15313200802258216

Mogro-Wilson, C., Rojas, R. and Haynes, J. (2016) 'A cultural understanding of the parenting practices of Puerto Rican fathers', *Social Work Research*, 40(4), 237–248. DOI: 10.1093/swr/svw019

Moreno-Mínguez, A., Romero-Balsas, P. and Laß, I. (2022) 'Labour markets, families and public policies shaping gender relations and parenting: introduction to the Special Issue', *Journal of Family Research*, 34(3), 847–863. DOI: 10.20377/jfr-842

Murphy, R., Tao, R. and Lu, X. (2011) 'Son preference in rural China: patrilineal families and socioeconomic change', *Population and Development Review*, 37(4), 665–690. DOI: https://doi.org/10.1111/j.1728-4457.2011.00452.x

Nieto, G. (2003) 'The Chinese in Spain', *International Migration*, 41(3), 215–237. DOI: 10.1111/1468-2435.00247

Onyeze-Joe, C., O'Neill, S. and Godin, I. (2022) 'Redefining fatherhood in a migratory context: a narrative inquiry into the experiences of African first-time fathers in Belgium', *American Journal of Men's Health*, 16(5). DOI: 10.1177/15579883221110355

Perrons, D., Plomien, A. and Kilkey, M. (2010) 'Migration and uneven development within an enlarged European Union: fathering, gender divisions and male migrant domestic services', *European Urban and Regional Studies*, 17(2), 197–215. DOI: 10.1177/0969776409357362

Qi, X. (2018) 'Floating grandparents: rethinking family obligation and intergenerational support', *International Sociology*, 33(6), 761–777. DOI: 10.1177/0268580918792777

Qin, D.B. (2009) 'Gendered processes of adaptation: understanding parent–child relations in Chinese immigrant families', *Sex Roles*, 60(7/8), 467–481. DOI: 10.1007/s11199-008-9485-4

Riessman, C.K. (2008) *Narrative Methods for the Human Sciences: Narrative Methods for the Human Sciences*. Thousand Oaks: Sage.

Robles-Llana, P. (2018) 'Cultural identities of children of Chinese migrants in Spain: a critical evaluation of the category 1.5 generation', *Identity*, 18(2), 124–140. DOI: 10.1080/15283488.2018.1447481

Sáiz López, A. (2011) 'Mujeres chinas en España: El capital social y su impacto en las estrategias productivas y reproductivas', *Papers. Revista de Sociologia*, 97(3), 591. DOI: 10.5565/rev/papers/v97n3.434

Sáiz López, A. (2012) 'Transnationalism, motherhood, and entrepreneurship: Chinese women in Spain', in *Social Production and Reproduction at the Interface of Public and Private Spheres*. Leeds: Emerald Group Publishing, pp 39–59.

Sanders, J.M. and Nee, V. (1996) 'Immigrant self-employment: the family as social capital and the value of human capital', *American Sociological Review*, 61(2), 231–249. DOI: 10.2307/2096333

Schieckoff, B. (2023) 'The labour market entry of immigrant women in Germany: disentangling the determinants of labour force participation', *Journal of Ethnic and Migration Studies*, 1–26. DOI: 10.1080/1369183X.2023.2222915

Schoppe-Sullivan, S.J. and Fagan, J. (2020) 'The evolution of fathering research in the 21st century: persistent challenges, new directions', *Journal of Marriage and Family*, 82(1), 175–197. DOI: 10.1111/jomf.12645

INE (Spanish National Institute of Statistics) (2022) *Cifras de Población a 1 de Julio de 2022. Estadística de Migraciones. Primer Semestre de 2022*. Available from: https://www.ine.es/prensa/cp_j2022_ p.pdf

Strier, R. and Roer-Strier, D. (2005) 'Fatherhood and immigration: perceptions of Israeli immigrant fathers from Ethiopia and the former Soviet Union', *Families in Society*, 86(1), 121–133. DOI: 10.1606/1044-3894.1884

Telve, K. (2018) 'Absent or involved: changes in fathering of Estonian men working in Finland', *Gender, Place & Culture*. DOI: 10.1080/0966369X.2018.1450227

Wang, L. and Keizer, R. (2024) '"I am a traditional but caring father": narratives of paternal masculinity in urban Chinese families', *Journal of Gender Studies*, 1–16. DOI: 10.1080/09589236.2023.2300426

Wang, X. (2020) 'The difficult transition to the "new" caring fatherhood: an examination of paternity leave', *Social Sciences in China*, 41(1), 182–202. DOI: 10.1080/02529203.2020.1719739

Wu, M. and Del Rey Poveda, A. (2024) 'Harsh choices: Chinese migrant families' childcare strategies in Spain', *Journal of Ethnic and Migration Studies*, 1–18. DOI: 10.1080/1369183X.2022.2159349

Xhaho, A., Bailey, A. and Çaro, E. (2022) 'Who takes care of the children? Albanian migrant parents' strategies for combining work and childcare in Greece', *Journal of Balkan and Near Eastern Studies*, 1–21. DOI: 10.1080/19448953.2022.2037963

Yuan, C. and Zhang, D. (2023) 'Moving towards gender equality in China: the influence of migration experiences on rural migrants' gender role attitudes', *Demographic Research*, 49, 355–384. DOI: 10.4054/demres.2023.49.14

Żadkowska, M., Kosakowska-Berezecka, N. and Szlendak, T. (2020) 'When migrant men become more involved in household and childcare duties: the case of Polish migrants in Norway', *Journal of Family Studies*, 1–21. DOI: 10.1080/13229400.2020.1712222

15

Refugee fathers' parenting to protect, nurture and train under resettlement in Sweden

Disa Bergnehr

Introduction

The epitome of parenthood is change and adaptation. While a parent has a fixed status as a parent to the child throughout life, his or her experiences and parental practices develop and are adapted continuously (Kuczynski and de Mol, 2015). The child grows older as does the parent, and external factors affect the everyday family life. But some things influence life more than others. Forced migration to a faraway country results in great change and affects most families in life-altering ways. This study explores narratives of refugee fathers from the Middle East on how they *protect*, *nurture* and *train* their children and how they adapt their *parental care* to new socioeconomic circumstances and Swedish society.

Sara Ruddick (1995) has pinpointed universal characteristics of what parenting entails: to *protect*, *nurture* and *train*. To survive, develop and gain social acceptability – the basic needs of a human being – the child 'demands' that parents attend to these needs and adapt their parental practices accordingly. However, what protection, nurturing and training mean in the specific societal and social context depends on varying aspects (Barlow and Chapin, 2010; for a more elaborate discussion, see Twamley et al, Chapter 1, this volume), and how parents come to parent also depends on individual resources– financial, social, cognitive, physical and psychological (Kuczynski and De Mol, 2015) – as well as on individual preferences grounded in experience and ideology (Ruddick, 1995).

Ruddick's theoretical framework for understanding parenthood has inspired the analysis of the present study. Together with theories on change (Kuczynski and de Mol, 2015) and cultural context (Barlow and Chapin, 2010), it has been helpful for exploring how certain parents come to parent, and how parenting evolves and is adapted to new circumstances. Ruddick's theorising has been particularly helpful for conceptualising *care* as protection, nurturing and training. Children ' "demand" that their lives be preserved and their growth fostered' (Ruddick, 1995: 17), and the social group(s) to whom the parents belong demand that the parents raise their child in an acceptable manner. 'These three demands – for *preservation, growth,* and *social acceptability* – constitute maternal work' (Ruddick, 1995: 17, emphasis in original). The demands intertwine and can be in conflict, which provokes parents to reflect on their strategies and alter their actions (Ruddick, 1995). Moreover, parenting is a bidirectional practice in which the child is also involved and has a great part in forming the outcomes. Thus, parents are prone to meet resistance and to be forced to negotiate, and at times must leave things be. Parents must accept that they are not in full control of the outcomes of their parental strategies (Kuczynski and de Mol, 2015).

Ruddick has argued that *maternal practices* and *maternal thinking* are suitable concepts to use when referring to how parents tend to their children and reason about, reflect on and learn from their practices. By doing so, she wanted 'to recognise and honour the fact that even now, and certainly through most of history, women have been the mothers. To speak of "parenting" obscures that historical fact' (Ruddick, 1995: 44). Furthermore, she has claimed that men who practise 'mothering' challenge the 'ideology of masculinity' since they 'to some extent take on the female condition and risk identification with the feminine' (Ruddick, 1995: 45). However, the results of the present study do not support Ruddick's reasoning, and I will use the terms *parents, parenting* and *parenthood* rather than *mother/fathers, mothering/fathering* and *motherhood/fatherhood*. I will refer to *parental care* rather than *maternal care*, since I propose the importance of exploring how men in different ways, in different social and societal contexts, have contributed and contribute to the care of children.

Andrea Doucet (2015, 2018; see also Doucet, Chapter 2, this volume) has noted that it is hard to estimate how much and in what ways mothers and fathers are involved in their children's care. Moreover, parenthood is not static; on the contrary, parental care changes and entails different things for different parents (or other caregivers) at different times and situations as the child grows and other circumstances change (Kuczynski and de Mol, 2015). By analysing interviews and diary notes that were collected over three years in Sweden with Middle Eastern refugee fathers, this study widens our understanding of fathering and parenting under resettlement, and how fathers who struggle with limited economic and/or cultural capital and a decline in social status partly change their care practices and paternal/parental thinking. Theoretically, the study contributes to the discussions on gendered parenthood. It questions the notion that fathering and mothering (fathers and mothers and their care for children), necessarily and universally are different.

Refugee and immigrant parenthood in Sweden and beyond

In Sweden, the state provides great support to parents in terms of generous parental leave insurance, a monthly child allowance, subsidised childcare, free education, free dental care and healthcare, and free parent support programmes (Bergnehr, 2023). In turn, Swedish parents – mothers as well as fathers – are expected to engage in paid labour as well as in the everyday care of children and home. Parents with a refugee background face great challenges in Swedish society. Those with a residence permit are granted universal family support to the same extent as citizens, but unemployment among immigrants of non-European origin is high. Thus, many refugee families are dependent on economic support, either the 'resettlement benefit' (*etableringsersättning*) that refugees can apply for up to a maximum of two years while they study the Swedish language and apply for work, or, after the two years have passed, the 'social assistance' (*försörjningsstöd*) that individuals that reside in households with no income or assets can apply for. The benefits include help with housing and paying the rent. Those who rely on social assistance must apply for work and take trainee positions; they are not allowed any asset of high value such as a car, or to take a vacation, for instance, to visit relatives abroad (Bergnehr, 2016a).

Life on social welfare restricts everyday family life and parenting. Mothers of Iraqi origin with a refugee background who I have interviewed in previous studies express despair and frustration at being 'deprived of the Swedish way of living' and 'of their independence, mobility and agency' (Bergnehr, 2016a: 24). Despite years of striving to obtain employment and self-sufficiency, they and their spouses have great difficulty in finding jobs. The mothers give examples of how their parenting is obstructed by limited finances and welfare regulations; they raise concerns about lax discipline at school and anti-authoritarian ideals that make children disregard adult authority which, to them, risks school failure and deviant behaviour (Bergnehr, 2016b). Other studies with newly arrived mothers and fathers with a refugee background show that these parents experience similar challenges during resettlement in Sweden (Bergnehr, 2018; Wissö and Bäck-Wiklund, 2021; Bergnehr, 2022).

The Swedish fauna and climate are comparatively benign, and the welfare state provides free vaccination programmes and check-ups for all children. As a parent, much effort is put into nurturing the child's development through informal and formal education and leisure time activities. There is a child-centred, anti-authoritarian parenting ideal that influences parenting and professional advice (Bergnehr, 2008). The risk that refugee parents face concerns not having the resources or capacity to nurture the child's health and development to the extent that society demands, and/or to train the child for social and societal acceptability (Bergnehr, 2016b, 2018, 2022).

Previous research from other national contexts on immigrant parenthood where the parents have immigrated to rich countries from comparatively poor ones predominantly focuses on labour migrants in Anglo-Saxon nations such as the US, the UK, Australia and New Zealand. Clearly, forced migration differs from labour migration, but there are also similarities to consider. The research shows that less well-off labour immigrants, like refugee migrants (cf. Bergnehr, 2016b), often experience downward social mobility and new challenges such as insufficient skills in the majority language, decreased support from social networks, low-paid jobs and less time to care for the home and children (Kim, Conway-Turner, Serif-Trask and Woolfolk, 2006; Park, 2008; Wu, 2011). The altered circumstances make mothers and fathers reconstruct their parenting strategies. They appropriate new ideals and habits while they resist others or combine new ways with old ones (Gedalof, 2009). It appears common to refute Western ideals of individual rights and anti-authoritarian child-adult relations. Parental firmness and discipline are brought up as vital strategies for protecting children from drugs, criminality and school failure. A dominant notion appears to be that a child's sense of belonging and responsibility comes from him or her learning to value the family unit and traditions from the culture of origin (Bermudez et al, 2014).

Thus, research on labour migrants from low-income countries having immigrated to high-income countries shows similarities in how parents experience and adapt to new challenges and societal demands. Swedish studies indicate that welfare-dependent refugee parents – mothers as well as fathers – face additional challenges with scarce resources and restricted mobility due to welfare dependence (Bergnehr, 2016b, 2018, 2022). A literature review on experiences of parenthood among refugees, asylum seekers and undocumented migrants shows that most research is conducted in high-income countries, mainly the US, and that more research is needed that involves fathers (Merry, Pelaez and Edwards, 2017). The paper finds similar challenges of migration to those raised earlier: migration means leaving what is known and stable behind for uncertain futures and new hardships (see also Naguib, 2018).

Data and methods

The present study is based on mixed-methods qualitative longitudinal data. The interviews and diary notes that were analysed were obtained from a larger project called 'Resettlement strategies in families: immigrant parenting, adolescent development and psychological health', supported by the Swedish Research Council for Health, Working Life and Welfare (grant number 2015-00581) and approved by the Ethics Committee (Dnr 2016/4-31). The project involved mothers, fathers and teenage children from the Middle East (mostly Syrian but also some Iraqi and Palestinian, some Christians and some Muslims) who had been granted residency in Sweden due to refugee status.

The families had been in Sweden for one to five years at the time of the first interview. Some obtained their residence permit just before or shortly after the data collection started, while others had lived in the country for some years with a residency permit. In Sweden, asylum-seeking children have the right to attend school, but adults need a residence permit to be admitted to official Swedish language training.

The participants were recruited as families with the assistance of school personnel who informed them about the project; one or two parents from 15 families agreed to participate, of which all resided in low socioeconomic areas in a middle-sized city in Sweden. Longitudinal data were collected over three years with consecutive interviews each year and diary notes that were taken for one to two weeks each year during the first two years. The length of the diary entries varied – some participants were rather explicit in their writings, while others were brief. The interviews were conducted at the children's school with the assistance of an interpreter.

Ten fathers agreed to participate: four of these were employed or gained employment during the data collection, and the others were dependent on the resettlement benefit or social assistance. The fathers were 40–56 years of age with varying educational and occupational backgrounds, ranging from six years of elementary school to a degree in higher education, and from having previously obtained a low-skilled job to having been a high-skilled professional or affluent businessman. All were married and had dependent children who attended school. In their country of origin, their spouses had been stay-at-home wives.

The amount of data varied among the participants; some were interviewed once, while others were interviewed three times, some took diary notes, but others did not, since how and to what extent they wished to participate was a matter of their personal choice. Some of the fathers were fluent in English and the interviews were held partly in English. Like most studies based on data collected directly with research participants, some participants provided 'richer' data than others in the sense that they provided elaborate answers and/or they chose to participate over several years, and/or they took diary notes as well as participated in interviews. Table 15.1 provides an overview of the data.

The interview guide and the questions that directed the diary notes were centred on family life and relationships, with questions about everyday activities including occupation and school, for example: what have you been up to today? Who did you meet, and what did you do? Was there anything that happened today that was particularly fun, exciting or joyful, or boring, hard or difficult, and if so: what and why? Is there anything in life that worries you? What gives you the most happiness in life? What do you wish for in the future? How would you describe your relationship with your children? What worries you the most and what gives you the most joy as a parent? Probe questions were asked.

Table 15.1: Overview of interview data

Father (pseudonym)	Interviews	Diary notes
Jacob	3	1
Samuel	3	2
Marcus	1	2
David	2	1
Paul	3	2
Jay	3	0
Kabir	2	1
Karam	1	0
Naazim	1	0
Aasim	1	1

Analysing narratives

A 'narrative is an evolving and emergent process, an interpretive action, that comes into being when persons, along with others, attempt to make sense of self and the world. Narrative is best thought of as a verb, "to narrate", or the derived form, "narrating"' (Schiff, 2017: 72). A researcher cannot take what is said at face value – that is, words do not necessarily reflect action or what has 'really' happened (Bruner, 2004). In any given social context, there are presumptions and (mutual or conflicting) understandings of what can and cannot be said and stated – for instance, understandings of what constitutes good or bad parenthood and thus what can or cannot be spoken about (Bergnehr, 2008; Doucet, 2018). Yet, on the other hand, you cannot presume that talk does not reflect practice. Thinking and reasoning about a certain phenomenon, such as parenting, come from experience and from practice, and practice is in turn informed by thinking – that is, reflection on experience that can lead to new or altered activities (Ruddick, 1995). As Schiff (2017: 92) has proposed:

> Despite the disjuncture between experience and telling, narrating is closely tied to lived experience and our reflections on life. Narrating is, arguably, the closest that we can get to experience and our understanding of those experiences ... There is no denying the fact that narrations are constructions, but they are constructions that articulate aspects of our lived experience, and they become active forces in our internal dialogue and in the field of social life.

Moreover, parental practices and thinking are responses to a 'child in a particular social world' (Ruddick, 1995: 14), and individuals 'make sense of their activities to themselves by means of concepts and values that are developed socially' (Ruddick, 1995: 15). As such, thinking as well as practice are produced socially, and 'narrating is an interpretive action, articulated in space and time' (Schiff, 2017: 74). To analyse narratives is thus to analyse individual thinking and social discourse, but also to some extent practice. The analytical focus here has been on the fathers' talk about caring practices and, more specifically, how in the narratives we can discern their strategies to protect, nurture and train their child. Narratives on practices are analysed in relation to the father's social and financial situation as well as to the wider societal context in which he parents.

The analytical focus of this chapter was on how the different forms of care came across and evolved in the fathers' narratives. It can be referred to as a theory-driven thematic and narrative analysis (cf. Riessman 1993; Braun and Clarke, 2006). The interview and diary note data were coded for how the fathers referred to (1) preservation, (2) growth and (3) social acceptability (Ruddick, 1995). The analyses were further elaborated by considering the societal context and the fathers' particular circumstances (employed, unemployed, in training, their wife's occupation and so on).

Parents are continuously triggered to reflect on their parental strategies – that is, to engage in *parental thinking* (Ruddick, 1995). In the interviews that were conducted in the present study, the fathers were encouraged to reflect on as well as express experiences about their parenting through the questions that were asked and the interaction that evolved. '[O]ne of the primary functions of narrating is to "make present" life experience and interpretations of life in a particular time and space' (Schiff, 2017: 72). The fathers articulated aspects of their lived experiences (Schiff, 2017: 92), and it is these articulations that have been analysed. In the results section that follows, the analyses of protection, nurturing and training are presented under separate headings, but include discussions on how and when they intertwine or may be in conflict.

Refugee fathers' parental care

Protection

One essential aspect of parental care is to protect the child from harm. 'Meeting the demand presupposes a minimal attentiveness to children and an awareness that their survival depends upon protective care' (Ruddick, 1995: 18). I argue here that (protective) care involves *direct* as well as *indirect* strategies that parents use, for instance, to avoid risks and promote the chances that the child will survive and thrive. The strategies vary depending on the child's age and other circumstances.

The fathers in this study emigrated with their families due to conflict, war and political or religious prosecution. Some of the fathers from Syria mentioned that the main reason for leaving at the time they did was that their eldest son was facing military conscription. All fathers referred to the safety of their children as the reason for leaving. Karam, a well-off, successful Iraqi physician raised the risk of his children being kidnapped for ransom or in other ways being harmed by military groups that disliked his position and political views: 'It was the children's future we thought of … For them to live without war or threats.' In Sweden, it took him three years to gain sufficient skills in the Swedish language and a position as a doctor, and three years of welfare dependence and residing in a small apartment with his wife and four children in a disadvantaged area, but also three years of slowly realising that his children were safe and could move around freely without risk.

The fathers' narratives illustrate that protective care – to protect the child from harm or death – is ongoing and an essential part of parental practice and thinking. They indicate that protective care can be the reason for life-altering decisions such as immigration to a foreign, unknown country and that parents use strategies to protect older children as well as younger ones. However, it also shows that the outcome of one's strategies is seldom certain or possible to foresee. Samuel, for instance, fled to protect his oldest son from compulsory military service, but when arriving in Sweden as asylum seekers, his son had turned 18 and was no longer defined as a minor, but as a single adult to which other immigration laws applied. Samuel, his wife and their younger children gained permanent residence permits swiftly, while his older son had to wait more than a year for a temporary residence permit. The waiting, for an unknown decision, caused a great deal of stress for the son and the rest of the family, and the son started to show signs of depression. In the diaries and interviews, Samuel described how he tried to support his son in this difficult situation. In the diary from the first year in Sweden he writes:

> I stayed at home with my [eldest] son all day yesterday. He was under the weather, so I stayed at home with him, talked to him. In the evening, we had dinner together. I worry about him, about him not being allowed to go to school [like his younger siblings], about him not feeling well. It is frustrating not being able to do anything for him that would change his situation.

Samuel's (and his wife's) strategy to protect his son did not result in the expected outcome at first – the son was still at risk of being sent back to Syria to join the army. However, eventually, the strategy worked, at least to some extent, and the son finally received a temporary, one-year permit to stay in the country.

There are other unforeseen outcomes of migration that appear in the fathers' narratives that are raised again and again in the (consecutive) interviews and diaries. Many are connected to the changed everyday life situation. Prior to migration, their spouses had been stay-at-home wives, but in Sweden both parents were occupied by studies or paid employment, thus having less time and energy to engage with their children. Also, some, prior to migration, had lived in an extended family, but in Sweden all were living in a nuclear family arrangement with only two adults in the household. Jacob answered the question on what he found most difficult to live in Sweden in the following way:

> I'm always so tired here, and there is so much stress. Yesterday, my youngest daughter spilled hot water on her hand, she got burnt, and I was at work while my wife was home alone. That was very stressful because I was at work, but finally I got in touch with a relative who was able to help my wife and daughter and get them to hospital … And this morning, my son urgently had to see a dentist, and I had to help him but also I had to go to work. You run here and there all the time, it is stressful, there is so much to do most of the time. That is different from how it was in Syria.

Jacob's narration points at new challenges to protect his children in Sweden caused by a decreased social network and diminished social support. He also raises a concern that is raised by most fathers – that is, how to protect the children from engaging in deviant behaviour, due to new influences in the new societal context. Jacob, the father of two teenage daughters, stresses his worries in all three interviews: 'There is so much stress here, so much you have to do, it is hard to keep track of the children's whereabouts, to nurture them, to help out with schoolwork.' Time and resources for protecting, as well as nurturing and training, come across as being scarce for the fathers in Swedish society, compared to their previous family life in their countries of origin. Paul's narration is another example of this. He raises serious concerns about how (not being able) to protect his eldest, teenage son from criminality, school failure and harmful development. Protection is here intertwined with nurturing and training. Paul appears to feel that he failed to protect his child and that the son resisted his efforts. In all three interviews, Paul mentions that in Swedish society, children have 'too much freedom' to do what they wish without consequences, at home and at school. To him, too much freedom increases the risk of school failure and criminality; the anti-authoritarian adult-child relationship ideal has left him at a loss in his parenting and he feels deprived of his parental authority.

Nurturing

Children's cognitive and physical development – their bodies, minds and psyches – is complex and demands nurturance. Their minds and cognitive capacities develop gradually and although they to some extent develop naturally, growth requires favourable conditions and adult recognition that 'each child grows in her or his distinctive, often peculiar way'. However, what nurturing entails 'appears to be historically and culturally specific' (Ruddick, 1995: 19).

The fathers note that they experience great differences in parenting and gender equality ideals between Swedish society and their countries of origin (see also Miller and Dermott, Chapter 13, this volume). New societal demands have caused the fathers to reflect on their parenting and to adapt their care practices. They have become more comprehensive and direct in their nurturing, in that they engage more in household chores and childcare compared to previously. In the diaries and interviews they enumerate everyday activities such as shopping for groceries, preparing meals, cleaning, leaving and picking up children from preschool or school, taking the children to the playground, and helping out with schoolwork; they also give examples of other (indirect and direct) caring activities, which are related to nurturing, such as picking up a child's bike, taking the child to the dentist and taking the children to the swimming pool and out for dinner. One example is a brief quote from Aasim's diary:

> Monday: I went to my language studies in the morning. Got home and helped my wife to prepare lunch. She did not go to school today since she was home with our sick child … Then I went out for groceries and other things for our home … Then I washed the car … At night we sat together, all of the family, and discussed certain issues.

> Tuesday: I went to language studies and the Employment Agency. I got home and when I got home, my wife was at school [language studies]. I prepared the meal and picked up my son from preschool. We got home and I fed my son. After, I spent time with my son.

In the interviews, it became evident how the fathers engage in parental care and thinking. They reflect on their practices and make sense out of them. The first interview with Kabir was held just days before got his residence permit. In response to the question 'So, what do you do during an ordinary day?', he answers:

> I buy groceries. I take my younger son to the playground and play with him a bit … And I go with [my older son] to watch his soccer games … And then, about every fortnight, I take them [the children] to the indoor play centre. They need that because it would be monotonous for them only to go between school and home, school and home.

The fathers reflect on what they do and why they do it, as the example from Kabir shows. They also reflect on how they have changed their parenting, including nurturing practices, in Sweden. Samuel, an affluent businessman in Syria but unemployed, welfare-dependent and having a hard time learning the Swedish language, answers the question on how he found fatherhood in Sweden: 'I am more of a father here. I see the children more, we socialise more, I have more time for my children. I worked all the time in my country.' Jay, employed in his old profession as an engineer, reasons in the same way.

> I was close to my children in my home country as well but not through everyday chores. It was more like, I took them to the movies. I didn't help them with their clothing, I didn't cook or shop groceries or clean, things like that ... Before, I did only the fun things ... I am not used to this way, but for the Swedes, it [is] normal, they don't think twice about it ... For me, I sort of lose the energy to do the fun things. I want to give them the energy [of doing fun things], but it is so stressful and tiring, all the things you must do before you get out.

In Jay's narrative, we see how fatherhood to him has become more demanding, involving more chores and direct care, which requires more out of him in terms of time and energy, but we also see how he reflects about this having made him closer to his children; the father-child relationship had become more like the mother-child relationship in terms of emotional closeness.

Although the fathers had become more involved in direct care under resettlement in Sweden, many of them were unable to provide the financial and material standards that they regarded to be important for a good family life and auspicious childhood; their possibilities for nurturing were restricted. Paul, for instance, shows increasing frustration and despair in the interviews over the years. In the third interview, he answers the first question 'How do you find life in Sweden now?' in the following way:

> I am not happy, not happy. Who can be happy and content when you move from your homeland where you could speak the language and had a job. Here, I don't have a job, I can't speak the language, and I'm sick and tired of all the hundreds of papers we have to fill in for the social services [for the social assistance]. We want jobs so that we don't have to deal with the social services. Now, we are not allowed to have a car, so you can't do things, and a family needs a car, how are you supposed to live [without a car].

Paul cannot financially provide for his family as he could in his country of origin, and the restrictions of the social services restrain the family's mobility. In addition, new parenting ideals have diminished his parental authority. His narrative suggests that his nurturing abilities are heavily circumscribed. However, he refers to having tried new ways of nurturing, such as talking more to his children rather than being strict and saying 'no' upfront, but sometimes to no avail.

Training

'Social groups require that [parents] shape their children's growth in "acceptable" ways. What counts as acceptable varies enormously within and among groups and cultures' (Ruddick, 1995: 21). 'If a group demands acceptable behaviour that, in a [parent's] eyes, contradicts her children's needs for protection and nurturance, then the [parent] will be caught in painful and self-fragmenting conflict' (Ruddick, 1995: 22). This seems to be the case for the fathers in the present study. Jacob, who, like many of the other fathers, raises concerns about the Swedish parenting ideals, says: 'I have tried, here in Sweden, to have a friendly relationship [to the children], to make them trust me and tell things to me. That is what I want.' In later interviews, he raises this issue again, together with his concerns that his children are not developing and flourishing in what he considers to be desirable ways, for instance, regarding their educational achievements. He struggles with trying to find successful parenting strategies, to combine what he understands to be the ideal in Sweden, 'to be friends with your children', with parental authority:

> In my experience, it is really hard to be friends with them and at the same time a father, because I feel that I have to reprimand them about their studies, sitting with the iPad, and all that. I get angry and yell at them sometimes but then I have regrets and make jokes. I think it is really hard, really hard, to be a father and at the same time be friendly.

The fathers' notions of parental authority and what constitutes good training are based on their own cultural references but can also be affected by them residing in disadvantaged areas with high rates of school failure, criminality and gangs (cf. Bergnehr, 2016b). The fathers' dilemmas with training may also be the result of them learning about the new culture at the same time as their children – they, as parents, are not in the know about how things work, as they were in their country of origin. One example that illustrates this is the quote from Jay. I asked how things were with his family, and he answered: 'It works out well, but possibly my children are acclimatising to Swedish culture faster than me and my wife. It is good, but I'm afraid they will take all their ideas from Sweden and dismiss our culture.'

The fathers state that they wish for their children to adapt to Swedish society, but not at the expense of losing ideals that they find pertinent from their country of origin. Their children are also trained (that is, *encultured* or *socialised* – see Barlow and Chapin, 2010) outside the family, but ideals from the wider societal context are not always in accordance with the fathers' notions of what is best and appropriate.

There are certain challenges for parents to train children in a new and unknown country. Although they know what is generally required for social acceptability (educational achievement, self-provision and individual rights for self-determination), some ideals in the new context may be against ideals from the home country, while other training activities can be difficult as a parent to achieve due to lack of knowledge and/or other resources. Despite several challenges, the diaries and interviews suggest that the fathers engage in the training of their children on an everyday basis. The training is closely interrelated with nurturing and stimulating cognitive development. For instance, when the fathers take the children to play in the park or to the swimming pool, such activities benefit the children's physical development and health, and include training in social skills (how to behave at the pool and when playing with others). When the fathers help their children with schoolwork or do household chores with a child (often noted in the diaries), nurturing intertwines with training.

When Jay in an interview talks about everyday life as a parent, he refers to him taking the son to the swimming pool to train for a swimming test at school. He connects this activity not only to something that will increase the child's chances of passing the test and educational success, but to something that will lead to a stronger bond between him and his son; through this training activity, they get to spend time together, they get a memory to share and something to talk about in the present and in the future.

Training is multidirectional and collective, something accomplished among the family members and through encounters with others that do not belong to the family. Moreover, parents are subjected to training (to learn anew, to change and to adapt) as much as their children (Kuczynski and de Mol, 2015). Married/cohabiting parents train and nurture their children together (although not always in the same way or without conflict), and the fathers refer to this mutual parental care. As Karam expresses it: 'Me and their mother usually talk to our children about their future, encouraging them to fight to gain good grades.' Moreover, training is executed through interaction with external actors. For example, Jay and Kabir both have children with special needs, and they talk about how they have gained training from professionals (teachers, psychologists and healthcare personnel) in how to parent their children. Thus, parental training practices are dynamic and may differ depending on the child. The fathers' narratives also illustrate that training is discussed and effectuated in collaboration with their spouses, and is influenced by the social and societal context and the parents' financial and cultural capital.

Conclusion

In this chapter, I have explored refugee fathers' narration on how they protect, nurture and train their children. The study illustrates some of the gains and strains that fathers experience in their parental care during resettlement in Sweden. It shows how their parenting involves challenges, adaptation and unforeseen outcomes. Moreover, it suggests that the fathers actively engage in protection, and in nurturing and training of their children. Their fathering can be conceptualised as *comprehensive*, although it is conducted with limited resources (Bergnehr, 2022). The fathers come across as being *active parents* (for example, involved/committed/engaged); they are men who in different ways care (cf. Hanlon, 2012) and adapt to new circumstances (Inhorn and Naguib, 2018).

There are different ways to care. The fathers in the present study appear very much involved in the daily care of their children, in what I refer to as *direct care* such as picking up their children from school, preparing meals, helping out with homework and going to the playground. They are also involved in *indirect care*, such as shopping for groceries, cleaning and cooking, and (trying) to provide financial stability (see Doucet, Chapter 2, this volume, for an elaborate discussion on different forms of care). What comes across is that the fathers' commitment to direct care appears to have increased in Sweden out of necessity, since their wives attend language studies and/or engage in paid labour. The fathers have appropriated the Swedish gender equality ideal of both parents having occupations outside the home; they appear at ease with their increased involvement in household chores and childcare that this has resulted in (cf. Miller and Dermott, Chapter 13, this volume; Wu and Del Rey Poveda, Chapter 14, this volume). However, they mentioned that everyday life had become more stressful with both parents being occupied in studies and/or work. Also, they felt that Swedish parenting ideals restricted their parental authority – that children get 'too much freedom' – which is not always helpful in the fathers' efforts to protect, nurture and train their children. Such experiences are also found among immigrants in other national contexts (for example, Kim et al., 2006; Gedalof, 2009; Wu, 2011; Bermudez et al, 2014), as well as in Swedish studies on immigrant refugee mothers from the Middle East (Bergnehr, 2016b, 2017, 2018).

To conclude, the present study shows different ways that fathers care for their children, that they are capable and willing to engage in parental practices, and that they adapt their parenting to new circumstances. The study raises questions such as: is it appropriate to point out – that is, would it be a surprise – that fathers (and other men) are capable and willing to care (Henriksson, 2010; cf. Hanlon, 2012; Doucet, 2018)? Is fathers' care in research unacknowledged because few have been interested in examining men's parental practices and connecting these to *care*? Ruddick (1995) has suggested that we use *maternal* rather than *parental* or *paternal* when conceptualising parents' care, but this raises an additional question: do we as researchers contribute to the production of stereotypical gendered descriptions of men and women's parental practices by our research questions and focus? Who says and has the right to claim that (some) care is 'manly/

masculine' while other care is 'womanly/feminine'? Would it be more appropriate to scrutinise and discuss *parental practices*, and how they evolve in a particular social and societal context, with an intersectional lens rather than to refer to maternal/feminine or paternal/masculine parenting? Well, my answer to the last question is: I believe so.

References

Barlow, K. and Chapin, B. L. (2010). The practice of mothering: an introduction. *Ethos*, 38, 324–338.

Bergnehr, D. (2008). *Timing Parenthood: Independence, Family and Ideals of Life*. Linköping: Linköping University.

Bergnehr, D. (2016a). Unemployment and conditional welfare: exclusion and belonging in immigrant women's discourse on being long-term dependent on social assistance. *International Journal of Social Welfare*, 25(1), 18–26.

Bergnehr, D. (2016b). Mothering for discipline and educational success: welfare-reliant immigrant women talk about motherhood in Sweden. *Women's Studies International Forum*, 54, 29–37.

Bergnehr, D. (2017). Omsorg för dagen och fostran för en framtid: Irakiska mödrars strategier för att skapa tillhörighet i Sverige [Caring in the present and fostering for the future: Iraqi mothers' reconstruction of belonging during resettlement in Sweden]. *Sociologisk forskning*, 1–2, 51–68.

Bergnehr, D. (2018). Children's influence on wellbeing and acculturative stress in refugee families. *International Journal of Qualitative Studies on Health and Well-Being*, 13(1), 1564517. hAasttps://doi.org/10.1080/17482631.2018.1564517

Bergnehr, D. (2022). Adapted fathering for new times: refugee men's narratives on caring for home and children. *Journal of Family Studies*, 28(3), 934–949. https://doi.org/10.1080/13229400.2020.1769708.

Bergnehr, D. (2023). Stöd till alla föräldrar – historisk framväxt och samtida utveckling. In T. Forkby S. Enell and J. Thulin (eds) *Prevention med barn och unga: teori och praktik för socialt och pedagogiskt arbete*. Lund: Studentlitteratur, pp 155–173.

Bermudez, M. J., Zak-Hunter, L. M., Stinson, M. A. and Abrams, B. A. (2014). 'I am not going to lose my kids to the streets': meanings and experiences of motherhood among Mexican-origin women. *Journal of Family Issues*, 35, 3–27.

Braun, V. and Clarke, V. (2006). Using thematic analysis in psychology. *Qualitative Research in Psychology*, 3(2), 77–101.

Bruner, J. (2004). Life as narrative. *Social Research*, 71(3), 691–710.

Doucet, A. (2015). Parental responsibilities: dilemmas of measurement and gender equality. *Journal of Marriage and Family*, 77, 224–242.

Doucet, A. (2018). *Do Men Mother? Fathering, Care, and Parental Responsibilities*, 2nd edn. Toronto: University of Toronto Press.

Gedalof, I. (2009). Birth, belonging and migrant mothers: narratives of reproduction in feminist migration studies. *Feminist Review*, 93, 81–100.

Hanlon, N. (2012). *Masculinities, Care and Equality: Identity and Nurture in Men's Lives*. Basingstoke: Palgrave Macmillan.

Henriksson, H. (2010). *New Fathers? Contemporary American Stories of Masculinity, Domesticity, and Kinship*. Newcastle: Cambridge Scholars Publishing.

Inhorn, M. C. and Naguib, N. (2018). *Reconceiving Muslim Men: Love and Marriage, Family and Care in Precarious Times*. Oxford: Berghahn Books.

Kim, S. et al (2006). Reconstructing mothering among Korean immigrant working-class women in the United States. *Journal of Comparative Family Studies*, 37, 43–58.

Kuczynski, L. and de Mol, J. (2015). Dialectical models of socialization. In W. F. Overton, P. C. M. Molenaar and R. M. Lerner (eds) *Handbook of Child Psychology and Developmental Science: Theory and Method*. Chichester: John Wiley & Sons, pp 323–368..

Merry, L., Pelaez, S. and Edwards, C. N. (2017). Refugees, asylum-seekers and undocumented migrants and the experience of parenthood: a synthesis of the qualitative literature. *Globalization and Health*, 13, 75. https://doi.org/10.1186/s12992-017-0299-4

Naguib, N. (2018). Casualties of fatherhood: Syrian refugee men and nurturance in the Arctic. In M. C. Inhorn and N. Naguib (eds) *Reconceiving Muslim Men: Love and Marriage, Family and Care in Precarious Times*. Oxford: Berghahn Books, pp 279–297.

Park, K. (2008). 'I can provide for my children': Korean immigrant women's changing perspectives on work outside the home. *Gender Issues*, 25, 26–42.

Riessman, K. C. (1993). *Narrative Analysis*. London: Sage.

Ruddick, S. (1995). *Maternal Thinking: Towards a Politics of Peace*. Boston: Beacon Press.

Schiff, B. (2017). A new narrative for psychology. *Oxford Scholarship Online*. DOI: 10.1093/oso/9780199332182.001.0001.

Wissö, T. and Bäck-Wiklund, M. (2021). Fathering practices in Sweden during COVID-19: experiences of Syrian refugee fathers. *Frontiers in Sociology*, 6, 721881. https://doi.org/10.3389/fsoc.2021.721881

Wu, B. (2011). *Whose Culture Has Capital? Class, Culture, Migration and Mothering*. Lausanne: Peter Lang.

16

Queer fathers and parents' caring path to parenthood in the Netherlands and Switzerland

Carole Ammann

Introduction

Research on caring fathering tends to implicitly refer to the parenting practices of heterosexual, cisgender men. Less empirical attention has been paid to gay, bisexual, trans and queer fathers and nonbinary parents. Their parenting experiences and practices are too often absent from research on fatherhood and parenthood. In this chapter, I focus on the narratives of queer fathers and parents in the Netherlands and Switzerland who became parents either within a co-parenting arrangement or through surrogacy. I analyse these individuals' caring ways of 'doing family' before the conception of their children, within structures and normative frameworks geared towards cis-heterosexual, two-parent families.

Building on the practical turn in family studies, 'doing family' asserts that people do not just have families, but do families (Morgan, 2011; Jurczyk, 2014) in their everyday lives. As will be shown, gay, bisexual, trans and queer men and nonbinary people did not become parents by chance (Goldberg et al, 2012; Pralat, 2020). On the contrary, their initial 'doing family' revolved primarily around the question of *how* to become parents. As queer people without a uterus cannot bear children, this highly conscious process is characterised by weighing up the various options, as well as intensive negotiation and decision making with their partners and/or co-parents, starting from the moment they want to become parents. All the gay, bisexual, trans and queer men and nonbinary people in this study have had to invest a lot of time, energy and emotion, and have faced many obstacles, doubts and detours on their journey to parenthood (Anttila et al, 2023a). Not only did they have to reflect deeply on their decision to become parents (Silveira et al, 2024), they also had to show much willingness, perseverance and, in the case of surrogacy, considerable resources to pursue their desire to have children.

In many European countries, the number and also the visibility of queer parents has increased, not least due to recent legal changes relating to the issues of marriage and parenthood, as well as the emergence and legalisation of new reproductive technologies (Dahl and Gabb, 2019). This is also the case in the Netherlands and Switzerland. In the past, gay, bisexual, trans and queer fathers and nonbinary parents mostly had their children in the context of a (former) heterosexual relationship. However, in the last two decades, younger generations have increasingly become parents as self-defined queer people, through adoption, fostering and surrogacy, within a co-parenting arrangement (Tornello and Patterson, 2015), or through a pregnancy by a trans person with a uterus (Riggs et al, 2021). Despite new options, gay, bisexual, trans and queer men and nonbinary people may still bury their parental aspirations due to a lack of information, legal options and role models (Berkowitz and Marsiglio, 2007). Overall, they still face many challenges on the path to parenthood and during parenting (Goldberg and Allen, 2020; Teschlade et al, 2023) and, as such, the reproductive possibilities have 'radically changed for some but remain unchanged for others' (Heaphy, 2019: 23).

Drawing on the narratives of 32 gay, bisexual, trans and queer fathers and nonbinary parents who have pursued parenthood either through surrogacy or co-parenting, this chapter expands and diversifies the dominant notion of caring fatherhood. Because the queer intended fathers extensively imagine themselves as future fathers and reflect about how they will best care about and for their future offspring, I argue that they are already caring fathers even before the conception of their children. Queer parents thus provide, in Stacey's (2006: 30) words, 'frontier terrain for exploring contemporary transformations in the meanings and motives for paternity'.

First, I review the literature on caring fathers and caring masculinities. Second, I provide an overview of family policies and LGBTQIA+ (lesbian, gay, bisexual, trans, queer, intersex, asexual and further people who do not identify as heterosexual and/or as cisgender but do not fit into the categories mentioned)[1] parenting rights in the Netherlands and Switzerland. Third, I review the relevant literature on gay, bisexual, trans and queer men and nonbinary people's parenting, with a particular focus on co-parenting and surrogacy. Fourth, I explain my methodological approach and provide some sociodemographic information about the research participants. While the majority of them identified themselves as 'fathers', a minority used the gender-neutral term 'parents'. In this chapter, I will follow the emic terms they used. Overall, I illustrate how queer fathers retrospectively describe their investment in their future paternal identities prior to the conception of their children by navigating the complexities within a cis-heteronormative environment. Finally, I discuss the findings in the conclusion.

Caring fathers and caring masculinities

Over the past two decades, research on fathering has been shaped by emerging forms of fatherhood (Inhorn et al, 2015). In particular, research on caring fathers in countries of the so-called Global North has highlighted the shift away from the dominant image of fathers as providers to the ideal of fathers as more active caregivers to their children. In this context, scholars have debated whether today's fathers can be described as 'new' (for example, Eerola and Huttunen, 2011; Johansson, 2011) or 'involved' (for example, Faircloth, 2014; Farstad and Stefansen, 2015) due to their increased presence and caregiving in their children's lives. Research has also highlighted the differences between ideals of an equal division of work, caregiving and domestic tasks between mothers and fathers, and how this plays out in practice (for example, Johansson and Klinth, 2008; Cannito, 2020). Studies have further explored the impact of being a primary caregiver on fathers' masculine identities and gender relations (for example, Medved, 2016; Hunter et al, 2017). Building on Tronto (1993, 2013), Doucet (Chapter 2, this volume) emphasises that care is processual and relational, and therefore should not be assessed in terms of time or specific tasks performed; rather, care should be understood as a 'habit of mind'. According to Tronto (1993, 2013), care has five dimensions: care about and be attentive to the needs of others (care about); take responsibility and be willing to meet those needs (care for); respond to them through concrete (competent) actions (caregiving); be cared for (care receiving); and care together or (collectively) be in solidarity with (caring with).

In parallel with the increased attention to fatherhood and gendered identities, Elliott (2016) has coined the concept of caring masculinities. The concept seeks to explain how men who engage in care work automatically resist hegemonic masculinities (Connell and Messerschmidt, 2005), where their affective relationships are fostered through care work. Elliott (2016: 252) has defined caring masculinities 'as masculine identities that exclude domination and embrace the affective, relational, emotional, and interdependent qualities of care'. Furthermore, she has argued that care work has the potential to transform gender relations as caring masculinities are fostered among men.

However, concerns have been raised that the concept idealises, and therefore neglects, the diversities among and hierarchies within caring relationships (Baumgarten et al, 2020). It has also been argued that caring masculinities do not necessarily reject hegemonic masculinities and the two can be intertwined in manifold ways (Hunter et al, 2017; Baumgarten et al, 2020). Jordan (2020), for example, has shown how caring can be coded as masculine in troubling ways, as it simultaneously transgresses and reinforces dominant gender norms. Roberts and Prattes (2023) take up such critique and demonstrate that they depart from the concept of caring masculinities as proposed by Elliott (2016) as both embracing care and rejecting domination. However, they do not address Elliott's (2016: 255) assumption that it is irrelevant 'if men do not "care about" (have nurturing attitudes and emotions) to begin. By "caring for" (doing care work), nurturing attitudes and emotions can develop in men'.

LGBTQIA+ families in the Netherlands and Switzerland

The Netherlands is known as a very liberal country when it comes to LGBTQIA+ rights. Same-sex couples have been able to register their partnership since 1991, and in 2001, the Netherlands was the first country in Europe to allow same-sex couples to marry. 'The acceptance of homosexuality has become a defining feature of the Dutch national self-image' (Duyvendak, 2016: 289), but not without having negative consequences, namely that LGBTQIA+ rights have become a battleground in debates about immigration and multiculturalism, and that a large part of Dutch society denies the persistence of homophobia (Mepschen, 2016). In addition, the increased visibility of trans and gender nonbinary people has exposed transphobia, leading to stigmatisation, harassment and violence (Vijlbrief et al, 2020).

In the Netherlands, the number of children with LGBTQIA+ parents is thought to be increasing (Jak et al, 2023), although no specific figures are available. In 2006, Meer dan Gewenst (More Than Wanted), an organisation that supports LGBTQIA+ families, became independent from the main Dutch organisation that supports LGBTQIA+ rights. Research has shown that the social acceptance of LGBTQIA+ families is increasing (Yerkes et al, 2018). In the Netherlands, same-sex couples and individuals have access to sperm and egg donation. Commercial surrogacy is prohibited, but private surrogacy is allowed. International adoption is very difficult for LGBTQIA+ couples due to the laws in most of the children's countries of origin (Jak et al, 2023). In 2016, the Dutch government committee recommended the introduction of more than two legal parents (Bremner, 2021; Cammu, 2019), but the government is still assessing the possible consequences of its introduction (Gehem and van den Berg, 2023).

It is unclear how many children grow up in LGBTQIA+ families in Switzerland (Nay, 2021), but estimates put the number at 30,000 (von Känel, 2023: 26). According to the Federal Statistical Office (Bundesamt für Statistik, 2021: 11), around 0.1 per cent of children live in households with same-sex couples. However, these data do not represent the full range of LGBTQIA+ parent families (Nay, 2021). In 2010, the Dachverband Regenbogenfamilien (Rainbow Families Umbrella Organisation) was founded to promote the social and legal equality of rainbow families. In 2018, the adoption of stepchildren was liberalised for same-sex couples. Since the introduction of the 'marriage for all' in July 2022, same-sex couples can also adopt children. However, in Switzerland, the number of Swiss parents who wish to adopt is always much higher than the number of children given up for adoption. In addition, children born as a result of a sperm donation from a Swiss sperm bank can have both same-sex parents legally recognised from birth. Same-sex married parents who have conceived their child through private sperm donation, sperm donation from a foreign sperm bank or surrogacy (abroad) can still only start the process of adopting a stepchild after one year.[2] In Switzerland, surrogacy is prohibited and multiple parenthood is not legally recognised. Overall, LGBTQIA+ (prospective) parents living in Switzerland still face many uncertainties (Büchler and Cottier, 2020).

Research on queer fathers and parents' parenting

Research on gay, bisexual, trans and queer fathers and nonbinary parents in Europe and beyond has increased, particularly since the 2010s. In her review, Reczek (2020) identifies several main areas of research, namely the relationship of these parents to their families of origin, the relationship between the couples and their division of household labour, the pathways to parenthood, and parenting dynamics. Carneiro et al (2017) also mention the following topics: motivations for fatherhood, sexual identity disclosure, gender and paternal identities, and paternal psychosocial adjustment. The qualitative literature review of the challenges faced by gay fathers shows the complex influence of sociocultural factors (Silveira et al, 2024).

Although the number of co-parenting arrangements is increasing, there is little research on how they are formed and experienced. Elective co-parenting provides an alternative for gay, bisexual, trans and queer men and nonbinary people who do not wish to or do not have the financial means to pursue surrogacy. Recent studies have investigated the motives for co-parenting arrangements, as well as their opportunities and challenges (Wimbauer, 2021). For some, the aim is to provide their children with (at least) a mother and a father who are biologically related to them (Erera and Segal-Engelchin, 2014: 449; Herbrand, 2018). Cammu (2021) has shown how the 'doing family' of families with more than two parents is characterised by display work.

In their survey of members of an online matchmaking platform for prospective parents in the US, Jadva et al (2015) show that women want their future children to live with them, while this is not necessarily the expectation of men. The study of gay fathers in the Netherlands shows a similar result: slightly less than two thirds report that their children mostly stay with their mothers, while the rest report that they share childcare equally (Bos, 2010). Herbrand (2018: 322) confirms this 'primacy of maternal connection' in her study on co-parenting in Belgium. Like the gay fathers in Erera and Segal-Engelchin's (2014) research, the participants in this research were actively involved in caregiving: with the exception of one, the children spent at least two days a week with the father(s), and often more.

There has been a recent surge in research on gay men who have built their families through surrogacy. Important topics include the motivations for using surrogacy (Blake et al, 2017), the path to parenthood (Smietana, 2018), the transition to parenthood (Bergman et al, 2010), the importance of biogenetic connections (Dempsey, 2013), the fathers' relationships with the surrogates (Carone et al, 2017), the parents and the surrogates' experiences (Kneebone et al, 2022), single gay fathers (Tsfati and Adital, 2021) and experienced discrimination (D'Amore et al, 2023). When gay men use surrogacy, privilege and vulnerability intersect due to race, class and geographical inequalities (Nebeling Petersen, 2015; Lustenberger, 2017). Due to its high cost, most gay, bisexual, trans and queer men and nonbinary people who use surrogacy are white and middle class (Berkowitz, 2020: 184).

Researching queer fathers and parents' parenting

The data for this chapter come from two anthropological research projects: one on fatherhood in the Netherlands, and one on gay, bisexual, trans and queer fathers and nonbinary parents in the Netherlands and Switzerland. Because of this chapter's focus on the path to parenthood, I only included those research participants who identified as queer before the birth of their children. Thus, I excluded those participants who did not yet identify as gay, bisexual, trans, queer, and/or nonbinary at the time of becoming parents. The chapter is based on in-depth, biographical interviews with 32 research participants, including four couples,[3] which I conducted between April 2020 and July 2023. With five of the research participants, I had a follow-up conversation several months after the initial interview.

The sample consists of 14 people living in the Netherlands and 18 living in Switzerland (see Table 16.1), 14 of whom were born outside these countries. Eight research participants became parents through surrogacy, 18 were parents in a queer co-parenting arrangement, one fostered, and three trans persons with a uterus were pregnant themselves. I also included two men who were not yet parents at the time of the interview, but who were on their way to parenthood with their male partners, one through surrogacy and one through adoption. Due to the large number of participants who were using surrogacy or living in a co-parenting arrangement, this chapter focuses on them. The queer co-parenting arrangements, by which I mean family constellations that are not based on a romantic and/or sexual relationship and in which at least one person identifies as gay, bisexual, trans, queer and/or nonbinary, were highly diverse: two lived in one household and 13 in two different ones. Five arrangements consisted of two people, seven of three people, and three of four people.

The majority of the research participants identified as gay and cisgender. The people in my sample were older than the average in both countries when they became parents. Only six of the research participants worked

Table 16.1: Research participants' demographics

Place of birth	The Netherlands	Switzerland	EU	The Americas
	11	7	12	2
Place of residence	The Netherlands	Switzerland		
	14	18		
Way of conception	Surrogacy	Co-parenting	Trans pregnancy	Fosterage/adoption
	8 (1)	18	3	1 / (1)
Number of children	0	1	2	3
	2	16	10	4
Age of oldest child	0–5	6–11	12–17	18+
	18	8	2	2
Sexuality	Homosexual	Bisexual	Pansexual	
	29	1	2	
Gender identity	Cisgender	Trans	Nonbinary	
	28	3	1	
Age at time of becoming a parent	30–39	40–49	50–59	
	19	10	1	
Degree	Not finished secondary school	Secondary school	Applied university	University
	1	3	9	19
Level of employment	< 50%	50–70%	80–90%	100%
	1	12	13	6

full time. The majority of the interviewees were highly educated (with the exception of one), middle class, and read as white (with the exception of three). I anonymised all research participants by giving them pseudonyms. The author is a white, highly educated, cisgender woman in her early forties who grew up in Switzerland and is not part of the LGBTQIA+ community.

Imagining caring fathering and parenting before the children's conception

The example of queer co-parenting arrangements

A few months after Novan and Michael – a Swiss-Dutch binational couple living in a Swiss city – became a couple, they jokingly imagined themselves having children. Seven years later, they started discussing the different ways that they could become fathers. It became clear that they preferred co-parenting in a 50/50 care arrangement. First, they looked among their friends to see if there was a suitable female co-parent, but there was not. Then, they created a profile on an online dating site for prospective parents. Their first date was with Melanie, with whom they had a good connection. After a year of getting to know each other, they decided that they wanted to have a child together. However, getting pregnant proved to be a challenge and they started looking for medical support. They found a gynaecologist who agreed to help them with illegal insemination, but Melanie did not get pregnant.

In the end, creating a co-parenting arrangement with Melanie did not work out and Novan and Michael had to start the whole process all over again. They dated lesbian couples and (single) women and finally met Anna. Novan and Michael saw Anna regularly and, on several occasions, they went to the mountains together for a few days to get to know each other better. They shared their ideas about parenting and possible future care arrangements, covering topics such as prenatal diagnosis, abortion, diet, religion, medicine, holidays, finances and school. Michael explained: 'We ended up making a family document listing all these issues. Each of us did an individual document first, and then we put them together.' (Vignette based on an interview, July 2023)

Co-parenting arrangements deviate from the bourgeois ideal of the nuclear family as they are not based on a romantic and/or sexual relationship and can involve more than two parents (Wimbauer, 2021: 23–24). Despite the information provided by organisations such as the Dachverband Regenbogenfamilien and Meer dan Gewenst, there is no blueprint for this type of family and how to become a caring father in a queer co-parenting arrangement. As a result, it requires a deep engagement with all the involved persons' family preferences and parenting ideals, and negotiating rules and processes that work for everyone (Wimbauer, 2021). Michael recalled:

For me, it was really like [sitting in front of] a blank sheet of paper. You are completely free in terms of what you want to do ... This is an opportunity, but also a difficulty because you always have to negotiate and find out: What are the possibilities? What feels right and what doesn't? (Interview, July 2023)

Anttila et al (2023a: 1645) identify four stages that characterise the path to parenthood for LGBQIA+ people: '(1) parental desires, (2) considering the practices, (3) reflecting on the decision, and (4) concrete actions toward bringing a child into the family'. Novan and Michael's family-building process was long and circuitous. The first stage, their desire to be parents became visible as they began to imagine concrete situations as future caring fathers. While for some respondents, it was clear that they would one day fulfil their aspirations to become fathers, even if they did not yet know how to go about it, others buried their parental desires when they identified as queer. This echoes a study of procreative attitudes among gay men in the US (Berkowitz and Marsiglio, 2007).

An important stage for Novan and Michael was the second phase, namely the concrete search for a suitable co-mother (or co-mothers). As this bond is not based on a romantic relationship, they put a lot of effort into the third phase, carefully considering whether they could imagine a future together as co-parents. They negotiated their choices by getting to know each other's ideas and values about parenting. During these intense discussions, intended gay, bisexual, trans and queer fathers and nonbinary parents care about and for their partners and the co-parents, and imagine caregiving to their future children. They also imagine caring with everyone involved for the wellbeing of their future family. In addition, they care about and for themselves by exploring deeply their own hopes, desires, expectations and fears as future parents. This contrasts with the interviews I conducted with 67 cisgender, heterosexual fathers in the Netherlands, many (but not all) of whom said that they had not thought too much about their role as future fathers before conception. For example, Olav, who grew up in Eastern Europe and had moved to the Netherlands, stated: 'I started working and I met my wife and then it [pregnancy] just happened. It was never like, okay we need one [a child], and then we need another [one], [we] never discussed things like that' (interview, April 2020). Because of their intense reflection on their desire to have children (Silveira et al, 2024), gay, bisexual, trans and queer fathers and nonbinary intended parents already care about and for their future offspring even before their conception. They also engage in practices of self-care related to their future parenthood.

Novan and Michael imagined themselves as caring fathers, raising their child with Anna in a 50/50 care arrangement. While both emphasised that they liked their jobs, they only worked between 50 and 70 per cent – much less than the Swiss average, where 87 per cent of the fathers worked full-time (90–100 per cent) in 2023.[4] Thus, Novan, Michael and the other gay, bisexual, trans and queer fathers and nonbinary co-parents I interviewed clearly fit into the notion of caring fathers who do not prioritise their role as providers, but aim to be actively and extensively involved in emotional and physical caregiving.

Lack of information (Berkowitz, 2020: 148) and legal barriers (Cammu, 2021) are common obstacles for gay, bisexual, trans, queer, and nonbinary intended parents on their journey to parenthood. Indeed, the challenges that these prospective parents face in procreating were a constant theme in the interviews. In the fourth stage, the concrete activities of bringing a child into the co-parenting arrangement, Novan, Michael and Melanie had to navigate structures geared towards cis-heterosexual couples. In practice, this meant finding a gynaecologist who would carry out an illegal insemination. Gerben, a trans man, his husband Dennis, and Marieke, their co-mother, faced similar challenges in the Netherlands. When Gerben transitioned, sterilisation was no longer compulsory, but the possibility of getting pregnant at a later stage was not discussed with him. This meant that after his transition, he no longer had his reproductive organs and therefore could not have a biologically related child. When Gerben, Dennis and Marieke wanted to become parents, they had to go to a hospital because Marieke's only chance of getting pregnant was through in vitro fertilisation. The three feared that they would not be able to access assisted reproductive technology because their family constellation consisted of a single woman and a male couple, one of whom was trans. Fortunately, they were able to access it, but they were still constantly confronted with a system that was geared towards two parents. Gerben explained: 'What we were doing literally all the time was asking for or just grabbing an extra chair … And in the hospital's registration system, there was only room for two names' (interview, February 2021) As Gerben was not biologically related to his child, he was not registered as its father.

Gerben's story illustrates the vulnerability of the gay, bisexual, trans and queer fathers and nonbinary parents' doing family. He and the other respondents who were not legally recognised as their children's parents experienced this process as very hurtful and unsettling. Like the participants in Anttila et al's (2023a) study, they felt dependent on the will of the legal mothers, even more so in the event of conflict. In a heteronormative environment that sees the mother as the primary caregiver, it is difficult to imagine becoming and being a caring queer co-parenting father and parent. In Switzerland, a two-week paternity leave period was only introduced in 2021. However, as there is no legal recognition of multiple parenthood, Novan and Michael could not both take the two weeks of paternity leave when their child was born – only the legal father could.

The example of gay couples using gestational surrogacy

> Carter, a Black man who grew up in the US, knew already he was gay as a teenager. His husband, Horst, a white man who grew up in a European country, did not come

out as bisexual until he was in his early 30s. On their first date, they discussed their desire to have children. For about four years, they researched the possibility of adoption, but it became clear that this was not an option in Switzerland. When they met a gay couple who had two children through surrogacy, a new possibility opened up. 'We had all the prejudices. We thought surrogacy was for celebrities', said Horst. 'For our friends, it worked really well, they had a great relationship with their surrogate. So we thought, "This is apparently a possibility" and we looked into it.' In the end, Horst and Carter opted for commercial surrogacy in the US.

First, they looked for a suitable agency and 'selected a relatively small one' where they felt 'less like a business client', as Horst put it. Second, they spoke to four doctors working in different surrogate clinics and chose one of them. Third, they had to complete questionnaires from the agency and the clinic. Fourth, the agency matched Carter and Horst with Ashley, their surrogate. Fifth, they chose an anonymous egg donor from a catalogue. Carter explained their choice as follows: 'We wanted to make sure that the baby could look biologically as if it could be from us, it should be somewhere in the middle [between Black and white].' When Ashley was pregnant with Carter and Horst's child, the three of them had a ritual of video calling each other every Sunday night to catch up. 'Normally we would have planned to be there for at least one of the ultrasounds but that was in the middle of the lockdown', Horst said. 'It was an exciting time but we felt extremely helpless being so far away.' Before the baby was born, Carter quit his job to look after the baby. He planned to return to work on a 60 per cent basis when the child was six months old. Horst continued to work full time, but cut back on his overtime. (Vignette based on an interview, November 2021)

The first step on the path to parenthood according to Anttila et al (2023a), namely the revealing of their parental desires, had already taken place when Carter and Horst first met. The next phase, considering the practicalities, took more time. It was clear to both that they wanted to become a family as a couple. Imagining a future family of two caring fathers and no mother disrupts the gendered notions of motherhood and fatherhood, for example because there is no clear allocation of who is the primary breadwinner and who is the primary caregiver. Research on same-sex parents has shown that they share domestic and paid work more equally than heterosexual couples (Bergman et al, 2010; Reczek, 2020: 307). However, this does not necessarily mean that same-sex parents are more caring than their heterosexual counterparts.

Initially, Carter and Horst wanted to adopt a child, but at the time of their family planning, adoption was not available to same-sex parents in Switzerland. Gabor and his husband Milan, who both grew up in an Eastern European country and were living in the Netherlands at the time of the interview, had a similar experience. In 2012, they started thinking about adoption or transnational surrogacy to become parents. Although Dutch law allowed same-sex couples to adopt, Gabor and Milan found it very complicated and ultimately they decided to make use of gestational surrogacy in the US. Overall, the legal context in many countries is not supportive of queer caring fatherhood, as encountering legal barriers is a typical challenge faced by gay, bisexual, trans and queer men and nonbinary people on their path to parenthood (Berkowitz, 2020: 148) and during parenting (Cammu, 2021).

For Carter and Horst, commercial surrogacy only became 'thinkable' (Smietana, 2022) as a possibility when they met another gay couple who had used it. Thanks to the exchange with them and the information provided by the Dachverband Regenbogenfamilien, the third stage of their family-building process, the discussion of their decision (Anttila et al, 2023a), did not take place on a blank page. Unlike Novan and Michael, who decided to co-parent without knowing anyone who had done so, Carter and Horst had a role model at the start of their journey to parenthood through surrogacy, but they had to find a script that suited them.

When choosing an egg donor, one of the most important criteria for Carter and Horst was that the baby's skin would be neither Black nor white. Carter explained: 'We wanted it not to feel like more related to one or the other. We also wanted people to see it as our child and not as his child or my child' (interview, November 2021). In her research on lesbian couples, Nordqvist (2010) has confirmed the importance of physical resemblance. This strategy can also be considered as an assimilation practice to prevent anticipated discrimination (Teschlade et al, 2023). Carter and Horst did not reveal the identity of the biological father. This strategy is common in places where biogenetic ties form the normative and legal basis for what constitutes a family (Berkowitz, 2020: 149).

For Gabor and Milan, the path to parenthood was very long and emotional. After 'a lengthy procedure' of about five years, during which they changed surrogates and clinics due to unsuccessful attempts at in vitro fertilisation, they finally became parents in 2020. Gabor recalled: 'It was difficult, putting ourselves together and starting again and again and again' (interview, May 2020). The examples of queer people using transnational gestational surrogacy illustrate that they too have to do a lot of emotional labour and have to overcome many obstacles on their journey to becoming parents. Like the gay, bisexual, trans and queer men and nonbinary people who choose to co-parent, they are forced to repeatedly question their own and their partners' motivation to become caring queer fathers and parents. All of them invested early in their future identities as caring fathers as they navigated complex legal barriers imposed by heteronormative norms in the Netherlands and Switzerland.

Conclusion

The literature on caring fatherhood has typically analysed fathers' intimacy and attachment to their young children. Scholars have extensively discussed questions about the novelty of the fathers' caring attitudes (for example, Eerola and Huttunen, 2011; Cannito, 2020) and how caregiving affects masculinities and gender relations (for example, Elliott, 2016; Beglaubter, 2021). However, the gender identities and sexual orientations of these fathers are usually not mentioned, as heterosexuality and cisgenderism are assumed to be the norm. In this chapter, I have offered a reading of how fathers care about and for their future offspring by exploring two issues: first, I analysed gay, bisexual, trans and queer fathers and nonbinary people; and, second, I focused on the journey to parenthood before the conception of their children rather than during pregnancy or the early stages of fatherhood. Using empirical examples, I have shown how gay, bisexual, trans, queer and nonbinary prospective parents understand, experience, negotiate and enact their 'doing family' (Jurczyk, 2014; Morgan, 2011), and thus imagine caring fathering before the birth of their children. In doing so, I give a voice to people who are underrepresented in research on fatherhood and widen the scope for theorising caring fatherhood in non-hegemonic contexts.

The insights into the family formation processes of the interviewees illustrate that queer intended fathers and parents lack 'cultural scripts' (Pralat, 2021: 291) and their paths to parenthood are therefore 'uncharted territories' (Nordqvist and Smart, 2014: 29). Intended queer parents lack role models, and this is even more the case for co-parenting arrangements. Their imagining of being a caring father is always shaped by the hegemonic family norm, based on the cisgender, heterosexual, two-parent family. Carter and Horst, and the other participants who used surrogacy, could not imagine forming a co-parenting family and having to share their parenting with someone else. In fact, surrogacy makes the gay couple the sole fathers, a form that resembles the cis-heterosexual, two-parent family.

However, sitting in front of a blank page, as Michael framed their experiences, also opens up new possibilities to reinvent 'doing family'

(Morgan, 2011) and being a caring father in new and personal ways – in line with the individualisation of contemporary fatherhood among the middle class in Western European countries (Gillies, 2005). Similar to Herbrand's (2018) study on co-parenting, the examples presented show that queer parenting offers the possibility to be adapted to the wishes and ideas of the parents involved. For all but one of the interviewees, their ideological commitment to a caring fathering and parenting identity is initiated right from the outset. They care about and for their future offspring and imagine themselves to be actively involved in everyday caregiving. At the same time, they reinforce existing gender norms to a certain extent, such as when it comes to the primacy of biogenetic ties or the (partial) primary caregiving role of the biogenetic mother. We can therefore say that gay, bisexual, trans, queer and nonbinary prospective parents simultaneously transgress and reproduce 'traditional' family patterns in their family-building processes (Heaphy, 2018; Teschlade et al, 2023).

The participants in this study did not become parents by chance. Pralat (2020: 161) argues that their 'inability to have a child by accident makes the prospect of creating a family not only more complicated but also subject to greater scrutiny'. Indeed, the participants' family-building processes often took years, and so their advanced age at parenthood compared to the Dutch and Swiss averages is no coincidence. Their path to parenthood involved extensive deliberation, planning, negotiation and decision making at all four stages identified by Anttila et al (2023a). First, they revealed and discussed their parental aspirations. Second, they considered the practicalities by gathering information from friends, the internet and organisations such as Meer dan Gewenst and Dachverband Regenbogenfamilien. Third, they discussed the pros and cons of different ways of becoming a parent within the legal framework and the social realities of their country of residence. The gay, bisexual, trans, queer and nonbinary research participants based their decisions on norms of what constitutes a 'good' family, such as the importance of biogenetic ties or the number of parents. They also considered issues of access and cost and the expected duration of their journey to parenthood. And fourth and finally, they took concrete actions to become parents.

Particularly in the second and the third stages, the queer intended parents carefully considered their ideas about family and parenting and discussed them with others involved. I argue that this can be seen as a practice of self-care as intended parents. Furthermore, by creating intimacy with their future child, they are imagining themselves as caring fathers and therefore care about and for their future offspring, even before the child is conceived. Elliott (2016) suggests that caring masculinities are fostered among men through everyday caring practices. In contrast, the results presented show that gay, bisexual, trans, queer and nonbinary prospective parents already imagine themselves as caring fathers and parents, and thus demonstrate caring masculinities before the actual caregiving takes place.

Acknowledgements

I am indebted to all the participants who contributed to this research. I am also grateful for valuable remarks from Paula Vermuë, Anna Tarrant, Mengyao Wu, Leo Valentin Theissing and the editors on earlier drafts of this chapter. This study was supported by the Swiss National Science Foundation (SNSF), grant nos. 186629 and 203051.

Notes

1. Here, I have included the L for lesbian, the I for intersex, and the A for asexual as I will be writing more generally about queer families in this section.
2. The Swiss Parliament has decided to change this, but it remains unclear when this will happen.
3. I interviewed the couple together, making it a total of 28 interviews.
4. https://www.bfs.admin.ch/bfs/de/home/statistiken/wirtschaftliche-soziale-situation-bevoelkerung/gleichstellung-frau-mann/erwerbstaetigkeit/teilzeitarbeit.assetdetail.32331900.html

References

Anttila S et al (2023) 'I didn't even realize I agreed to meet the child so rarely': negotiations and parental desires in LGBTQ family forming processes. *Journal of Family Issues* 44(6): 1637–1661.

Baumgarten D, Lengersdorf D and Meuser M (2020) Caring Masculinities? Zum Wandel (des Verständnisses) väterlicher Verantwortung. In A Buschmeyer and C Zerle-Elsäßer (eds) *Komplexe Familienverhältnisse – Wie sich das Konzept ‚Familie' im 21. Jahrhundert wandelt*. Münster: Verlag Westfälisches Dampfboot, pp 63–86.

Beglaubter J (2021) 'I feel like it's a little bit of a badge of honor': fathers' leave-taking and the development of caring masculinities. *Men and Masculinities* 24(1): 3–22.

Bergman K et al (2010) Gay men who become fathers via surrogacy: the transition to parenthood. *Journal of GLBT Family Studies* 6(2): 111–141.

Berkowitz D (2020) Gay men and surrogacy. In AE Goldberg and KR Allen (eds) *LGBTQ-Parent Families.: Innovations in Research and Implications for Practice*, 2nd edn. New York: Springer, pp 143–160.

Berkowitz D and Marsiglio W (2007) Gay men: negotiating procreative, father, and family identities. *Journal of Marriage and Family* 69(2): 366–381.

Blake L et al (2017) Gay fathers' motivations for and feelings about surrogacy as a path to parenthood. *Human Reproduction* 32(4): 860–867.

Bos HH (2010) Planned gay father families in kinship arrangements. *Australian and New Zealand Journal of Family Therapy* 31(4): 356–371.

Bremner PD (2021) Gay and lesbian collaborative co-parenting: recognising multiple parents in the Netherlands and the UK. In H Wahlström Henriksson and K Goedecke (eds) *Close Relations: Family, Kinship, and Beyond*. New York: Springer, pp 37–52.

Büchler A and Cottier M (2020) Transgender, Intersex und Elternschaft in der Schweiz und im Rechtsvergleich. Ein Plädoyer für die Aufhebung der Mutter-Vater-Dyade. *La pratique du droit de la famille* 4: 875–889.

Bundesamt für Statistik (2021) *Familien in der Schweiz. Statistischer Bericht 2021*. Available from: https://www.bfs.admin.ch/bfs/de/home/statistiken/bevoelkerung/familien.assetdetail.17084546.html

Cammu N (2019) 'Legal multi-parenthood' in context: experiences of parents in light of the Dutch proposed family law reforms. *Family & Law*. DOI: 10.5553/FenR/.000042s

Cammu N (2021) 'We are three parents, but legally two': absent legality, present display. *Journal of Family Issues* 42(5): 1007–1028.

Cannito M (2020) Beyond 'traditional' and 'new': an attempt of redefinition of contemporary fatherhoods through discursive practices and practices of care. *Men and Masculinities* 23(3–4): 661–679.

Carneiro FA et al (2017) Are the fathers alright? A systematic and critical review of studies on gay and bisexual fatherhood. *Frontiers in Psychology* 8: 1636.

Carone N, Baiocco R and Lingiardi V (2017) Italian gay fathers' experiences of transnational surrogacy and their relationship with the surrogate pre-and post-birth. *Reproductive Biomedicine Online* 34(2): 181–190.

Connell RW and Messerschmidt JW (2005) Hegemonic masculinity: rethinking the concept. *Gender & Society* 19(6): 829–859.

D'Amore S et al (2023) European gay fathers via surrogacy: parenting, social support, anti-gay microaggressions, and child behavior problems. *Family Process*: 1–24. DOI: 10.1111/famp.12950

Dahl U and Gabb J (2019) Trends in contemporary queer kinship and family research. *Lambda Nordica* 24(2–3): 209–237.

Dempsey D (2013) Surrogacy, gay male couples and the significance of biogenetic paternity. *New Genetics and Society* 32(1): 37–53.

Duyvendak JW (2016) The pitfalls of normalization: The Dutch case and the future of equality. In CA Ball A (ed) *After Marriage Equality: The Future of LGBT Rights*. New York: New York University Press, pp 288–305.

Eerola P and Huttunen J (2011) Metanarrative of the 'new father' and narratives of young Finnish first-time fathers. *Fathering* 9(3): 211–231.

Elliott K (2016) Caring masculinities: theorizing an emerging concept. *Men and Masculinities* 19(3): 240–259.

Erera PI and Segal-Engelchin D (2014) Gay men choosing to co-parent with heterosexual women. *Journal of GLBT Family Studies* 10(5): 449–474.

Faircloth C (2014) Intensive fatherhood? The (un)involved dad. In E Lee et al (eds) *Parenting Culture Studies*. London: Springer, pp 184–199.

Farstad GR and Stefansen K (2015) Involved fatherhood in the Nordic context: dominant narratives, divergent approaches. *NORMA: International Journal for Masculinity Studies* 10(1): 55–70.

Gehem M and van den Berg D (2023) *Waarden en wensen bij een wetswijziging meerouderschap en -gezag. Een verslag van gesprekken over wat er op het spel staat voor meeroudergezinnen en professionals*. Available at: https://www.rijksoverh eid.nl/documenten/rapporten/2023/10/06/tk-bijlage-1-waarden-en-wen sen-bij-een-wetswijziging-meerouderschap-en-gezag

Gillies V (2005) Raising the 'meritocracy' parenting and the individualization of social class. *Sociology* 39(5): 835–853.

Goldberg AE, Downing JB and Moyer AM (2012) Why parenthood, and why now? Gay men's motivations for pursuing parenthood. *Family Relations* 61(1): 157–174.

Goldberg AE and Allen KR (2020) *LGBTQ-Parent Families: Innovations in Research and Implications for Practice*, 2nd edn. New York: Springer Nature.

Heaphy B (2018) Troubling traditional and conventional families? Formalised same-sex couples and 'the ordinary'. *Sociological Research Online* 23(1): 160–176.

Heaphy B (2019) Family, kinship and citizenship: change and continuity in LGBQ lives. In P Aggleton et al (eds) *Youth, Sexuality and Sexual Citizenship*. New York: Routledge, pp 19–33.

Herbrand C (2018) Ideals, negotiations and gender roles in gay and lesbian co-parenting arrangements. *Anthropology & Medicine* 25(3): 311–328.

Hunter SC, Riggs DW and Augoustinos M (2017) Hegemonic masculinity versus a caring masculinity: implications for understanding primary caregiving fathers. *Social and Personality Psychology Compass* 11(3): e12307.

Inhorn MC, Chavkin W and Navarro J-A (2015) Introduction: globalized fatherhood. emergent forms and possibilities in the new millennium. In MC Inhorn, W Chavkin and J-A Navarro (eds) *Globalized Fatherhood*. Oxford: Berghahn Books, pp 1–28.

Jadva V et al (2015) 'Friendly allies in raising a child': a survey of men and women seeking elective co-parenting arrangements via an online connection website. *Human Reproduction* 30(8): 1896–1906.

Jak L, Griffin L and Coster S (2023) *Regenboogouderschap: gezinnen van nu*. Available from: https://www.movisie.nl/sites/movisie.nl/files/2023-09/ handreiking-Regenboogouderschap-gezinnen-van-nu.pdf

Johansson T (2011) The construction of the new father: how middle-class men become present fathers. *International Review of Modern Sociology* 37(1): 111–126.

Johansson T and Klinth R (2008) Caring fathers: the ideology of gender equality and masculine positions. *Men and Masculinities* 11(1): 42–62.

Jordan A (2020) Masculinizing care? Gender, ethics of care, and fathers' rights groups. *Men and Masculinities* 23(1): 20–41.

Jurczyk K (2014) Doing Family–der Practical Turn der Familienwissenschaften. In: A Steinbach, M Hennig and O Arránz Becker (eds) *Familie im Fokus der Wissenschaft*. Wiesbaden: Springer, pp 117–138.

Kneebone E, Beilby K and Hammarberg K (2022) Surrogates' and intended parents' experiences of surrogacy arrangements: a systematic review. *Reproductive Biomedicine Online*. DOI: 10.1016/j.rbmo.2022.06.006

Lustenberger S (2017) 'We are citizens': vulnerability and privilege in the experiences of Israeli gay men with surrogacy in India. *Journal of Comparative Family Studies* 48(3): 393–403.

Medved CE (2016) Stay-at-home fathering as a feminist opportunity: perpetuating, resisting, and transforming gender relations of caring and earning. *Journal of Family Communication* 16(1): 16–31.

Mepschen P (2016) Sexual democracy, cultural alterity and the politics of everyday life in Amsterdam. *Patterns of Prejudice* 50(2): 150–167.

Morgan D (2011) *Rethinking Family Practices*. Basingstoke: Palgrave Macmillan.

Nay YE (2021) *Zusammenschau der Forschung zu 'Regenbogenfamilien'*. Available from: https://www.regenbogenfamilien.ch/fakten/

Nebeling Petersen M (2015) Between precarity and privilege: claiming motherhood as gay fathers through transnational commercial surrogacy. In V Kantsa, G Zanini and L Papadopoulou (eds) *(In)Fertile Citizens: Anthropological and Legal Challenges of Assisted Reproduction Technologies*. Mytilini: Univesity of the Aegean, pp 93–100.

Nordqvist P (2010) Out of sight, out of mind: family resemblances in lesbian donor conception. *Sociology* 44(6): 1128–1144.

Nordqvist P and Smart C (2014) *Relative Strangers: Family Life, Genes and Donor Conception*. Dordrecht: Springer.

Pralat R (2020) Parenthood as intended: reproductive responsibility, moral judgements and having children 'by accident'. *Sociological Review* 68(1): 161–176.

Pralat R (2021) Sexual identities and reproductive orientations: coming out as wanting (or not wanting) to have children. *Sexualities* 24(1–2): 276–294.

Reczek C (2020) Sexual-and gender-minority families: a 2010 to 2020 decade in review. *Journal of Marriage and Family* 82(1): 300–325.

Riggs D et al (2021) Trans parenting. In A O'Reilly (ed.) *Maternal Theory: Essential Readings*. Ontario: Demeter Press, pp 823–832.

Roberts S and Prattes R (2023) Caring masculinities in theory and practice: reiterating the relevance and clarifying the capaciousness of the concept. *Sociological Research Online*. DOI: 10.1177/13607804231205978

Silveira GB, Roggia GB, Rigue J, and Kruel CS (2024) Male homoparenting and its challenges: an integrative literature review. *Ciência & Saúde Coletiva* 29(4): e19382023.

Smietana M (2018) Procreative consciousness in a global market: gay men's paths to surrogacy in the USA. *Reproductive Biomedicine & Society Online* 7: 101–111.

Smietana M (2022) Having children as a matter of Pride: gay men, surrogacy and queer reproductive justice. Available from: https://www.lucy.cam.ac.uk/events/livefromlucy-pride-month-having-children-matter-pride-gay-men-surrogacy-and-queer

Stacey J (2006) Gay parenthood and the decline of paternity as we knew it. *Sexualities* 9(1): 27–55.

Teschlade J, Motakef M and Wimbauer C (2023) Discrimination and normalization as an effortful social practice: an analysis of LGBTQ+ families in Germany. *Sexualities*: 1–19. DOI: 10.1177/13634607231205819

Tornello SL and Patterson CJ (2015) Timing of parenthood and experiences of gay fathers: a life course perspective. *Journal of GLBT Family Studies* 11(1): 35–56.

Tronto CV (1993) *Moral Boundaries: A Political Argument for an Ethic of Care.* New York: Routledge.

Tronto CV (2013) *Caring Democracy: Markets, Equality, and Justice.* New York: New York University Press.

Tsfati M and Adital B-A (2021) Single gay fathers via surrogacy: the dialectics between vulnerability and resilience. *Journal of Family Studies* 27(2): 247–260.

Vijlbrief A, Saharso S and Ghorashi H (2020) Transcending the gender binary: Gender non-binary young adults in Amsterdam. *Journal of LGBT Youth* 17(1): 89–106.

Von Känel, M (2023) Familienvielfalt erkennen und befähigen – Denkanstösse für eine qualitative Unterstützung. *SozialAktuell*: 26–28.

Wimbauer C (2021) *Co-Parenting und die Zukunft der Liebe. Über postromantische Elternschaft.* Bielefeld: transcript Verlag.

Yerkes MA, Dotti Sani GM and Solera C (2018) Attitudes toward parenthood, partnership, and social rights for diverse families: evidence from a pilot study in five countries. *Journal of Homosexuality* 65(1): 80–99.

17

Fathers caring in families with children with disabilities

Jesús Rogero-García, Gerardo Meil and Pedro Romero-Balsas

Introduction

Men's involvement in childcare is an issue of growing interest. Research has shown that fathers' involvement in their children's care has grown significantly in recent years both in Spain and in Western societies in general, mainly for two reasons. The first one is the progressive increase in public interest in promoting men's participation in caregiving to reduce gender inequality in this area and the penalisation at the workplace experienced by women after childbearing (Fernandez-Cornejo et al, 2018; Cukrowska-Torzewska and Matysiak, 2020). The second one is the well-documented finding of a significant relationship between fathers' involvement and education, namely the transmission of gender equality values (Cano and Hofmeinster, 2023), the creation of closer emotional bonds between fathers and children, the emotional wellbeing of both (O'Brien, 2009; Twamley et al, 2013), and children's educational outcomes (McBride et al, 2005; Hill, 2015).

In Spain, fathers have increased their involvement in caregiving during the last two decades (Meil and Rogero-García, 2015; Cano, 2019). Despite the interest in men's caregiving and the increase in their involvement, there are significant gaps in the research in this field. One of them is the lack of knowledge about the role played by fathers in families with children with disabilities. The Survey on Disability, Personal Autonomy and Dependency Situations 2020 estimates that in Spain, 4 per cent of children between the ages of two and five have some type of limitation: 0.2 per cent hearing, 0.3 per cent visual, 2.8 per cent communication, 1.7 per cent learning, 0.7 per cent mobility and 1.6 per cent interaction and personal relationships (INE, 2023). The percentage of children with disabilities is significantly higher in low-income households (Observatorio Estatal de la Discapacidad, 2023). In these cases, childcare demands tend to increase substantially and affect both the organisation of daily time and the economic situation of families, as well as the level of stress, cohesion and family wellbeing. This implies additional challenges for parents, both in terms of family caregiving and in their relationship with educational and care institutions.

This chapter specifically addresses childcare involvement of fathers living in families with children with disabilities in Spain. We will analyse the effects of having a child with disabilities on care practices and in particular its impact on: (1) the amount of childcare provided by fathers; (2) the distribution of care within the couple; and (3) the level of participation of nonparental agents in childcare (grandparents, nursery schools, paid caregivers and other nonremunerated persons).

Literature review

Although fathers are often less involved than mothers in parenting practices, their involvement has a critical influence on the functioning of a family with children with disabilities in several respects (Boyd et al, 2019; Rankin et al, 2019). Fathers' involvement can have a positive impact on the mental and emotional health of the rest of the family members, alleviate the pressure experienced by mothers, and improve the overall functioning of the family system (Flippin and Crais, 2011). Their increased involvement is associated with lower levels of family stress (Parette et al, 2010) and depression among mothers (Laxman et al, 2015), and with higher levels of parents' own wellbeing (Boyd et al, 2019).

In addition, it has been shown that the involvement of fathers in parenting is a predictor of better developmental outcomes in children, including better emotional regulation and cognitive and language development (Tamis-LeMonda et al, 2004). In this regard, in the context of autism spectrum disorders (ASD), fathers have been found to have unique interaction styles that enhance positive effects on their upbringing and development (Flippin and Crais, 2011).

Despite this, fathers are underrepresented in childhood disability research (Bogossian et al, 2019; Rankin et al, 2019; Acar et al, 2021), and their involvement and its effects on family life need to be investigated in greater depth (Meadan et al, 2013; Davys et al, 2017). Most of studies in this field use samples consisting only of fathers and/or mothers of children with disabilities, but very few compare their situation with that of families with children without disabilities.

Previous research has explored whether fathers are more, less or similarly involved in childcare depending on whether they have a child with disability. The results of this research are mixed. Some of the studies suggest similar paternal involvement in families of children with and without disabilities. For example, the study by Mavrogianni and Lampropoulou (2020) found no significant differences in the overall level of involvement in childcare between fathers of deaf children and those of the other groups. Similar results were obtained by Ozgun and Honig (2005), Young and Roopnarine (1994) and Pelchat et al, (2003) for families with children with various types of disabilities in Turkey, New York and Canada, respectively. The longitudinal study by Dyer et al (2009) also found no evidence that fathers of children with disabilities were less or more involved than others in the US. Olsson et al (2006), using a Swedish sample, also found no differences in the division of tasks in families with and without children with intellectual disabilities.

In contrast, Bristol, Gallagher and Schopler (1988) found in the US that fathers of children with communication and behavioural limitations assumed fewer caregiving responsibilities compared to fathers of children without disabilities, even in families where the woman was employed. This reduced involvement was related to the severity of the child's atypical behaviours. Along these lines, Konstantareas and Homatidis (1992) also found in the US that fathers of children with autism and maturational delay spend less time with their children compared to other fathers.

As shown, the results of the literature review point in different directions, showing the need for more exhaustive research to better understand how having a child with a disability affects family dynamics and, in particular, the involvement of fathers in caregiving. This is even more necessary in the Spanish case, where no research has been found that addresses these objectives.

Methodology

This study is based on the Quidan Survey, which was conducted online among 3,100 parents with children under the age of seven living in Spain. While the questionnaire was designed by Quidan research team (https://quidan-project.com), fieldwork was carried out by NETQUEST, a market research company, following International Organization for Standardization (ISO) standards during May and June 2021. Sample quotas were established and distributed uniformly by sex and age of the minor child, and proportionally to educational level and place of residence, to guarantee that enough information of these subgroups was gathered. Weighting factors were calculated and applied to adjust the sample size to the real population distribution, using the Eurostat Labour Force Survey as a source. The use of self-administered online surveys has been shown to be more reliable than face-to-face surveys for the study of family relationships (Schumann and Lück, 2023). Validity is also achieved through the introduction of control questions and duration control, rejecting those who answer randomly and so-called speeders (who finish the questionnaire 20 per cent earlier than normal). Recaptcha and a specific ID for every interviewed was used to avoid automatic supplantation of identity and those who tried to answer the questionnaire twice. A total of 11 per cent of the initial sample size was rejected. The final sample consists of fathers and mothers of at least one child aged 0–6 speaking Spanish, spread over the whole country. Only respondents who lived with a partner in the same household were selected, in order to eliminate the possible bias in the estimation of childcare time introduced by couples who do not live together, totalling 2,908 parents. The number of families with children with disabilities captured by the survey is 76.

The participation of the different agents in childcare is measured through the *daily minutes dedicated* by fathers, mothers, nursery schools, grandparents, hired persons, extracurricular activities and other unpaid persons. To collect this information, we used the 'activity diary' technique (Robinson, 1999) adapted to the study of caregiving, which we have called the 'childcare diary'.

In the 'childcare diary' respondents were asked to indicate which persons or institutions 'took care (were in charge of him/her, etc.)' of each of their children between 7 am and 11 pm, in 15-minute intervals, during the last working day, with a representative sample from Monday to Friday. Information was collected for each child and the care of the same child by several agents was counted and, when a person cared for more than one child at the same time (in the same time slot), only one time slot was recorded. The dependent variable is the daily time spent by each agent caring for all respondent's children. This methodology has the advantage of collecting information more accurately and reliably than other methodologies (Robinson, 1999; Gershuny, 2000). Its application to the specific study of childcare is a novel methodological approach that has rarely been applied globally.

The main independent variable is the *presence of at least one child with disabilities*, measured as having *difficulties in carrying out daily activities*, which comes from the following question: 'Do you have any child with a chronic or physical problem, illness or disability that makes it difficult for him/her to carry out daily activities?' Possible answers were 'yes', 'no' or 'I prefer not to answer'.

The relevant variables identified in the literature that act as control variables in the relationship between the presence of children with disabilities and fathers' involvement are as follows:

- *The father's educational level*, which has been observed to be an element that promotes fathers' involvement in caregiving (Brągiel et al, 2014) and facilitates the family's adjustment to the children's disability situation (Trute, 1990). The *educational level of the mother* has also been incorporated, assuming that it may also be relevant.
- *The age of the youngest child*, since it has been found to be fundamental to understanding the intensity of care needed by children with disabilities, as well as the involvement of different agents, both formal and informal (Parette et al, 2010). Although it is not possible to know for sure whether the age of the youngest child corresponds to that of the child with a disability, we can say that it does in most cases, as 46 per cent of the

sample includes parents with only one child. The *age of the father* was also included in the models, which may have an impact on his economic activity and his general approach to caregiving.
- *The father's employment status* and the *mother's employment status* have an impact on the time available to care for their children and on the distribution of these responsibilities within the couple (Pelchat et al, 2003).
- *Net monthly household income* has also been identified as a relevant factor (Fox et al, 2015).
- *The existence of siblings in the home*, as this has direct effects on the dedication of the father and mother to care, among other consequences for the family.
- *Time to reach the nearest grandparents' home* has been observed to play an important role, as they are an important support to care grandchildren in Spain (Meil and Rogero-García, 2015).
- *The size of the municipality*, which is related to the availability of formal childcare services, as bigger cities have more resources and more diversified social policies, mainly for children aged 0–3 (Sola-Espinosa, Rogero-García and Meil, 2023).

The categories of these variables can be seen in Tables 17.2 and 17. 3. For some variables, it was necessary to include 'not applicable or no response' as a category in the models in order to guarantee a sufficient number of cases and ensure representativeness. Previously, it was ensured that all variable categories with missing data were of sufficient size to meet the statistical requirements of binary logistic regression models (Garson, 2016).

The methodological strategy consisted of the design of several binary logistic regression models relative to the dependent variables described: two models with the dependent variables 'daily time spent by the father' and 'daily time spent by the mother', whose dichotomous categories were: '6 hours or less' (value 0) and 'more than 6 hours' (value 1); another model with the dependent variable 'difference in daily time between father and mother' whose categories were '2 hours or less' (value 0) and 'more than 2 hours' (value 1); and five models on daily care by agents external to the couple: 'grandparents, nursery schools, hired persons, and other relatives or acquaintances', whose categories were 'none or less than 15 minutes' (value 0) and 'at least 15 minutes' (value 1); and a model aggregating daily care time by all agents external to the couple, with the categories '6 hours or less' (value 0) and 'more than 6 hours' (value 1).

In addition, ANOVA analyses were performed to further explain the results obtained with the following independent variables:

- *Weekly hours of paid employment by mother and father*. The information was extracted from the questions, 'Including overtime, how many hours a week do you normally work?' and 'What about your partner?'. In this

case the information comes from a question in which the respondent calculates the time spent in employment in a typical week.
- *Compatibility of work schedule with family commitments*. This comes from the question: 'To what extent is your work schedule compatible with your family commitments?', in which the response scale ranged from a maximum of 1 (very compatible) to 5 (not at all compatible). Thus, the higher this indicator, the more incompatible the work schedule is with family commitments.
- *Degree of satisfaction with the couple's relationship*, on a scale of 1 to 10 (1 not at all satisfied, 10 totally satisfied).
- Variables about *frequency of arguments in the couple*: (a) *about the division of childcare*; (b) *about the model of childrearing/education*; (c) *about the division of household chores*; and (d) *about the time and attention to the couple*. In all these four items, the possible answers ranged from 1 (never) to 10 (continuously).

Results and discussion

Table 17.1 presents the daily amount of time in minutes devoted by different caregivers on childcare, depending on whether the child has a disability or chronic illness. The results show that fathers devote significantly less time to caring for their children with disabilities than the rest: on average, they spend 354 minutes a day compared to 440 minutes – that is, 86 minutes less than those who do not have children with disabilities. On the other hand, mothers with children with disabilities spend 57 minutes more than other mothers, although the difference is not statistically significant at the conventional level of significance of 0.05. On the other hand, the gender differences in the time spent on care by fathers and mothers in both types of households are statistically significant, being much higher in families with children with disabilities: 333 minutes of difference in these compared to 189 in the rest of the households. In turn, although they do not reach the conventional significance level of 0.05, differences are observed – almost all of them below the 0.1 level – indicating that in households with children with disabilities, there is greater participation of caregivers other than parents: hired persons, extracurricular activities and other unpaid persons. However, this does not include grandparents or kindergarten attendance.

After controlling for the main relevant variables, the logistic regression models confirm that fathers with children with disabilities spend significantly less time caring for children than other fathers, while mothers of this type of children spend more time than other mothers (Table 17.2). In these households, greater inequality in caregiving within the couple is also observed. The first model shows that fathers with a child with a disability are 47 per cent less likely to devote more than six hours of care compared

Table 17.1: Daily minutes of childcare help provided by different agents depending on the presence of a child in special need with daily activities due to disability or chronic illness

	No children with disabilities	With children with disabilities	Total	Sig.
Father	440	354	438	0.045
Mother	630	687	631	0.146
Grandmothers/grandfathers	108	123	109	0.598
Children's school	220	224	220	0.899
Hired person	12	29	12	0.057
Extracurricular activities	18	40	18	0.051
Other nonremunerated persons	22	51	23	0.072
Difference between mother and father	*189*	*333*	*193*	*0.008*
Time of use of agents external to the couple	*380*	*467*	*382*	*0.091*
N	2,832	76	2,908	

Source: Quidan survey, 2021

to other fathers. The second model shows that, in contrast, mothers are 2.38 times more likely to care for more than six hours when they have a child with a disability. The third model shows that in these cases gender inequality in time devoted to childcare increases significantly: compared to households without children with disabilities, in these households, mothers are 86 per cent more likely than fathers to dedicate at least two hours more to caregiving than fathers.

These results are in line with previous studies such as Bristol et al (1988) and Konstantareas and Homatidis (1992) for the US, but contradict the evidence of Mavrogianni and Lampropoulou (2020) for Greece, Ozgun and Honig (2005) for Turkey, Young and Roopnarine (1994) for New York, and Pelchat et al (2003) for Canada, who found no differences in parental involvement in families with and without children with disabilities.

Our results are in line with research that has analysed the differences in the role of men and women in the care of their children with disabilities. In this regard, it has been observed that fathers usually serve as help or support for the main caregiver (Pelchat et al, 2003) and that they provide direct care only when mothers are ill or busy with their work (Navalkar, 2010). Likewise, for Sweden, Olsson et al (2006) observed that mothers of children with intellectual disabilities were more negatively affected in employment than fathers, which indirectly reveals a lower involvement of the latter in the family. Therefore, according to these results, the trend towards a change of model towards a greater involvement of fathers in caregiving activities

Table 17.2: Logistic regression models on daily time spent by the father and the mother, and the difference between the two

	Father (0 = 6 hours or less; 1 = more than 6 hours)		Mother (0 = 6 hours or less; 1 = more than 6 hours)		Difference mother–father (0 = 2 hours or less; 1 = more than 2 hours)	
	Sig.	Exp(B)	Sig.	Exp(B)	Sig.	Exp(B)
Do you have children in special need of help with daily activities? (ref: No)	0.015	0.531	0.037	2.378	0.017	1.856
Father's age	0.553	1.005	0.910	0.999	0.769	1.003
Father's level of education (ref: no education, primary or 1st stage secondary)	0.003		0.039		0.006	
2nd stage secondary education	0.001	1.603	0.033	0.667	0.002	0.630
University studies (all levels)	0.001	1.671	0.341	0.821	0.004	0.631
Father's employment status (ref: permanent contract)	0.000		0.001		0.000	
Temporary contract, self-employed, ERTE* or working without a contract	0.492	0.931	0.075	0.798	0.802	0.975
Unemployed or other situation	0.000	2.113	0.001	0.502	0.000	0.435
Mother's level of education (ref: no education, Primary or 1st stage secondary)	0.121		0.080		0.424	
2nd stage secondary education	0.902	0.978	0.362	1.217	0.319	1.202
University studies (all levels)	0.348	1.194	0.062	1.517	0.668	1.085
Mother's employment status (ref: permanent contract)	0.000		0.000		0.000	
Temporary contract, self-employed, ERTE* or working without a contract	0.456	1.088	0.107	1.246	0.444	1.088
Unemployed or other situation	0.000	0.493	0.000	1.797	0.000	2.469
Net monthly household income (ref: less than €1,101)	0.020		0.447		0.006	
Between €1,001 and €2,700	0.087	1.339	0.705	1.083	0.140	1.286
More than €2,071	0.013	1.608	0.562	0.873	0.573	0.898

Table 17.2: Logistic regression models on daily time spent by the father and the mother, and the difference between the two (continued)

	Father (0 = 6 hours or less; 1 = more than 6 hours)		Mother (0 = 6 hours or less; 1 = more than 6 hours)		Difference mother–father (0 = 2 hours or less; 1 = more than 2 hours)	
	Sig.	Exp(B)	Sig.	Exp(B)	Sig.	Exp(B)
No response	0.488	1.141	0.938	0.982	0.666	1.085
Size of municipality (ref: fewer than 20,000 inhabitants)	0.003		0.195		0.000	
20,001–100,000 inhabitants	0.004	1.394	0.089	0.783	0.012	0.751
More than 100,000 inhabitants	0.001	1.392	0.137	0.823	0.000	0.585
Distance to grandparents' home (ref: less than 15 minutes)	0.511		0.020		0.697	
15–40 minutes	0.199	1.145	0.105	1.241	0.496	1.074
More than 40 minutes	0.983	0.997	0.646	1.097	0.612	1.084
Not applicable or no response	0.739	0.962	0.049	0.762	0.544	0.931
Age of youngest child in months	0.081	0.996	0.147	0.996	0.490	0.999
Presence siblings (ref: No)	0.000	1.552	0.000	1.512	0.478	0.941
Constant	0.027	0.397	0.003	4.464	0.917	1.044
R2 Nagelkerke	*0.101*		*0.049*		*0.097*	
Hosmer and Lemeshow test	0.271		0.407		0.485	
N	2,810		2,810		2,810	

Note: * ERTE = Expedientes Temporales de Regulación de Empleo (Temporary Employment Regulation Files)

(Doucet, 2006; Dermott, 2008; Kaufman, 2013) is challenged in families with children with some type of disability.

Two reasons can be formulated that may explain or, at least, be related to the reduced involvement of fathers with children with disabilities. The first possibility is that in these couples, the man devotes more time to paid work or finds it more difficult to balance employment with family demands. According to this reasoning, in these households, mothers would devote more time to caring for their children, while men would intensify their involvement in paid work in order to secure the economic resources that would allow them to afford the cost of services (therapeutic treatments, special care, academic reinforcement and so on) and technical aids (wheelchairs, home adaptations and so on) that may be required to meet the needs of their children. This would be in line with previous studies which have observed that, traditionally, the way in which parents were involved in the lives of their children with disabilities was not through direct physical care, but through the provision of economic resources (Pelchat et al, 2003; Navalkar, 2010). In fact, paid work is still perceived by many parents as an indirect way to be involved in the education of their children with complex disabilities (Pancsofar et al, 2019).

Although this explanation seems plausible, our results do not show statistically significant differences between the time that fathers of children with disabilities devote weekly to employment compared to the rest of fathers. The same results apply to mothers (Table 17.3), so we cannot confirm this hypothesis. However, it could be that these men have schedules with a similar duration to the rest, but that are less compatible with family life, which would explain their reduced involvement in caregiving. However, the results obtained do not confirm this second reasoning either, since they do not refer significant differences in the degree of difficulties for balancing working and family commitments (Table 3), so that we are still unable to explain the lower paternal involvement in caregiving through his relationship with employment.

A third reason could be related to lower satisfaction with their family life. Recent studies exploring the degree of regret about having children among men and women in Spain point in this direction. Meil, Romero-Balsas and Muntanyola (2023a, 2023b) have found that fathers of children with disabilities regret parenthood more frequently than other fathers, unlike what happens among mothers, who show a similar degree of regret to the rest of mothers. In fact, according to data from the survey analysed, the proportion of fathers who disagree with the statement 'parenting is a source of satisfaction' and who affirm that 'having children has more disadvantages than advantages' is significantly higher ($p < 0.05$) among fathers who have children with disabilities than among the others.

Our results suggest that there is indeed a relationship between having a child with a disability and some indicators of family conflict. In particular, in

Table 17.3: Weekly hours of paid work and degree of compatibility of working hours with family commitments, according to sex and presence of children in special need of help with daily activities

	Fathers							Mothers					
	No children with disability	With children with disability	Total	Sig. ANOVA	N without disability	N with disability		No children with disability	With children with disability	Total	Sig. ANOVA	N without disability	N with disability
Hours per week dedicated to paid work	34.45	32.69	34.40	0.378	2759	78		22.85	22.49	22.84	0.867	2.836	78
Compatibility of work schedule with family commitments	2.61	2.84	2.62	0.247	1435	38		2.55	2.35	2.55	0.262	1.424	41

these families there is a higher frequency of arguments over the division of childcare (although in the case of the mother, the difference is not statistically significant) and over the time and attention devoted to the couple (Table 17.4). Although not statistically significant at conventionally accepted levels, the results also point to a lower satisfaction with the couple's relationship among fathers with children with disabilities, something that is not observed among women. These results may be related to the higher prevalence of stress and anxiety found among mothers and fathers of children with intellectual and developmental disabilities (Olsson and Hwang, 2001; Scherer et al, 2019).

Regarding the involvement of caregivers other than the parents, the analyses carried out (see Table 17.5) show that the presence of a child (or children) with disabilities multiplies the probability of hiring a person for caregiving by 2.4. In the rest of the models, no statistically significant relationship is observed between the presence of child (or children) with disabilities and the involvement in caregiving by other external agents. Therefore, the results suggest that having a child with disabilities increases the probability of hiring an external person to care for them or provide specific services, but is not related to greater care by grandparents, nursery schools or other agents. Previous studies have found that these families invest significantly more money than the rest in the care and health of their children (Newacheck et al, 2004), which is related to higher levels of stress (Fox et al, 2015; Lima-Rodriguez et al, 2018).

The absence of a relationship between having a child with a disability and a longer attendance time in nursery schools is, in part, consistent with the results of Booth-LaForce and Kelly (2004) in the US, who found that children with disabilities tended to enter nursery school at a later age and attend for fewer hours per day than other children. Reasons for not attending earlier included difficulty in finding good-quality and affordable care, transportation problems, and difficulties adjusting them with other services required by these children. In contrast to our results, this study found a greater involvement of grandparents in caregiving in families with children with disabilities. In the Spanish case, our results are consistent with the trend we have identified towards a more occasional involvement of grandparents in the care of children and to resolve emergency situations rather than for continuous and intense care (Meil and Rogero-García, 2015).

Conclusion

The main objective of this study is to analyse the impact of having children with disabilities on the degree of involvement of fathers in their care, on gender inequality in these families and on the distribution of this care among different agents. Our results show that in households with children with disabilities, there is less involvement of the father in their care, which

Table 17.4: Different indicators of family satisfaction and conflict, according to sex and presence of children in special need of help with daily activities

	Fathers						Mothers					
	No children with diff.	With children with diff.	Total	Sig. ANOVA	N without diff.	N with diff.	No children with diff.	With children with diff.	Total	Sig. ANOVA	N without diff.	N with diff.
Degree of satisfaction with the couple's relationship	8.27	7.80	8.26	0.136	1403	38	8.00	8.08	8.00	0.800	1.392	40
Frequency of discussions over childcare sharing	4.09	5.33	4.13	0.005	1406	38	4.55	4.97	4.56	0.320	1.394	40
Frequency of discussions about the model of child rearing/education of the child(ren)	4.02	4.29	4.03	0.546	1403	38	4.41	4.81	4.42	0.362	1.397	40
Frequency of arguments over the sharing of household chores	4.51	4.89	4.52	0.395	1401	38	5.07	5.56	5.08	0.254	1.388	40
Frequency of discussions about time and attention to partners	4.38	5.41	4.41	0.018	1376	34	4.64	5.66	4.67	0.015	1.133	29

Note: diff. = difficulties

Table 17.5: Logistic regression models on daily time spent on childcare by noncouple agents

	Grandparents (0 = none; 1 = at least 15 minutes)		Nursery school (0 = none; 1 = at least 15 minutes)		Person hired (0 = none; 1 = at least 15 minutes)		Other people (0 = not at all; 1 = at least 15 minutes)		Extracurricular (0 = none; 1 = at least 15 minutes)		Agents external to the couple (0 = 6 hours or less; 1 = more than 6 hours)	
	Sig.	Exp(B)	Sig.	Exp(B)	Sig.	Exp(B)	Sig.	Exp(B)	Sig.	Exp(B)	Sig.	Exp(B)
Do you have children in special need of help with daily activities? (ref: No)	0.778	1.084	0.938	1.022	0.049	2.424	0.405	1.503	0.199	1.664	0.412	0.803
Father's age	0.262	0.989	0.204	1.012	0.607	1.011	0.256	0.977	0.356	0.985	0.573	1.005
Father's level of education (ref: no education, primary or 1st stage secondary)	0.700		0.038		0.000		0.345		0.019		0.150	
2nd stage secondary education	0.399	0.872	0.191	1.228	0.161	4.894	0.572	1.213	0.019	2.819	0.463	0.893
University studies (all levels)	0.512	0.891	0.019	1.490	0.018	14.501	0.705	0.865	0.006	3.469	0.638	1.081
Father's employment status (ref: permanent contract)	0.185		0.089		0.115		0.037		0.777		0.047	
Temporary contract, self-employed, ERTE or working without a contract	0.724	1.041	0.029	0.788	0.246	1.351	0.012	1.767	0.491	0.868	0.025	0.785
Unemployed or other situation	0.087	0.680	0.551	0.890	0.114	0.244	0.946	0.968	0.788	0.903	0.151	0.760
Mother's level of education (ref: no education, primary or 1st stage secondary)	0.989		0.005		0.068		0.331		0.116		0.720	
2nd stage secondary education	0.989	1.003	0.194	1.297	0.929	0.931	0.284	0.681	0.284	1.688	0.536	1.130
University studies (all levels)	0.930	1.019	0.009	1.701	0.438	1.839	0.140	0.573	0.096	2.249	0.426	1.174
Mother's employment status (ref: Permanent contract)	0.000		0.000		0.001		0.749		0.015		0.000	
Temporary contract, self-employed, ERTE or working without a contract	0.143	1.190	0.012	0.749	0.098	0.625	0.950	1.017	0.433	1.160	0.702	0.958

Table 17.5: Logistic regression models on daily time spent on childcare by noncouple agents (continued)

	Grandparents (0 = none; 1 = at least 15 minutes)		Nursery school (0 = none; 1 = at least 15 minutes)		Person hired (0 = none; 1 = at least 15 minutes)		Other people (0 = not at all; 1 = at least 15 minutes)		Extracurricular (0 = none; 1 = at least 15 minutes)		Agents external to the couple (0 = 6 hours or less; 1 = more than 6 hours)	
	Sig.	Exp(B)	Sig.	Exp(B)	Sig.	Exp(B)	Sig.	Exp(B)	Sig.	Exp(B)	Sig.	Exp(B)
Unemployed or other situation	0.000	0.426	0.000	0.348	0.000	0.159	0.461	1.205	0.010	0.512	0.000	0.285
Net monthly household income (ref: less than €1,101)	0.538		0.000		0.012		0.207		0.324		0.000	
Between €1,001 and €2,700	0.726	0.933	0.000	2.539	0.038	0.356	0.062	2.407	0.715	1.174	0.371	1.181
More than €2,071	0.289	0.793	0.000	3.718	0.115	0.453	0.102	2.348	0.347	1.532	0.004	1.808
No response	0.487	0.857	0.003	1.920	0.003	0.164	0.035	2.919	0.897	1.062	0.652	1.098
Size of municipality (ref: fewer than 20,000 inhabitants)	0.557		0.735		0.196		0.299		0.479		0.000	
20,001–100,000 inhabitants	0.288	0.872	0.547	0.929	0.641	1.170	0.688	1.122	0.371	0.826	0.248	0.870
More than 100,000 inhabitants	0.454	0.917	0.945	1.008	0.103	1.590	0.145	1.442	0.239	0.802	0.011	1.314
Distance to grandparents' home (ref: less than 15 minutes)	0.000		0.001		0.251		0.014		0.932		0.159	
15–40 minutes	0.000	0.560	0.696	1.044	0.471	1.198	0.140	0.650	0.971	0.993	0.108	0.840
More than 40 minutes	0.000	0.250	0.034	1.435	0.045	1.957	0.585	1.230	0.620	1.145	0.313	0.846
Not applicable or no response	0.001	0.637	0.005	0.704	0.779	1.095	0.023	1.751	0.752	0.932	0.046	0.782
Age of youngest child in months	0.026	0.995	0.000	1.017	0.756	1.002	0.624	0.998	0.000	1.028	0.095	1.004
Presence of siblings (ref: No)	0.000	1.553	0.000	2.123	0.000	3.156	0.017	1.669	0.000	2.781	0.000	1.939
Hosmer and Lemeshow test	*0.047*		*0.046*		*0.330*		*0.029*		*0.002*		*0.040*	
N	*2,810*		*2,810*		*2,810*		*2,810*		*2,810*		*2,810*	

is compensated by a greater dedication of the mother and the use of paid caregivers, but not by a greater involvement of grandparents.

This results cannot be attributed to the prevalence of a traditional Mediterranean family model in Spain, which is more reluctant to embrace gender equality and more reliant on the extended family. As argued before, fathers' involvement in childcare in Spain has increased substantially among parents in the last decades, gender inequality in housework has also decreased and childcare support by grandparents has evolved to be more an emergency resource for young parents, rather than a regular one, following the tendency in all developed Western countries. Therefore, our results are not only country-specific, but reflect general patterns of family childcare.

Based on this finding, we explored the possible reasons why fathers spend less time caring for their children in these situations. First, we tested the hypothesis that less paternal involvement may be related to greater dedication to employment, but the results obtained do not confirm it. Nevertheless, future studies with larger samples should explore this relationship further. Second, we analysed to what extent the satisfaction of these fathers with their family life could influence their lower involvement in childcare. Our results show that parents with children with disabilities have greater couple conflict due to childcare and the quality of their couple relationship. This suggests that the greater needs of the disabled child are a source of conflict that could contribute to lower family satisfaction, which would affect their motivation – but not that of women – to become involved in the care of their children.

If we assume these premises, a key question is why men experience greater discomfort than women when they have a child with a disability. One hypothesis, which could be tested in future studies, is that men find it more difficult to develop their role as fathers in its most expressive aspect (playing with their children, spending time with them in other leisure activities and so on) due to the difficulties derived from their children's limitations. Mothers, on the other hand, would maintain unchanged, or even pronounced, their role as providers of basic care in a context in which this is even more necessary. Future research should explore what the reasons are behind these different approaches to caring and identify ways of promoting convergence.

Finally, our work has found that in households with children with disabilities there is a greater likelihood of hiring external caregivers or providing specific services, but not a greater involvement of grandparents. These results suggest that these families invest more economic resources in the care and health of their children, which has been related to higher levels of stress among parents. This could reflect significant shortcomings on the part of public administrations in the provision of support services for families with children with disabilities, which are not compensated by family solidarity and which force families to pay for many of these services privately. This introduces significant inequalities between families according to their economic resources (Observatorio Estatal de la Discapacidad, 2023) that would generate educational inequity at a crucial stage of children's development.

In terms of research, we believe that future studies should corroborate the lower paternal involvement in these households and, if confirmed, explore its causes to identify solutions. As was noted earlier, the father's involvement has a direct impact on the likelihood of depression in the mother, on the cognitive and emotional development of the children, and on the general wellbeing of the entire family. Our results suggest the importance of promoting public policies to support families with children with disabilities through resources and services to alleviate the burden of care. Due to the design of the questionnaire, we could not measure and analyse the availability and impact of different public support resources for these families. However, this is a crucial element, as has been illustrated before. Future research should focus on this topic, analysing its impact not only on subjective wellbeing and caring attitudes, but also on practices, identifying those measures that work best to reduce gender and economic inequalities in these families. Another limitation of this study is that it does not identify different levels of difficulty or specific types of disabilities, which would provide more precise information about the relationship between the children's need for assistance and fathers' involvement. This should be also addressed in future studies. Despite these limitations, this chapter presents novel and relevant findings about fathers' childcare in families with disabled children, with significant implications in terms of public policy.

References

Acar, S., Chen, C. I. and Xie, H. (2021) 'Parental involvement in developmental disabilities across three cultures: a systematic review', *Research in Developmental Disabilities*, 110: 103861.

Bogossian, A., King, G., Lach, L. M., Currie, M., Nicholas, D., McNeill, T. and Saini, M. (2019) '(Unpacking) father involvement in the context of childhood neurodisability research: a scoping review', *Disability and Rehabilitation*, 41(1): 110–124.

Booth-LaForce, C. and Kelly, J. F. (2004) 'Childcare patterns and issues for families of preschool children with disabilities', *Infants & Young Children*, 17(1): 5–16.

Boyd, M. J., Iacono, T. and McDonald, R. (2019) 'The perceptions of fathers about parenting a child with developmental disability: a scoping review', *Journal of Policy and Practice in Intellectual Disabilities*, 16(4): 312–324.

Brągiel, J. and Kaniok, P. E. (2014) 'Demographic variables and fathers' involvement with their child with disabilities', *Journal of Research in Special Educational Needs*, 14(1): 43–50.

Bristol, M. M., Gallagher, J. J. and Schopler, E. (1988) 'Mothers and fathers of young developmentally disabled and nondisabled boys: adaptation and spousal support', *Developmental Psychology*, 24(3): 441–451.

Cano, T. (2019) 'Changes in fathers' and mothers' time with children: Spain, 2002–2010', *European Sociological Review*, 35(5): 616–636.

Cano, T. and Hofmeister, H. (2023) 'The intergenerational transmission of gender: Paternal influences on children's gender attitudes', *Journal of Marriage and Family*, 85(1): 193–214.

Cukrowska-Torzewska, E. and Matysiak, A. (2020), 'The motherhood wage penalty: a meta-analysis', *Social Science Research*, 88–89, 102416. DOI: 10.1016/j.ssresearch.2020.102416

Davys, D., Mitchell, D. and Martin, R. (2017) 'Fathers of people with intellectual disability: a review of the literature', *Journal of Intellectual Disabilities*, 21(2): 175–196.

Dermott, E. (2008) *Intimate Fatherhood: A Sociological Analysis*. New York: Routledge.

Doucet, A. (2006) *Do Men Mother? Fathering, Care and Domestic Responsibility*. Toronto: University of Toronto Press.

Dyer, J. W., McBride, B. A., Snatos, A. M. and Jeans L. M. (2009) 'A longitudinal examination of father involvement with children with developmental delays. Does timing of diagnosis matter?', *Journal of Early Intervention*, 31: 265–281.

Fernandez-Cornejo, J. A., Del Pozo-García, E., Escot, L. and Castellanos-Serrano, C. (2018) 'Can an egalitarian reform in the parental leave system reduce the motherhood labor penalty? Some evidence from Spain', *Revista Española de Sociología*, 27(3): 45–64. DOI: 10.22325/fes/res.2018.33

Flippin, M. and Crais, E. R. (2011) 'The need for more effective father involvement in early autism intervention: a systematic review and recommendations', *Journal of Early Intervention*, 33(1): 24–50.

Fox, G. L., Nordquist, V. M., Billen, R. M. and Savoca, E. F. (2015) 'Father involvement and early intervention: effects of empowerment and father role identity', *Family Relations*, 64(4): 461–475.

Garson, G. D. (2016) *Partial Least Squares: Regression and Structural Equation Models*. Asheboro: Statistical Associates Publishers.

Gershuny, J. (2000) *Changing Times: Work and Leisure in Post-industrial Society*. Oxford: Oxford University Press.

Hill, N. E. (2015) 'Including fathers in the picture: a meta-analysis of parental involvement and students' academic achievement', *Journal of Educational Psychology*, 107(4): 919–934.

Instituto Nacional de Estadística (2023): 'Encuesta de discapacidad, autonomía personal y situaciones de dependencia 2020'. Available from: https://ine.es/dynt3/inebase/es/index.htm?padre=8494.

Kaufman, G. (2013) *Superdads: How Fathers Balance Work and Family in the 21st Century*. New York: New York University Press.

Konstantareas, M. M. and Homatidis, S. (1992) 'Mothers' and fathers' self-report of involvement with autistic, mentally delayed and normal children', *Journal of Marriage and the Family*, 54: 153–164.

Laxman, D. J. et al (2015) 'Father involvement and maternal depressive symptoms in families of children with disabilities or delays', *Maternal and Child Health Journal*, 19: 1078–1086.

Lima-Rodríguez, J. S., Baena-Ariza, M. T., Domínguez-Sánchez, I. and Lima-Serrano, M. (2018) 'Discapacidad intelectual en niños y adolescentes: influencia en la familia y la salud familiar. Revisión sistemática', *Enfermería Clínica*, 28(2): 89–102.

Mavrogianni, T. and Lampropoulou, V. (2020) 'The involvement of fathers with their deaf children', *International Journal of Disability, Development and Education*, 67(1): 45–57.

McBride, B. A., Schoppe-Sullivan, S. J. and Ho, M. H. (2005) 'The mediating role of fathers' school involvement on student achievement', *Journal of Applied Developmental Psychology*, 26(2): 201–216.

Meadan, H., P. Parette, H. and Doubet, S. (2013) 'Fathers of young children with disabilities: experiences, involvement and needs', in *Father Involvement in Young Children's Lives: A Global Analysis*, New York: Springer, 153–167.

Meil, G., and Rogero-García, J. (2015) 'Does paternal childcare replace grandparental support in dual-earner families?', *Family Science*, 6(1): 31–37.

Meil, G., Romero-Balsas, P. and Muntanyola-Saura, D. (2023a) 'Regretting fatherhood in Spain', *Journal of Family Research*, 35: 37–52.

Meil, G., Romero-Balsas, P. and Muntanyola-Saura, D. (2023b) 'Las bases sociales del arrepentimiento de la maternidad en España', in D. Becerril Ruiz, J. Serrano and J. Jiménez Cabello (eds) *Amores, desamores y rupturas*. Valencia: Tirant Humanidades, pp 282–306.

Navalkar, P. G. (2010) 'Fathering a child with a disability in India: a perspective from Mumbai', *Childhood Education*, 86(6): 389–393.

Newacheck, P. W., Inkelas, M. and Kim, S. E. (2004) 'Health services use and health care expenditures for children with disabilities', *Pediatrics*, 114(1): 79–85.

O'Brien, M. (2009) 'Fathers, parental leave policies and infant quality of life: international perspectives and policy impact', *Annals of the American Academy of Political and Social Science*, 624(1): 190–213. DOI: 10.1177/0002716209334349

Observatorio Estatal de la Discapacidad (2023) *El despliegue de la garantía infantil en las niñas y niños con discapacidad: programa de acción. Informe de resultados*. Observatorio Estatal de la Discapacidad.

Olsson, M. B. and Hwang, C. P. (2001) 'Depression in mothers and fathers of children with intellectual disability', *Journal of Intellectual Disability Research*, 45(6): 535–543.

Olsson, M. B. and Hwang, C. P. (2006) 'Well-being, involvement in paid work and division of childcare in parents of children with intellectual disabilities in Sweden', *Journal of Intellectual Disability Research*, 50(12): 963–969.

Ozgun, O. and Honig, A.S. (2005) 'Parental involvement and spousal satisfaction with division of early childcare in Turkish families with normal children and children with special needs', *Early Child Development and Care*, 175(3): 259–270.

Pancsofar, N., Petroff, J. G., Rao, S. and Mangel, A. (2019) '"What I want to do as a father is be there": constructions of school involvement for fathers of children with complex disabilities', *Research and Practice for Persons with Severe Disabilities*, 44(3): 153–168.

Parette Jr., H. P., Meadan, H, and Doubet, S. (2010) 'Fathers of young children with disabilities in the United States: current status and implications', *Childhood Education*, 86(6): 382–388.

Pelchat, D., Lefebvre, H. and Perreault, M. (2003) 'Differences and similarities between mothers' and fathers' experiences of parenting a child with a disability', *Journal of Child Health Care*, 7(4): 231–247.

Rankin, J.A. et al (2019) 'Fathers of youth with autism spectrum disorder: a systematic review of the impact of fathers' involvement on youth, families and intervention', *Clinical Child and Family Psychology Review* 22: 458–477.

Robinson, J. P. (1999) 'The time-diary method: structures and uses', in W. E. Pentland, A. S. Harvey, M. Powell-Lawton and M. A. McColl (eds) *Time Use Research in the Social Sciences*. New York/London: Kluwer Academic/Plenum Publishers, pp 47–89.

Scherer, N., Verhey, I. and Kuper, H. (2019) 'Depression and anxiety in parents of children with intellectual and developmental disabilities: a systematic review and meta-analysis', *PloS One*, 14(7): e0219888.

Schumann, A. and Lück, D. (2023) 'Better to ask online when it concerns intimate relationships? Survey mode differences in the assessment of relationship quality', *Demographic Research*, 48(22): 609–640.

Sola Espinosa, I., Rogero-García, J. and Meil Landwerlin, G. (2023) 'El uso de servicios formales de cuidado infantil entre 0 y 3 años en España', *RES. Revista Española de Sociología*, 32(1): a144.

Tamis-LeMonda, C. S., Shannon, J. D., Cabrera, N. J. and Lamb, M. E. (2004) 'Fathers and mothers at play with their 2- and 3-year-olds: contributions to language and cognitive development', *Child Development*, 75(6): 1806–1820.

Trute, B. (1990) 'Child and parent predictors of family adjustment in households containing young developmentally disabled children', *Family Relations*, 292–297.

Twamley, K., Brunton, G., Sutcliffe, K., Hinds, K. and Thomas, J. (2013) 'Fathers' involvement and the impact on family mental health: evidence from Millennium Cohort Study analyses', *Community, Work & Family*, 16(2): 212–224. DOI: 10.1080/13668803.2012.755022

Young, D. M. and Roopnarine, J. L. (1994) 'Fathers' childcare involvement with children with and without disabilities', *Topics in Early Childhood Special Education*, 14(4): 488–502.

18

Accounting for lack of emotional engagement: adults reconceptualising fatherhood

Ann Phoenix

Introduction

Over the last few decades, researchers, practitioners and policy makers have come to take it for granted that fathers are central to family lives and children's wellbeing. 'In many locations, (good) fatherhood is increasingly understood not just in terms of provision but also in terms of "stepping into" domesticity; as spending time with one's children, and as offering care and nurture' (Henriksson, 2019: 321). Yet, despite the plethora of publications on fathers and fatherhood, there remains much that we do not know about differences between fathers and the contexts in which they live. This chapter aims to contribute to understandings of how fatherhood and fathering are positioned within fathers' and children's everyday lives, and differences between groups of fathers. It draws on studies of adults who grew up in 'non-normative', minoritised ethnic group households and retrospectively make meanings of the fathering they received. It examines the gap between models of 'new fathers' and everyday practices of fathers, and how these are received by children (Faircloth, 2023). The chapter highlights multiple ways in which understanding of fatherhood require it to be contextualised, including historically and intersectionally.

The chapter is informed by adult children's perspectives on the fathering they received and their accounts of its impact on them, focusing particularly on cases where children have not been emotionally engaged with their fathers. The following analyses help to illuminate the ways in which children can be unconsciously affected by the fathering they receive in ways that have implications for the generations to follow and, in the case of participants from Caribbean backgrounds, that are part of long legacies of enslavement and colonialism (Smith, 2011).

Background

The shift towards 'more caring, intimate and emotionally engaged ways of being a father' has been recognised across social science disciplines as part of intensive parenting (Dermott and Miller, 2015). While the terminology differs in psychology, some researchers have also shifted from a focus on assessments of 'father involvement' to considerations of 'father–child relationship quality', including relations of care (Palkowitz, 2019). It has become commonplace to recognise the importance of high-quality fathering to children's wellbeing and development, and that many fathers want to spend time with their children (Burgess and Goodman, 2023). Many studies found that, during lockdowns in the global COVID-19 pandemic, fathers were more able to realise that ideal and spent more time interacting with their children than they previously had (Oppenheim and Rehill, 2020). 'Traditional' ideas of fatherhood are thus being increasingly unsettled, but relatively little is known about how the model of the 'new father' promoted by experts and policy makers is played out in the everyday (Faircloth, 2023).

As Diniz et al (2021) point out from a systematic review of father involvement in early childhood, much of the research available still focuses on 'unidimensional evaluations' of fathers' involvement in play, expressions of affection or leisure activities. This leaves unexplored whether fathers play an independent role in caring for their children or are mostly 'helpers' in mothers' work and managerial roles, doing what some still consider as 'babysitting' their children (Lewington et al, 2021). Gendered differences in conceptualising parenting and in parenting practices thus remain central. In concert with this, Doucet (2020: 27) argues that it continues to be taken for granted that the concept of father involvement 'has developed within oppositional binaries of care and breadwinning, rather than through an acknowledgement of the relationality of these concepts'. Fathers thus often continue to be seen as breadwinners, not carers. Conceptually, this also removes making economic provision from care, even though children cannot thrive unless they have access to material provision and a lack of material resources prevents parents from parenting in ways that are considered socially ideal (Cooper, 2021). Yet, internationally, the provider function is a central component of fatherhood (Henriksson, 2019). As Henriksson (2019) indicates, the provider role is not attainable for men who are unemployed or living in poverty. In addition, for those who have to migrate in order to earn money for their families, 'father absence' is a form of 'responsible fathering'. Therefore, it is important to consider the situatedness of fatherhood behaviours and consider meanings as well as effects in complex ways, since the same behaviour does not necessarily have the same meanings or impacts for different children. Doucet suggests that the binarisation of care and economic provision matters because concepts are performative, shaping as well as describing social life. Yet, while there are calls to rethink fatherhood, there remains a great deal that has not been conceptualised or researched. Strier and Perez-Vaisvidovsky (2021: 334), for example, suggest that while contemporary fatherhood research recognises fatherhood 'as a multifaceted, dynamic social, and cultural construction, deeply affected by class, race, and gender inequalities', dominant theories on fatherhood continue to be developed from the experiences of 'middle-class, Anglo-centered, dominant, and mainstream fatherhood, whereas non-hegemonic, marginalized father groups have remained undertheorized'. Equally, there remains insufficient evidence about fatherhood where parents do not live together (East et al, 2020; Graf and Wojnicka, 2023).

Tracey Reynolds (2009) conducted pioneering research on Caribbean fathers in the UK, starting from the understanding that fatherhood has changed across all social groups. Thus, nonresident fathers, who have long been common in Caribbean culture because of histories of forcible separation in enslavement and postslavery poverty, are no longer 'deviant'. In modern Caribbean and UK Caribbean households, Reynolds found that many apparently 'absent' fathers have 'visiting unions' and 'friendling' relationships where fathers (and stepfathers) keep in contact with mothers and children, although they are not co-resident. Reynolds suggests that nonresident fathers are part of networks of trust, values and reciprocity that help to make families and communities functional and sustain connections that bind societies together. Therefore, it is important to nuance understandings of Caribbean fathers and to avoid reproducing taken-for-granted pathologising.

Equally, it is important to recognise the ways in which different groups of fathers differ because they have very different histories. The British Caribbean psychoanalyst Barbara Fletchman Smith (2011) drew on clinical examples of British Caribbean people and historical analysis of slavery to examine how histories of enslavement have contemporary impacts on men's roles in families. Smith shows how the psychic impact of everyday practices in slavery have been communicated in complex ways down generations, with insidious effects on men and women, fathering, mothering and grandmothering. In transatlantic enslavement, there were two main ways in which notions of fatherhood came to be sedimented into Black American and Caribbean bodies and cultures. First, enslaved women and girls had very little control over their reproductive bodies. Enslavers and their entourage fathered children as a byproduct of their felt entitlement to do what they wished to Black bodies. While some of the resulting children were given lighter work as, for example, 'house slaves', enslaver fathers modelled lack of care and lack of responsibility for their children.

The second main way in which fatherhood came to be divorced from care and responsibility for enslaved children and mothers was that relationships between men and women were discouraged or not taken seriously. Men could be ordered to father children if enslavers wished, and fathers, mothers and children could be sold at will:

> Basically, the system used separation of mothers from their babies, of loving couples from each other, as a conscious and unconscious method of creating anxiety, depression and hopelessness. Under this system the development of togetherness in families was foreclosed. One of the consequences, as we see today, was that it became possible for African Caribbean men to make babies with willing women with no intention of providing for them in any way. The making of babies became an option for the propping up of a masculinity that felt undermined or attacked.
>
> ... During slavery, any children the adults had together were not theirs but belonged to their owners, a situation which would have led to difficulties over the concept of 'belonging' for both the child and the adult. For African men in the Caribbean, the disconnection from paternity compromised the father's authority over his family. (Smith, 2011: 51)

While this deliberate production of lack of paternal care for the enslaved was cruelly inhumane and dehumanising, it was not essentialising: 'the destructiveness of slavery was never a total success ... The wish to be treated as human and to lead a good life was asserted and continues to be asserted down the generations' (Smith, 2011: 49). Smith's refusal to treat the impact of enslavement in absolutist ways alerts us to the importance of recognising that destructive histories haunt the present, but that this history does not determine contemporary cultures and relationships.

From a US study on Black fathers living away from their children from their own perspectives, Jennifer Hamer (2001: 220) concludes that:

> Inevitably, what poor and working-class Black live-away fathers actually do for their children rests with society's ability to provide them access to sufficient economic means. It is equally contingent on the legitimacy and support granted to their paternal status ... For those men who have little else to offer, the provision of nurturance, love, and affection are priceless aspects of fatherhood.

Recent ethnographic work taking an ecological perspective on Black US fatherhood embeds their everyday practices in the context of their families and community, and indicates that intersections of racialisation, place and low income are central. Abdill (2017) argues that longstanding negative perceptions of Black fathers in the inner city impact on their performances of masculinity and fatherhood, but that the increasing visibility of fathers with their children opens up new possibilities for them to be able to publicly show their care. Edin and Nelson (2013) conducted a seven-year ethnography with 110 Black and white fathers living away from their children. They found that the fathers are often resolved to play a vital role in their children's lives, but that this is often harder than they expect. Many are determined to 'be there', to show love and spend quality time, and have tried to forge fatherhood in ways that fit their circumstances. Yet, the circumstances in which they have lived have militated against continuous father–child relationships.

From children's perspectives, there has long been evidence that many want to spend more time with both parents than they currently do (Bhopal et al, 2000). They sometimes go to great lengths to maintain connections with separated parents (Smart, 2006) and often feel great sadness if they do not have regular contact with their fathers (Frosh et al, 2002). A holistic understanding of fatherhood requires explorations of fathers and children's intersectional positioning, the centrality of gender differences between parents, differences between fathers, between children, across and within racialised, ethnicised and social class groups. It also requires an understanding of children's and fathers' own perspectives.

This chapter makes visible some groups generally rendered silent in discussions of fatherhood in the affluent Minority World. It takes an intersectional perspective in recognition of the fact that everyone is simultaneously positioned in multiple social categories, including gender, social class and racialisation. These categories are not independent of each other, but intersect and mutually construct each other, producing qualitatively different meanings and experiences (Collins, 2019). Intersectional perspectives thus enable a holistic analysis of experiences of fatherhood. Methodologically, the chapter focuses on the narratives of adult children about their fathers and, for some, their own fatherhood. It examines fathering where father–child emotional engagement can be viewed as lacking and how children and fathers account for this in their narratives.

The chapter reuses retrospective narrative accounts from a study of adults who had three types of 'non-normative' childhoods: migrating later than their parents as serial migrants from the Caribbean; young people of different ethnicities who were language brokers for their parents and adults who, as children, lived in households where members were visibly ethnically different. The chapter is divided into three sections. The first describes the studies that inform the study. The second addresses fatherhood in context, showing why intersectionality is central to holistic understandings by drawing on the accounts of two men who grew up in visibly ethnically different households. The third considers adult narratives of fatherhood experienced in Caribbean serial migration childhoods. It focuses on the experiences of some of those who have not experienced intimate and emotionally engaged fathering. It examines how one man accounts for the fathering he received and accounts for his (lack of) emotional engagement with his children. The section draws on Gunilla Halldén's (1991) conceptualisation of children as their parents' intergenerational projects. In an interview study of 34 parents of four-year-olds, Halldén found that while parents were interested in their children in the present (as being), they also invested in their children as potentiality (as projects) in different ways. The section uses Halldén's notion of 'child as project' to examine ways in which caring can be separate from intimacy and emotional engagement in fathering. It considers both how children can feel alienated from fathers who are not emotionally engaged with them and give accounts of consciously seeking to 'do' fatherhood differently and of not developing intimate relationships with their own children. It introduces analyses done by Valerie Walkerdine and colleagues (2013) of one of the serial migration study participants to deepen the contextualisation of fatherhood and fathering practices by historicising them. The fourth and final section briefly concludes the chapter.

The chapter argues that understanding fathers' care practices and how they are experienced requires analysis of fatherhood in context, viewing it performatively as part of everyday practices, as historically located and as intersectional and differentiated. It shows that paternal emotional engagement and care are complex and inextricably linked to the power relations associated with men and masculinities.

The research

The study that informs this chapter addresses the question of how adults negotiate their identities as they re-evaluate 'non-normative' childhood experiences. It was funded by the Economic and Social Research Council as a professorial fellowship ('Transforming experiences: re-conceptualising identities and "non-normative" childhoods') to the author, funded from 2007 to 2010 and continued throughout the 2010s. The study brings together findings from studies of three sets of 'non-normative' childhoods. The aim was to understand the psychosocial factors that produce adult citizens who lead 'ordinary' everyday lives despite having childhood experiences that are often viewed as 'non-normative'.

Participants were encouraged to construct full, narrative accounts of their experiences. Individual interviews focused on experience and on psychological and social processes, personal biography and positioning. They explored how people are affected by their awareness of what 'society' thinks of them (the canonical) and justify their individual positioning. They also elicited discussions of how narratives of social and emotional contexts and experiences change over time and the place of anticipated futures in these changes and in identity projects. The samples comprised 53 serial migrants

(39 women and 14 men), 41 who grew up in visibly ethnically different households and 40 language brokers (23 women and 17 men).

Most interviews were held in participants' homes in a range of locations in southern England, with a few in Australia, Italy, Sweden and the US. The final sample was recruited from varied backgrounds, including in terms of educational backgrounds, employment, ethnicised and language groups. Interviews lasted from just under an hour to over six hours, with most lasting about two hours. Researchers wrote fieldnotes to contextualise the interview data and facilitate psychosocial analyses.

Interviews were fully transcribed, including nonlinguistic features to allow analysis of the interactional dynamics of the interview. Summaries were prepared as a first stage of analysis, followed by thematic analysis and line-by-line narrative analysis for some interviews and some questions (Riessman, 2008; Andrews et al, 2012). Following the individual interviews, participants were invited to one of seven feedback sessions which functioned as focus groups (including 5–12 participants), at which the participants' discussion was recorded and transcribed (with informed consent and anonymously). A further focus group was held in Los Angeles. Group discussions helped the identification of 'well-worn' stories and canonical narratives, and highlighted areas of consensus, conflict and negotiation. The focus groups were recorded and transcribed as standard prose in order to save time and transcription costs.

Some of the interviews were analysed jointly in the project team (Elaine Bauer, Stephanie Davis-Gill, Leandra Box from the Race Equality Foundation and Pat Petrie covering maternity leave) and some with other project groups. In addition, some of the serial migration interviews were reused as part of the parenting project in the Narratives of Varied Everyday Lives and Linked approaches node of the National Centre for Research Methods (Phoenix et al, 2021). One serial migration interview was jointly analysed by ten researchers at the Norwegian Centre for Advanced Studies in Oslo, where Hanne Haavind and Harriet Bjerrum Nielsen successfully gained a large grant that enabled 20 researchers to work as co-investigators for periods of six months or one month, and the author worked for six months at the same time as Valerie Walkerdine and other colleagues whose publication on that interview is discussed later on in this chapter.

Contextualising fatherhood: the importance of intersectionality

It is well recognised that there are differences between different groups of fathers. However, general comparisons of, for example, working-class and middle-class fathers give limited insights into everyday fatherhood. The example in this section starts from the everyday lived experience of fatherhood from a man in his 40s, who is of mixed Black-white parentage. His parents (white mother and Black father) separated early in his childhood and he talks about his father during a long narrative in response to the request to tell his story of growing up in a visibly ethnically different household where his mother and all his older brothers were white. Early on in his narrative, he begins to talk about his identity and the mismatch between his racialised-class intersectional identification and the ways in which his identity is (not) generally recognised:

> One of the strongest parts of my identity I would say is, I I feel I've been socialised in a predominantly white working-class background, so I identify strongly with white working-class lads from that background. *However* when I'm outside of [area in Manchester], people think I'm, because I'm mixed race and I looked mixed race. People don't naturally associate me as connected with the white working-class side of my cultural identity which to me is stronger than my mixed race identity. Because it's something I've lived with more and I think something around which I've built my identity. And as I've gotten older I've added more things to myself but the core of me, is that …
>
> What I did do at some point was internalise external opinions of my identity. And I learnt that via the other adults around me, within the extended white family and also within my Jamaican family. Never been Black enough to be Black or white enough to be white and whenever an issue or discussion would happen around mixed identity, people would say oh stop trying to make yourself special, stop … talking about it. They would dismiss it so I would in some ways have to minimise anything which was, externally different to a white background. So if I'd been to my father's for the weekend I would have to minimise talking Jamaican patois or the way I would walk or the way I would move because I was obviously looking to my father for some kind of behavioural identity. When I bring that behaviour back to my mum's it was always frowned upon, or I'm sure it wasn't on a conscious level, I'm sure it was very unconscious thing because lots of my family didn't understand my experiences within my Jamaican family, outside of them. So I had an absolute definite different experience with my father at weekends, than I did when I was back with my other white brothers … And yeah it's just fascinating to see how I've kind of absorbed all those experiences and I wasn't able to articulate any of these emotions, feelings, thoughts at the time. I used to explain to my older white brothers that they were er … they were always in a majority. I felt I was in a majority when I was at home, within my family house but when I came out of there I was in a minority and because they were male, they were quite strong, and good looking guys they were never in a minority so they didn't understand that experience. And again I would have my identity brought into question, and get into trouble around

that because people called me 'Nigger' or 'Paki' or all that ridiculous stuff that people do ... Yeah and that's how I learnt.

... I have a great relationship with my dad and his wife and his children. Er, yeah and it was just nice to be at my dad's and eat rice and peas, but also my dad's identity – he's assimilated massively to the point where actually I realised when I was about 15, or 16, there wasn't anything I could get from him, I had to do it myself. ('Isaac', UK-born, 40s, mixed parentage)

It is striking that Isaac's story does not result from my asking about his experiences of being fathered, but that we learn about fatherhood and Isaac's experience of it as part of his narrative about growing up as visibly ethnically different from the rest of his family. In a context where his parents have been separated for most of his life, he has long had a visiting relationship with his father. Valerie Walkerdine and colleagues (2013) made a similar point from analyses of one serial migrant woman interviewed by the author as part of the Transforming Experience study.

'Angela's way of introducing her father is interesting, as she actually puts it off: 'I'll tell you about my father in a minute'. And instead, she goes on and tells the interviewer about meeting up with her father at an airport after a long separation. It is not a story she would have told if asked about her father (which is probably why she says she will tell the interviewer about her father in a minute, making him at that moment a minor character in the event she discusses). (Walkerdine et al, 2013: 285)

Stories about fatherhood that are produced as part of telling other stories can thus help to produce contextualised understandings of fatherhood. In Angela's case, it was part of a five-hour unbroken narrative where she took seriously the invitation to tell her story as she wished. In Isaac's case, it is part of a story of forging his identities. Isaac is clear that he enjoys being with his father and his father's family, but that his father did not provide the support for his identity that he sought in his childhood and teenage years. As he says, 'I was obviously looking to my father for some kind of behavioural identity', so when he had been to his father's home for the weekend, he would return to his mother's home talking Jamaican patois and walking and moving like a Jamaican. This is necessarily intersectional, in that his talk about walking and moving like a Jamaican is gendered as well as racialised. Yet, because his father, according to Isaac, has 'massively assimilated', Isaac found himself unable to learn identity from his father. In terms of belonging, he considered himself to be alone, particularly since a large part of his identity is as white, working class and masculine. This is an identity that others frequently exclude him from, although he considers it central to his upbringing and his belonging with his mother's family and particularly his white, working-class brothers. When he was interviewed for this study, Isaac no longer had anything to do with his white brothers since they consistently refused to accept that racialisation and racism is of importance in society and to him.

Isaac's story was not unusual in the visibly ethnically different study. Other mixed-parentage men looked to their fathers to help them navigate racialised masculinities, but, retrospectively, told of fathers who were not emotionally available to them and who did not provide them with the racialised/gendered 'role models' they sought. 'Paul's' narrative exemplifies this:

> Very sort of absent father in the household type thing ... And I guess my dad was the only route to anything Indian. Because it wasn't like you could say I didn't get on with my dad, but we've got a nice uncle, or there were nice people in the neighbourhood because there was no one so he was our *only* sort of pathway to Indianness, to brownness to anything to do with that. I guess it's a big pressure for him but it didn't go well. (Paul, 40s, mixed Indian-white parentage)

Isaac and Paul (who, in their 40s, had not become fathers themselves) gave narratives that highlight how emotional engagement with fathers is necessarily intersectional. For Isaac, although he has a 'great relationship' with his father, he could not get the support he wanted in terms of his racialised identity as 'mixed' and in relation to the racism he encountered. He had to learn his self-positioning over time from different sources. An important point is that however much time Isaac's father spent with him and whether or not his father provided care for him, Isaac felt that his father refused to acknowledge racialised identities. It is important to recognise that learning fatherhood is only one of the things that boys might want to learn from their fathers.

This is an example of how the context in which fathering occurs is crucial and intersectional. For boys and men who can take for granted that they fit normative models in UK society because they are white and middle class, researchers may erroneously interpret practices as only gendered when they do not recognise the situated intersectional contingency of fatherhood and sonhood. As Wojnicka (2024) suggests, 'intersectionality and masculinities studies, go together like a horse and carriage'.

Different forms of distanced/engaged fatherhood across generations

This section explores the account of a man who considers that his painful 12-year separation from his parents had a very marked impact, intensified by his struggle with poverty and having to work for money as a child.

Accounting for lack of emotional engagement

Anthony:	'Cos 12 years is a long bloody time.
Interviewer:	Mm.
Anthony:	It was a long time ... So when- you know when they came erm came you know all that ... sense of love anymore because you cannot err you have to harden yourself to ... go through life ... You're OK. You don't have that hug that kiss that ... you know we're children. People don't think it doesn't matter but it does matter when you ... you grow up with no parents and [interviewer coughs] you hurt yourself [interviewer coughs] just one little kiss on your – and you're better ... and that – ... Imagine hurting like hell probably for your parents but they [inaudible] and kiss it ... It was better. You didn't have any more pain ... Yeah it was no resent, all my children when they born – all my children were born in [west of England] so when they born I used to go and take them to my father ... introduce them and – and er to my father in London ... So everything were just ('comfortable'). After I met him I didn't have any resentment. Erm ... that were gone. I just know that he's my father ... My mum ... was no resentment after a while, but – but the love wasn't there ... That love you're supposed to have ... Leaving Jamaica erm getting leaaaving Jamaica by myself it does ... affect in a way in mentally – mentally because when I came up I was like jealous of my siblings ... because I – like I didn't know my father until I came up at 17 ... And I have erm ... one sister and two brother erm from my father's side ... and my sister by – by my mother's side ... Erm where with erm – erm – sight of erm envy them or jealous of them about was education ... because I didn't get the education ... So I was ... like in a limbo for quite a *while* actually.
Interviewer:	... So- so would you say that erm ... your experience of ... you know your – your mother leaving and so on had any impact on how you were as a father, at all ... and – your mother and your father?
Anthony:	I don't know. It's – it's erm it's very hard to say because errrm they say you need some erm ... family structure and if you have a family structure ... they you're going to have something to relate to [Interviewer: Mm], which I- I didn't have a ... er er a broad enough family structure to- so I can take a – a – a example frooom.

> [Interviewer: Mm] You know. I just ... were blundering in – in the dark as a *parent* ... what I know now I would ... stood up more like a erm as a father ... in a ... I'd do it differently ... Errrm ... I – my – my son would erm was speaking to me the other night and said ... erm his son is ... supposed to know his table ... and erm he told him he was lazy so therefore ... he talk to him and he didn't know his tables and he said he didn't know his *seven* times ... and he said to him ... say ... 14 him a certain time ... to leaaarn not only seven time but to 14 ... his fourteen times, as well ... So he took away his – all his ... and say if he don't know it by the end then the television will be gone ... Every time he don't know it something else *gooo* ... And within that period of *tiiiime* ... he didn't know only the seven time but he know the 14 time as well ... And probably if I do that with them...

Unlike the majority of the serial migration sample who were left with relatives they loved and hated to leave, Anthony largely had to fend for himself. As a result, he had a very unhappy childhood and very little schooling. When he arrived in the UK, he deeply resented his younger siblings born in the UK who were better educated. In adulthood, he worked to gain basic qualifications. However, as he said, he had difficulties with emotional relations because he had to harden himself to survive.

Anthony had six children with three wives. He explained that he lived with all his children for some time and that all his children and grandchildren know where he is and have his phone number. His account graphically shows that he has learned from his son how it is possible to do fatherhood. His unfinished sentence in the preceding quote, 'And probably if I do that with them...', suggests that he does look back on his own fatherhood and think about what he could have done differently. Yet, while one son has severe problems as an adult, two of his children have done exceptionally well professionally.

Anthony's narrative underlines the fact that inconsistent contact with fathers does not determine poor outcomes for children, but that it can be extremely painful and have emotional impacts. It also indicates that it can be difficult to know how to 'do' fathering when one has not experienced consistent fathering. However, this is not a simplistic story, in that these experiences are intersectional. The difficulties Anthony faced that affected his emotional life and educational opportunities are related to the intersection of poverty and serial migration with gender and racialisation.

There is a further intersection that it is important to consider for the serial migrants: historical positioning. In their secondary analysis of Angela's interview (one of the serial migrants in the study), Walkerdine et al say that:

> We are arguing for an approach in social research that can potentially understand the indissolubility of the psychic and the social. Our presentation of the large history makes sense of the small historical details that Angela presents in the interview and shows us how such material is transmitted intergenerationally through its unwitting actors … The link to historical processes is crucial because it produces a mode of explanation that does not attempt to reduce complex historical forces and processes to the family …
>
> What is important about the history is that it allows the possibility of moving beyond two-dimensional thinking in which a complex and destructive relationship between a father and daughter is presented. History walks into the room because it could be argued that her body 'knows' that history through the embodiment of the small histories that she recounts …
>
> In our case, the Caribbean history of slavery with its consequences for poverty, family life and masculinity is not just a backdrop for such an analysis, but concretely interwoven in the event, and therefore in the present. Thus, with respect to Angela's relationship with her father, other men, her siblings and her children, we can begin to understand how the small or micro histories recounted by her appear through resonance in the research encounter. (Walkerdine et al, 2013: 293, 294, 295)

Walkerdine et al's (2013) analysis fits with many currents of social science work. Much decolonial work, for example, shows that histories of slavery and colonialism are inextricably linked to academic disciplinary understandings. Many disciplines came into being as part of dominant forms of knowledge production that produced and reproduced colonial difference, and the idea that the colonised were inherently inferior to the colonisers (Meghji, 2021; Bhambra, 2022). Psychosocial theorists like Walkerdine et al (2013) concerned with these 'connected histories' attend to the link between micro- and macro-theories.

Conclusion

This chapter has contributed to examining the gap between models of 'new fathers' and everyday practices of fathers, and how these are received by children (Faircloth, 2023). It has discussed the importance of intersectional analyses of fatherhood that recognise how children and their fathers are simultaneously positioned in racialised/gendered/social class and national contexts that are historically located. Four decades ago, Elder et al (1985) showed that the context in which fathering occurs is crucial and situated in life course perspective. Their analyses showed a link between stressful socioeconomic circumstances, paternal behaviour and child outcomes.

In keeping with this, this chapter has used narratives from retrospective studies of 'non-normative' childhoods to show the multiplicity of ways in which fatherhood needs to be contextualised to provide a holistic and intersectional understanding. It argues that considering the impact of fatherhood as implicitly the result of decontextualised fatherhood practices ignores five crucial aspects of fatherhood: first, children's perspectives on what they are looking for from their fathers; second, the wider community of adults and family members who children consider important to their identities and may provide them with parenting; third, some of what may be seen as poor fatherhood, such as leaving children behind when parents migrate, or organising for them to migrate without their parents, may be important to seeing children as part of economic and educational projects (Halldén, 1991) that aim to give children better lives; fourth, it does not clarify how the pain of not being emotionally engaged with their fathers impacts on children in different ways, including their own parenting; and, fifth, the decontextualising of fatherhood ignores the ways in which fatherhood is linked to histories that have continuing impacts – in this case, of enslavement and racisms. As a result, many boys from minoritised ethnic groups look to their fathers to provide them with understandings of how to 'do' racialised masculinities and the associated power relations, rather than viewing masculinities and fathering in isolation.

The analyses of the narratives discussed here show that not having fathers who are emotionally engaged with children does not determine how children parent when they become adults. However, the participants in the study were positioned outside normative childhoods and families by virtue of their serial migration, growing up in visibly ethnically different households or doing childhood language brokering. For those who had Caribbean parents, particularly those living in poverty, histories of enslavement also meant that they did not have access to long histories of fathers being emotionally engaged with their children. As a consequence, they have to forge parenthood in their own ways, drawing on the resources available to them. In keeping with suggestions from many fatherhood researchers, it is thus necessary to take multidimensional theoretical and methodological approaches to engaging with the complexity of making connections between embodiment, subjectivity and the sociocultural (Johansson, 2023) to attend to the 'social and cultural ecology of fathers, children, and family life' (Volling and Palkowitz, 2021: 427). The examples given in this chapter attend to this complexity by considering fathering in circumstances generally ignored in research on normative, 'new fathers'. They show the importance of taking non-essentialist, intersectional approaches to studying fatherhood that do not limit or prescribe fatherhood practices in exclusionary ways.

References

Abdill, A. M. (2017). *Fathering from the Margins: An Intimate Examination of Black Fatherhood*. New York: Columbia University Press.

Andrews, M., Tamboukou, M. and Squire, C. (2013). *Doing Narrative Research*. London: Sage.

Bhambra, G. K. (2022). Relations of extraction, relations of redistribution: empire, nation, and the construction of the British welfare state. *British Journal of Sociology*, 73(1), 4–15.

Bhopal, K., Brannen, J. and Heptinstall, E. (2000). *Connecting Children: Care and Family Life in Later Childhood*. New York: Routledge.

Burgess, A. and Goldman, R. (2023). *The kids Are Alright: Adolescents and Their Fathers in the UK – Research Review*. Fatherhood Institute. Available from: https://www.fatherhoodinstitute.org/_files/ugd/efff1d_a73fee1a9 f1c429da6cef60dd9cc0a8d.pdf

Collins, P. H. (2019). *Intersectionality as Critical Social Theory*. Durham, NC: Duke University Press.

Cooper, K. (2021). Are poor parents poor parents? The relationship between poverty and parenting among mothers in the UK. *Sociology*, 55(2), 349–383. https://doi.org/10.1177/0038038520939397

Dermott, E. and Miller, T. (2015). More than the sum of its parts? Contemporary fatherhood policy, practice and discourse. *Families, Relationships and Societies*, 4(2), 183–195.

Diniz, E., Brandão, T., Monteiro, L. and Veríssimo, M. (2021). Father involvement during early childhood: a systematic review of the literature. *Journal of Family Theory & Review*, 13(1), 77–99. https://doi.org/10.1111/jftr.12410

Doucet, A. (2020). Father involvement, care, and breadwinning: genealogies of concepts and revisioned conceptual narratives. *Genealogy*, 4(1). https://doi.org/10.3390/genealogy4010014

East, L., Hutchinson, M., Power, T. and Jackson, D. (2020). 'Being a father': constructions of fatherhood by men with absent fathers. *Journal of Family Studies*, 26(3), 477–487. https://doi.org/10.1080/13229 400.2018.1459308

Edin, K. and Nelson, T. J. (2013). *Doing the Best I Can: Fatherhood in the Inner City*. Berkeley: University of California Press.

Elder Jr., G. H., van Nguyen, T., and Caspi, A. (1985). Linking family hardship to children's lives. *Child Development*, 361–375.

Faircloth, C. (2023). Intensive fatherhood? The (un)involved dad. In E. Lee, J. Bristow, C. Faircloth and J. Macvarish (eds) *Parenting Culture Studies*. Cham: Springer International Publishing, pp 241–265

Frosh, S., Phoenix, A. and Pattman, R. (2002). On the way to adulthood: relationships with parents. In *Young Masculinities*. London: Routledge, pp 225–255.

Graf, T. E. and Wojnicka, K. (2023). Post-separation fatherhood narratives in Germany and Sweden: between caring and protective masculinities. *Journal of Family Studies*, 29(3), 1022–1042. https://doi.org/10.1080/13229400.2021.2020148

Halldén, G. (1991). The child as project and the child as being: parents' ideas as frames of reference. *Children & Society*, 5(4), 334–346.

Hamer, J. (2001). *What It Means to Be Daddy: Fatherhood for Black Men Living away from Their Children*. New York: Columbia University Press.

Henriksson, H. W. (2019). Exploring fatherhood in critical gender research. In *Routledge International Handbook of Masculinity Studies*. Abingson: Routledge, pp 320–330.

Johansson, T. (2023). Theorising fatherhood: challenges and suggestions. *Families, Relationships and Societies*, 12(1), 49–59. https://doi.org/10.1332/204674321X16693961177375

Lewington, L., Lee, J. and Sebar, B. (2021). 'I'm not just a babysitter': masculinity and men's experiences of first-time fatherhood. *Men and Masculinities*, 24(4), 571–589.

Meghji, A. (2021). *Decolonizing Sociology: An Introduction*. Chichester: John Wiley & Sons.

Oppenheim, C. and Rehill, J. (2020). How are the lives of families with young children changing. *Nuffield Foundation*. Available from: https://www.nuffieldfoundation.org/publications/changing-lives-families-young-children

Palkovitz, R. (2019). Expanding our focus from father involvement to father–child relationship quality. *Journal of Family Theory & Review*, 11(4), 576–591.

Phoenix, A., Brannen, J. and Squire, C. (2021). *Researching Family Narratives*. London: Sage.

Riessman, C. K. (2008). *Narrative Methods for the Human Sciences*. London: Sage

Smart, C. (2006). Children's narratives of post-divorce family life: from individual experience to an ethical disposition. *Sociological Review*, 54(1), 155–170.

Smith, B. F. (2011). *Transcending the Legacies of Slavery: A Psychoanalytic View*. London: Karnac Books.

Strier, R., and Perez-Vaisvidovsky, N. (2021). Intersectionality and fatherhood: theorizing non-hegemonic fatherhoods. *Journal of Family Theory & Review*, 13(3), 334–346. https://doi.org/10.1111/jftr.12412

Volling, B. L., and Palkovitz, R. (2021). Fathering: new perspectives, paradigms, and possibilities. *Psychology of Men & Masculinities*, *22*(3), 427–432.

Walkerdine, V., Olsvold, A., and Rudberg, M. (2013). Researching embodiment and intergenerational trauma using the work of Davoine and Gaudilliere: history walked in the door. *Subjectivity*, *6*, 272–297.

Wojnicka, K. (2024). Intersectionality and masculinities studies, go together like a horse and carriage. *NORMA*, 1–5.

19

Conclusions: Towards more nuanced understandings of fathers' care

Petteri Eerola, Henna Pirskanen,
Pedro Romero-Balsas and Katherine Twamley

In the summer of 2022, the four editors came together to plan an edited collection in which care as a conceptual tool would be at the centre of its inquiry. We wanted to go beyond the dominant scholarly focus on Anglo American and European middle-class fathers to think widely about how care is practised, understood and experienced by a range of individuals. As discussed in Chapter 1, we noted that while many studies on fatherhood have explored men's understandings and practices of 'new', involved and caring fatherhood, this research has often lacked a conceptual understanding of care. Rather, fathers' involvement in care has tended to be studied through an examination of their time spent on childcare tasks. We noted that the concept of care was sparsely and inconsistently applied, even when there is increasing understanding that men's involvement in care could have a transformative impact on gender relations within and beyond the family (Tronto, 1993; Elliot, 2016). Our aim then was to achieve a more nuanced understanding of contemporary fatherhood and fathers' care, as well as the circumstances which facilitate such care. Now, as we write this concluding chapter during a residency at the Kone Foundation's Saari Residence in Mynämäki, southern Finland in September 2024, we revisit these diverse chapters to consider what this volume has added to our understandings of fathers' care across a wide variety of contexts and positionalities, and to outline the work that is still left to be done.

We find that although our book is called *Caring Fathers in the Global Context*, we were never of course going to be able to include chapters from every country and region. In fact, we have more chapters from Europe than from other contexts, reflecting our own networks despite our efforts to reach out more widely. Still, we have collected together chapters with data from an impressive range of international contexts, including China, Canada, South Africa, Russia, Somalia, Chile and the Faroe Islands, and those that include migrant fathers from a range of countries including Syria, Afghanistan and the Caribbean, among others. Moreover, the chapters in this book draw on data collected from diversely situated fathers (such as gay and trans fathers;

nonresident fathers and 'young' fathers) along with data from relational others who are cared for and care with men, in particular their children and partners. There are of course multitudes of fathers and families. Our biggest regret has been an inability to find a contribution which focused particularly on fathers with disabilities, as we consider this a key gap in the literature. It is estimated that around 16 per cent of people worldwide live with a significant disability (WHO, 2023) and previous research has demonstrated how disabilities can impact on fathering experiences (Kilkey and Clarke, 2010). We suggest this as a fruitful area for further scholarly development.

We were also concerned to think widely about how care may be methodologically addressed (and 'measured', as Doucet writes in Chapter 2). The different methods and methodologies used by authors in the book together enable as comprehensive a picture as possible of caring fatherhood, including the various personal, relational, cultural and structural aspects across macro-, meso- and micro-levels which shape fathers' care. At the macro-level, for example, Koslowski (Chapter 11) examines what different parental leave legislation can tell us about how localised conceptualisations of gender and care are institutionalised, creating the boundaries around parents' opportunities to care. And Ammann's qualitative study with GBTQ fathers in the Netherlands and Switzerland explores how policies around same-sex adoption and surrogacy shape men's care labour as they navigate conception.

More meso-level studies, as exemplified by those chapters which examine migrant fathers' experiences, help us to unpack how individual and community-level norms come together to shape men's care. For example, Wu and Del Rey Poveda (Chapter 14) detail how Chinese migrant fathers in Spain take on 'new' responsibilities of hands-on care for their children while sharing financial responsibilities with their wives, since in Spain they are unable to draw on other networks which enable more gendered divisions of labour in China. Two quantitative studies in the book examine the relationalities between different circumstances associated with increased presence of men at home (via parental leave take-up: see Saarikallio-Torp et al, Chapter 12) and men's time in spent in 'charge' of their child (Rogero-García et al, Chapter 17). In the former we see that fathers' traditional views on gender roles decrease their use of parental leave, while the latter chapter suggests that men with children with disabilities spend less time with their children than other fathers. While these studies do not tell us about care as practised per se, they do signal different associations with father presence and therefore future areas for more in-depth research on fathers' care. More generally, we can see across the volume that there are more qualitative than quantitative studies included here. This is in response to our overall volume aims, which suggest a more conceptual and explorative approach around care processes in this budding area of research, and thus a qualitative approach. Yet, as discussed by Doucet in Chapter 2 and demonstrated by these chapters, there is certainly a place for quantitative studies in this endeavour and we call for more experimentation in quantitative and mixed methods studies on fathers and care.

The experience of rupture has also been called upon by authors to understand better social behaviour, showing how a change in situation may bring into sharp relief the taken-for-granted aspects of care which men may not have articulated in 'ordinary' circumstances. This was clear in chapters which examine the experiences of migrant fathers, but also in the two chapters which explore family life under COVID-19 lockdown periods: the chapters by Twamley and Haffejee (Chapter 9) and Zhang and his co-authors (Chapter 7) allow us to analyse fatherhood in a novel way, when changes produced in the social environment trigger changes in fatherhood, at least at the temporal level. These analyses allow us to consider why temporary changes remained at the superficial level, without the often hoped-for more radical *transformation* in practices. For Twamley and Haffejee, this lack of transformation can partly be explained by the lack of the intention around these policies and among the parents themselves to shift normative gendered caring relations. This suggests that an ideal of more equal and caring fatherhood is an important first step in transformational change, not simply being (or forced to) be present. This then echoes the chapter by Doucet, in which she carefully lays out how we may conceptualise fathers' care, beyond 'time or tasks'. These findings are further borne out by Saarikallio-Torp and colleagues in Chapter 12, in which they found that, in addition to socioeconomic characteristics, fathers' caring attitudes increase fathers' shared parental leave use, while traditional gender role attitudes decrease it. These are important relational contexts to consider when designing family policies.

At the more micro-level, studies drawing on interviews and essays convey different perspectives, meanings and experiences of caring fatherhood, from a subjective and intersubjective stance of different family members. Moreover, in-depth interviews and surveys with different family members (such as in Eerola et al, Chapter 8; Phoenix, Chapter 18; Tiilikainen, Chapter 4; Ammann, Chapter 16; Zhang et al, Chapter 7) or together in the same interview (see Twamley and Haffejee, Chapter 9) highlight the shared and sometimes conflicting meanings on different aspects of fatherhood. As Bergnehr reminds us (Chapter 15), it is important to consider how children themselves influence and shape fatherhood, and this is clearly revealed in multiple chapters, reflecting the relational nature of fathers' care (Doucet, Chapter 2).

The temporal nature of fathers' care, as revealed in the longitudinal study by Tarrant and colleagues (Chapter 10) or the studies which interrogate how adult children now reflect back on their own experiences of being fathered (such as Phoenix, Chapter 18) help to historicise current discourses around fatherhood and consider why and in what ways care practices and ideals may change over time. Relatedly, our book has shown the wide variety of care that men undertake that changes across the life course, from pre-pregnancy (Ammann, Chapter 16) to the 'empty nest' stage (Żadkowska et al, Chapter 6). In Ammann's study (Chapter 16), for instance, despite the absence of a child or pregnancy, we read about the ways in which men build relationships with other caregivers, such as their partner, the mother of the child or surrogate, and social institutions, in setting up circumstances which will facilitate future care that they perceive will meet the needs of their future child.

Thus, the chapters provide a rich and varied interrogation into fathers and care. We now move on to consider what the chief conclusions are from this body of work and the future directions in research which they provoke.

Understanding care beyond time and tasks

We have argued for a more precise and theorised approach to care – not just time or tasks (Doucet, Chapter 2) – to better understand care and its relation to gendered transformation (Elliot, 2016). Through in-depth nuanced analysis with fathers, their children and partners, the authors in this volume have highlighted the various ways in which differently positioned fathers may engage in care, pushing us to consider 'absent' or invisible ways in which fathers may engage in fathering. For example, Żadkowska and colleagues (Chapter 6) describe in their chapter how 'empty nest' fathers in Poland navigate the care of adult children, managing their own emotional needs and desires in order to prioritise those of their children. This could look like a lack of care without the careful analysis of the authors. Similarly, in Russia, Ivanova (Chapter 5) reveals how nonresident fathers may choose for their children to live primarily with the mother as they consider this to be in the best interests of the child. These examples highlight how apparent 'nonpresence' may in fact be undertaken with a caring disposition, in response to the perceived care needs of children. However, as seen in the chapter by Phoenix (Chapter 18), such practices conceived of as care by fathers, in this case sending their children from the Caribbean to the UK for a better life, may not be perceived as 'enough' by the children who miss a more emotionally engaged relationship with their father. Moreover, the two chapters which detail fathers' experiences and practices during the COVID-19 lockdowns, Twamley and Haffejee (Chapter 9) reporting on the UK and South Africa and Zhang et al (Chapter 7) on China, shows how fathers' increased presence in the home did not necessarily entail more care for their children or any transformational change in gendered divisions of care. Thus, these chapters illustrate how presence or absence of 'time' and 'tasks' is not enough to 'measure' or demonstrate care or its absence.

As Doucet discusses in her chapter (Chapter 2), typically breadwinning has been situated as outside of care, in fact sometimes as 'evidence' of men's disengagement in care. Yet breadwinning came up time and again in the chapters of this book as being of central importance to men as they conceive of themselves as fathers. Several chapters in the book delve into the nexus of breadwinning and care in order to consider how and when we may collapse the two. Here, the responsive and relational context of breadwinning is key to its constitution as care (Tarrant et al, Chapter 10). However, we will discuss in more detail later on, the ideological importance placed on breadwinning can also act as an impediment to men's involvement in (others aspects of) care.

A global discourse of intimate and emotionally engaged fatherhood

Based on the chapters in the volume, we argue that a discourse of caring, intimate, emotionally engaged fatherhood has global reach, beyond the normative middle-class white Anglo European contexts in which such theories were first developed (for example, Dermott, 2008). In case examples from different countries, caring fatherhood is seen to be widely understood through the ideas of emotional involvement and engagement with children. This is evident in the chapter by Gaini (Chapter 3), who shows how Faroese youth emphasise the importance of emotional commitment as a key element of a 'caring father', and in the chapter by Tiilikainen (Chapter 4) which also illustrates how (mostly adult) Somali men and women living in Canada and Finland understand the father's role through the ideals of intimate fatherhood and do not feel that financial provisioning is 'enough' in their assessments of a 'good' father.

Nonetheless, there is also important evidence of fathers who rally against this ideal, drawing on alternative norms of fatherhood, notably in the chapter by Miller and Dermott (Chapter 13) who have conducted research with Syrian refugee fathers in the UK and some evidence from Tiilikainen's study (Chapter 4) that fathers in Somalia may not aspire to intimate fatherhood as much as their children do. These chapters demonstrate how, despite the cultural dominance of this ideal, it is not ubiquitous, though they do suggest that perhaps younger generations are more inclined to aspire to emotionally involved father–child relations than older generations.

The global discourse of caring, intimate and emotionally engaged fatherhood reflects and links up closely with another common discourse, both scholarly and popular, of change in fathers' care and fathering practices. This discourse has been widely discussed in sociological research on fathers and families during the last few decades (Dermott, 2008; Miller, 2011; Brannen et al, 2023;). Many authors comment on how fathers and children call on this narrative of 'change' or 'progress' in interpreting or reflecting on their experiences of fathering and being fathered (see, for example, Gaini, Chapter 3). Though this progressive narrative seems to have global acceptance, not all men welcome this change or engage in it. In part, these differences reflect the intersectional inequalities between differently positioned fathers. For example, Bergnehr (Chapter 15) notes that migrant fathers in Sweden negotiate with localised discourses of child-centred emotionally involved fathering, but worry that their children are exposed to multiple risks (such as delinquency and drugs) which they argue necessitate more authoritarian parenting.

An additional important contextualising factor is the extent to which discourses of intimate fatherhood are linked to ideals of gender equality in family life. 'Change' in emotional engagement may be tied to 'change' in gendered parenting practices, as men are expected to take on a greater role in care compared to fathers of previous generations. This is illustrated in the chapter by Eerola and colleagues (Chapter 8) where mothers and fathers express an underlying assumption that gender equality is an assumed desire and part of being a 'good father'. However, other chapters included in the volume show how emotional involvement or engagement does not necessarily mean that a father would engage in discourses of gender equality or embody a caring masculinity (see Elliott, 2016). In the chapter by Miller and Dermott (Chapter 13), who explore Syrian refugee fathers' practices and perspectives on care after migration to the UK, they report that participants struggle to engage in paid work due to various immigration and language conditions, and are thus engaging in more hands-on 'feminine' care work, such as cooking for their children. The fathers emphasise how this is ideally a temporary state, as they prefer to engage in paid work as part of their role as fathers, which gives them legitimacy and potentially authority as father figures. Some fathers also find their changing gender roles particularly stressful and come to view their dual responsibilities as a burden, as discussed by Wu and Del Rey Poveda (Chapter 14) in their study of migrant Chinese fathers in Spain. These authors show how increased involvement in care activities can be primarily driven by the changing demands, such as mothers' limited time availability and fathers' sense of obligation to take responsibility in situations in which there is 'no choice'. Here we see that dominant ideologies of gender and family are challenged, but not necessarily sufficiently transformed. These chapters also show how practices may change, without a concomitant shift in ideals and underlying norms.

The inclusion of studies based in different countries allows us to consider the relevance of the nation state as a unit of analysis. For those chapters which focus on the interplay of policy and everyday care practices, the country context is foregrounded in the analysis. Looking overall, we can see certainly that national policies can play a role in facilitating or impeding fathers' care (as seen in Koslowski, Chapter 11; see also Twamley et al, 2023), but that research on fathers and care must also go beyond considerations of the nation state. The chapters which include migrant fathers help us to consider the interplay between cultural understandings and family circumstances with wider national situations, as does the chapter by Twamley and Haffejee (Chapter 9) exploring similarities and differences of fathers' experiences during COVID-19 lockdowns in the UK and South Africa. Drawing on the work of Doucet and Phoenix (both this volume), we argue that context, relationality and intersectionality are key to aspects which must be attended to when studying fathers and care. Some research questions will necessarily gravitate more towards nation-state analysis, but the richness of this volume is through the multiple studies which together complicate and nuance this enquiry. Overall, these chapters demonstrate that engagement in care practices, whether 'hands-on' care as in the case of migrant fathers (Miller and Dermott, Chapter 13) or earning as part of a commitment to care among young fathers (Tarrant et al, Chapter 10), does not necessarily indicate a shift to 'caring masculinities' and perhaps rather that 'expressions and practices of caring and hegemonic masculinities ... sit alongside one another' (Tarrant et al, Chapter 10). This may be heightened in cases where fathers experience marginalisation and challenges in financially providing for their children, when perhaps their marginalised position increases the pressure to (be seen to) earn. This may lead us to question, as Tarrant and colleagues do, whether 'caring masculinities' are more easily available to a subset of privileged fathers.

Constraints for fathers' further involvement in care

Many of the chapters in this volume are concerned with why fathers do not do more or different kinds of care. There is an enduring concern that fathers are not contributing to care to the same extent as women. Nonetheless, we do not see the black-and-white assumption that a caring father is only one who is as equally involved as the mother or one who undertakes similar tasks. Rather, the nuanced accounts consider what situational and personal factors create situations of uneven involvement in care. For example, Zhang and colleagues (Chapter 7) argue that an intertwining of ideologies and traditional gender roles makes it challenging for urban Chinese dual-income couples to alter the gender structural inequalities in their parenting practices. And the chapter by Zadkowska et al (Chapter 6) on fathers of adult children in Poland shows how fathers' concerns to preserve the independence and privacy of their children may mean that they appear less emotionally engaged with their children than mothers. These studies help to contextualise findings from, for example, Saarikallio-Torp et al's chapter (Chapter 12) on fathers' involvement in parental leave – it may not just be a straightforward lack of 'care about' children that shapes men's take-up of parental leave, but also their sense of what is better for their children.

Despite the global reach of discourses on intimate fatherhood, the chapters in this book show that emotional presence-oriented care is more available to some fathers than others and that there are multiple factors which work against fathers' further involvement in care. This may be a temporary but material barrier to care, such as the biological and embodied aspects of care discussed in Eerola and colleagues' chapter (Chapter 8, on breastfeeding as an impediment to men's night-time care) or Ammann's chapter (Chapter 16, where men who are not in a relationship with a woman or person with a uterus must navigate various barriers to the adoption or conception of a child).

More commonly, the chapters discuss how the gendered ideologies of care shape how men enact and perceive their care role. In particular, several studies note the enduring ideological importance attached to men's role in financial provisioning (or breadwinning), as discussed earlier. While breadwinning may on the one hand be enacted within a caring disposition (Doucet, Chapter 2 in this volume; Schmidt, 2018), it may also disrupt men's ability to engage in other forms of care as they struggle to financially support their family. Thus, as reported by Tarrant and colleagues (Chapter 10), even when young men in the UK take on a primary care role, they consider themselves a 'failed father' and prefer to get back into an earning role.

Another factor discussed in the chapters is the policy context, as discussed earlier. Policies both reflect and reinforce cultural gendered discourses on care, as demonstrated in Ivanova's chapter (Chapter 5) where postseparation policies in Russia do not support shared residence or sole residence with the father. The fathers themselves in Ivanova's chapter appear to agree that the children are best placed with the mother, thus relegating fathers to a reduced involved role in care. Similarly, Koslowski in her chapter (Chapter 11) shows how policies, in this case relating to parental leave, embody gendered attitudes to care, such that fathers may be considered on a par with mothers (such as in Sweden) or relegated to a secondary care role (such as in Chile). In turn, these policies limit fathers' ability to take leave and develop individual responsibility for their children. However, as has already been discussed, parental leave or time spent with a child does not necessarily equate to 'care', or may be 'care' without the underlying transformational potential of caring masculinities.

While there is a story of transformation that looms large across the chapters, there are also popular discourses of deficient or feckless fathers, which can act as a constraint on fathers' care. For example, in Tarrant et al's (Chapter 10) and Ivanova's (Chapter 5) studies, they report how such stereotypes of fathers about young fathers in the UK and nonresident fathers in Russia impact on their fathering experiences. In Gaini's chapter (Chapter 3), children are aware of the stories attached to Faroan fathers as unmodern and, perhaps in part in reaction to such discourses, emphasise how their fathers are emotionally involved. Such stories of lack of capability create further barriers to fathers, who must overcome and/or demonstrate their competence to care to be given the chance to do so. This was also apparent in the chapter by Ann

Phoenix (Chapter 18), who draws on narratives from retrospective studies of 'non-normative' childhoods examining how children and fathers account for a lack of father-child emotional engagement. Here we see how racism and histories of enslavement have disrupted father-child relations, with ongoing impacts on Caribbean men's experiences of fathering. Participants lacked histories of emotionally engaged fathers to draw on in caring for their own children and describe their efforts to forge caring fatherhood in their own ways. This chapter demonstrates how individuals may overcome barriers to care by drawing on other resources available to them.

Despite the many constraints which men face in terms of practising care, the authors in this volume highlight that men often have more choice or agency regarding their involvement in care than women. This is hinted at, for example, in the chapter by Rogero-García and colleagues (Chapter 17), where fathers with children with disabilities take care of their children for less time than mothers, and less time than fathers of children without disabilities. And in the chapter by Eerola, Mustosmäki and Pirskanen (Chapter 8), where some fathers were seen to opt out of night-time care. Sometimes the boundaries between opting out of care due to a preference to engage in easier aspects of care or those that lend more power (such as breadwinning) and men's adoption of ideologies which lead them to assume that children are better off being primarily cared for mothers are difficult to pick apart, as Ivanova (Chapter 5) discusses so eloquently in her chapter on nonresident fathers in Russia (see also Miller, 2011).

Directions for future research on fathers' care

The chapters in this edited collection highlight the need for a comprehensive approach to care in order to achieve a more nuanced and theoretically sound understanding of fathers' care in different international contexts. We argue that future research should follow this lead. We conclude the book by identifying what we think is still missing from current sociological fatherhood research and highlighting which aspects of fathers' care we think should receive greater attention in future research.

While the volume includes chapters from various international contexts, it is evident that the focus in research remains primarily on Anglo-American and European contexts. The chapters from contexts beyond this narrow field (or majority world contexts, as some scholars call it) as well as from migrant chapters newly moved to them demonstrate what can be added by studying more culturally diverse fathers. Thus, for a better understanding on global developments on fathers' role in care, more research especially from the minority world is needed. Further, as argued by Ammann in her chapter (Chapter 16), most of the research is still very heteronormative, excluding fathers from gender and sexual minorities. The chapters also show that most of the research focuses primarily on fathers with a biological link to the child, while, for example, adoptive fathers, nonbiological LGBTQ+ fathers, grandfathers, male kin and other father figures have received notably less attention. Research on fathers' care and men's parenting is also focused mainly on fathers with young children, while studies on fathering older children is lacking, but as seen in, for example, the chapter by Zadkowska et al (Chapter 6), such studies can richly enhance our understanding of fathers' care and its temporal dimensions.

As we have outlined, the chapters in this book suggest that a more emotionally involved ideal of fathering is widely available to fathers and their children. To better understand the varying roles of men in care and different ideals of fatherhood, it would be important to also study fathers and families who do not aspire to intimate or equal fatherhood.

We also note that many of the chapters here focus in particular on person-to-person care in father-child relations. In a time of ecological catastrophe, environmental crises and wars occurring in various parts of the world, it would also be crucial to pay more attention to how fathers invest their time in caring for the planet, supporting their communities and fostering peace, as well as modelling such behaviours for future generations. We see this as a key area of future research which could be enhanced by sociological research on fathers during ruptured moments and disadvantaged life situations.

This book has studied fathers' care through divergent country and policy contexts, and through the accounts of differently positioned men, women and children. Based on the chapters in this book, we have argued that the discourse of caring, intimate and emotionally engaged fatherhood has a global reach. The chapters have also shown that a more nuanced understanding of care, which goes beyond time and tasks, is inevitably needed to comprehend the multifaceted nature of fathers' care. Additionally, the chapters have highlighted how understandings of 'good care' may differ among men, women and children. As many questions remain open and new ones continue to arise, we would not like this book and its chapters to be seen as an endpoint for research, but rather as an open call for fellow researchers to further develop a more nuanced understanding of fathers' care and fatherhood in contemporary societies. As societies, policies and cultural understandings continue to evolve and significant gaps in research exist, ongoing attention to fathers' care is more important than ever.

References

Brannen, J., Faircloth, C., Jones, K., O'Brien, M. and Twamley, K. (2023). 'Change and continuity in men's fathering and employment practices: A slow gender revolution', in C. Cameron A. Koslowski, A. Lamont and P. Moss (eds) *Social Research for Our Times: Thomas Coram Research Unit Past, Present and Future*. London: UCL Press, pp 227–242.

Dermott, E. (2008) *Intimate Fatherhood*. Abingdon: Routledge.

Elliott, K. (2016) 'Caring masculinities: theorizing an emerging concept', *Men and Masculinities*, 19(3), 240–259. https://doi.org/10.1177/1097184X1557620

Kilkey, M. and Clarke, H. (2010) 'Disabled men and fathering: opportunities and constraints', *Community, Work & Family*, 13(2), 127–146. https://doi.org/10.1080/13668800902923738

Miller, T. (2011). *Making Sense of Fatherhood: Gender, Caring and Work*. Cambridge: Cambridge University Press.

Schmidt, E.-M. (2018) 'Breadwinning as care? The meaning of paid work in mothers' and fathers' constructions of parenting', *Community, Work & Family*, 21(4), 445–462. https://doi.org/10.1080/13668803.2017.1318112

Tronto, J. (1993) *Moral Boundaries: A Political Argument for an Ethic of Care*. New York: Routledge.

Twamley, K., Iqbal, H. and Faircloth, C. (2023) *Family Life in the Time of COVID: International Perspectives*. London: UCL Press.

WHO (World Health Organization) (2023) Disability facts. Available from: https://www.who.int/news-room/fact-sheets/detail/disability-and-health

Index

References to tables appear in **bold**.

A

accessibility 28, 73, 100 *see also* availability
adoption 285–286, **288**, 292, 293
adoption leave 203
adult children
  engagement of fathers of 101, 107
  on fathers 325, 328–330, 331–333
  see also 'empty nest' phase
Ammann, Carole 13, 339, 341, 345, 346
ANOVA analyses 305, **311**, **313**
Anttila, S. 290, 291, 292, 295
attentiveness 9, 31, 33, 284
Australia **199**, 199–200, 205, 206, **206**
availability
  definitions of 28
  emotional 214, 330
  of fathers 72, 125, 160, 185, 225

B

'being there' 177–179, 180, 182, 183, 185, 325
Bergnehr, Disa 12–13, 74, 340, 343
birth of child, father's presence at 47
bisexual people *see* LGBTQIA+ parents
Bjarnadóttir, V.S. 121
Black fathers
  emotional engagement of 321, 322, 325–326, 330–332, 334
  narratives of 328–330, 331–333
  scholarship on 324–325
blurring protective authority 103–105, 109
Booth-LaForce, C. 312
Brandth, B. 9, 49
Brannen, Julia 3, 5, 27, 55, 154, 252, 342
breadwinning *see* paid work
breastfeeding 141–142, 146, 148
Bristol, M.M. 303, 307

C

Canada 10, 35, 64, 68, 69, 74–75
care
  definitions of 4, 29, 32, 279
  direct care 5, 29, 272, 275, 276, 279, 307
  5 dimensions/phases of 33, 284
  indirect care 32, 34, 215, 243–244, 272, 275, 279
  parenting frameworks of 266–267
  see also engagement/interaction; fathering involvement; scholarship

care ethics
  author's overview of 30–31
  caring fathers and 31–32, 179
  research, how to 33–35
  see also 3 Rs of care ethics
care work
  housework as 29
  measuring of 29–30
  mental load of 125–127
Caribbean people
  emotional engagement of fathers 321, 322, 325–326, 330–332, 334
  enslavement history of 323–324, 333, 334, 346
  narratives of fathers 328–330, 331–333
  scholarship on fathers 324–325
caring fathers
  author's overview of 28–29, 213, 217
  examples of 22–23
  research on 218, **219**, 220, **221**, 223, 224
  see also Black fathers; Caribbean people; caring masculinities; hedonistic fathers; hegemonic masculinities; 'new father' model; parental leave; parental night shift; protective masculinities; refugees; research; responsibilities; scholarship; 'traditional father' model; *specific countries (e.g., Finland, China)*
caring masculinities
  author's overview of 3, 99–100, 213–214
  COVID-19 pandemic 153
  'empty nest' research and 103, 105–108, 109–110
  LGBTQIA+ parents 295–296
  parental leave and 214, 345
  scholarship on 284–285
  young fathers 175, 176, 177–179, 182–183, 184, 186, 189–190, 344
child as project concept 326
children *see* young people
children with disabilities *see* disabilities, children with
child support
  as care 86–88
  gender divisions of labour and 80
Chile **199**, 200–201, 205, 206, **206**
China
  COVID-19 on, impacts of 118–124, 129
  cultural values 116, 127–128, 250
  fathers, role of 115–116, 257

gender divisions of labour 124–127, 128, 129, 251, 344
migration to Spain 250, 252–253, 255–258, 258–259
parenting modes in, research on 114–115, 116, **117**, 118, 129–130
chronobiological rhythms **141**, 143, 147
classes *see* middle classes; working classes
classes, intersectionalities of 7–8
cognitive labour 143, 149
see also mental load
Colaizzi's descriptive phenomenological method 118
competence 22–23, 33, 284, 345
compulsory leave 197, 200, 201, 206–207
concerted cultivation 7
co-parenting
family separation and 79, 186–188
LGBTQIA+ arrangements 286, 287, **288**, 288–291, 294–295
COVID-19 pandemic
FACT-COVID study 153, 156–157
gender divisions of labour and 124–127, 154–156, 159–161, 162–163, 165, 167, 168–169
impacts of 118–124, 129, 153
paid work and 159–161, 163–164, 168
parenting modes during 114–115, 116
young fathers 180, 181
cultural logic 7
cultural values
China 116, 127–128, 250
Faroe Island 46–47, 56–57
Finland 214–215
influence of 245
Somalia 64, 70, 72, 75
Spain 250
Sweden 279

D

Del Rey Poveda, Alberto 12, 339, 343
Dermott, Esther 12, 56, 342, 343
descriptive phenomenological method 118
diaries
childcare/activity diaries 13, 304
multimodal diaries 157, 158, 159–163, 164–167
notes from refugee fathers 267, 269–270
direct care 5, 29, 272, 275, 276, 279, 307
disabilities, children with
author's overview of 301
fathering involvement, research on 303–306
fathers, role of 13
paid work and 310, **311**
regret 310
scholarship on 302–303

time spent caring for 306, **307**, **308–309**, 310, **314–315**
disabilities, fathers with 7, 339
divisions of labour *see* gender divisions of labour
divorce *see* family separation
doing family 282, 286, 291, 294–295
Doucet, Andrea
care 4, 267, 284, 339–340
caring fatherhood 10, 64, 80, 91–92, 114, 344
on nurturing 56
on paid work and care 80, 244, 322–323, 341–342

E

ecological approaches 10, 25–26, 32, 34, 35, 36, 324–325
Eerola, Petteri 11, 49, 343, 345, 346
Elder, G.H. 334
Elliott, K. 3, 30, 284, 285, 295, 343
emerging adulthood theory 98
emotional availability 214, 330
emotional engagement *see* engagement/interaction
'empty nest' phase
adult children, fathering 103–105, 105–108, 109–110
research on 98, 102–103
scholarship on 100–101
engagement/interaction
adult children, of fathers of 101, 107
COVID-19 pandemic and 123, 124, 126–127
definitions of 28
emotional engagement 321, 322, 325–326, 330–332, 334, 342–344
factors that influence 115–116, 119, 120
involvement as 100
of non-resident fathers 84, 90
of young fathers 186–187, 189–190
equal sharers 22, 28–29, 138, 197, 204, 206
ethics of care *see* care ethics
Ewald, A. 9–10

F

FACT-COVID (Families and Community in the time of COVID) 153, 156–157
family practices 156, 169
family separation
child support 80, 86–88
co-parenting relationships 79, 186–188
COVID-19 on, impacts of 168
nonresident fathers on 83–84
property division 89
roles of fathers after 79–80, 84–86, 89–91
see also nonresident fathers

Index

family values 46–47, 128
Faroe Islands
  author's overview of 46–47
  fathers, role of 47–48, 51–52, 56–57
  narratives of fathers, young
    people's 52–55
  parenting information for fathers 45
  values, cultural/family 46–47, 56–57
fathering involvement
  author's overview of 99–100
  'being there' (social engagement)
    177–179, 180, 182, 183, 185, 325
  as care 4
  children with disabilities 302–303,
    303–306, **307**, **308–309**, 310, **314–315**
  definitions of 28, 49
  migration and 68–73, 235, 242,
    245–246, 255–259, 322, 325–327
  of nonresident fathers 84–86, 89–91
  refugee families 235–236, 239–243,
    243–245, 245–246
  scholarship on 99–100, 245, 284,
    322–326
  young people on 68–73
fathers *see* Black fathers; caring
  masculinities; hedonistic fathers;
  hegemonic masculinities; 'new father'
  model; parental leave; parental night
  shift; protective masculinities; refugees;
  research; responsibilities; scholarship;
  'traditional father' model; *specific
  countries (e.g., Finland, China)*
father's quota *see* Finland; parental leave
feminist care ethics *see* care ethics
Finland
  cultural values 214–215
  fathers, role of 138–139, 149–150
  father's quota (parental leave) 212, 216,
    218, 220, **221**, 222–224
  intensive parenting, research on 218,
    219, 220, **221**, 223, 224
  parental leave 138, 144, 147, 212, 216
  parental night shift, research on 135,
    139–140, **141**
  use of parental leave, research on 213
Fisher, Bernice 32, 33
5 dimensions/phases of care 33, 284
flexible working 5, 8, 9–10, 253
forced migration *see* refugees
FYFF ('Following Young Fathers
  Further') 175, 179–180, 182–183,
  185–186, 1867–188

G

Gaini, Firouz 10, 342
gay people *see* LGBTQIA+ parents
gender divisions of labour
  adult children, parenting 103–105

author's summary of 344–346
caring fatherhood and 22, 23, 26–27,
  28–30, 35
children with disabilities 306, **307**,
  308–309, 310
and child support 80
disciplinary matters 125
on Faroe Islands 51–52
in Finland 138–139
migration and 249–250, 255–256
parental leave and 156, 195–196
parental night shift 136–138, **141**,
  141–144, 149–150
refugee families 240–241, 243
re-gendering of care 178, 186, 190
scholarship on 136–138, 215–216
in Somalia 62–63
in transnational families 69–70
trends in, research 136
see also China; COVID-19 pandemic;
  parental leave
Gilligan, Carol 30, 31, 33
Global North
  narratives in, fatherhood 26, 56, 284
  scholarship on fatherhood/fathers 4, 5,
    7, 9, 45–46, 48–49, 234
Global South 49, 153

H

Haffejee, Sadiyya 11, 129, 340, 344
hedonistic fathers 115
hegemonic masculinities 9, 97, 106–107,
  179, 189, 214, 258, 284
Herbrand, C. 286, 295
historical positioning 333
Homatidis, S. 303, 307
homosexual people *see* LGBTQIA+ parents
Honig, A.S. 302, 307
Household Portraits 22, 23–24, 36n2
housework 29

I

In a Different Voice (Gilligan) 30
indirect care 32, 34, 215, 243–244, 272,
  275, 279
intensive parenting
  author's overview of 213, 217
  by fathers 213, 215, 224, 322
  research on 218, **219**, 220, **221**, 223, 224
interaction *see* engagement/interaction
*The International Review of Leave Policies and
  Research* 196, 198
interpretative repertoires 135, 140, **141**,
  141–144, 144–147, 149
intersectionalities
  of Black fathers 324–326, 327–330,
    332–334
  of class 7–8

of fathers 6–8, 93, 176, 183, 343, 344
historical positioning 333
and masculinities 330
of parental leave 204–205
scholarship on 6–8
interviewees
   on adult children 103–105, 105–108
   on child support 86–88
   on co-parenting 289, 290, 291
   on COVID-19 and parenting 118–124, 159–163, 164–167
   on cultural expectations 66–68
   on death of a father 71, 239
   on family separation 83–84
   on fathers, adult children 325, 328–330, 331–333
   on fathers, young people 49–50, 51–55, 56–57, 58
   on gender divisions of labour 24, 124–127, 128, 240–241, 243
   on good fatherhood 182–184
   on integration experiences (as refugees) 236–238
   on involvement of fathers 68–73, 84–86, 89–91, 239–243
   on mental load 125–127
   on migration experiences 255–257, 258–259
   on mothers 70, 72–73
   on night-time care work 141–144, 144–147, 147–149
   on nurturing 275–276
   on paid work 159–161, 163–164, 168, 184–186, 238–239, 241–242
   on property division 89
   on protection 273–274
   on responsibilities 242–243, 256, 259
   on surrogacy 292, 293
   on training 277–278
   see also research; scholarship
intimate fatherhood 5, 56, 64, 73, 75, 136, 178, 244, 322, 342–344
involvement *see* fathering involvement
Islam 62, 67–68, 70, 75
Ivanova, Ekaterina 11, 341, 345, 346

J
Japan **199**, 201–202, 205, **206**, 206–207

K
Kaufman, Gayle 204, 310
Konstantareas, M.M. 303, 307
Koslowski, Alison 12, 339, 345

L
Lammi-Taskula, Johanna 12, 215
Lampropoulou, V. 302, 307
leave *see* parental leave

LGBTQIA+ parents
   adoption 285–286, **288**, 292, 293
   author's overview of 283
   co-parenting 286, 287, **288**, 288–291, 294–295
   doing family 282, 286, 291, 294–295
   parental leave 198, 200, 201, 203, 204
   path to parenthood stages 290, 295
   rights 207, 285–286
   scholarship on 285–287
   surrogacy 285, 286, 287, **288**, 291–294
life course studies 98, 334
Lifeline method 23, 24
literature *see* scholarship
logistic regression models 305, 306–307, **308–309, 314–315**
longitudinal research 21, 153, 156, 175, 180–181, 224, 269, 270, 303

M
masculinities *see* caring masculinities; hegemonic masculinities; protective masculinities
maternal leave *see* parental leave
maternal practices/thinking 267, 279–280
Mavrogianni, T. 302, 307
Meil, Gerardo 13, 310
Mencare 196–197
mental load of care work 5, 125–127, 136, 138–139, 178
middle classes 7–8, 99, 123, 179, 260, 287, 288, 295, 323, 327
migration
   adult children on nonresident fathers 328–330, 331–333
   and fathering involvement 68–73, 235, 242, 245–246, 255–259, 322, 325–327
   fathering practices, research on 253–255, **254**, 255–259, 259–260
   fathers, role of 73–75, 343–344
   gender divisions of roles and 249–250, 255–256
   impacts of 62–63, 249–250, 250–252, 255–259
   as responsible fathering 322
   scholarship on 63, 250–252, 255, 269
   self-employment and 252–253, 255–256, 258–259
   see also refugees
Miller, Tina 12, 342, 343
moral obligation 87
moral responsibilities 5–6
Morgan, David 80, 156, 282, 294, 295
mothering 267
mothers
   children with disabilities 306–307, **307, 308–309**, 310, **311**, 312, **313**

Index

COVID-19 on, impacts of 121, 123, 124, 125, 159–163, 163–167
family separation and 83–84, 91, 92, 186–188
interviewees on 70, 72–73
mental load of care work 5, 125–127, 136, 138–139, 178
migration experiences of 255–256
moral responsibilities of 5–6
paid work 127–128, **199**, 216, 251, 252
parental night shift 136–137, 138, **141**, 141–144, 144–147, 147–149
regret 310
see also gender divisions of labour; interviewees; parental leave
multimodal diaries 157, 158, 159–163, 164–167
multinomial regression analysis 218, 220, **221**
Mustosmäki, Armi 11, 346

N

narratives
of adult children on fathers 325, 328–330, 331–333
analysis of 271–272
of caring fatherhood 29, 45
of change/process and fatherhood 342–343
cultural 214–215
definitions of 271
of fatherhood 5, 213–214, 345–346
historical, mapping of 26–27
of marginalisation of Russian fathers 80–81
on non-resident fathers 323
relational approach to 25
of young people on fathers 49–50, 51–55, 56–57, 58
natural growth 7
Nelson, T.J. 325
Netherlands 285, 286, 287, **288**, 290, 291, 293
'new father' model
Faroe Islands 48, 49, 52, 56, 57
gaps in 321, 322, 333–334
Poland 97–98, 99, 101
night shift *see* night-time care
night-time care work
author's overview of 135
fathers, role of 141–144, 144–147, 147–149
paid work and 143–144, 146–147, 149
research on 139–140, **141**
scholarship on 136–138
nonbinary people *see* LGBTQIA+ parents
non-normative childhoods 326–327, 330–333, 333–335, 345–346

non-resident fathers
adult children on 328–330, 331–333
engagement of 84, 90
on family separation 83–84
fathering involvement 84–86, 89–91
narratives of 323
responsibilities 80–81, 86–89, 92
see also family separation
nurturing
fathers as 149, 150, 176, 178, 179, 184, 186–187, 285
as parenting characteristic 266–267, 268
by refugee fathers 274–276, 277, 278–279
shift towards by fathers 212–213, 214, 225
types of 56

O

obligatory leave 197, 200, 201, 206–207
O'Brien, M. 9, 196, 215, 301
'old father' model *see* 'traditional father' model
Olsson, M.B. 303, 307
overnight *see* parental night shift
Ozgun, O. 302, 307

P

paid work
as caring 6, 32, 80, 244, 310, 341–342
children with disabilities and 310, **311**
and child support 80, 86–88
COVID-19 pandemic and 159–161, 163–164, 168
cultural expectations 66–67
flexible working 5, 8, 9–10, 253
mothers 127–128, **199**, 216, 251, 252
and parental night shift 143–144, 146–147, 149
and parenting dimensions **219**, **221**
participation rates of women/mothers **199**
refugees, experiences of 238–239, 241–242
scholarship on 27
self-employment 252–253, 255–256, 258–259
young fathers and 184–186, 345
pandemic *see* COVID-19 pandemic
parental leave
adoption leave 203
Australia 199–200
author's overview of 195, 197, 198
caring masculinities and 214, 345
Chile 200–201
compulsory/obligatory leave 197, 200, 201, 206–207
eligibility 8, 138, 198–199, 199–200, 201–202, 202–203, 203–204, 207
Faroe Islands 47, 48
fathers' use of 8–9, 22–23

and gender divisions of care 156, 195–196
Japan 201–202
and migrant fathers 63
parenting dimensions and 213–214, 217–218, **219**, 220, **221**, 223, 224
policies 195–197, 199–205
scholarship on 8–9, 215–216
South Africa **199**, 202–203, 205, 206, **206**
Sweden **199**, 203–204, 205, 206, **206**, 207
United States (US) 204–205
well-paid leave 205, 206, **206**, 207
see also Finland; gender divisions of labour
parenthood
moral responsibilities and 5–6
theoretical frameworks for 266–267
parenting *see* caring fathers; co-parenting; intensive parenting; 'new father' model; parenting modes; 'traditional father' model
parenting dimensions *see* parental leave; research
parenting modes
author's overview of 114
in China 115–116
COVID-19 pandemic impact on 118–124
research on 116, **117**, 118
paternal leave *see* parental leave
Pearson's correlation coefficient 218
Pelchat, D. 302, 307
Petts, R.J. 215–216
Phoenix, Ann 13, 57, 341, 344, 345–346
Pirskanen, Henna 11, 346
Poland
caring masculinities in 105–108
'empty nest' phase in, research on 98, 102–103, 109–110
fathers, role of 101, 344
protective masculinities in 103–105, 109–110
policies *see* parental leave
pragmatic fathers 115
Prattes, R. 284–285
protection
as parenting characteristic 266–267, 268
by refugee fathers 272–274
protective masculinities 98, 99–100, 103–105, 109–110
provisioning *see* paid work

Q

qualitative research
ANOVA analyses 305, **311**, **313**
author's overview of 11–12, 13, 27

challenges with 28–29
childcare diaries/activity diaries 13, 304
creative writing/essay method 50–51
diaries 157, 158, 159–163, 164–167, 267, 269–270
emerging adulthood theory 98
focus groups 327
interpretative repertoires 135, 140, **141**, 143, 144, 146, 147, 149
interviews 102–103, 114–115, 116, 117, 120, 129–130, 139–140, **141**, 253–254, 326–327
life course studies 98, 334
literature reviews 286
logistic regression models 305, 306–307, **308–309**, **314–315**
longitudinal studies 21, 153, 156–157, 175, 179–181, 186–187, 269–270
multinomial regression analysis 218, 220, **221**
repeat interviews 233, 235
social engagement framework 176, 177–178, 179
surveys 303
thematic narrative analysis 82–83, 253–254
see also research
quantitative research 12, 27, 28, 30, 35, 49, 223, 339–340
queer people *see* LGBTQIA+ parents

R

reciprocity 64, 72, 75, 323
refugees
fathering involvement of 235–236, 239–243, 243–245, 245–246
integration experiences of 236–238
Iraqi 268, 273
nurturing of children by 274–276, 277, 278–279
paid work experiences of 238–239, 268
parenting experiences of 268–269
protection of children by 272–274
scholarship on 234–235, 269
training of children by 277–278
see also migration
re-gendering of care 178, 186, 190
regret 310
relational approaches 10, 25, 31, 34, 55–56, 63–64, 91–92, 114, 284, 339, 340
relationalities 31, 32, 33, 34, 35, 129, 156, 344
relational ontologies 25
repertoires *see* interpretative repertoires
research
author's overview of existing 5–8
author's suggestions for future 35, 317, 339, 346–347
author's summary of 338–342

and care ethics 33–35
on caring fathers 21, 23–24, 24–26
children with disabilities, on fathers of 303–306, 306–312, **307**, **308–309**, **311**, **313–315**, 316–317
on COVID-19 and care 156–158, 168–170
on COVID-19 and parenting modes 114–115, 116, **117**, 118–124, 124–127, 129–130
on 'empty nest' phase 98, 102–103
on gender divisions of domestic labour 26, 27
Household Portraits 22, 23–24, 36n2
intergenerational research on fathers 46, 49–51, 63
on LGBTQIA+ parents 287, **288**, 288–291, 291–294, 294–295
Lifelines 23, 24
on migrant fathers 253–255, **254**, 255–259, 259–260
on non-normative childhood experiences 326–327, 330–333, 333–335
on nonresident fathering 81–83, 83–86, 87–89, 90–93
on parental leave 197–198, **199**, 199–205, 205–207, **206**, 217–225, **219**, **221**
on parental night shift 139–140, **141**
on parenting dimensions 218, **219**, 220, **221**, 223, 224
on refugee fathers 235–236, 236–238, 238–239, 239–245, 246, 269–270, **271**
responsibilities of researchers 35
task-based approaches 4
on transnational families 63, 64–65, **66**, 66–73
trends in gender divisions of care 136
on young fathers 179–182, 182–186, 189–190
see also ecological approaches; interviewees; qualitative research; quantitative research; relational approaches; scholarship; time use studies
respect 33, 64, 67–68, 70, 71, 73, 75
responsibilities
care ethics and 31, 32, 33, 34, 114, 214–215, 284
of Chinese fathers 115–116, 249–250, 250–251
COVID-19 pandemic, during 157, 159–163, 164–165, 168–169
cultural 64, 66–67, 68, 71–72, 75, 214, 240, 257
definitions of 28, 100
gendered 62, 99, 125–127, 128, 129, 236

interviewees on 242–243, 256, 259
measuring of 28, 29–30
migration as responsible fathering 322
nonresident fathers 80–81, 86–89, 92
parental leave policies on 195–196, 207
parental night shift 135, 136, 138, 142–144, 145–150
parenting modes during COVID-19 pandemic 118–119, 120–121, 123–124, 126–127
of researchers 35
responsiveness
care ethics and 31–32, 33–34, 36, 64, 124
parental leave and 9
Roberts, S. 284–285
Rogero-García, Jesús 13, 346
Romero-Balsas, Pedro 13, 310
Roopnarine, J.L. 302, 307
Ruddick, Sara 266–267, 279
Russia
child support 86–88
family separation in 79–80, 83–84
marginalisation of fathers 80–81, 345
nonresident fathers, research on 81–83, 84–86, 91–93
property division 89

S
Saarikallio-Torp, Miia 12, 340, 344
same-sex couples *see* LGBTQIA+ parents
scholarship
author's overview of 3
on Black fathers 324–325
on caring masculinities 284–285
on children with disabilities 302–303
on co-parenting relationships 186–188
on COVID-19 and care 155–156, 322
on 'empty nest' phase 100–101
on family separation 79–80
on fathering involvement 99–100, 245, 284, 322–326
on flexible working 9–10
on gender divisions of care 136–138, 215–216
global research on fatherhood 48–49
on intersectionalities 6–8
on LGBTQIA+ parents 285–287
on marginalisation of Russian fathers 80–81
on migration 63, 250–252, 255, 269
on paid work and caring 6
on parental leave 8–9, 215–216
on refugees 234–235, 269
rise in 26
on unpaid work 27
on young fathers 176–177, 178–179
see also Global North; interviewees; research

self-employment *see* paid work
separation *see* family separation
slavery 323–324, 333, 334, 346
sleep 137–138, 142–143, 145–146, 147–149
Smith, Barbara Fletchman 323, 324
social engagement framework 176, 177–178, 179
Somalia
 cultural values in 64, 70, 72, 75
 fathers, role of 62–63, 66–67, 73, 74–75
 transnational families from, research on 63, 64–65, **66**, 66–73
South Africa
 care during COVID-19, research on 158, 163–167
 COVID-19 on, impacts of 154–156
 parental leave **199**, 202–203, 205, 206, **206**
Spain
 Chinese migrants from 250, 252–253, 255–258, 258–259
 cultural values 250
 fathers, role of 301, 316
stereotypes
 of fathers 5, 12, 53, 98, 179, 345
 gender 128, 129, 182
 of Muslim men 63
Strier, R. 323
surrogacy 285, 286, 287, **288**, 291–294
Sweden
 cultural values 279
 parental leave **199**, 203–204, 205, 206, **206**, 207
 refugees in, research on 267, 269–270, **271**, 272–278
 state support 268
 'Swedish Dad' model 235
Switzerland 285–286, 287, **288**, 291, 292, 293
Syrian refugees
 fathering involvement of 235–236, 239–243, 243–245, 245–246
 integration experiences of 236–238
 paid work experiences of 238–239
 refugee seekers from 234, 272–273
 research on 235–236, 269–270

T

Tarrant, Anna 12, 340–341, 344, 345
teenagers *see* young people
thematic narrative analysis 82–83, 253–254
3 Rs of care ethics 22, 31, 35, 36, 64, 114, 129 *see also* relationalities; responsibilities; responsiveness
Tiilikainen, Marja 10, 342
time, caring as 4, 29

time use studies
 children with disabilities, fathering involvement 306, **307**, **308–309**, 310, **314–315**
 COVID-19 pandemic, during 153, 155
 limitations of 4, 6
 parental night shifts 136–137, 138
 results of 3
 unpaid care work and 27–28, 29–30
'traditional father' model
 author's overview of 213–214, 217
 China 116, 128, 257
 Faroe Islands 52, 54–55, 56, 57
 Finland 213–215
 Poland 97–98, 101, 104, 108
 research on 218, **219**, 220, **221**, 223, 224
 Somalia 62–63
training
 as parenting characteristic 266–267, 268
 by refugee fathers 277–278
transnational families *see* migration; refugees
trans people *see* LGBTQIA+ parents
Tronto, J. 4, 6, 31, 32, 33, 163, 284
Twamley, Katherine 11, 129, 340, 341, 343–344

U

United Kingdom
 care during COVID-19, research on 157–158, 159–163
 COVID-19 on, impacts of 154–156
 young fathers, research on 179–182, 182–184, 189–190
United States **199**, 204–205, 206, **206**, 303
unpaid work 27–28, 29 *see also* care work; paid work
Utrata, J. 80–81, 93

V

values *see* cultural values; family values

W

Walkerdine, Valerie 326, 327, 329, 333
well-paid leave 205, 206, **206**, 207
Wetherell, M. 48, 140
Wojnicka, K. 99, 330
women *see* mothers
working classes 7–8, 179, 324, 327–328, 329–330
Wu, Mengyao 12, 339, 343

Y

Young, D.M. 302, 307
young people
 on cultural expectations 66–68
 on death of a father 71

on equal care 51–52
expectations for fathers by 74
as fathers 175–176, 176–179, 182–184, 184–188, 196
on good fatherhood 182–184
on involvement of fathers 68–73
narratives of fathers by 49–50, 51–55, 56–57, 58
on paid work 184–186
scholarship on young fathers 176–177, 178–179
see also disabilities, children with

Z

Żadkowska, Magdalena 11, 341, 344, 347
Zhang, Guanli 11, 340, 341, 344

www.ingramcontent.com/pod-product-compliance
Lightning Source LLC
Chambersburg PA
CBHW051524020426
42333CB00016B/1770